THOMAS KINSELLA:
THE PEPPERCANISTER POEMS

THOMAS KINSELLA: THE PEPPERCANISTER POEMS

Derval Tubridy

University College Dublin Press
Preas Choláiste Ollscoile Bhaile Átha Cliath

First published 2001 by University College Dublin Press,
Newman House, 86 St Stephen's Green, Dublin 2, Ireland
www.ucdpress.ie

ISBN 1 900621 52 5 (hardcover)
1 900621 53 3 (paperback)

Cataloguing in Publication data available from the British Library

Typeset in Ireland in 10/12 Sabon and Palatino
by Elaine Shiels, Bantry, Co. Cork
Index by John Loftus
Printed in Ireland by Colour Books, Dublin

For

Lilian McGoran Tubridy

CONTENTS

Acknowledgements   ix
Abbreviations   xi

INTRODUCTION   1

1 ELEGIAC CONCERNS   13
  Butcher's Dozen   14
  A Selected Life   25
  Vertical Man   32
  The Good Fight   41

2 PSYCHIC GEOGRAPHY   56
  One   56
  A Technical Supplement   75
  Song of the Night and Other Poems   94
  The Messenger   105

3 HISTORICAL PARTICULARS   118
  Songs of the Psyche   120
  Her Vertical Smile   132
  Out of Ireland   146
  St Catherine's Clock   154

4 POLITICAL MATTERS   166
  One Fond Embrace   166
  Personal Places   174
  Poems from Centre City   183
  Madonna and Other Poems   195
  Open Court   206

CONCLUSION   215
   The Pen Shop   216
   The Familiar   221
   Godhead   224

Notes   230
Selected Bibliography   254
Index   264

ACKNOWLEDGEMENTS.

I would like to thank Thomas Kinsella for his kind permission to quote from his copyrighted work and to reproduce the images and illustrations of the Peppercanister editions. I thank him also for thoughtful and considered conversation, and for his and Eleanor Kinsella's warm hospitality. My thanks go also to Louis le Brocquy for kind permission to reproduce his 'Reconstructed Head of Thomas Kinsella' on the cover.

I am very grateful to the Ireland–United States Commission for Educational Exchange for the Fulbright Ireland McCourt scholarship in literature which facilitated my research at Emory University, Atlanta, and Glucksman Ireland House, New York University. My warm appreciation goes to all the staff at Special Collections, Woodruff Library, Emory, especially Steve Enniss, for their professionalism and enthusiasm. Working on the Thomas Kinsella papers there was indeed a pleasure

My thanks also go to Goldsmiths College, University of London, for granting me research leave, and to my colleagues at the Department of English for their advice and encouragement. For her patience and good guidance I would like to thank Barbara Mennell of University College Dublin Press. I am very grateful also to J. C. C. Mays for his perceptive reading of the manuscript and for his valuable suggestions.

The support and appreciation of friends and family have been vital to the book. My deepest thanks to John Fitzgerald whose careful eye and keen humour kept me going. My greatest debt is to my mother, Lilian McGoran Tubridy, for her wisdom and guidance.

Derval Tubridy
Goldsmiths College
London
June 2000

ABBREVIATIONS

C *Thomas Kinsella: Collected Poems 1956–1994* (Oxford: Oxford University Press, 1996).

P Refers to the page number of the Peppercanister edition under consideration, or to the named Peppercanister edition of the quotation it follows.

Each quotation from the Peppercanister poems is followed by the page number from the Peppercanister edition and from the *Collected Poems* edition. Where there are variants between both versions this is signalled by the abbreviation 'var.' after the appropriate letter.

Quotations from Kinsella's earlier work which does not form part of the Peppercanister series are taken from the *Collected Poems*. Variants between the first editions of these poems and the versions in the *Collected Poems* are not signalled.

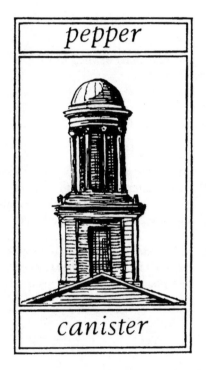

pepper

canister

INTRODUCTION

The shape of Kinsella's career is distinctive among Irish poets, moving from early celebration to muted appreciation as critics and readers responded to the increasingly allusive and complex poetry which has characterised his work since the early 1970s. This study takes as its starting point Kinsella's decision to found his own press, The Peppercanister Press, from which all of his subsequent work has issued. Peppercanister is not simply a press: it is a series of distinctive and interconnected poetic sequences that build together to form a loosely structured whole, which links with Kinsella's early work to form a continuing project in which art, self and society are subjected to rigorous scrutiny. The power of Kinsella's work lies in its ability to avoid the generalisation or the grand gesture. By maintaining a fidelity to the minutiae of life the poet looks behind the constructs of history, society and the self to discover the rhythms and processes from which each arise.

Kinsella began as a lyricist in the manner of the early W. H. Auden and W. B. Yeats, writing finely crafted poems celebrating 'love, death and the artistic act'.[1] An example of work written 'specifically in Auden's manner' is 'A Lady of Quality' from Kinsella's first collection, *Poems*, 1956:[2]

> In hospital where windows meet
> With sunlight in a pleasing feat
> Of airy architecture
> My love has sweets and grapes to eat,
> The air is like a laundered sheet,
> The world's a varnished picture.
>
> (C 8)

For Kinsella, Auden provided an entry point into poetry: 'Reading Auden, it occurred to me that there was a need in myself, and that I could write poetry.'[3] Kinsella's early writing received wide acclaim, winning the Poetry Book Society recommendation on two occasions with *Another*

September in 1958 and *Nightwalker and Other Poems* in 1967. *Another September*, for which he received the Guinness Poetry award, established Kinsella as 'the most distinguished younger poet writing in Ireland', displaying an increased confidence and ambition in work which acknowledged a debt to Ezra Pound and T.S. Eliot.[4] To these influences Dillon Johnston adds the mark of Keats in *Poems* and *Another September*, and Shelley and Austin Clarke in the 1962 volume *Downstream*.[5] Already, Kinsella's work was being compared with that of Robert Lowell, Richard Wilbur and Wallace Stevens.[6] The 1958 volume was followed in 1960 by *Moralities*, a collection which considers faith, love, death and song, and two years later by *Downstream*, in which Kinsella probes behind peaceful domesticity to find a world of death and decay, as in 'Chrysalides':

> To the unique succession of our youthful midnights,
> When by a window ablaze softly with the virgin moon
> Dry scones and jugs of milk awaited us in the dark,
>
> Or to lasting horror: a wedding flight of ants
> Spawning to its death, a mute perspiration
> Glistening like drops of copper, agonised, in our path.
>
>   (C 52)

Kinsella's voice gains in strength and complexity as he moves towards looser and more open sequences of poems in which self-exploration plays a central role. The interim collection, *Wormwood*, which was incorporated two years later into *Nightwalker and Other Poems*, won him the Denis Devlin Memorial Award in 1967. The poems of *Nightwalker* operate in what he calls 'the violent zone, between the outer and the inner storms, where human life takes place'.[7] Within this zone, concerns of love and the artistic act mitigate the poet's increasing sense of life as ordeal. His address to the beloved with which *Wormwood* opens indicates the apocalyptic vision from which the collection takes its name:[8] 'Sensing a wider scope, a more penetrating harmony, we begin again in a higher innocence to grow toward the next ordeal' (C 62).

The language of these poems moves from what Edna Longley has called the 'mellifluous cadences' which characterised his earlier work, towards a free verse in which received forms and rhyme play a very minor part.[9] Yet still, Auden and Eliot make their mark through an 'echo from Auden's "Nones" and the persona of intellectual *noctambule*' which, in John Montague's opinion, 'is depressingly close to early Eliot'.[10] However, reviewing *Nightwalker and Other Poems*, Eavan Boland remarks on how the collection confirms Kinsella's change of direction towards a more abrupt, less lyrical line, and notes that:

If there is at times a disquieting repression of lyricism in this volume, a banishing of the grace which one associated with Kinsella's early work, yet there is a new strength to replace it. One does not doubt that Kinsella has increased his own stature by exploring so relentlessly what, in his own lovely phrase, he calls "the stagger and recovery of spirit."[11]

Kinsella confirms his conscious decision to abandon traditional poetic structures of the well-made poem saying, 'Yes, I kicked the whole scheme asunder at a certain point, realizing that the modern poet has inherited wonderfully enabling free forms.'[12] An important influence on Kinsella's poetic development was his move in 1965 from his life in Dublin as a senior civil servant in the Department of Finance to a position as writer-in-residence in Southern Illinois University where he could devote himself full time to writing. Living in the US opened Kinsella's ear to the American voice, and in particular to the voice of William Carlos Williams. Auden's 'grace and eloquence, obeying the requirements of stanza form and rhyme with gaiety and expertise' joined with Yeats's 'carving of poems into a regular sequence of objects' to provided Kinsella with an exemplary poetic apprenticeship.[13] But both poets gave way to Williams's rangy line which provided Kinsella with a 'sort of leverage out of a rather clamped tradition – with very few exits for poetry – into a state of thinking, and attitude where anything is possible'.[14] Robert Lowell's *Life Studies* showed him how to develop a poetic sequence that 'develops a progressive experience shared with the audience.'[15] Ezra Pound's *Cantos* also provided Kinsella with an example of what is possible in poetry. He points to the 'revolutionary energy' in Pound's subject matter and technique and indicates three aspects of the *Cantos* which influenced his later work, especially the Peppercanister poems: 'their extraordinary scope, their reliability in local detail and their capacity to keep going'.[16]

The idea of keeping going is integral to Kinsella's writing. Part of the development of his poetry involves a move away from collections of discrete poems towards sequences of poems which are open-ended and interactive. As Kinsella puts it: 'I hope the echoes of one poem or sequence go on and get caught up by the next. The poems I'm writing now will, I hope, gather up previous work as well as move forward.'[17] The last poem of *Nightwalker and Other Poems*, 'Phoenix Park', incorporates this open-endedness into its structure. The last line of 'Phoenix Park' ends with a comma – 'Delicate distinct tissue begins to form,' – inviting the reader onward to the first line of Kinsella's next sequence of poems, 'Notes from the Land of the Dead', which begins in lower case with 'hesitate, cease to exist, glitter again' (C 94–5). And, as Maurice Harmon points out, the epigraph to *Notes From the Land of the Dead* when it appeared in the 1973 volume *New Poems* is taken directly from the last lines of 'Phoenix Park':

A snake out of the void moves in my mouth, sucks
At triple darkness. A few ancient faces
Detach and begin to circle. Deeper still,
Delicate distinct tissue begins to form,

(C 94)[18]

Reviewing Kinsella's 1996 *Collected Poems*, Floyd Skloot underlines the extent to which revision and incorporation are integral to Kinsella's poetry: 'At any given point – in the various editions of selected poems, in the assembling of smaller, privately published books into more comprehensive, larger books, or in this collected edition – poems mutate, adjacencies shift. These are not just cosmetic changes; they reflect new understandings of what his work means.'[19]

Kinsella's writing moves from what Longley calls the 'static pose'[20] of the contained lyric to a more fragmented form in which beginnings and endings are less easily defined, eschewing melody in favour of a shifting rhythm which lies closer to its subject matter. He explains the development of his style as a shift away from 'the notion of decorative language, of poetry as linguistic entertainment', which he terms 'facile rhetoric, or "music" or mimesis for its own sake', towards a 'totality of imaginative response with the merely linguistic characteristics deleted so that one is brought closer and closer to the data and to the form and unity embodied in the data.'[21] While praising *Notes from the Land of the Dead* for its ability to grapple 'with the complex plight and destructive energies of our society' John MacInerney criticises the occasional 'clotted phrasing' and 'obscure personification' of the poem.[22] Seamus Heaney, reviewing the anthology of Irish poetry *An Duanaire 1600–1900: Poems of the Dispossessed*, acknowledges the shift in tone and diction in Kinsella's poetry and attributes it partly to his work translating Middle Irish poetry:

> He has strenuously punished the lyricist in himself who carried off such stylish performances in the early books. As the influence of Pound and indeed of Ó Rathaille has taken hold, he has gradually evicted traces of Audenesque, iambic – strictly English – melody, in order to find a denser, more laconic, more indigenous way with the poetic line.[23]

Kinsella's work with Seán Ó Tuama on *An Duanaire* is part of a longstanding commitment to translation from Irish which began with *Longes Mac nUsnig: Being the Exile and Death of the Sons of Usnech*, and *The Breastplate of Saint Patrick*, both published in 1954, and followed by *Thirty-three Triads* the next year. Translation, for Kinsella, became both an act of commitment to a tradition of literature by giving it a 'new currency' in which it is made available to contemporary readers, and 'the best way', as he notes, 'of appreciating the work itself'.[24] One of Kinsella's great achievements of translation, and one with which he remains imaginatively involved, is his translation of the Old Irish epic Táin Bó Cuailnge, *The Táin*. Kinsella's work on *The Táin* involved extensive research in early Irish literature and mythology, the influence of which is evident particularly in the poetry such as *Notes from the Land of the Dead* and Peppercanister sequences such as *One*, which have as their backbone stories of Ireland's prehistory from the ninth century *Lebor Gabála Érenn* or *The Book of Invasions*. As he emphasises, the 'historical element' that the research for translations revealed became part of the subject matter of his own poetry.[25] However, Kinsella's increasing use of mythical material provided, for some, an obstacle to the understanding of his poetry. As Dillon Johnston explains, it was not always evident to critics that poems such as 'Survivor' from *Notes from the Land of the Dead* were, what he calls, 'loose renditions' of episodes from Irish mythology.[26] 'Survivor', for example, draws on an episode from the *Lebor Gabála Érenn* which tells of Fintan, last survivor of Cessair's people:[27]

> By twilight everything was destroyed,
> the only survivors a shoal of women
> spilled onto the shingle, and one man
> that soon – as they lifted themselves up
> and looked about them in the dusk –
> they silently surrounded.

(C 115)

Kinsella's translation of the *Táin* arose through his involvement with Liam Miller's Dolmen Press, which had issued much of Kinsella's early poetry and all of his translations.[28] Miller prompted Kinsella to find and translate 'manuscripts of myths, legends, or stories in Irish which deserved publication in English'.[29] By founding Dolmen Press in 1951, Miller revived a tradition of Irish publishing that had ended with Maunsel & Roberts in 1926, and provided a vital publishing outlet for Irish writers.[30] Asked by Peter Lennon of *The Guardian* whether those who published with Dolmen had been refused by publishers abroad, Miller replied: 'Not at all. Several of them have had offers from England and America, but they continue to publish with us.'[31] Kinsella explains how,

> from the beginning the Press set itself the object of publishing work by Irish writers, and it soon found itself dealing with a new Irish poetry. For the next three decades it provided professional primary publication in Ireland for poetry and drama, with commentary on Irish and Anglo-Irish literature.[32]

Dolmen focused on fine printing and good design and its editions of work by poets and playwrights including J. M. Synge, Brian Coffey,

Austin Clarke and John Montague were often illustrated by artists such as Pauline Bewick, Harry Clarke and Louis le Brocquy (whose brush drawings for the *Táin* contributed to its success). A year after its foundation, Kinsella's *Three Legendary Sonnets* appeared under the Dolmen imprint. With the exception of *Notes from the Land of the Dead*, which was published by the Cuala Press in 1972, all of Kinsella's European editions of poetry came from Dolmen, with *Downstream*, *Nightwalker and Other Poems* and *Selected Poems 1956–1968* appearing also in association with Oxford University Press. His US editions at this time included *Poems and Translations* from Atheneum, New York in 1961, *Nightwalker and Other Poems* from Knopf in 1968, *Tear* from the Pym Randall Press in Cambridge, Mass. in 1969 and *Notes from the Land of the Dead* again with Knopf in 1973.

In 1964 the Dolmen Press was incorporated, and Kinsella, along with Liam Miller and Liam Browne, became one of its founding directors. This placed the poet in a difficult position since as a director he could not justify Dolmen publishing all of his work.[33] He needed to find another outlet for his poetry and, rather than moving to another publishing house, Kinsella decided to found his own imprint, the Peppercanister Press in 1972. There were other reasons for the establishment of Peppercanister. In his preface to Stephen Enniss's bibliography of Peppercanister, Kinsella expresses his frustration with magazine publications that do not always present work in the best way, and points to the need to publish work quickly and at regular intervals in order to get a sense of its progress. Kinsella explains how publishing with Peppercanister offers him the kind of interim publication usually provided by magazines and journals through which he can assess the progress of his work: 'Peppercanister became an alternative to the publication of poetry in literary journals. I had always found this unsatisfactory, with the poems placed between stories and articles and disappearing with a particular issue.'[34] By founding the Peppercanister Press, Kinsella follows in the tradition of small Irish presses such as Austin Clarke's Bridge Press, run from his home in Templeogue.

The Peppercanister Press takes its name from St Stephen's church on Upper Mount Street, Dublin, known locally as 'the Peppercanister'. The church is visible from Kinsella's home at the time on Percy Place, parallel to the Grand Canal, from where Peppercanister began issuing 'occasional special items'.[35] Kinsella explains the genesis of the press:

> The idea originated with *Butcher's Dozen*, written in April 1972 in response to the Widgery Report on the "Bloody Sunday" shootings in Derry. The poem was finished quickly and issued as a simple pamphlet at ten pence a copy; cheapness and coarseness were part of the effect, as with a ballad sheet.[36]

There followed two poems in commemoration of the Irish composer, Seán Ó Riada, *A Selected Life* and *Vertical Man*, the first of which raised funds for the Seán Ó Riada Foundation. The last of these occasional pamphlets was a poem called *The Good Fight* written for the tenth anniversary of the assassination of John F. Kennedy which was, like *A Butcher's Dozen*, issued as a small public pamphlet. Peppercanister retained a close connection with the Dolmen Press. *Butcher's Dozen* was printed at the Elo Press in Dublin and distributed by Dolmen, but the subsequent three pamphlets were both printed and distributed by Dolmen.

The character of the Peppercanister publications changed in 1974 with the publication of the fifth Peppercanister, *One*. For the next thirteen years the Peppercanister Press produced editions of poetry which matched the high standard of design and production notable in Dolmen editions. Kinsella acknowledges Miller's influence, saying 'I had admired Liam Miller's commitment to quality in materials and design, and for a while this was confused with the Peppercanister idea'.[37] *One* and *A Technical Supplement* contained illustrations, the first by Irish artist Anne Yeats and in the second plates were taken from Denis Diderot's eighteenth-century *Encyclopédie*. In all of the Peppercanisters great attention was paid to the covers, some of which, like *The Messenger*, display a virtuosity of design which contributes significantly to the understanding of the text inside. Peppercanisters five to twelve were each published in deluxe and trade editions, with some volumes also coming out in limited or library editions. The deluxe editions were printed on handmade paper, bound in calf, basil or vellum, and often presented in a slip case. Frequently, Kinsella included an additional verse written in the author's hand to the text of the deluxe editions. These lines then became part of the main text when the poem was reprinted in the larger collections issued by Oxford University Press or Wake Forest.

The two volumes of 1978, *Song of the Night and Other Poems* and *The Messenger*, were the last of the Peppercanisters to be printed at the Dolmen Press. The next four volumes, *Songs of the Psyche* and *Her Vertical Smile* of 1985, and *Out of Ireland* and *St Catherine's Clock* of 1987 were set by Raymond and Nuala Gunn and printed by Reprint Ltd in Dublin for the Peppercanister Press. It was at this point that Kinsella took full control of the design and layout of the Peppercanisters, drawing on Liam Miller's expertise and advice to make sure that the 1985 volumes matched the high standards of the previous Peppercanisters. On 9 March 1984, Miller sent Kinsella 'notes towards a general specification for Peppercanister books', to help him plan the editions. These notes described the format of the Peppercanisters as US royal octavo, the type as Photoset Pilgrim Roman with Italic, printed on Artlaid Natural paper which was threadsewn in sections and then bound.[38]

Kinsella's publicity material for Peppercanister divides the editions into a number of series. The first series comprises the first four occasional poems, *Butcher's Dozen*, *A Selected Life*, *Vertical Man* and *The Good Fight*. The next three Peppercanisters, *One*, *A Technical Supplement* and *Song of the Night and Other Poems* form the second series; *The Messenger*, *Songs of the Psyche* and *Her Vertical Smile* the third.[39] There is a small discrepancy between the information included in the 1985 brochure, and that produced two years later. In 1985 Kinsella announces that the fourth series will begin with *One Fond Embrace* and *Out of Ireland*. By 1987 this information has been revised to read that the fourth series will open with *Out of Ireland* and *St Catherine's Clock*. This change of plan is indicative of the more complicated publishing history of the Peppercanister Press at this time. In 1980, two years after the last editions to be printed at the Dolmen Press under Liam Miller's supervision had appeared, Kinsella was in correspondence with Peter Fallon of Gallery Press with a view to publish the poet's work.[40] In 1981 a version of *One Fond Embrace* was issued by Gallery Press, in association with the Deerfield Press of Massachusetts. However, Gallery did not assume the relationship with Peppercanister that Dolmen had in the past, preferring only to print those editions that would be published under Gallery's imprint.[41] When it seemed that the Peppercanister imprint was on less than secure ground, John F. Deane of Dedalus Press agreed to print and distribute Kinsella's work, which would continue to be published initially by the Peppercanister Press. Kinsella was careful to distinguish Peppercanister from Dedalus, refusing to be included in Deane's anthology of Dedalus poets and taking exception to the *Times Literary Supplement* review of *Personal Places* and *Poems from Centre City* which attributed the volumes to the Dedalus Press.[42] This misunderstanding no doubt arose from the fact that neither volume contains the usual colophon giving publication details, and indeed the previous volume, *One Fond Embrace*, states in its colophon that 'Peppercanister 13, One Fond Embrace, has been printed by the Carlow Nationalist and published by The Dedalus Press.' In 1988 a revised version of *One Fond Embrace* was published as the thirteenth Peppercanister. A regular series of subsequent volumes followed, distributed by Dedalus: *Personal Places* and *Poems from Centre City* in 1990; *Madonna and Other Poems* and *Open Court* in 1991. After a break of five years during which Kinsella published an essay on poetry and politics in Ireland called *The Dual Tradition*, which was issued by Carcanet Press in Manchester as Peppercanister number 18, Kinsella returned with a volume of poetry called *The Pen Shop*, which was published by Peppercanister in 1997. The two most recent Peppercanisters are *The Familiar* and *The Godhead*, which appeared in April 1999.

Though perhaps not initiated with this purpose directly in mind, Peppercanister quickly became an ideal format for the longer sequences of poems which are characteristic of Kinsella's writing. The loosening of stanzaic form and the introduction of narrative and dramatic passages into his writing suited the more adaptable format of Peppercanister. As Kinsella indicated, the Peppercanisters are a valuable form of interim publishing, allowing the poet to revise the work before it is published commercially. The initial four Peppercanister volumes were published together by Dolmen in association with Oxford University Press under the title *Fifteen Dead*. The next three were published similarly under the title *One and Other Poems*. Both of these editions were published in 1979. With the demise of the Dolmen press following Liam Miller's death in 1987, Peppercanister continued Dolmen's association with Oxford University Press issuing the volume *Blood and Family* in 1988, which gathered together *The Messenger, Songs of the Psyche, Her Vertical Smile, Out of Ireland* and *St Catherine's Clock*. In 1994 Oxford University Press published *From Centre City*, which brings together *One Fond Embrace, Personal Places, Poems from Centre City, Madonna and Other Poems* and *Open Court*. In each of these commercial editions Kinsella has revised the poetry, sometime extensively, especially with the later writing. In 1996 Oxford University Press produced a paperback volume, *Thomas Kinsella: Collected Poems 1956–1994*, in which the poet once again revises and reworks the poems, providing the reader with another version of the work-in-progress.[43] In his review of the *Collected Poems*, Floyd Skloot describes how Kinsella avails himself of the different forms in which his poems are published to constantly refer back to his earlier work, absorbing previous work into the current writing.[44] Skloot argues that while 'many critics since roughly 1968 have accused Kinsella of brooding himself to pieces, the presence here of the entire work shows how the pieces all fit':

> The impression is of a fully realized, cohesive endeavor that both concerns and enacts fragmentation, that mounts temporary incursions into chaos despite the futility of the undertaking, and that restlessly stalks peace.[45]

Thomas Kinsella's Peppercanister poems are vital to understanding how 'the pieces all fit'. With these slim volumes Kinsella develops the themes and references which link together apparently disparate works and provide an undertow to the surface movement of his poems. Until recently, criticism of Kinsella's poetry concentrated on the early writing, including *Notes from the Land of the Dead* and perhaps the first few Peppercanister pamphlets. Notable among early studies is Maurice Harmon's excellent study of 1974, *The Poetry of Thomas Kinsella*, which examines Kinsella's writings and translations from 1958 to 1974. The greater part of critical writing on Kinsella since this time has taken the form of journal articles or chapters in books such as Robert F. Garratt's paper on 'Fragilities and Structures: Poetic Strategy and Thomas Kinsella's "Night-Walker" and "Phoenix Park"' published in *Irish University Review* in 1983, Dillon Johnston's (whose association with Kinsella arises through the Wake Forest Press which published Kinsella's early work in the US) part-chapter of Kinsella in *Irish Poetry after Joyce* in 1985, and Seamus Deane's chapter on Kinsella in *Celtic Revivals: Essays in Modern Irish Literature 1880–1980* of the same year. In 1987 John F. Deane produced a special issue of *Tracks* devoted to Kinsella, which included criticism, poetry and an interview with the poet. In 1980 Carolyn Rosenberg completed her compendious PhD dissertation 'Let Our Gaze Blaze: The Recent Poetry of Thomas Kinsella'. Rosenberg's research is exhaustive and comprehensive, providing invaluable information on Kinsella's family history and the influence of Jungian psychology and Irish mythology on his work. Her work has provided important ground-work for most subsequent scholars. Yet it was not until the latter part of the 1990s, forty-three years after Kinsella's first publication, *The Starlight Eye*, that complete critical surveys of Kinsella's work have been published. The first of these, Thomas H. Jackson's *The Whole Matter: The Poetic Evolution of Thomas Kinsella* pays particular attention to Kinsella's early writing, evaluating the Jungian and mythological basis of the poetry, and providing important local contextualisation for readers not familiar with Dublin. As part of Twayne's English Authors Series, Donatella Abbate Badin's *Thomas Kinsella*, published in 1996, is an ideal introduction to the reader unfamiliar with Kinsella's work. She plots out the main themes and approaches of his writing and provides a clear and comprehensive bibliography. Indispensable to Kinsella scholarship is Brian John's study of the same year, *Reading the Ground: The Poetry of Thomas Kinsella*, which meticulously draws together the key threads of the poet's work, and argues persuasively for Kinsella as an 'essential voice of our time'.[46]

These critical works provide a foundation for this present study of Kinsella's Peppercanister poems, which explains the genesis and develop-ment of the work and analyses each volume in detail within the context of the ongoing Peppercanister series. Drawing on material available in the Thomas Kinsella Papers held at Emory University, Atlanta, it sources the diversity of research which underpins Kinsella's poetry and explores how publication under the Peppercanister imprint has affected the direction and development of the poet's work. An informed reading of Kinsella's work requires an understanding of the scholarly framework in which it is written. This study hopes to make evident the breadth and richness of Kinsella's inquiry which enables him to write a poetry of great subtlety, rigour and engagement; and to provide a starting point for research into areas such as Kinsella's prosody and questions of how his handling of the poetic sequence compares with that of poets such as Ezra Pound or William Carlos Williams.

Adopting a chronological approach, the study examines the Pepper-canister volumes under the general rubrics of tradition, subjectivity, history and politics. The chapters of this study do not adhere strictly to the sequences into which Kinsella arranged his writing since the structure that underpinned that arrangement was modified, and eventually dispensed with, as the writing developed. And indeed, as is pointed out above, practical circumstances on occasion intervened to change the planned order of publication. However, there are certain foci around which the Peppercanister volumes resolve. Chapter one reads the first four Peppercanisters, *Butcher's Dozen*, a satire on injustice, *A Selected Life*, *Vertical Man*, elegies for Seán Ó Riada, and *The Good Fight*, a commemoration of John F. Kennedy, through the lens of tradition. In each of these volumes Kinsella brings together visions of the past and of the future and explores the negotiations that the present must undergo in order to reconcile both. Chapter two examines the four volumes that continue Kinsella's inward turn begun in *Notes from the Land of the Dead*. Though quite distinct in context and tone, *One*, *A Technical Supplement*, *Song of the Night and Other Poems* and *The Messenger* each explore the idea of subjectivity in the context of family and society. It is here that we see Kinsella's attention to the visual aspect of his work at its most pronounced with, for example, deft arrangement of illustrations from Diderot's *Encyclopédie* interwoven with the text of *A Technical Supplement*, and visual puns on the cover of *The Messenger*. Chapter three opens with Kinsella's first Peppercanister volume after a seven-year period, *Songs of the Psyche*. This volume connects with the psychological exploration of the previous volumes and points toward Kinsella's greater engagement with larger historical contexts that inform the subsequent poems, *Her Vertical Smile*, *Out of Ireland* and *St Catherine's Clock*. Once again the figure of Seán Ó Riada takes a pivotal position in Kinsella's poetry, here joined by another composer Gustav Mahler, the ninth-century philosopher Johannes Scotus Eriugena, and Robert Emmet in a juxtaposition which allows Kinsella to question the validity of historical narrative and the position of the individual within that narrative. The fourth chapter explores the shift in Kinsella's focus from the historical to the contemporary in *One Fond Embrace*, *Personal Places*, *Poems From Centre City*, *Madonna and Other Poems*, and *Open*

Court. Situated in and around Dublin, these poems interweave the personal and the political in a poetry which is often darkly critical of contemporary Irish society. The study concludes with an examination of Kinsella's most recent Peppercanister volumes, *The Pen Shop*, *The Familiar* and *Godhead*, which signal a turning away from the sharp criticism of the early 1990s poetry towards a more lyrical meditation on the relationships that sustain the self.

1
ELEGIAC CONCERNS

At the opening session of Poetry International 1973 six poets including Thomas Kinsella met to discuss poetry and politics. Commenting that poetry necessarily included a private and a public aspect, Kinsella argued that poetry needed to be able to respond to public events, even if the poetry itself might not be able to effect change. He concluded with a view of human nature which conveys much of the attitude behind Kinsella's first four Peppercanisters, *Butcher's Dozen*, *A Selected Life*, *Vertical Man*, and *The Good Fight*, as Hugh McFadden of *The Irish Times* reports:

> Some actions were so brutal that they demanded comment. But he did not believe that brutality could be cured by any action of the poet. The evidence was piling up that peace and non-aggression were not the normal states of human behaviour. Man was naturally inclined to brutality and he did not think it was 'treatable.'[1]

Kinsella's comments come only a year after his long poem *Butcher's Dozen* responded to bloodshed in Northern Ireland, and two years after the death of his close friend the Irish composer Seán Ó Riada, in whose memory he wrote two elegies, *A Selected Life*, and *Vertical Man*. Violence, whether it is the sharp brutality of a state against its citizens, or the slow indifference of self-destruction, informs each of these three poems. The fourth poem, *The Good Fight*, continues the theme in an exploration of random and isolated violence targeted against public office. In 1979 these first four Peppercanister volumes, or 'occasional poems', were gathered by Dolmen Press into an edition called *Fifteen Dead*. The title of the Dolmen volume marks the sense of elegy and mourning which identifies all of these poems. The first thirteen dead signalled by the title are the thirteen civil rights protesters shot in Derry in 1972. The fourteenth is Seán Ó Riada, who died on 6 October 1971, and the fifteenth is the assassinated US President, John Fitzgerald Kennedy. Though radically different in tone and style each poem commemorates the dead and seeks to explore and understand how public death, whether death in public or death of a public figure, challenges our ideas of community and identity.

Butcher's Dozen

A Lesson for the Octave of Widgery

Butcher's Dozen, the first of Kinsella's Peppercanister volumes, is a satire in rhyming couplets written as an immediate response to the findings of the Widgery Tribunal of Inquiry into the shooting by the British Army of thirteen civil rights demonstrators in Derry[2] on 30 January 1972. The title puns bitterly on the term 'baker's dozen' and the subtitle, as Brian John explains, refers both to the speed with which Kinsella wrote the poem ('finished, printed and published within a week'),[3] and to 'the week of devotion and spiritual preparation (as in the octave of Pentecost or of the Epiphany)' integral to Catholicism.[4] In his commentary on the poem, Kinsella emphasises that it was not written in response to the shootings, but rather to the findings of the tribunal which exonerated the British Army and cast suspicion over the victims:

> The poem was written response to the Report of the Widgery Tribunal. In Lord Widgery's cold putting aside of truth, the nth in a historic series of expedient falsehoods – with Injustice literally wigged out as Justice – it was evident to me that we were suddenly very close to the operations of the evil real causes.[5]

Butcher's Dozen appeared as a simple pamphlet of eight pages which was sold for ten pence. The cover features the outline of a coffin in black, on which the figure '13' is written. The cover image was taken from the design of a badge 'issued at the Civil Rights protest march in Newry on 6 February' which Kinsella attended.[6] *Butcher's Dozen* was printed at the Elo Press in order that a large quantity might be produced with speed, and was distributed by the Dolmen Press under the imprint of the Peppercanister.[7] The importance of ensuring the widest possible readership for the poem is reflected in the price, which covered simply the production costs and nothing more. In correspondence with Mr Carey McWilliams, editor of *The Nation* in New York, Kinsella notes that:

> the main aim is to get the poem to the largest possible circulation, as you will have deduced from the price . . . [which] allowed for minimum booksellers' discount only, employing the cheapest printer we could find, taking no royalty or designer's fee, etc.[8]

Liam Miller of the Dolmen Press emphasised the importance of distribution and affordability when he commented to Desmond Rushe of the *Irish Independent* that 'It is marvellous to see a poet of the quality of Tom Kinsella so deeply concerned in the affairs of his country. I want to see his poem get the widest possible circulation.'[9] And this the poem did. David McCullough, reviewer for the *News*, attests to the poem's ubiquity when on a visit to Dublin in the Spring of 1972. Everywhere he turned he 'seemed to encounter a small buff-colored pamphlet decorated with a black coffin bearing the number 13.[. . .] It cost only ten pence, and you could buy it just about anywhere, bookstores, small shops, anywhere.'[10] However, the impossibility of financial gain with such a project was not immediately evident to all, as is shown by one particularly vituperative, and anonymous, critic of *Butcher's Dozen* who characterises the poem as a 'vile way of making money'.[11] James Simmons, in a parody of *Butcher's Dozen*, mounts a personal attack on Kinsella accusing him of seeking to increase his reputation and his coffers through the misery of others: 'That ought to boost my reputation / In England and the U.S.A. / Where the cash is anyway.'[12]

The poem was reprinted in *The Sunday Press*, on 30 April 1972, four days after its initial publication, and somewhat later in *The Irish News and Belfast Morning News* on Thursday 4 May, and again in *Fortnight* on 11 May. Sections of the poem, with an accompanying review, were carried by *The Evening Press*, and *The Irish Press* on 27 April 1972, and by the *Irish Independent* the next day. The *Irish Independent* reports a first edition of 2,000 copies, and an undated clipping in Thomas Kinsella papers states that '*Butcher's Dozen* appeared in an issue of 10,000 copies at 10p and is almost sold out', a reference which Stephen Enniss understands to refer to the numbers of the first and second trade editions combined.[13] *Butcher's Dozen* was published in two trade editions, the first on 26 April 1972, the second in August of the same year. Shortly after the first trade edition, a limited edition of 125 copies was published 'almost as an afterthought'.[14] This was the first edition to feature the image of the Peppercanister Church which has been associated with Kinsella's poetry since then. Two years later, in September 1974, a library edition of 175 copies of the poem was published, once again with the

Peppercanister imprint. All of these initial editions were printed by the Elo Press in Dublin.[15]

When the poem was printed in *The Sunday Press* and *The Irish News and Belfast Morning News,* a note remarked that the text was patterned on Alexander Pope's *The Dunciad.* A review by Kevin Sullivan in *The Nation* magazine disputed the comparisons between *Butcher's Dozen* and *The Dunciad* saying, 'nothing could be less like the elegant heroic couplets of Alexander Pope than these rattling octosyllabics in which a form of doggerel is made at times to parody itself'. Sullivan instead suggests parallels with Shelley's 'Mask of Anarchy',[16] Butler's *Hudibras* and Joyce's *The Holy Office*, 'but from line to line one is above all aware of the indignant spirit of Jonathan Swift informing the whole: *saeva indignatio*'.[17] While *The Dunciad* and *Butcher's Dozen* share the compulsion of rhyming couplets, the former's even pentameter is not mirrored by the latter, which is written in a persuasive four-stress line or, as Edna Longley puts it, 'broadsheet doggerel'.[18] On this last point Kinsella and Longley agree. He explains the genesis of the poem in these terms: 'One changed one's standards, chose the doggerel route, and charged'.[19] Kinsella remembers the writing of *Butcher's Dozen*, and his choice of form, in the 1990 poem 'The Stranger' in *Poems From Centre City*:

> A simple form,

> adjusted easily to the situation,
> open to local application; weakened
> by repetition; ridiculed and renewed

> at last in parody. My pen quickened
> in a pulse of doggerel ease.

> (P 12, C 313–14 var.)

Brian Lynch, writing in *The Evening Press*, points to the difficulty of writing political poetry in modern times and criticises Kinsella's use of Pope and Swift as exemplars, writing that 'Pope and Swift are dead and so is their method'.[20] Almost a decade later commentators were still comparing *A Butcher's Dozen* with the work of Alexander Pope. In an interview with Thomas Kinsella, Elgy Gillespie describes *A Butcher's Dozen* as 'a much lesser piece of doggerel in literary terms as the Popean "Dunciad" it was modelled upon'. In his notes to *One Fond Embrace*, Kinsella denies the influence of Pope and cites Brian Merriman instead: 'it is Merriman. No Pope here.' This note becomes a draft stanza for *One Fond Embrace,* which was omitted from the Peppercanister version: 'that saw a lame Dunciad in a rigid patrol / raging with Merriman through bloody Derry / – no Pope Here . . .'. [21]

If we are to look for precedents of *Butcher's Dozen*, we must reach back to other writers of the eighteenth century, to the work of Brian Merriman, Aogán Ó Rathaille and Jonathan Swift. The rhythm of *Butcher's Dozen*, with its four-beat rhyming couplets, echoes poems such as Swift's acerbic satire 'Ireland':

> Remove me from this land of slaves,
> Where all are fools, and all are knaves;[22]

While public commentators were quick to see the influence of Swift in Kinsella's poem, it was the poet himself who drew the reader's attention to Irish language exemplars in the work of Ó Rathaille and Merriman:

> Reaching for the nearest aid, I found the *aisling* form – that never quite extinct Irish political verse-form – in a late, parodied guise: in the coarse energies and nightmare Tribunal of Merriman's *Midnight Court*.[23]

The *aisling* is a traditional Irish verse form in which the poet has a vision of a beautiful woman who is seen as the personification of Ireland.[24] It has late medieval origins, but was most widely practised from the seventeenth to the nineteenth centuries. In *The Hidden Ireland* Daniel Corkery explains that:

> The word 'Aisling' means vision; and the vision the poet always sees is the spirit of Ireland as a majestic and radiant maiden . . . Ireland is in all the 'aisling' poems; and the only lines in them that strike fire from us are those of her sorrows.[25]

This form was used effectively in the political verse of Ó Rathaille in which the apparition foretells the arrival of the Stuart King.[26] The later work of Brian Merriman uses the *aisling* form to satirise sexual politics and religious celibacy. The subversive power of Merriman's poem is attested to by the fact that English language versions of 'The Midnight Court' were still banned in Ireland at the time that David Marcus's translation was published by Dolmen in 1966.[27] Merriman subverts the vision of the young woman into that of a terrible harridan:

> A hellish, hairy, haggard hank,
> . Bearded, bony, long and lank;
> Her height I'd estimate for sure
> At twenty feet, and maybe more[28]

The grotesque visions described by Merriman are echoed by Kinsella:

> Then from left and right they came,
> More mangled corpses, bleeding, lame,
> Holding their wounds. [. . .]

(P 2, C 137)

but where Merriman finds wit, Kinsella finds only anguish and despair. In a harshly ironic tone Kinsella echoes the form of *The Midnight Court* by allowing the dead to speak for themselves, thereby indicting and subverting the explanations of the Widgery Report.

The poem opens with a description of the poet's visit to the place of the shooting.[29] The poet announces his point of view from the very outset – 'I went with Anger at my heel' – an approach which is further reinforced by the phrase 'murder smell' to describe the atmosphere of the Bogside at that time (P 1, C 137). Pathetic fallacies such as 'sullen steps' and 'brutal place' combine to set the tone as the poet surveys the place of death:

> And when I came where thirteen died
> It shrivelled up my heart. I sighed
> And looked about that brutal place
> Of rage and terror and disgrace.
>
> (P1, C 137)

The voices of seven phantoms, and three corpses speaking as one, are heard in the poem, each setting out an argument to discredit both the events of the previous months, and of the previous centuries. Kinsella divides the poem into two parts which deal, through the first three voices and the corpses, with the specific incidence of violence and, through the last four voices, with the system which gives rise to that violence. The first voice speaks from 'a ghostly pool of blood', describing the shootings in the Bogside in terms of an excessive use of force: 'Here lies one in blood and bones, / Who lost his life for throwing stones' (P 1, C 137). Next to bear witness are three corpses who are envisioned in a viscerally immediate yet grotesque form as they emerge 'red and raw, / from dirt and stone', saying:

> 'Behind this barrier, blighters three,
> We scrambled back and made to flee.
> The guns cried *Stop*, and here lie we.'
>
> (P 2, C 137)

The second single voice, 'soiled and white', tells of how the soldiers found weapons on the bodies of the dead where doctors examining them previously had found nothing (P 2, C 137). Maurice Harmon emphasises the direct link between the tribunal's report and Kinsella's satire when he points out that 'the poem's main device is to allow the words of the thirteen dead to contradict the spurious findings of the report'.[30] Harmon links a passage from the report with one from the poem. The report makes this statement:

> The Medical Officer made a more detailed examination afterwards but on neither occasion did he notice anything unusual in Donaghy's pockets.

After another short interval, and whilst Donaghy's body still lay on the
back seat of Mr Rogan's car, it was noticed that he had a nail bomb in one
of his trouser pockets (as photographed in RUC photographs EP5A/26
AND 27).[31]

The full force of Kinsella's contempt is evident in the passage, spoken by
the second voice, which rewrites this incident:

> When the bullet stopped my breath
> A doctor sought the cause of death.
> He upped my shirt, undid my fly,
> Twice he moved my limbs awry,
> And noticed nothing. By and by
> A soldier, with his sharper eye,
> Beheld the four elusive rockets
> Stuffed in my coat and trouser pockets.
>
> (P 2, C 138)

The third voice describes the lack of due care with which the bodies of
the wounded and the dead were treated by the authorities, making the
serious charge that certain wounded may in fact have suffocated while
being transported in the armoured cars: 'We three met close when we were
dead. / Into an armoured car they piled us / Where our mingled blood
defiled us, / Certain, if not dead before, / To suffocate upon the floor'
(P 2, C 138). Recent findings on the events of 30 January 1972 suggest
that the concerns about the Widgery report to which Kinsella gives voice
may soon become part of the official record. On 16 September 1999
The Belfast Telegraph carried reports of new evidence from the Saville
inquiry which casts 'doubt on allegations that one of the dead, . . . was
carrying nail bombs when he was shot'. The forensic scientist, who pro-
vided the data which implied that the victims had been handling
weapons, now indicates that these findings are unreliable since further
tests reveal 'that exhaust fumes from motor vehicles could have caused
the same contamination as handling weapons'. These reports, allied with
further evidence that certain victims had been shot while lying face
down, or in the back of the head with ammunition which is illegal under
the Geneva Convention, underline Kinsella's courage in speaking out in
Butcher's Dozen at a time when circumspection was often considered
the wiser option.

The fourth voice focuses on the Widgery Tribunal itself, asking: 'Does
it need recourse to law / To tell ten thousand what they saw?' (P 3, C 138).
Kinsella points up the hypocrisy of co-opting the law to justify a violence
which is direct contravention of that law. In passages which have subse-
quently been omitted from the 1996 *Collected Poems* Kinsella makes his
indignation clear:

Law that lets them, caught red-handed,
Halt the game and leave it stranded,
Summon up a sworn inquiry
And dump their conscience in the diary.
During which hiatus, should
Their legal basis vanish, good,
The thing is rapidly arranged:
Where's the law that can't be changed?

(P 3)

The fifth voice of *Butcher's Dozen* deals with the legacy of imperialism in Ireland. Taking as his image the contents of a witch's cauldron, the poet gives us a recipe for colonial disaster. The ingredients comprise 'a bunch of stunted shoots, / A tangle of transplanted roots, / Ropes and rifles, feathered nests, / Some dried colonial interests' (P 4, C 139). The poet acerbically concludes: 'Now, to crown your Irish stew, / Boil it over, make a mess. / A most imperial success!' (P 4, C 139).[32] At this point in *Butcher's Dozen* the voice of the poet intervenes to explain the point of view of 'sympathetic politicians' who argue that obsessions with past wrongs can only lead to further trouble: 'Backward looks and bitterness / Keep us in this dire distress' (P 4, C 139). But this opinion is swept aside by the harsh voice of the fourth spirit who exposes the contradictions inherent in a society which is responsive and alert only to the threat of violence, but then refuses to talk to those who have participated in that violence:

We rap for order with a gun,
The issues simplify to one
– Then your Democracy insists
You mustn't talk with terrorists!

(P 5, C 140)

The vitriolic tone continues in the voice of the sixth ghost who sets out the logic of imperialism in a curse on 'the cunning and the bland', and lays the blame for postcolonial disaster firmly at the door of the colonisers who 'keep the natives on their paws / With ready lash and rotten laws; / Then if the beasts erupt in rage / Give them a slightly larger cage' (P 6, C 140). Yet through his anger, the poet attempts to provide an element of balance. While the sixth voice denigrates the Orange Order as the 'slops and scraps' of the 'Empire-builder', the seventh voice, who is the 'thirteenth corpse', swiftly mitigates this opinion:

Doomed from birth, a cursed heir,
Theirs is the hardest lot to bear,
Yet not impossible, I swear,
If England would but clear the air

(P 7, C 141)

Kinsella's ire is directed not at the communities involved in the conflict, but at the political process which helps perpetuate that conflict. The poem ends on a conciliatory tone which seeks to bring together the communities of Ireland: 'We are what we are, and that / Is mongrel pure. What nation's not' (P 8, C 142 var.). The contradiction inherent in the phrase 'mongrel pure' points up the futility of establishing a tradition of exclusion and essentialism from any religious, cultural or political perspective. As it closes, the poem shifts its focus to the earth, which is both a common denominator and a divider, and looks back to a time before sectarian division:

> The gentle rainfall drifting down
> Over Colmcille's town
> Could not refresh, only distil
> In silent grief from hill to hill.
>
> (P 8, C 142)

Reactions to *Butcher's Dozen* were mixed and volatile. The high praise of associates like Liam Miller and contemporaries such as Eilís Dillon,[33] were echoed by reviewers such as Desmond Rushe, who called the poem a 'remarkable publication' and praised Kinsella for reacting to 'events of the day so speedily, and with such concern, sorrow, power and pity'.[34] Gerald Dawe explains how vital the poem was to those struggling to comprehend the killing of the civil rights marchers on what is known as 'Bloody Sunday':

> . . . it was with a sense of outrage and disgust that the people read the Widgery Report. It had turned reality inside-out by making the unarmed marchers into a guerilla force and the Paratroopers into a restrained and disciplined army. *Butcher's Dozen*, which was handed around in its frail pamphlet form, summed up that nightmarish world [. . .] The ballad cauterized the wound.[35]

However, not all reviewers were of this opinion. In *Fortnight* James Simmons characterises *Butcher's Dozen* as 'a nasty piece of work' and objects to Kinsella's denunciation of the continuing effects of imperialism. In a perverse move for a review which purports to repudiate violence, Simmons berates the Irish for their ineptitude in battle:

> The sons of Imperialists are as much saddled with their burden as the sons of the corrupt and incompetent Irish leaders who could not defend their country and who botched their rebellions. The Irish are not traditionally against war and so on. They are just not very good at it. So how can any sane Irish man feel morally indignant?[36]

Simmons's ethnic essentialism is exactly the kind of attitude that Kinsella seeks to question in *Butcher's Dozen* which, through its focus on the

mechanics of power and authority rather than on supposed tribal anti-
pathies, moves the conflict of Northern Ireland from the realm of mythic
inevitability into an arena of political possibility. *Butcher's Dozen*
touched on more than a few raw political nerves. Professor M. Roberts
of the Department of Modern History in The Queen's University of Belfast
refused to accept a copy of the poem sent to him by Professor D. Greene,
MRIA. Writing in the third person, Roberts neatly elaborates the political
demarcations which were troubled by Kinsella's poem:

> As a historian, he [Roberts] is unsympathetic to myth-making; as a patriot,
> he does not read propaganda emanating from a country which has so
> ostentatiously manifested its enmity to his own.[37]

While Roberts characterises *Butcher's Dozen* as propaganda, others saw
the poem as one of the few ways in which what they saw as propaganda
of another kind could be counteracted. The news bulletin of the Northern
Ireland Civil Rights Association, *Civil Rights*, announces the publication
of *Butcher's Dozen* with the prediction that Kinsella's 'account of the
Derry massacre will long outlive British Propaganda efforts to cover up
the murder of civil rights marchers'.[38] In the light of recent developments
arising from the new inquiry into Bloody Sunday under the chairman-
ship of Lord Saville of Newdigate, the questions that Kinsella raises in
Butcher's Dozen are still very relevant to contemporary political analysis.[39]

In his commentary on the poem in *Fifteen Dead* Kinsella takes on
board some of the criticism levelled against *Butcher's Dozen* – 'it did
not put adequate emphasis on the Civil Rights campaign in the north; it
did not lament the "Protestant dead"' – and voices some of his own regrets:

> I failed to fit in a reference to the culpable silence of the Catholic Church,
> North and South, in the face of Northern injustice during the long build-
> up to the current troubles. The poem doesn't bring out properly the price
> paid by the Northern majority for its long, grim dominance: its mediocrity,
> due to the exodus of its best intelligences.[40]

Seventeen years after Bloody Sunday, Kinsella reaffirms the poem's roots
in the reaction against injustice, and refutes the charge that it condones
terrorism:

> Northern Ireland is an unjust society and I see nothing unreasonable about
> saying this, on one of its brutal occasions. The idea of the poem being in
> support of terrorism or that kind of thing is a misreading, probably a
> deliberate one.[41]

Again, in his foreword to the reissue of *Butcher's Dozen* in 1992, on the
twentieth anniversary of the Widgery Report, the poet reaffirms the
poem's relevance to the social and political situation in Northern Ireland:

Northern Ireland, twenty years after Bloody Sunday, is still an unjust and violent society. The injustice is official and structured, based on the threat of Unionist violence at the establishment of the Northern state, and on a system of sectarian discrimination since then. The current violence is an outcome of this, and continues to increase.[42]

Butcher's Dozen is unusual in both its function and form. Written as a deliberate poetic intervention in a particular political process, the poem gives voice to concerns and attitudes which were not officially sanctioned and still remain at odds with the official version of events. It is a public poem, and a political poem; a poem designed to reach the largest audience, and to provoke strong reactions. By engaging so closely with public matters in *Butcher's Dozen* Kinsella has, in many critics' eyes, sacrificed aesthetics for politics. Badin characterises *Butcher's Dozen* as a poem 'singularly lacking in emotion and sounding too much like a political treatise in iambic tetrameters'.[43] Other critics have found the surfeit, rather than the lack, of emotion problematic in the poem. In *We Irish*, Denis Donoghue identifies *Butcher's Dozen* and Brian Friel's *The Freedom of the City* as examples of works which 'come from the primitive demand, the insistence upon unmediated rage', and which suffer by being so swiftly conceived in response to an atrocity.[44]

Such criticisms provoke a very important question: what do we expect from poetry? Must poetry always be the result of reflections in tranquillity? Is it acceptable for a poet to take a public political stand? What is the relationship between politics and aesthetics? These questions, in turn, bring us to a consideration of the relationship between the artist and his or her community. Writing in his introduction to *The Faber Book of Political Verse*, Tom Paulin comes close to refuting the attitude of Donoghue's criticism when he observes that 'one of the dogmas of the ahistorical school of literary criticism is the belief that political commitment necessarily damages a poem.'[45] Using John Dryden's *Absalom and Achitophel* as an example, Paulin argues for the necessity of the political poem, one which 'often begins in a direct response to a current event' and reminds us that 'in certain societies to write poetry is to act socially, not to turn one's back on contingency'.[46] In a review of Kinsella's and Seán Ó Tuama's anthology of Irish writing, *An Duanaire*,[47] Seamus Heaney makes a direct connection between *Butcher's Dozen* and the tradition of disaffected political poetry of the seventeenth and eighteenth centuries. He argues that 'much of the work of Ó Bruadair, Ó Rathaille, Seán Clárach MacDhomhnaill and others has the same rage and certitude as Kinsella's own Bloody Sunday poem'.[48] To mark the twenty-fifth anniversary of the shootings on 30 January 1972 Heaney sent an abbreviated version of a ballad which he wrote in response to the events of 1972 to the *Derry Journal* which appeared on 1 February 1997:

My heart besieged by anger, my mind a gap of danger,
I walked among their old haunts, the home ground where they bled;
And in the dirt lay justice like an acorn in the winter
Till its oak would sprout in Derry where the thirteen men lay dead.

In an earlier interview with Seamus Deane, Heaney emphasises the importance of integrity and control at the point where art and politics meet. He argues against art serving 'any particular momentary strategy' within politics, but concedes that 'poetry and politics are, in different ways, an articulation, an ordering, a giving of form to inchoate pieties, prejudices, world-views'.[49]

In a 1974 broadcast for Radio Éireann Kinsella spoke of Ireland as a 'necessary burden':

> [It is] a place I must keep coming back to, I must keep trying to understand. It gets less and less rewarding, but it becomes more and more necessary.'[50]

The need to understand underlies all of Kinsella's poetry, but it is here, in *Butcher's Dozen*, that the necessity becomes a burden. The poem has gained a notoriety which threatens to obscure Kinsella's wiser and more complex poetry, and its overt political attitudes have pigeonholed the poet in the eyes of many readers. In a review of *Butcher's Dozen*, Floyd Skloot emphasises the relevance, and importance, of the poem for Kinsella's own poetic development and for the wider cultural community:

> As the first product of a major, internationally published poet's venture at self-publication, *Butcher's Dozen*, with its public and political character, provides a useful reminder that despite his sojourn in America, Kinsella – the twenty-year public servant – is deeply concerned with the life of his people. It brings him back home, loud and clear, and it initiates a sequence that will prepare him to publish, with a 'mature unsureness', poems that focus on the outer and inner processes of his country and himself.'[51]

As the first of the Peppercanister series, *Butcher's Dozen* marks an abrupt shift from the psychologically motivated poetry of *Notes from the Land of the Dead*. However, as the Peppercanister series develops we can connect *Butcher's Dozen* with Kinsella's other satires, *One Fond Embrace* and *Open Court*, to see how the poet's occasional sharp criticism of Ireland's states of affairs is of a piece with his more allusive and interior poetry. In *Butcher's Dozen* Kinsella made a firm judgment on a fraught and complex situation. The politically controversial opinions voiced by the poem mark him as a poet of conviction and integrity. Fittingly for a poet who is as concerned with the development of society as he is with the development of the self, these opinions are now being supported by the revised historical record.

A Selected Life

The public and political character of *Butcher's Dozen* highlighted by Skloot gives way to a more personal yet still socially engaged poetry with the next two Peppercanister pamphlets, *A Selected Life* and *Vertical Man*, in which Kinsella explores a private friendship in terms of larger social and cultural influences. Writing on elegiac poetry in the works of Crane, Kinsella and Nemerov, Celeste M. Schenck describes the modern elegy as a poem which 'offers lyric-philosophical pronouncements on mortality, art, language, and loss'.[52] All of these four facets are integral aspects of Kinsella's two elegies for Seán Ó Riada, *A Selected Life* and *Vertical Man: A Sequel to A Selected Life*. The public and private loss of Ó Riada's premature death at the age of forty is mourned in an appreciation of his gift for music and language which is framed within the poet's psychic journey through the landscape of Dublin and West Cork.

Born into a family of traditional musicians in Adare, County Limerick in 1931, Ó Riada was Ireland's foremost composer who also had a vital influence in the revival of traditional music. As Kinsella explains, Ó Riada 'restored life and nobility to it by his analytic ear for its essential melodic excellence and by his great personal gift for presentation'.[53] Part of this presentation was the founding of the music group Ceoltoirí Chualann which worked to give Irish music a new direction, 'releasing the original airs from the metronomic conventions of the céilí band.'[54] As Kinsella alludes to in *One Fond Embrace*, Ó Riada's work with Ceoltoirí Chualann is continued today with the popular traditional group The Chieftains (P 13, C 289). He also wrote a number of scores for films, the most renowned of which is *Mise Éire*, 1959. Ó Riada's work in the classical tradition included settings of poems by Hölderlin in the tradition of German Lied, a work for orchestra, 'Hercules Dux Ferrariae', which uses the contemporary technique of serialism, and the series *Nomos 1–4* for orchestra and choir, the second of which is often considered his best work. He is described as a composer who had

> this breadth and this depth, and the ability to tackle with imagination and technical skill broad philosophical themes which go beyond the regional and the finite, and reach into questions of time, of the ultimate, of the hereafter.[55]

Ó Riada worked at Radio Éireann and the Abbey Theatre before taking up a lectureship at University College Cork. He moved from Dublin to the Cork Gaeltacht (Irish speaking area) of Cúil Aodha where Irish became his vernacular. Ó Riada's shift from from English to Irish was part of a growing movement among his generation to embrace Irish as a living language, a shift which Kinsella felt drawn towards but unable to embrace. Kinsella's reasons for continuing to live and work through English have to do with the role of language in contemporary life. Switching from English to Irish would entail, for Kinsella,

> a commitment to the Irish language; to write in Irish instead of English. And that would mean loss of contact with my own present – abandoning the language I was bred in for one which I believe to be dying. It would also mean forfeiting a certain possible scope of language: English has a greater scope, if I can make use of it, than an Irish which is not able to handle all the affairs of my life.[56]

However, through his translations of poetry in Irish, from the early *Longes Mac Unsnig*, *Thirty-three Triads* and *Faeth Fiadha* to the later seminal anthologies, *An Duanaire 1600–1900: Poems of the Dispossessed* and *The New Oxford Book of Irish Verse*, Kinsella has brought Irish literature into the hands and language of his contemporaries, much as Ó Riada's work with Irish traditional music brought it from the edges of the Gaeltacht into the heart of the cities. John Engle describes Ó Riada as one who 'acted as a lightening rod for the cultural energy of a people' who came to represent 'both radical innovation and a humbling, fundamental return to pure traditionalism.'[57]

Ó Riada's achievement is seen by Kinsella as both personal and communal:

> His more notable achievements in music have always involved others – the musicians and poets of the Gaelic past, his own Ceoltóirí, his adopted community in Coolea.[58]

With this remark Kinsella emphasises the interrelationship between the artist and society which he considers to be integral to art and vital for community. Ó Riada's death had a significant impact on people from all walks of Irish life, and the importance of his contribution to Ireland's culture was celebrated by his contemporaries. In the same year that Kinsella's *A Selected Life* appeared, John Montague dedicated 'Patriotic Suite', the eighth part of his poem *The Rough Field*, 'for Sean O Riada'.[59] A few years later, Seamus Heaney's poem 'In Memoriam Sean O'Riada' appeared in the 1979 collection *Field Work*.[60] Aidan Mathews emphasises the public importance of Ó Riada when he writes that:

> Most of our more senior poets have made encomia to the memory of Sean O'Riada: for Kinsella, he is 'the vertical man'; for Montague, he represents

a mythic coalescence of O'Carolan's music, renaissance recklessness and the usages of the great Gaelic houses in the seventeenth century. Heaney's notation is less aristocratic, but it encapsulates a similar ambition – that of establishing a cultural epitome and, in consequence, an affective norm in one's art.[61]

A Selected Life, described by Kinsella as 'a funeral poem', appeared in August 1972.[62] Possible alternative titles for the poem were 'Sound and Echo' and 'Moments Musicaux'.[63] It was issued in both a limited and a trade edition and the proceeds from both went to a foundation established in Ó Riada's name: Fundúireacht an Riadaigh. The cover features an image of Ó Riada which was derived from a medallion by the sculptor Seamus Murphy based on the death mask of the composer. It is a haunting image which captures Ó Riada's profile in chiaroscuro, eyes closed as if in meditation rather than death. The sense of peace, and stasis, conveyed by the image of the composer on the cover of the volume, contrast with the taut portrait Kinsella sketches of him in the opening section of A Selected Life: 'He clutched the shallow drum / and crouched forward, thin / as a beast of prey' (P [7], C 143). This section gives us Ó Riada the musician. His instrument and his body become one, folded into each other. The skin of the bodhrán is stretched as tightly as Ó Riada's own shirt over the taut body which crouches forward, waiting. Kinsella describes Ó Riada as a beast of prey, tense and alert as it moves in for the kill, his eyes 'stared / to one side, toward the others' (P [7], C 143). The very act of making music is imbued with a sense of threat and danger. Ó Riada begins to play, striking the bodhrán 'cruelly' with his nails, and the instrument responds with an 'answering arid bark' (P [7], C 143). Here, the music which Kinsella describes is a music of animal instinct. It is a music born of necessity: out of a hunger which, like that of the beast of prey, must be satisfied. The taut assonance of 'shirt / stretched' and 'struck the skin', and the surprising rhyme of 'Sharp' and 'bark' combine to convey the sense of urgency and rigour which Kinsella attributes to Ó Riada's work (P [7], C 143).

The opening section of the poem is set in Galloping Green, a suburb of Dublin about eight miles from the city centre. It is May 1962 and Ó Riada is gathered together with the Ceoltóirí Chualann making the music for which he, and the other members of the group, and indeed its successor 'The Chieftains', would be best known. The second part of A Selected Life moves from Dublin to Cúil Aodha, just as Ó Riada himself had done. It is now 6 October 1971, three days after Ó Riada's death at the age of forty in a London hospital. It is his funeral. In the Bulletin of the Department of Foreign Affairs Kinsella describes the funeral as 'remarkable':

From every part and every element of the country many hundreds came to take their leave of Seán Ó Riada, a young man who had laid extraordinary hold on their emotions.[64]

The second section is called 'Coolea: 6 October 1971' and it opens with the poet's view of the funeral scene. In lines that have been described as 'both chiseled and numinous' Kinsella writes:[65]

> A fine drizzle blew
> softly across the tattered valley
> onto my glasses, and covered
> my mourning suit with tiny drops.

(P [8], C 143)

The formality of the occasion is emphasised by the echo of 'morning suit' contained in the phrase 'mourning suit', and it also conveys the idea of the poet clothed in mourning just at the valley is clothed in mist. A series of observations follow which link together to connect the private grief for a friend lost with the public grief of a nation. The 'tiny drops' which cover the poet become emblematic of Ireland's grief as the sounds of the instruments played at the funeral mingle with the cries of the animals outside.

In the second stanza of this section a crow emerges from the undergrowth with a 'dark groan'. In Celtic mythology the crow has strong associations with war and death. Here, the crow's voice emanates from both the animate and the inanimate parts of the world: 'It croaked: a voice out of the rock / carrying across the slope. Foretell' (P [8], C 143). The word 'foretell' is repeated in the first line of the third stanza, where it announces the scenes immediately prior to the funeral. Once again Kinsella starts from a point on the furthest horizon, taking the Sullane river as a route through which to bring the eye 'through the fields' and down behind Ó Riada's house to where the preparations and greetings are under way:

> cars parking in the lane; a bare yard;
> family and friends collecting in the kitchen;
> a shelf there, concertinas sprawled in the dust,
> the pipes folded on their bag.
> The hole waiting in the next valley.
> That.

(P [8–9], C 143)

Kinsella's cinematic eye gives us the overview and the detail in one. A sense of expectancy is conveyed by the patient positions of the musical instruments, and by the growing crowd in the kitchen. The focus of the anticipation is an absence rather than a presence. The funeral about to begin has 'The hole waiting in the next valley' as its final justification (P [9], C 143). A single word, 'That', brings the stanza to a halt in an attitude of meditation and ineffability.

The crow of this stanza does more than announce the imminent funeral. It harks back to pagan times when Mórrígan the war fury would assume the shape of a crow, bringing together in this metamorphosis the twin poles of life and death. The crow introduces to the poem another vertical man in the shape of Cúchulainn who wished to die standing up 'feet on the ground, eyes facing the foe'. Cúchulainn lashed himself to a pillar stone, and his death was only noticed by his enemies when a hooded crow landed on his shoulder.[66] The focus of the poem shifts abruptly from the general observations of the funeral preparations to the very particular description of a dead rat lying 'on its side in the wet'. In death the distinctions between inside and outside which maintain the integrity of the body have been violated: 'the back torn open. A pale string / stretched on the gravel' (P [9], C 144). This is not a Keatsian easeful death, for the face of the rat is 'wrinkled back in hatred', and the dead rat itself is described in ambiguous terms as a 'Devil-martyr' (P [9], C 144). The responsibility for the quiet horror of this scene is laid by the poet directly at the feet of the crow:

> I have interrupted
> some thing . . . You! Croaking
> on your wet stone. Flesh picker.
>
> (P [9], C 144)

Once again the focus shifts as 'The drizzle came thick and fast suddenly' and the poet's gaze moves to the site of the funeral where 'Down in the village the funeral bell began to beat' (P [9], C 144). By addressing the crow directly – 'You!' – Kinsella establishes a communion with this foreteller of death, and links it with the subject of the poem: 'And you. Waiting in the dark chapel' (P [9], C 144). Like a character from Dante or Beckett, Ó Riada is 'Packed and ready' for a journey to the other-world, or the underworld. But he is also, literally, packed and ready in his coffin awaiting burial. This darkly accurate description becomes poignant as Kinsella develops the parallel between death and a journey. Ó Riada is 'Leaving' but, as with most leavetakings, a 'few essentials' are forgotten (P [9], C 144).

The remaining four stanzas of this section enumerate these forgotten essentials which include 'a standard array of dependent beings' (P [9], C 144). The tone of detached observation evident in the phrase 'standard array' is emphasised by the description of these dependents as 'small, smaller, pale, paler, in black' (P [9], C 144). It is as if Kinsella cannot bear to approach the grief which all, including the poet, share. And so he remains distant, giving us observations and descriptions which each convey a particular and discrete perspective. The following stanzas give us an almost cubist view of the funeral. First comes the music which strikingly evokes the gestures of mourning:

> [. . .] a piercing
> sweet consort of whistles crying,
> goosenecked wail and yelp of pipes,

> (P [10], C 144)

Then follows the wake, lit by a firelight which plots 'in the dark; hugger mugger' (P [10], C 144). Firelight conflates with mourners who are unexpectedly illuminated by the fire as they collapse back in a laughter which is quickly choked by 'Angry goblets of Ireland's tears' (P [10], C 144). Music, laughter and tears are all underpinned by drink which eases the pain as 'Men's guts ignite and whiten in satisfaction' (P [10], C 144). The last stanza of this section closes in an atmosphere of drunken grief, while also describing a scene of Ó Riada working while drunk:[67]

> – a workroom, askew: fumbling at the table
> tittering, pools of idea forming.

> (P [10], C 144)

The instruments of the third last stanza give way to the voice of a contralto filling the room with the strains of Gustav Mahler's *Das Lied von der Erde* or 'The Song of the Earth'. For Kinsella, 'the memory of the music, and the context of drunkenness, is one of the "essentials" he [Ó Riada] is leaving behind.'[68] The phrase 'Earth's autumnal angst' brings together the titles of the first two songs: 'the drinking song of the earth's sorrows' and 'the lonely one in autumn'.[69] The lines which follow evoke an atmosphere of Mahler's work conveyed by lines from *Das Lied von der Erde*: 'Autumn mists drift over the lake; / every blade of grass stands covered with rime: / It is as if an artist had strewn jade-dust / over the delicate blossoms.'

As the poet draws a veil over the scenes of the wake, we move to '*St. Gobnait's Graveyard, Ballyvourney: that evening*'. The poet stands alone, observing how the grass trampled by the funeral returns to normal: 'The trampled grass, / soaked and still, was disentangling / among the standing stones / after the day's excess' (P [11], C 145). Nature recovers and continues. The limitations of human life, so eloquently explored by Mahler's song, are underscored by the parallel Kinsella makes between the standing gravestones which surround him, and the standing stones of pre-christian Ireland which attest to an endurance of culture and community, if not of the individual. Once again the crow appears, this time in the company of a flock who 'circled / the church tower, scattered / and dissolved chattering / into the trees' (P [11], C 145). The crows are satiated: 'Fed'. The slight horror conveyed by the word's isolation brings us back to the image of the disembowelled rat, and then leads us forward to a contemplation of the buried remains of the composer.

Death is always linked to the carnal as the poet contemplates 'His first buried night', which is both fearful 'And welcome' (P [11], C 145). The ambiguity contained in the stanza connects the sorrow of the mourners in their loss of family and friend with a sense of relief after suffering.[70] But all at once Ó Riada appears again, a music-hall 'Pierrot limping forward in the sun / out of Merrion Square' (P [11], C 145). This thumbnail sketch of the composer presages his passing as he appears 'pale as death from his soiled bed' (P [11], C 145). And once again he is drawn back to the earth from which he came:

> swallowed back: animus
> brewed in clay, uttered
> in brief meat and brains, flattened
> back under our flowers.
>
> (P [12], C 145)

Here Kinsella encapsulates the cycle of life in a movement of embodiment and disintegration. The noetic animus becomes material as it is 'brewed in clay'. Echoing Judeo-Christian theophany, the self is 'uttered' into existence, the word becoming 'meat and brains' in a brief existence before being 'flattened / back under our flowers' (P [12], C 145). The bathos of 'flattened' undercuts the grand abstractions of the 'animus' which, as Brian John points out, combines the idea of reason or purpose with a concomitant notion of hostility or hatred:

> Moreover, while 'animus' is synonymous with 'rancor' or 'enmity' (as in 'animosity'), its meaning here includes the Latin one of 'reason' or 'intellect' or the spiritual principle, and the brief span allowed to humanity in which to develop one's intellectual or spiritual life.[71]

In contrast with this vision of growth and decay, the image of Ó Riada given in the penultimate stanza of the poem presents him as immutable: 'Gold and still he lay' (P [12], C 146). But this is not an image of death, for he is only on his 'secondlast bed'. The exchange between Ó Riada and Kinsella is distinguished by the plain and the italicised print as the former addresses the latter with the affectionate '*Dottore!*' which harks back to earlier conversations (P [12], C 146). Montague's memoriam for Ó Riada also uses this address, in German: 'murmurs / Herr Doktor as / the wail of tin / whistle climbs against fiddle [. . .].'[72] As the poem concludes poet and composer speak with words which recall two decades of friend-ship and understanding, interchanging a multiplicity of languages in a toast of farewell:

> *Salut.*
> Slán.
> *Yob tvoyu mat'.*
> Master, your health.[73]

(P [12], C 146)

Vertical Man

A Sequel to A Selected Life

Vertical Man, published a year later in 1974, continues the elegy to Ó Riada. Kinsella takes as his title that chosen by Ó Riada for one of his recordings. It comes from a line in a poem by W. H. Auden called 'To Christopher Isherwood':

> Let us honour if we can
> The vertical man
> Though we value none
> But the horizontal one.[74]

The stark opposites of the vertical and the horizontal recall immediately the distinction between life and death, as Kinsella ruefully remarks that, though laid to rest, Ó Riada keeps reappearing: 'It seems it is hard to keep / a vertical man down' (P [5], C 147). We are brought back to another exemplary figure in Kinsella's poetry, this time from the early volume *Downstream* published in 1962. The figure is 'Dick King' in whose ghost the poet reads: 'That death roves our memories igniting / Love' (C 37). The redemptive qualities of death are emphasised by this figure who, like Ó Riada, 'was an upright man' (C 37), a man who, in Brian John's words, 'represents the heroic quester, the self struggling to stand upright against insurmountable odds, [. . .] while the world values only the horizontal, the literally or spiritually dead.'[75]

Vertical Man is subtitled 'a sequel to A SELECTED LIFE' and the continuity between both volumes is emphasised as the opening passage of the poem is given the number four to keep it in sequence with the previous three passages of *A Selected Life.* The image of Ó Riada's profile from the front cover of *A Selected Life* is reproduced in the first page of *Vertical Man,* with an epigraph drawn from the second Peppercanister: '. . . Master, your health' (P [4]). The poem is written in the spirit of one taking up an unfinished conversation. The opening of

Vertical Man invokes Yeats's poem 'All Soul's Night'. The toll of 'the great Christ Church Bell' becomes 'a sudden howling / of engines along Market Street' as bourbon replaces Yeats's 'two long glasses brimmed with muscatel'. The toast which Kinsella offers to Ó Riada: 'To you: the bourbon-breath' recalls Yeats's less certain invocation: 'A ghost may come; [. . .] To drink from the wine-breath / While our gross palates drink from the whole wine.' In their very different ways, Yeats and Kinsella both seek to create a structure through which the world can be understood and in which the self can be positioned and, though Richard Ellmann characterises Yeats's ambition in *A Vision* (of which 'All Soul's Night' is an epilogue) as one of comprehensive control, we must not ignore the poet's cautionary line which undercuts any sense of mortal mastery: 'No living man can drink from the whole wine'.

In *Vertical Man* the mournful valleys of Coolea from *A Selected Life* are replaced by the darkly ominous streetscape of Philadelphia. A variant title for the poem is 'The Ghost of Seán Ó Riada Attends a Private Musical Evening in Philadelphia'.[76] It is Ó Riada's first anniversary, and Kinsella is alone in his apartment high above the screeching traffic, drinking a toast to his lost friend. It is *'Philadelphia: 3 October 1972'* (P [5], C 147). The city is transformed into a place of foreboding as:

> [. . .] the night-monotony
> was startled below by a sudden howling
> of engines along Market Street,
> curséd ambulances intermixing their screams
> down the dark canyons.
>
> (P [5], C 147)

Like the rat and the crow of the previous poem who are invested with a sense of horror and otherworldly power, the fire-engines and ambulances of Philadelphia become animated with howls and screams as they traverse the streets which are now dark and unknowable canyons. The sounds of the city traffic recall the wail and cry of the musical instruments at Ó Riada's funeral. Here Kinsella conflates inner and outer states, investing the empirical with the subjective until the two are indistinguishable. This conflation of poet and city prepares the way for the reappearance of the remembered. The poet turns to the death mask of the composer and a cast of his left hand which he has brought to Philadelphia from Dublin, and to the sleeve of Ó Riada's recording, 'Vertical Man', which features a photograph of the composer 'sitting in his waistcoat, with cigar, and quizzical face averted, dangling a lay figure in front of him with surreptitious obscenity.'[77] The irreverence of this description is counterpointed by the solemnity of the death mask and the cast. These three objects – the first two imprints of the composer's body, the last a representation of it – provide a focus from which emerges the man himself: 'Over the gramophone your death-mask / was suddenly awake' (P [5], C 147). The Ó Riada who appears is an atmosphere rather than a vision, drawn in from the night:

> and I felt something of you
> out in the night, near and moving nearer,
>
> (P [5], C 147)

He who had been 'directed toward / crumbling silence' reappears to provoke the poet into sound as the poet raises a glass in his memory, and in his presence:

> To you: the bourbon-breath.
> To me, for the time being,
> the real thing . . .
>
> (P [5], C 147 var.)

The qualifying phrase 'for the time being' conveys the notion of life as a transitory existence, and death the final and irrevocable state. In this stanza life and death intersect in a moment of friendship and remembrance. The ellipses which close the stanza announce a shift in the poem from remembrance to what Kinsella terms 'offerings' 'to the ghost, in propitiation'.[78] The notion of appeasement or conciliation to this ghostly figure is reinforced by the menacing sounds from the street and combine to transform Ó Riada from a memory or transitory presence into a representative of an otherworldly force, both positive and negative, which Kinsella will explore further in One.

Like his earlier poems 'Downstream' and 'A Country Walk', the external circumstances of Vertical Man become a vehicle for an exploration of the subjective experience. The ambiguous status of death as both deliverance and damnation haunt the poet, who searches for a means through which it may be understood. In his eloquent and perceptive study of Kinsella's early poetry, Maurice Harmon draws our attention to one of the motivations behind Kinsella's work:

> Fundamentally, the problem is one of language, or of translating a concept of existence, of endurance, into words, since the quest for order, for love, for moral values amid appalling conditions of action and feeling, necessarily involves the search for a language adequate to the terms of that search and the nature of its motivations.[79]

The ineffability of the word 'That' in A Selected Life attests to the impossibility of talking about death, even when it is envisioned as a 'hole waiting in the next valley' (P [9], C 143). What we see in the Peppercanister poems is a poet working towards a means of expression, towards a way of communicating an understanding of experience. And in order to find that means of expression, that manner of communication, he must forge a poetic language which derives from detailed witness to that experience.

Kinsella structures *Vertical Man* through a series of aspects. In his commentary on the poem Kinsella outlines the elements which go to make up the body of the poem: 'two sentences from Plato's *The Laws*, from among the drafts of *The Good Fight*, and the "plot" of the long sequence I had been working on during the day.'[80] This long sequence becomes the 1974 publication *One*. The closing sections of *Vertical Man* return to the music which is playing at Ó Riada's funeral nearly a year ago, and which sounds again in the poet's Philadelphia apartment. This is Mahler's *Das Lied von der Erde* and, in particular, the opening movement called '*Das Trinklied vom Jammer der Erde*', or 'The Drinking Song of Earth's Sorrows'. *Vertical Man* shifts from the descriptive introduction of the first four stanzas into a less formally structured sequence of observations and meditations which arise from the above elements. These can be divided into five passages, each introduced by a capital. The opening quotation: '"There has grown lately upon the soul / a covering as of earth and stone, / thick and rough . . ."', is interrupted by the voice of the poet who explains that: 'I had been remembering / the sour ancient phrases . . .' (P [6], C 147). The exchange between the lines quoted from Plato and the lines in the poet's own voice mirrors the Platonic dialogue from which it derives: 'Very well, / seemingly the argument requires it: / let us assume mankind is worth considering . . .' (P [6], C 147). There follows a pause in which the single and isolated line announces: 'That particular heaviness' (P [6], C 148). The word heaviness can be taken on a number of levels here. It implies the seriousness of the matter under discussion – the worth of mankind – but it also gestures towards the inescapable materiality of mankind manifested in the weight of its mass. Taken figuratively, the word also incorporated the idea of existence as a burden. The next passage considers the worth of mankind in terms of the artistic process. The inevitable givens – 'That the days pass, / that our tasks arise, dominate our energies, / are mastered with difficulty and some pleasure' – are assumed and accepted for a moment before being swiftly devalued by the phrase 'and are obsolete' (P [6], C 148). The brief respite of the 'sweet stir / hurrying in the veins' emphasises in its rhythm a transient ecstatic conjunction, which gives way to a contemplation of the very pedestrian ground which 'grows dull to the tread' (P [6], C 148). Life as a trial, or even a torture is evoked by the phrase 'The ugly rack' which the poet accepts resignedly saying, 'let it ride' (P [6], C 148).

Once again the poet addresses his interlocutor with a line which is almost an invocation: 'That you may startle the heart of a whole people'

(P [6], C 148). Brian John reads this line as a reference to Ó Riada's achievement in writing a score for the film *Mise Éire*, which gave expression to the common emotion of an emerging nation.[81] Kinsella describes the composition and effect of this score as both critically and popularly significant:

> In the early sixties he was commissioned to write the music for a documentary film *Mise Éire* (I am Ireland); the film was to cover Ireland's struggle for political freedom and to reach a climax with the Easter Rebellion of 1916. Fully aware of the reserves of national feeling such a project might draw upon, Ó Riada went for his main theme to Ireland's great emblematic song of lamentation and pride, *Róisín Dubh* (The Black Rose); he virtually recreated it, and wrung from it, in full Mahlerian and Sibelian harmonies, every emotional possibility. It is a monument to his talent that the result, while devastating the audience for whom it was produced, remains a fine musical achievement.[82]

Though the commentary notes the score as an undoubted achievement, *Vertical Man* makes a more qualified judgement as the 'delicate, self-mocking' power of the composer is seen to be 'beating to a coarse pulse / to glut fantasy and sentiment' (P [6], C 148). What may be read as a criticism of the popular touch in art seems to contradict the value that the poet has already given to the close connection between artist and community, but ultimately Kinsella's focus is on the artistic process itself. This is a process which always starts from the point of zero. Success in the past is no guarantee of success in the future. But, more importantly, what made the work possible in the past, will not necessarily do so again:

> That for all you have done, the next beginning
> is as lonely, as random, as gauche and unready,
> as presumptuous, as the first,
>
> (P [6], C 148)

However, there is always a build-up of experience, what Kinsella calls 'a kind of residue', which informs the act of writing or the act of composing and which ensures a slightly less 'unready' beginning: 'a maturer unsureness, as we / prepare to undergo preparatory error' (P [6], C 148). The inclusive 'we' joins poet and composer in the act of composition, and underscores this passage's relevance for an understanding of the act of creation. But the repetition of the variations 'prepare' and 'preparatory' on the same line undercut the seriousness of the venture and emphasise the aspect of unknowing inherent in the work.

High seriousness gives way to humour as the poet's interlocutor cautions him not to become portly, a pun on the word 'heaviness' discussed above (P [6], C 148). The appellation 'D******' recalls Ó Riada's farewell 'Dottore' of A Selected Life (P [6], C 148). But it also, and more pertinently, refers to Ó Riada's and Kinsella's shared love of reading and their initial enthusiasm for Lawrence Durrell's 1957 novel, Justine, an enthusiasm which gave way to a sense of disappointment as 'the lush intellectual glamour' of Durrell's writing gave way 'to reveal the travelogue beneath' (P [6], C 148).[83] The second passage opens with the recent memory of that morning's attempts to write. The scene is lightly sketched; the 'rain-stained glass' through which the poet gazes, the tools and materials of his trade laid out on the desk (P [7], C 148). But at this point of preparation which, as Kinsella has already warned us is as likely to be 'preparatory error', the poet turns inward:

> [. . .] and bury
> my face in my hands, in self-devouring prayer,
>
> (P [7], C 148)

The quiet agony of this inward movement is mirrored by the external circumstances of a 'Night seething with / soft incandescent bombardment!' (P [7], C 148). Here Kinsella incorporates into his meditation on Ó Riada an examination of what is required by the creative process, both practically and mentally as he sets out what Floyd Skloot observes as the poet's 'attempt at understanding the imperatives of the artistic mission'.[84]

The charts pinned to the wall and the notes in the desk which lay inert in the daylight 'come crawling to life again' as night advances, vivified by the poet's inward turn (P [7], C 148). Kinsella gives us a glimpse here of how the research completed prior to writing is incorporated into, and transformed by, the poetic process. At once the scene changes and we are in an interior landscape recognisable from Kinsella's early work such as Wormwood. The quotation from the book of the Apocalypse which prefaces that volume does not seem out of place here:

> and a great star fell from heaven, burning as it were a torch; and it fell on the third part of the rivers and upon the fountains of waters; and the name of the star is called Wormwood[85]

In Kinsella's world every ending necessitates a beginning and in this passage we glimpse what Brian John calls 'a vision of process' through which the self, and the poetry, are born.[86] This passage is ostensibly what Kinsella has termed 'the "plot" of the long sequence I had been working on during the day',[87] and its concentration on the archetypal and and the psychic both echo the earlier Notes from the Land of the Dead evoke the subsequent volume One. Here the visceral intersects with the astrological as:

At the dark zenith a pulse beat,
a sperm of light separated wriggling
and snaked in a slow beam down
the curve of the sky, through faint
structures and hierarchies
of elements and things and beasts. [. . .]

(P [7], C 149)

The singular 'sperm of light' traverses the multiplicities of 'elements and things and beasts', becoming itself multiple as it divides and redivides (C 149). The 'sperm of light' becomes a 'multiple gold tear' which transforms into a 'bright Quincunx newly risen' (P [7], C 149). The quincunx is an arrangement of five objects with one at each corner of a rectangle or square and one at the centre. In an interview with Philip Fried in 1988 Kinsella explained the quincunx as that form which 'finds a unity in moving toward five. Five is four centred on one'.[88] After five, the process begins again at one. Kinsella connects the quincunx with Irish numerology and place names by pointing out that 'the Irish word for a province is the same as for a fifth'.[89] Arthur McGuinness traces the origins and uses of 'Quincunx' citing as a possible source for Kinsella's use of the figure in Plato's *Timeaus*, and also C. G. Jung's *Symbols of Transformation* in which the quincunx is the point at which 'the demiurge joins the parts of the world-soul together by means of two sutures, which form a chi (X)'.[90] McGuinness and Brian John agree that the Quincunx is 'a cosmic structure symbolizing the creative tension, "woman-animal," that constitutes the "self".'[91] Kinsella directly incorporates this symbol as he closes the passage with an image of the very same 'woman-animal' which fades to the 'far-off desolate call' of a child (P [7], C 149). Kinsella emphasises the otherworldly origin of this vision when he addresses Ó Riada once again, saying 'But that is your domain' (P [7], C 149). The communion between poet and composer hesitates as, in the opening of the fourth passage of the poem, Ó Riada's 'presence / turned back toward the night' (P [8], C 149). But the poet draws him in with the promise of one last rendition of the song that in Kinsella's writing epitomises Ó Riada: Mahler's *Das Lied von der Erde*.

In *A Vertical Man* Mahler is played on 'a decent record-player', and as the music sounds the poet is brought back in time to his youth in Dublin, in the company of the man he calls 'John Reidy':

> I remember the elaborate, opulent close of *Der Rosenkavalier* filling the mean little space: the unmade single bed, the dusty electric fire glowing in the grate, spattered with butts, Reidy's narrow, unfocussed face intent in the dark like an animal. I heard Mahler there for the first time. Reidy played *Das Lied von der Erde* again and again.[92]

Kinsella's writing in this passage mirrors the movement of the first song of work: *Das Trinklied vom Jammer der Erde* or 'The drinking song of earth's sorrows'. He captures the character of the piece with the lines:

> – into those bright cascades!
> Radiant outcry –
> trumpets and drenching strings – exultant tenor –
>
> (P [8], C 150)

The spatial arrangement of Kinsella's poem echoes the temporal arrangements of Mahler's work, in which a sweet delicacy mixes with terrible force. The fourth passage closes with the word '*Schadenfreude!*' picked out in italics. This pleasure derived from the misfortune of others recalls the theme of *Das Lied von der Erde* in which the beauty of the earth is contrasted with the terrible inevitability of death. That beauty can come from horror, and joy from grief, are contrariety lying at the foundation of *Vertical Man*.

With the fifth passage Mahler and Kinsella intertwine as the poet addresses Ó Riada:

> The golden bourbon winks in the glass. For the road.
> But wait, there is something I must show you first,
> a song of cark and care. A drinking – a drunken – song
> for the misery of this world . . . Not quite right yet
> – but very soulful. To give you a hollow laugh.
>
> (P [9], C 150)

The effects of the winking golden bourbon leak out through the syntax of Kinsella's writing, which rolls on emphatically to present the verses of a song that melds the lines and the sense of Hans Bethge's text for *Das Lied von der Erde* with Kinsella's own words. Kinsella rewrites the text of Bethge's *Das Trinklied vom Jammer der Erde*, which is a translation and adaptation of the work of Chinese poet Li-Tai-Po, thus situating himself at the centre of Mahler's work in which the grief of impending death is counterpointed, and emphasised, by the joys of drink, song and the ever-returning beauty of nature. The four sections of this passage mirror the four verses of Bethge's text, though in Kinsella's version of the last verse the imperative of the former – 'Look down there!' (*Seht dort hinab!*) – is changed to the interrogative – 'Would you care to share a queer vision I had?' (P [9], C 151). This question returns us to the cold graveyard of *A Selected Life*, and also to the 'woman-animal' of the quincunx, as Kinsella describes the apparition of a crouching 'ape-shaped' figure whose very cries are defined by paradox: 'demented, howling out / silent foulness, accurséd silent screams' (P [9], C 151). Here Kinsella underscores the sharp contrast that Bethge makes between the hideous cries of the ape and the beauty of life:

> [. . .] In the moonlight, on the graves,
> squats a wild, spectral figure –
> it is an ape! Hear how his howls
> pierce the sweet scent of life![93]

The accent Kinsella places on 'accurséd' recalls the 'curséd' ambulances the screams of which announced Ó Riada's presence at the outset of the poem.

The fifth, and final, passage of the poem contains three quatrains which recall events from the friendship between poet and composer. Each of these is outlined in Kinsella's commentary on *A Selected Life* and *Vertical Man*. The first recalls a night out in a place on the quays in Dublin when, goaded by inept playing on the piano, Ó Riada 'went up to the pianist and asked to play, then sat down and tore off the tops of his nails and played for a quarter of an hour to the admiration of the surrounding tables'.[94] The second recollection concerns the *sean-nós* singing of Jerry Flaherty whom Kinsella and Ó Riada met on a holiday to Ballyferriter, County Kerry, in 1959. Flaherty's singing is described by Kinsella thus:

> Nothing intervened between the song and its expression. The singer managed many difficult things, but the result was to focus attention on the song, not on the performance or on the quality of the voice. It was a special voice, adapted (like a reptile or an insect) to its function. Mere beauty of tone would have distracted, attracting attention for its own sake. And the singer's act of communication was thoroughly completed by his audience.[95]

While describing Flaherty's voice, Kinsella also describes a kind of art which is expressly designed for its purpose, in which the medium matches the method. It is an art which is communal rather than singular, for the circle of communication opened by the singer is closed and completed by his audience. Kinsella's remarks are relevant to his own writing in which the style is constantly being questioned and altered in order that it might better express the explorations which give rise to it, and in which, as Kinsella emphasises in the later volume *Out of Ireland*, the understanding of the reader is imperative. Kinsella's recollection of Flaherty's singing brings us back also to the early poem 'The Shoals Returning' from *Nightwalker and Other Poems* which elegises Flaherty's drowning in a fishing accident. The passage in *Vertical Man* is taken almost directly from the earlier poem in which Kinsella writes:

> A voice rises flickering
> From palatal darkness, a thin yell
> Straining erect, checked
> In glottal silence. The song
> Articulates and pierces.

(C 68)

The third, and final, section once again recalls that summer in Ballyferriter. Kinsella draws a sketch of himself and Ó Riada fishing for shrimp. The absolute and almost static sense of joy in life is recalled in Kinsella's commentary where he writes that Ó Riada turned to him and said: 'I feel as if I have never done anything else in my life.'[96] Here Kinsella contrasts utter contentment with absolute loss as prepares to drink a final toast: 'The golden goodness trembles'. And we are brought back to a contemplation of the great loss to friend, family and nation occasioned by Ó Riada's premature death, expressed in the almost inarticulate lines:

> [. . .] The waste!
> Abject. Irrecoverable . . .
> (P [8], C 150 var.)

The Good Fight

A Poem for the Tenth Anniversary of the Death of John F. Kennedy

The Good Fight mourns both the death of John Fitzgerald Kennedy and of a certain kind of optimism and confidence which he had come to embody. Through the figures of Kennedy and Lee Harvey Oswald the poem sets up a series of oppositions between the public and the private, the popular and the isolated, the politician and the poet, rhetoric and philosophy, only to undermine the clarity of that opposition through a complex intertextuality which draws on Plato's writing, near-contemporary accounts of the Kennedy administration, and journalism on the inauguration and assassination. Kinsella is clear-sighted in his analysis of democracy and alert to the risks inherent in a system which lays greater store on mass hysteria than on reasoned argument. Throughout, like one banished from Plato's republic, the figure of the poet circles the text.

On 22 November 1973, exactly ten years after Kennedy's assassination, *The Good Fight* was issued by Peppercanister Press in tandem with *Vertical Man*. The poem was begun, as Kinsella explains, soon after the Dallas assassination but was not completed until the tenth anniversary:

With this fifteenth death many things died, foolish expectations and assumptions, as it now seems. I began the poem soon after Kennedy's assassination – with how many other poems written for a while, as people roamed the nights to relieve themselves of obscure pressures. But the poem jammed and allowed time for the foolishness to digest.[97]

The 'foolishness' to which Kinsella refers is the way in which a single figure was invested with all the hopes and desires of a people longing for grand rhetoric and great deeds. In the poem Kinsella traces how Kennedy found a place for himself in the hearts of the people which was closer to the mythic rather than to the actual, and he asks some very important questions. What was the cost of such an investment? What happens when a leader comes to embody aspirations rather than realities? And what does it tell us about the nature of power and politics?

Kinsella explores these questions through a series of dualities. Using Plato's writings on justice which propose the philosopher as the ideal ruler, *The Good Fight* sets up a dialectical rhythm through which the contradictions inherent in the ideals of a democratic society are explored. Kinsella also develops a critique of Plato's theory of forms, arguing instead that the ideal is always contaminated by the contingent. As he writes in the drafts of the poem: 'Establish from the very beginning the closest tie between the idea and the animal'.[98] Kinsella also questions the relationship between art and politics as he explores how Kennedy is transformed by his own rhetoric and how that rhetoric leads to his undoing. Through the figures of Lee Harvey Oswald and Robert Frost, Kinsella draws our attention to the relationship between art and violence, and the difficulties of communication, whether on a private or public level.

In *The Good Fight* Kinsella develops the processes of appropriation and montage which will become characteristic of his Peppercanister poetry as he incorporates into his poem material from two studies on the Kennedy presidency: Theodore H. White's *The Making of the President 1960* and Henry Fairlie's *The Kennedy Promise*.[99] The intertextual aspect of the poem is integral to its sense for, as Brian John emphasises, 'the montage techniques, learnt from exemplars such as Ezra Pound and Thomas Mann, effectively embody the poet's search for structure, meaning, and harmony.'[100] In addition, Kinsella draws on Plato's *The Laws* and *The Republic* to provide a philosophical ground on which the poet's political analyses are traced. In his comparison between the politics of ancient Greece and those of the United States of the 1960s, Kinsella builds on the parallel drawn by Henry Fairlie who recognises that:

> There is an important sense in which John Kennedy and his brothers were subjected to a Platonic upbringing, in which they were nurtured and educated and trained to be the guardians of the state. Certainly, there was something in the atmosphere of the administration which was reminiscent of the gymnasium in ancient Greece, men set apart, endowed in

body as well as in mind with the capacity to excel, taking the state as their mistress.[101]

Set in opposition to the figure of Kennedy is the shadowy image of Lee Harvey Oswald as seen through the eyes of *Playboy* writer John Clellon Holmes, who uses Oswald's own 'Historic Diary' and the Warren Report in his analysis of the mind of the presumed assassin.

The poem is divided into four sections preceded by three epigraphs. It opens with a treatment of Kennedy's election campaign, and of the decisions and transformations necessary to gain and hold power. The second section focuses on the isolated figure of Lee Harvey Oswald, shadowed by images of the solitary poet, and ends with a discourse on the development of social organisation. The third and fourth sections reverse time by beginning with Kennedy's assassination and its effects on the populace, and ending with his inauguration. Once again the poet makes an appearance, here in the person of Robert Frost, reading a poem at the President's inauguration. Each section of the poem, and the cover, is marked by an image of Plato's head, taken from *The Portrait of the Greeks* by Gisela Richter. These images are drawn from Greek portrait statues held by museums in Cambridge, Aix en Provence, Athens and Syracuse.[102] Kinsella arranges the images in descending order, starting with a complete full frontal image of Plato's head, and progressing through stages of physical attrition by which the details of the face are progressively effaced until the last image looks little more than a skull. The gradual diminution of the images of Plato, whether through erosion or vandalism, evokes the waning power of his ideal Republic, ruled by philosophers trained for the purpose, and the rise to prominence of those who gain power through those routes most denigrated by Plato: wealth and democratic election.

The Good Fight is prefaced by three epigraphs drawn from Fairlie's book, Holmes's article, and a quotation attributed to Lee Harvey Oswald. These epigraphs encapsulate the primary motifs of *The Good Fight*: the desire of a community to invest its identity in a single figure or name, the alienation of the individual within that community, and the question of individual responsibility. Fairlie writes of how in 1962 the people of the United States 'began seriously to calculate that, if the three brothers took the Presidency in succession, it would carry the country to 1984 . . . the succession could then pass to the sons'.[103] This dynastic vision undermines the premises of elected representation on which the United States was founded and harks back to the monarchical associations evoked by the parallels drawn between Kennedy's White House and King Arthur's Camelot. In the publicity leaflet for the volume, Peppercanister quotes a review from *The Journal of Irish Literature* which makes this connection:

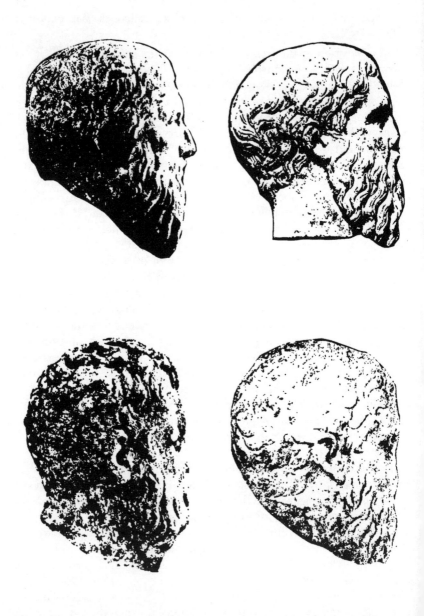

The images of Plato's head, with which Kinsella illustrates *The Good Fight*, are drawn from Greek portrait statues held by museums in Athens, Cambridge, Aix en Provence, and Syracuse (*The Portrait of the Greeks* by Gisela Richter).

In these post-Camelot days both the myth and the reality of the young American President, his short-lived administration, his assassination, shift as unpredictably as an oil-slick on a puddle of water.

This parallel is further strengthened by the echoes noted by Brian John between the lines drawn from Kennedy's speech in part I of the poem and the close of Tennyson's 'Morte d'Arthur'.[104] The quotation from Holmes's article on Oswald draws a subtle parallel between the assassin and the poet which is developed further in part II of the poem. The first two epigraphs situate the poem between hope and despair. The third, which is absent from Kinsella's *Collected Poems*, points to an ambiguity of responsibility which still haunts these events:

> No sir, I killed nobody.
> Lee Harvey Oswald, Dallas Police
> Headquarters, 22 November 1963.
>
> (P 4)

Though Kinsella focuses on the events of Kennedy's election campaign, his inauguration and his assassination, the poet's primary interest lies not so much with what actually happened, but with what was perceived to have happened, and the effect that perception had on society. Kinsella focuses on the figure of John F. Kennedy, but the ideas of leadership and ethics which the poem explores are drawn from Plato's writings. The dualism instigated by Plato's theory of forms is integral to the poem, and the notion of an unattainable ideal, matched with a flawed reality, characterises Kinsella's portrayal of Kennedy. The poem opens with the traditional fairy-tale phrase 'Once upon a time' (P 5, C 153), evoking a moral and educative perspective of the narrative while also emphasising the archetypical nature of the phantom protagonist. The repetition of the word 'certain' in the first sentence underlines the definite, but unnamed, identity of the protagonist who is at once a particular person – John F. Kennedy – and also an exemplar of the ideal democratic candidate. The phantom is described in an explicitly visceral manner. His search for power is portrayed in terms which evoke the process of fertilisation through phrases such as 'red-smelling corridors', and 'the smell of seed'. Kinsella sets up a tone of urgency in these opening lines, combining a sense of necessity with one of inevitability as the phantom 'swallowed / life and doom in the same animal action' (P 5, C 153).

Plato's distinction between the perfection of ideal forms and the imperfection of their physical manifestation is confounded by Kinsella, who describes a figure for whom the thirst for justice and for food is of equal measure:

([. . .], the human mouth
tasting Justice or a favourite soup[105]
with equal relish.)

(P 5, C 153)

Throughout his characterisation of Kennedy, Kinsella plays with an opposition between the visceral and the cerebral. Drawing on reportage from White's book on *The Making of the President*, Kinsella evokes a driven figure whose appetite for power is understood in a distinctly physical way, and whose body exhibits the toll of that appetite:

Once, he rolled up his sleeve
and looked at the calloused, scratched arm:
'Ohio did that to me.'
(One day in Philadelphia
his hand *burst* with blood.)[106]

(P 6, C 154)

Set against this grotesque image is the cool rationality of a candidate who always strives to be in control: 'asking: "Who made that decision? / Who had command decision then?"' (P6, C 154). However, the decisiveness exhibited by these questions is already undermined by the preceding line: 'and shook his head, not understanding' (P 6, C 154). The ambivalence of Kennedy's position is further emphasised as Kinsella evokes Plato's simile of the sea captain (*The Republic*, 7: 488):

Outside, half seen, the fields of stars
chilled his forehead, their millions centred on
the navigator.
                    Not commanding. Steering.

(P 5, C 153)

Through this simile Plato emphasises the incompatibility between running for elected office and governing a state since each of these pursuits requires different skills. As Plato explains, it is not possible 'for any one to acquire by skill or practice the art of getting control of the helm, . . . and at the same time to master the art of steering'.[107] Kinsella echoes Plato's lines:

Can we believe it possible for anyone
to master the art of steering while he must
at the same time expend his best skill
gaining control of the helm?

(P 5, C 153)

The person who has the skills and wisdom to hold high office does not necessarily also have the instinct and tenacity to obtain office. Kinsella places Kennedy in the impossible position between the navigator and the helmsman as one who must embody the high principles of the ideal leader but who needs to make the compromises necessary to obtain elected office. This incompatibility can also be understood in terms of appearance and reality whereby the image of the principled leader hides the ruthlessness and deception necessary to navigate the democratic process.

The second part of this first section of *The Good Fight* rewrites Kennedy's campaign speeches, focusing on the extravagant rhetoric which was to fire the American people:

> Ever free and strong
> we will march along, going to meet
> the harsh bright demands of the West, building
> a new City on a New Frontier,
>
> (P6, C 154)

The first two phrases are the opening lines of a popular song at the time, 'The New Frontier', which was also the catch phrase with which Kennedy sought to include all elements of the population in his bid for election:

> The New Frontier of which I speak is not a set of promises: it is a set of challenges. It sums up not what I intend to *offer* the American people, but what I intend to *ask* of them. [. . .] I am asking each of you to be new pioneers on that New Frontier.[108]

The metaphor of the new frontier was exploited to include states as diverse as New Hampshire and Alaska, and in the process became a little muddied. In Pocatello, Idaho, Kennedy proclaimed:

> I think the future of the United States is unlimited, and I say that after travelling to Maine on Friday, to the last frontier of Alaska on Saturday, and to the great industrial frontier of Michigan yesterday. I come today to the frontier of energy.[109]

Yet still, the rhetoric of the 'New Frontier' was powerful and inclusive. It sought to harness the patriotism of war in a time of peace and prosperity. The fire of Kennedy's exhortation in Towson, Maryland, that 'the New Frontier of which I speak is the opportunity for all of us to be of service to this great republic in difficult and dangerous times'[110] is captured in Kinsella's lines:

> 'Forward, then, in higher urgency,
> adventuring with risk,
> raising each other to our moral best,
> aspiring to the sublime
> in warlike simplicity, [. . .]'
>
> (P 7, C 155)

This stanza is placed in quotation marks, setting it off from the voice of the narrator who comments on the candidate's appearance and behaviour, and from the voice of the evaluator, placed in parenthesis, who remarks: 'It sounds as though it could go on for ever, / yet there is a shape to it – Appropriate / Performance' (P 7, C 155). Here Kinsella judges Kennedy against a Platonic standard, but also makes reference to his own poetic project which seeks to forge an appropriate performance adequate to experience. The harmony or 'pure pitch' (P 8, C 156) necessary between the 'two sinews of the Soul, / Body and Mind' (P 8, C 156) recall the harmony or 'right pitch' which is produced by the appropriate balance between the rigours of gymnastics and the rhythm of dance advocated in *The Republic* (3: 411–12).

The optimism of the first section turns to anxiety as Plato's voice interjects directly for the second time. Through this passage, delineated by italics, Kinsella underlines the risks inherent in the democratic process in which, according to Plato, the opinions of the populace will inevitably become the opinions of the candidate.[111] Plato's description of the young, wealthy and handsome candidate prone to such influence finds an apt personification in Kennedy:

> *What schooling will resist, and not be swamped*
> *and swept downstream? What can a young man do?*
> *Especially if he belong to a great city*
> *and be one of her rich and noble citizens*
> *and also fine to look upon, and tall?*
>
> (P 8, C 156)

The value of education is juxtaposed against experience as Kinsella closes the section with a glimpse of the 'specialists / chosen for their incomparable dash' (P 9, C 157) who formed the coterie of Kennedy's special advisers. These were the 'the best and brightest', whose education was not matched by experience, the consequence of which was to have enormous impact on global politics, not least the Vietnam War.

From the ebullience of the campaign trail and election success, *The Good Fight* shifts to an observation of Kennedy's nemesis: Lee Harvey Oswald. The opening lines of the second section set the scene: 'A lonely room. / An electric fire / glowing in one corner' (P 11, C 157). These lines evoke the 'night monotony' of *Vertical Man,* creating an echo which implicates the poet, newly arrived in Philadelphia, in the figure of Oswald.[112] The utter isolation of these lines contrasts strongly with the popular fervour of the previous section:

> Above and below him
> there are other rooms, with others in them.
> He knows nobody as yet, and has
> no wish to. Outside the window
> the street noises ascend.

(P 11, C 157)

The diction of this section is slow and measured as it describes the solitary figure negotiating his way in an unfamiliar city until a *'routine'* of living is established (P 12, C 158). The attention to detail, 'where to buy bread and tomatoes, / milk and meat', builds up an accumulated image of the mundane and the ordinary into which the consciousness of the subject abruptly breaks (P 11, C 157). The voice changes from the third to the first person as the figure who 'draws his journal to him / and revolves his pen meditatively' speaks (P 12, C 158). In his drafts to the poem, Kinsella announces the shift from third to first person with this description: 'A voice, solo. An inner whine, / insect, intent.'[113] This voice is at once the voice of Lee Harvey Oswald, and of the poet himself.[114] It is a voice which can be linked also with the creative voice characterised through the singular and purposive tones of *sean-nós* singing: 'The song / Articulates and pierces' (C 68).[115] However the act of communication necessary to art and to community cannot be completed by one who, in his absolute isolation, splits himself in two: 'I have seen myself, a "thing" / in my own eyes' (P 13, C 159). This rupture objectifies the self and makes a mockery of expression: 'opening / and closing my mouth / in senseless mimicry' (P 13, C 159).

Through Oswald, Kinsella poses a question: Is isolation the condition of man, or is it simply the position of one man? The condition of isolation 'in itself' with which the speaker is familiar, threatens to become an isolation from the greater whole of society of which he has never fully felt a part:

> I believed once that silence
> encloses each one of us.
> Now, if that silence does not
> enclose *each*, as I am led
> more and more to understand
> – so that I truly am cut off,
> a thing in their eyes also –

(P 13, C 159)

The contradictory solipsism of the first two lines gives way to an anxiety at the possibility of a community of which the speaker is not a part. Here, Oswald's isolation is sharply counterpointed against the illusion of community woven by Kennedy's 'New Frontier' rhetoric elaborated in the previous section. The logical conclusion to the argument the speaker articulates, is suicide: 'Soak wrist in cold water / to numb the pain. / Then slash my left wrist. / Then plunge wrist into bathtub of hot water' (P 14, C 159 var.). Here, Kinsella draws directly from John Clellon Holmes's article 'The Silence of Oswald' in which the writer quotes from Oswald's Historic Diary, complete with idiosyncratic spelling and punctuation:

> Soak rist in cold water to numb the pain, than slash my leftwrist. Than plaug wrist into bathtum of hot water . . . Somewhere, a violin plays, as I wacth my life whirl away. I think to myself 'How easy to Die' and 'A Sweet Death, (to violins).[116]

Holmes's analysis of Oswald's character – 'a man observing himself as if he were not himself' – leads him to the conclusion that 'such a man often becomes a melancholic, or an artist, or a killer'. Here, in the text which underwrites the second section of *The Good Fight*, art and violence are conjoined. However, the choice of suicide to music gives way to an alternative, a way of connecting: 'Or I might reach out and touch' (P 14, C 159). In the drafts of the poem Kinsella writes 'reach out and touch . . . (Plato) / and do what I can competently', and in this latter part of section two of *The Good Fight*, the poet enters into dialogue with the philosopher.[117]

Typographically, this is an interesting section. Kinsella separates the voice of the philosopher from his interlocutor or commentator by dividing the page into two columns. The voice of the interlocutor, in plain text, is placed on the left of the page. Plato's voice, in italics, is on the right. Drawing on G. Lowes Dickinson's *Plato and his Dialogues*, Kinsella interlinks passages from *The Republic* and *The Laws* to form a discourse on government, justice, and art. Kinsella draws on that part of *The Republic* in which Plato describes the decline of the Republic and the progression of society from timarchy (a society where honour is the dominant principle) to tyranny. Tyranny is, in Plato's view, the worst of all political evils, but is also the natural and inevitable product of democracy:

> *– Democracy cries out for*
> *Tyranny; and the Tyrant becomes*
> *a wolf instead of a man . . .*
> (P 15, C 160)[118]

Questions on the origin of crime, '*Passion, ignorance and concupiscence*', are linked with the divine nature of justice from which there is no escape: '*There is none so small or so high / but that he shall pay the fitting / penalty*' (P 14, C 160). Kinsella makes good use of Dickinson's evocative translation of Plato's discourse on the dangers of art, especially of poetry.

Placed against the injunction that '*Great crimes*' will cause the soul to '*sink into the / abyss*' of Hades, is a horrific vision of the corruptive capacity of art '*Images of evil in a foul / pasture . . .*' (P 14, C 160). Plato underscores the risks for the future politicians of the Republic:

> For we would not have our guardians reared among images of evil as in a foul pasture, [. . .] until at last a great mass of evil gathers in their inmost souls'[119]

Throughout this part, Plato's words are subject to commentary by the speaker whose words are placed as a gloss in the margin of the text. The speaker questions the value of society based on honour but not justice, and underlines phrases in Plato's part through the repetition of key words: 'squat!' (P 15, C 160). The final comment focuses on Plato's pronouncement that it is only the philosopher who is truly happy. Here, Kinsella draws together Lowes Dickinson's commentary on, and translation of, Plato in the stanza:

<table>
<tr>
<td>

The rest! The whole
world but one! An
impossible logic-being.
</td>
<td>

– The rest damned to a constant
flux of pain and pleasure. They
struggle greedily for their
pleasures, and butt and kick with
horns and hoofs of iron.
</td>
</tr>
</table>

(P 15, C 160).[120]

The exclamatory response in the left column draws attention to the inequity of a system based on privilege. Kinsella exaggerates Plato's division between the class of philosophers and the rest of society so that the division lies now between a single chosen figure, like the newly elected John F. Kennedy, and the rest of society which includes the alienated and excluded figure of Lee Harvey Oswald.

The contrast between the intellectual and the instinctive alluded to above is extrapolated further in the following passage. Kinsella plays on the words 'man' and 'beast', transposing and recombining the letters to form the words 'best', 'mean', 'team', and 'meat'. With the addition of the letters 'd' indicated by parentheses, 'r', and 'i', indicated by superscript, the poet elaborates the permutations to include the words 'damn' and 'brains'. From the two root words Kinsella draws out conflicting positions in society, such as the division between intellectual and physical capabilities, the distinction between good and evil, the relationship between the individual and the team, and, perhaps most significantly, the fear of damnation as a force for social control. Kinsella ends with a question which strikes at the heart of our concept of society as a *socius*, underlining the inherent conflict in a society based on the freedom of the individual:

I wonder what would
happen if somebody was
to stand up and say he
was utterly opposed not
only to the government
but to the people, to the
entire land and complete
foundations of his
society?

(P 15, C 161).

An unequivocal, if shocking answer to this question comes in part three of *The Good Fight*. The section opens with an image of Hellenic content-ment drawn from Henry Fairlie's *The Kennedy Promise* which portrays the politician in Washington as 'adorned and adored because he has no competitor.'[121] Against this image of order and calm is contrasted the disorientation and trauma which followed Kennedy's assassination. Kinsella draws significantly from Fairlie's book in stanzas three to five, and at times the poet's voice is subsumed under the weight of reportage from studies such as Martha Wolfenstein and Gilbert Kliman's *Children and the Death of a President*.[122] The same collective hysteria which made Kennedy's election campaign successful is manifest in the 'various forms of castration dreads' and 'unconscious parricidal wishes' which beset the mourners. It is not Kennedy the man, but Kennedy the image who is grieved for. Once again the conflict between the actual and the ideal is brought to the fore as the speaker of stanza six proclaims:

It was unhealthy – a distortion of normal attitudes.
Things had been exalted
altogether out of proportion. [. . .]

(P 18, C 162)

Here, Kinsella echoes Fairlie's observation that 'if its power and prestige are exalted, the American Presidency can be a dangerous office, exciting a false relationship with the people.'[123] Rather than portraying Kennedy as a victim, Kinsella implicates the President in his own death through his manipulation of a vision which could never become reality. In his inauguration speech Kennedy commits the United States to the pursuit and defence of liberty far beyond the abilities of its individual citizens:

Let every nation know, whether it wish us well or ill, that we shall pay any
price, bear any burden, meet any hardship, support any friend or oppose
any foe in order to assure the survival and success of liberty.[124]

The section ends with a composite scene from Kennedy's inauguration, bringing together the incident in which Cardinal Cushing's prayer for

Kennedy was interrupted by a short-circuited wire which ignited, causing
smoke to spiral from the lectern, and Robert Frost's attempt to read his
preface in verse written for the inauguration. Frost's eloquence was
thwarted by the wind which rustled his papers and the sunlight which
blinded his vision until he was forced to abandon his papers in favour of
a recitation of 'The Gift Outright'. It is Frost who totters 'forward /
scratching his head, and opening his mouth:' (P 18, C 162), but the
words are spoken in Kinsella's voice:

> I am in disarray. Maybe if I
> were to fumble through my papers again . . .
>
> I can no longer, in the face of so much
> – so much . . .
> It is very hard.
>
> (P 19, C 162)[125]

In the fourth and final section of *A Good Fight* Kinsella draws the
various strands of the poem together in a meditation on the point and
purpose of the poet. Kinsella's familiarity with the corridors of power
from his days as a senior civil servant, and his present perspective as
poet give him a particular insight into the two roles which, in Plato's
Republic, are conceived of as diametrically opposed: the philosopher-
ruler who is at the centre of society, and the artist who exists at the
fringes of, or is banished from, society. Kinsella stresses the need to
acknowledge, and deal with, the existence of both extremes of the moral
spectrum, embodied here in the figures of Kennedy and Oswald:

> The manipulation, the special pleading,
> the cross-weaving of these
> 'vessels of decision',
> the one so 'heroic',
> the other so. . .
>
> (P 19, C 163)

The poet's role is not to choose between both, but to 'wear them down
against each other' in order to 'get any purchase' on actuality or exper-
ience. And experience is limitless, since all we can be really sure of is:

> That all *un*reasonable things
> are possible. *Everything*
> that can happen will happen . . .
> (P 20, C 163 var.)

The portrait of the poet that Kinsella draws is not heroic. The opening
image of Frost in disarray, fumbling with his papers, is developed to
include all poets, including the speaker, who are described as 'huddled'

and 'feeble'. This self-depreciation extends to caricature: poets are ones 'who harp on Love and Art and Truth too often' (P 21, C 163). Kinsella argues for a movement away from the grand themes and appropriate perspectives of poetry, and towards an attention to the detail and particularity of experience: 'it is we, letting things *be*, / who might come at understanding' (P 21, C163). Yet by so doing, the poet will inevitably 'disappoint Plato' for whom balance, 'apportionment' and 'proper pitch' are as vital to the 'philosophic nature' of the ideal ruler as they are to the kind of art which is deemed acceptable in *The Republic*. However, as Plato realised when he came to write the more pragmatic *Laws*, society – and art – are rarely ideal, and it is to this flawed and disharmonious world that Kinsella turns his attention. As he emphasises in conversation with John Haffenden, 'I don't think graceful postures are adequate; you have to deal with the raw material.'[126]

Kinsella uses the phrase 'Appropriate / Performance' to describe the power of Kennedy's rhetoric. He describes it as 'Another almost perfect / working model . . . But it gets harder. / The concepts jerk and wrestle, back to back' (P 7, C 155). These are words that can be used equally to describe Kinsella's own work. For Kinsella 'significant work begins in eliciting order from actuality' and it is his very strong 'responsibility toward actuality' that drives him to develop poetry in which the form arises from the nature of the material, rather than being imposed on the material.[127] In *The Good Fight* we see Kinsella developing a form of writing which takes into account the 'inflexibilities, knots, impossible joints' of its material (P 8, C 155). The poet relies on patience and a good sense of direction to forge a poetry which uses the material of the 'secondary world' of experience to provide a glimpse of 'a primary world' of understanding:

> That is the source of our patience.
> Reliable first in the direction
> and finally in the particulars of our response,
> fumbling from doubt to doubt
> in an art of the necessary,
> one day we might knock
> our papers together, and elevate them
> (with a certain self-abasement)
> – their gleaming razors
> mirroring a primary world
> where power is also a source of patience
> for a while before the just flesh
> falls back in black dissolution in its box.
>
> (P 21, C 164 var.)

Throughout *The Good Fight* Kinsella balances Platonic idealism with contingent reality while making it clear that it is not a question of choosing one or the other, but rather of negotiating a path between them. The diverse and complex voice which Kinsella develops in these four poems, *Butcher's Dozen, A Selected Life, Vertical Man* and *The Good Fight*, enable him to explore what Seán Lucy terms 'public appetite and disappointment'.[128] In his review of the first four Peppercanister volumes Lucy describes Kinsella as an 'explorer of inner space', a poet who 'records human destiny, even public destiny, in terms of physical sensation and consciousness. His vision is a dark one, but it is neither cynical nor anti-human, but rather, tragic. It values courage, energy, intelligence, beauty and love, stating their value clearly against the inevitability of deterioration, loss and death.'[129] In *A Selected Life, Vertical Man* and *The Good Fight*, Kinsella questions the relationship between the artist and his audience, and the politician and his electorate. By drawing a parallel between art and politics the poet asks: to what extent does society project its needs onto these public figures? And at what cost to them? The intertextual nature (to varying degrees) of these four sequences signals the development of Kinsella's work away from a seamless synthesis, in which the poet's voice is predominant, towards a poetry in which the literary, philosophical or historical elements are placed in counterpoint with the poet's voice to form a montage in which, to paraphrase Kinsella's thoughts on *sean-nós* singing, it is the song and its expression which takes precedence over the beauty of the tone or the quality of the performance.

2

PSYCHIC GEOGRAPHY

In 1989 Kinsella spoke of his poetry as an ongoing project, a movement towards a unity which extends beyond the individual poem or sequence:

> One of the things that has disappeared, by comparison with the early work, is the notion of the 'complete' poem, the idea that a poem can have a beginning, middle and end and be a satisfactory work of art thereby. The unity is a much bigger one than that. And it isn't a sequence, or a set of connected long poems. It's a totality that is happening, with the individual poem a contribution to something accumulating.[1]

The volumes discussed in this chapter, *One, A Technical Supplement, Song of the Night and Other Poems* and *The Messenger* continue the work of appropriation and accumulation which characterises Kinsella's writing. From the elegiac concerns of public and private loss of the first four Peppercanisters, in which society is understood through its reaction to death and violence, the poet moves to a more private investigation of the self through the framework of Irish mythology in *One*, anatomy and bodies of knowledge in *A Technical Supplement*, Taoism and music in *Song of the Night and Other Poems*, and alchemy in *The Messenger*.

One

The process of accumulation and recovery through which Kinsella's poetry is written is particularly evident in the 1974 volume *One*. Here Kinsella reaches back to the concerns of *Notes From the Land of the*

Dead, to the framework of Celtic mythology and Jungian psychology which informs these poems. In a sense, we can read *One* as a direct continuation of that earlier writing, with the four occasional poems of elegy – *Butcher's Dozen*, *A Selected Life*, *Vertical Man* and *The Good Fight* – as a shift, but not a break, in the exploration of what Kinsella has called 'psychic geography'.[2] In his drafts of the poem Kinsella describes *One* as a 'sequel to "Notes from L. of D"'.[3] Brian John emphasises the thematic connections between the two works, describing *One* as the 'natural outcome of *Notes from the Land of the Dead*, where the questing self, in search of origins and understanding, proceeds downward and inward, into the darkness of the underworld, the realm of the self's unconscious or shadow'.[4] Indeed, *One* emerges quite literally from 'the land of the dead' since the voyage recounted in 'Finistère' originates there:

> The Celtic doctrine is that the first ancestor of the human race is the god of the Dead, and that this god inhabits a distant region beyond the ocean. . . .[5]

The title *One* announces a beginning which has already been preempted by the zero of *Notes from the Land of the Dead*:[6]

> – what shall we not begin
> to have, on the
> count of
> 0

One is part of the numerological system Kinsella has described as 'an enabling idea' that allows him to explore the 'profound personal and family matters' which concern his poetry. Influenced by Jung, Kinsella developed a system which draws together the isolation of the individual, its connection with the other, and the foundation of community, in a sequence from nought to five:

> One begins as zero, one develops as one, one meets another and becomes two, with luck, three emerges. [. . .] Something like a psychic zero is in an act of preparation, and something like a personal unit in its finding its way into existence. The scheme I have found most useful can count up to five; that is as far as it gets.[7]

The number five has important geographical significance in Ireland, which is divided into four provinces, called 'fifths', each intersecting at Tara, the seat of the High King, and commonly referred to as the fifth province.[8] In an interview with Philip Fried, Kinsella connects Irish mythology and geography with his poetic process:

> *The Book of Invasions* arranges the land of Ireland into four. But there is also a Fifth, the centre; in Old Irish, "Mide." There is a county of Meath in the centre of modern Ireland. I'm aiming toward the idea of middle.[9]

Though five names a multiplicity, it also marks the convergence of disparate entities in a central, singular, point. The number five represents the whole of Ireland, and is also the number of the first kindred, the five primeval peoples of Ireland: Cessair, Partholón, Nemed, the Fir Bolg and the Tuatha Dé Danann.[10] Five is associated with the quincunx of which Kinsella writes in *Vertical Man*, the 'principle of cosmic centre or order.'[11] The 'Prologue' with which Kinsella opens the Dolmen and Oxford editions of *One* sets the scene for the telling of 'the Voyage of the First Kindred'.

> The storyteller's face
> turned toward the fire.
> He honed his flickering blade.
>
> (C 165)

However, this ten-lined poem is absent from all but one of the editions of the poem published by Peppercanister in 1974. *One*, the fifth Peppercanister, was issued in three editions: trade, limited and deluxe, and is unpaginated. The deluxe edition contains the short poem written in the poet's hand, entitled 'The Storyteller's Face'. This poem is included, untitled, in the Dolmen edition of 1979 which collects *One*, *A Technical Supplement* and *Song of the Night and Other Poems*. It also appears in Wake Forest's collection of the same year, *Peppercanister Poems, 1972–1978*, and the more recent Oxford *Collected Poems, 1956–1994*, under the title 'Prologue'. In these two last editions the final poem of the sequence is given the title 'Epilogue'.[12] In 1972 the poem 'Finistère' was published separately by Dolmen Press in an edition accompanied by images of spiral motifs derived from the stone carvings of Newgrange and Knowth, County Meath, and Cardonagh, County Donegal

Each of the Peppercanister editions features seven line drawings by Anne Yeats, daughter of W. B. Yeats and, like Kinsella, a director of the revived Cuala Press. Yeats's drawings are spare and vigorous. They pick up on the historical and psychological thematics of the poem through images of the snake and the spiral, the sun or cell, the tree and the beast, the great stone of Mag Slechta, and a scattering of those origins of life itself: chromosomes. The drawings are interspersed among the poems of the sequence, which are divided into two sets of three, framed by an opening and a closing poem which is differentiated from the main text by its italic print. The first three poems, 'The Entire Fabric', 'Finistère' and 'The Oldest Place' draw primarily on the mythology of the first peoples of Ireland as explained in H. D'Arbois de Jubainville's *The Irish Mythological Cycle and Celtic Mythology*.[13] Like Joyce, who mentions de Jubainville in *Ulysses*, Kinsella looks to de Jubainville's reconstruction of Irish myth, and to his source material in the Lebor Gabála Érenn, and studies such as Geraldus Cambrensis's *Topographia Hibernica* and Geoffrey Keating's *History of Ireland*, for the source narrative of these poems. The importance of mythology in the exploration of the individual psyche is emphasised by Erich Neumann who links narrative with psychology: 'These myth figures are archetypal projections of the collective unconscious; in other words, humanity is putting something outside itself in its myths, something of whose meaning it is not conscious.'[14] The latter three poems, 38 Phoenix Street', 'Minstrel' and 'His Father's Hands' continue the theme of origin and descent from the perspective of the poet's own family. These six poems are bounded by an opening and a closing poem, which draws quite specifically on imagery from the analytic psychology of C. G. Jung. These three aspects of Kinsella's sequence – the psychological, the mythic, and the familial – combine to form a conceptual and creative framework through which the poet examines the self and the society of which he is a part.

The first of Yeats's drawings, on the frontispiece of the Peppercanister volume, depicts a snake draped on a tree. While evoking the story of Adam's and Eve's fall from grace in the book of Genesis, it points to a genesis of another kind which is represented more directly by the next image of a coiled snake with its offspring, or victim, emerging from its mouth. The image of the snake, representative of the world of instinct, evokes the Jungian symbol of origin: the uroboros,[15] the 'heavenly serpent' that 'slays, weds, and impregnates itself. It is man and woman, begetting and conceiving, devouring and giving birth, active and passive, above and below at once.'[16] Yeats's serpent image depicts the urgent energy of the creature in the opening poem of the Peppercanister volume:

> Up and awake. Up straight
> in absolute hunger
> out of this black lair, and eat!
>
> (P [5], C 165)

Emerging from the primordial darkness of its lair and 'driven rustling blind' into the 'grey sheen of light', the creature comes into being in a specifically visceral manner. The almost onomatopoeic compounds 'whimswift', 'Snapdelicious', and 'Throbflutter' combine with the assonance of 'fragments of old frights and furies' to convey a lepidopterous appetite and movement. With the satisfaction of 'the drive, the desire' comes a stasis and balance out of which appears the speaking subject.

The next four stanzas are written from the position of the 'I' who describes a dream in four parts. The first part relates to the distinction between self and other that appetite conveys. The second 'and deeper part' describes the speakers 'absorption' into a 'cosmic grip' and the

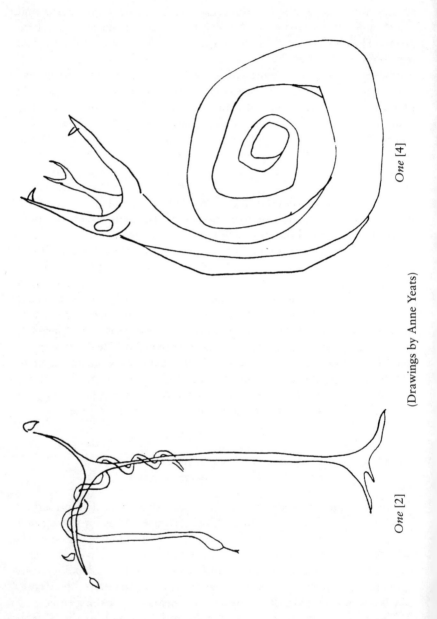

One [4]

(Drawings by Anne Yeats)

One [2]

gradual decay of its body. In the third part the speaker sees two disks of light which, as Brian John points out, alludes to the creation story in the Lebor Gabála Érenn: 'And god made two bright and great lights: He made the greater light that it might take over the day, and the lesser light in the night.'[17] The fourth, and last part of the dream depicts the speaker 'coiled in combat' with cosmic forces, escaping only by shedding his 'decrepit skin'. The upward movement with which the poem opens becomes a 'plunge downward' towards stasis:

> *Down! Like a young thing!*
> *Coil, now, and wait.*
> *Sleep on these things.*
>
> (P [6], C 166)

The dream described in the poem suggests the formation of the self, both in a Jungian and in a strictly physical sense.[18] The image which is set against the close of the poem depicts the head of a snake, or beast, or even perhaps a man, with a forked tongue. The ambiguity contained in the image enriches the complex interweaving of man, animal and archetype that Kinsella achieves in the sequence.

From this scene of creation in its cosmic and corporeal form the poet moves to a creation of another kind. In a poem which, while forming part of the first triad, offers us another introduction to the issues of creation and individuation central to the sequence, Kinsella sets us a Faustian scene. Drawing on the scene in the Knight's Hall from Goethe's *Faust*, the poet adopts the persona of a faintly ridiculous Faust 'sporting a striped jacket, / posed in confident quackery, bearded'.[19] In his company is 'a woman, drawn up like a queen, / rouged and spangled': a Helen of Troy whose beauty is artifice rather than authentic. This midnight scene of theatre and magic exposes the mechanics of the spectacle:

> a neglected pavement, an ivied corner
> with metal gates and temple pillars
> – a mean backdrop: [. . .]
>
> (P [9], C 167)

Kinsella's scene is a near-perfect simulacrum of Goethe's 'ancient temple' complete with 'serried rows of columns'.[20] And just as Faust is described as rising from a 'cavernous hole' so Kinsella's confident artificer emerges from a rusty and outworn lift:

> A tableau rattled up from the crypt:
> a man, sporting a striped jacket,
> posed in confident quackery, bearded;
> a woman, drawn up like a queen,
> rouged and spangled. [. . .]
>
> (P [9], C 167)

Perhaps the most important connection between 'The Entire Fabric' and Goethe's scene lies in the operations of the cauldron and the golden key. Carolyn Rosenberg draws our attention to the parallels between Goethe's cauldron of primaeval chaos 'brimming over with potential forms' and Kinsella's 'round pot'; and between Goethe's magic key which both protects and creates, and the object that 'flashed' in the right hand of Kinsella's Faustian protagonist:[21] 'His glowing key's no sooner touched the bowl / than smokelike haze obscures the stage' (lines 6439–40). These objects are the tools of Faust's explorations which, in Jung's view 'symbolize in a traditional manner a quest for knowledge of the self'.[22] In Kinsella's poem the Faustian poet-protagonist also touches the key to the bowl: 'he reached out / to touch the vessel's rim', but unlike the lucky Faust whose conjuring produces first Paris, then Helen, Kinsella's bearded figure fails to conjure up anything more than 'faint strains of music.' However this music is the 'Ariel tones' which proceed from the 'spirit-world' and which in Kinsella's poem can be likened to the music of the spheres as 'the entire fabric sang softly' (P [9], C 167).[23]

By drawing on Goethe and Jung to underpin this poem Kinsella makes clear his purpose of self-exploration. Goethe's *Faust* is apt in the distinctions it makes between artifice and creation, and also in the conflation of the role of poet and magician in the word 'sorcerer'.[24] We might also keep in mind that in Goethe's time the word 'conjurors' (line 6072) denotes 'printers' – a fitting connection given Kinsella's dual role of poet and publisher.[25] Kinsella closes the poem with characteristic irony. Having failed to conjure any apparitions, the protagonist steps forward,

> a hand cupped behind an ear,
> out at the waiting dark, as if
> searching the distance. He made to speak.
> (P [9], C 167)

but before he can get a word in edgewise, the lift makes to bear him away. Yet this is after all a prefatory poem and perhaps what the poet/ magician will succeed in conjuring up lies in the subsequent poems, or indeed, in the subsequent Peppercanisters.

The next two poems, 'Finistère' and 'The Oldest Place' draw on Celtic myths of the original peoples of Ireland. 'Finistère' retells the story of Ith, son of Bregon, who sights Ireland as a distant shape across the sea from the Land of the Dead, and whose story contains strong parallels with the Greek myth of Prometheus.[26] 'The Oldest Place' looks even farther back in time to the people of Partholón who also come to Ireland from the Land of the Dead but who all perish by a terrible plague. This poem includes references to the Formorians and the awful idol to whom children were sacrificed: Cromm Cruach.

Where *Notes from the Land of the Dead* closes with zero, 'Finistère' opens with the number one which, in the Peppercanister and Dolmen editions, is printed as 'I'. This character can be read as either the first number or the first person pronoun. The speaker is both an individual and also one of a community. Unfortunately, in the Oxford edition the character used is '1' which limits the ambiguity and richness of the text. Set against the opening stanzas of the poem is Yeats's line drawing of a seascape with a combination of moon, sun and clouds above. The vigour and intensity of Yeats' line echoes the power of Kinsella's diction in 'Finistère'.

The speaker of 'Finistère' is both Ith and Amairgin, but is also the poet himself. The 'bald boulder on the cairn top' is the tower of Bregon from which Ith catches a glimpse of Ireland and, fired with 'purpose / and predatory peace' the sons of Míl set forth across the ocean from the end of the world, or 'Finisterre'.[27] The question mark with which the stanza ends in the Peppercanister edition, 'A point of light?' is exchanged for the more definitive period in *The Complete Poems*. The connection between the visceral and the conceptual in this voyage of discovery, which is as much a journey of self-discovery as it is the discovery of Ireland, is neatly encapsulated in the short stanza: 'A maggot of the possible / wriggled out of the spine / into the brain' (P [10], C 168). The voyage described is at once a journey across rough and dangerous waters, and an exploration across uncharted psychic spaces. Kinsella's onomatopoeic language conveys powerfully the swell and thrust of the ocean:

> At no great distance out in the bay
> the swell took us into its mercy,
> grey upheaving slopes of water
> sliding under us, collapsing,
> crawling onward, mountainous.

> (P [10], C 168)

The power of nature is analogous to the power of the gods, and in particular the 'mild mother' to whom the voyagers pray in the midst of the storm. This deity recalls the Great Mother of Jungian thought, particularly in the work of Erich Neumann, who is associated with the 'watery abyss' from which all things come.[28] 'Mild Mother' also recalls the Mothers of Faust's scene in 'The Entire Fabric'. Though they do not figure directly in the poem (the 'Shades' refer to the Emperor and his court), Faust's Mothers 'are the guardians of the past, keepers of immortal images which once came forth into life and now exist as recollected ideals' and it is from their realm that the apparitions of Helen and Paris come.[29] The prayer to the Mother god outlines the ways in which she is glorified. Through the 'great uprights' or standing stones, the images of the síle-na-gig 'whose goggle gaze / and holy howl we have scraped / speechless on slabs of stone', and the spiral carvings at sacred sites such as Newgrange, the poem enumerates the ways in which glory is given to the one 'in whose outflung service / we nourished our hunger' (P [12], C 169). The language of this stanza is rich in assonance and alliteration until the words themselves seem to coil in the carved spirals or swift eddies of the water:

> in coil zigzag angle and curl
> river ripple earth ramp
> suncircle moonloop . . .
>
> (P [12], C 169)

The single journey described in 'Finistère' condenses the complexity of the invasion of the sons of Míl described in the Lebor Gabála Érenn as a number of landings and subsequent retreats. With a power that recalls Prospero in Shakespeare's *The Tempest*, the druids and filí of the Tuatha Dé Danann conjure the storm to prevent the Sons of Míl from landing in Ireland. Amairgin, the file among the voyagers, chants an invocation which sets the natural power of the land against the magic of its inhabitants:[30]

>   gale gullet
> salt hole
>   dark nowhere
> calm queen
>   pour peace
>
> (P [12], C 169)

The 'sunny breeze' which marks the end of the storm blows the travellers towards the shore of Ireland into the 'deep bay' of what is thought now to be Kenmare, County Kerry.[31] The lines '– three times we misjudged and were nearly driven / on the same rock' allude to the three landings the people of Míl made in their invasion of Ireland, hence a sense of familiarity: '(I had felt all this before)', and also to the difficulties they had landing on the final approach which required them to skirt Ireland three times before coming ashore.[32] But this *déjà vu* also draws on a sense of connectedness between the individual, the community and the land which is integral to mythology, and to the quest for self-knowledge that Kinsella's poetry pursues.

The poem shifts from the first-person plural to the first-person singular as the speaker assumes the voice of the ancient poet, Amairgin, filtered through a present-day sensibility. The ironic counterpoint between the Christian invocation and the pagan poem which follows establishes a kind of identity between contemporary poet and ancient file:

> I steadied myself. 'Our Father . . .', someone said
> and there was a little laughter. [. . .]
>
> (P [13], C 170)

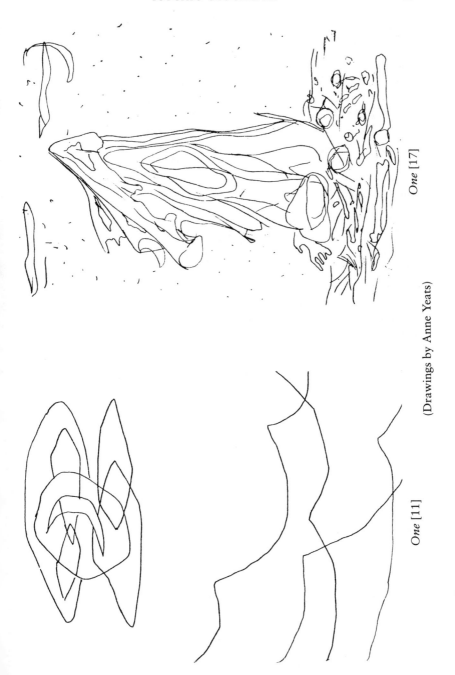

One [17]

(Drawings by Anne Yeats)

One [11]

The poet reaches back for the 'old words' which are also the 'right words' but as he steps onto the land his 'tongue stumbled'. Here Kinsella rewrites the scene where Amairgin, first poet of Ireland, chants a poem in honour of the 'divine science' which joins the poet with nature. The power and knowledge of the file enabled him to master the hidden forces of nature, and to control both the visible and the invisible world. Through this knowledge the file becomes one with nature for, as de Jubainville explains, 'to possess this science was to possess nature in her entirety'.[33] While Amairgin's poem list a series of identities, 'I am the wave of the Ocean; / I am the murmur of the billows', Kinsella's poem distances the speaker from the power of the file with the repeated interrogative: 'Who?':

> Who
>   is a breath
> that makes the wind
> that makes the wave
> that makes   this   voice?

> (P [13], C 170)

With this question Kinsella links the poet's words with the power of the wind and the ocean, each with an origin in the single 'breath' which animates the world. Yet this questioning demands an answer, and just as Amairgin's poem closes with a series of rhetorical questions, 'who telleth the ages of the moon?' so Kinsella's poem also implies the power of the poet:

> Who goes in full into
> the moon's interesting conditions?

> (P [14], C 171)

As the poem closes, parenthetical references to the scene at hand, '(the craft knocked behind me)', bring us back to the difficulties of landing and the uncertainties of the journey ahead, '(I went forward, reaching out)' (P [14], C 171).

The third poem of this first triad, 'The Oldest Place', derives its narrative from the story of earlier settlers of Ireland, the people of Partholón and later, of Nemed. Kinsella divides the poem into five sections which trace the history of Partholón and Nemed. The first three sections deal with Partholón's arrival in Ireland, the cultivation of the land, and the plague which wiped them out. The final two sections recall the descendants of Nemed (who came after Partholón) and their subjugation to the power of the terrible gods, the Fomorians. Partholón's history is pithily told in the History of the Britons by Nennius:

The first of them was Partholón, bringing with him a thousand companions, both men and women. Their number increased until there were four thousand of them; then a plague fell on them, and in one week they all perished, so that not one of them was left.[34]

The demise of this people is caused by something approaching an original sin. Partholón fled his homeland after killing his father and mother, and the plague which devastates his people is punishment for this crime. Their fate is sealed even as they arrive in Ireland for 'the stale reminder of our sin still clung' (P [14], C 171). In 'The Oldest Place' Kinsella complicates the relationship between land and people through which identity is formed:

> And there was something in the way the land behaved:
> passive, but responding. It grew under our hands.
> We worked it like a dough to our requirements
> yet it surprised us more than once
> with a firm life of its own, as if ..
> it used us.
>
> (P [15], C 172)

Here Kinsella writes of a land in which the development of the people and the development of the earth go hand in hand. He draws on the old Celtic doctrine of the origin of the world which 'represents the earth as assuming its actual form slowly and gradually under the eyes of the different human races that flourished on it'.[35] An act of mourning is transformed into a feature of the land as the grave dug for one of Partholón's sons becomes a lake, Loch Rudraige (P [15], C 172). The identity of a community and the identity of the physical terrain are formed in tandem. However, Kinsella's approach is evenhanded. It is not simply the people who change the land. The land itself has its own capacity for change, its own life and identity which endures through the successive invasions, even as it is changed by them.

In a plain and clear diction Kinsella describes the demise of Partholón and his people. As with the previous two sections, he draws significantly on de Jubainville's straightforward redaction of the myth:

> Year followed year.
> The first skin blemishes appeared,
> and it almost seemed we had been waiting for them.
> The sickness and the dying began again.
>
> (P [15], C 172)

The people gather on the first great plain of Ireland, Sen Mag, 'the bare plain we found first' in order to bury each other more easily as almost all die. As the section comes to a close the speaker shifts from the first person plural to the singular 'I':

> A day came when I fell down by the great stone
> alone, crying, at the middle of the stinking plain.
>
> (P [15], C 172)

The single survivor (necessary if the tale is to be told) is named Tuan and he recalls Fintan from 'Survivor' in *Notes from the Land of the Dead*, who was the only one left when Cessair's people perished in the flood.[36]

Tuan has a dream or vision which transports him ahead to the time of the next people of Ireland, the Nemed, who are under the thrall of the Formorians, gods of death, night, and storm, who demand annually two thirds of all the children born in one year:[37]

> Night fell, and I lay there face down,
> and I dreamed that my ghost stood up
> and faint starry shadows everywhere
> lifted themselves up and began
> searching about among themselves for something,
>
> (P [15], C 172)

Tuan's vision comes from sleep, but also from death, and it also reaches back to an even more remote period in Irish history in which identical human sacrifices were demanded by the idol Cromm Cruach or the Bloody Crescent. Tuan is an other-worldly witness to this sacrifice in which the supplicants become:

> – muscular nothingnesses,
> demons, animal-heads, wrestling vaguely toward me
> reaching out terrible gifts into my face,
> clawfuls of dripping cloth
> and gold and silver things.
> They passed through me . . .
>
>   To the stone,
> and draped it with their gifts, murmuring,
>
> (P [15–16], C 173)

The speaker's second dream in which he advances on the stone, 'hand on heart, / the other hand advanced', recalls St Patrick's power struggle with the old gods, but, unlike Christian rewriting, in the narrative of 'The Oldest Place' the old god remains pre-eminent:

>   And its glare
> gathered like a pulse, and struck
> on the withered plain of my own brain.
>
> (P [16], C 173)

The 'dark radiance' of the stone gives way to a 'complex emptiness shimmering' as the poem draws its focus tightly around the individual questing self, and away from the overlapping and multiple first peoples of Ireland. The nightmare dream with which the poem closes sees the standing stone of Cromm Cruach gain a vitality which is almost anthropomorphic: the 'eyes hovering' in the 'crumpled face / with forehead torn crisscross, begging' (P [16], C 173). In an image which conflates the terrible stone god with the figures of the *cailleach*, the goddess Mórrígan and the crow with which she is associated, Kinsella evokes the powers of creation and destruction integral to the great and terrible mother of Jungian archetype. Yeats's drawing, which faces 'The Oldest Place, conflates the standing stone with that of a ragged figure in an image which emphasises the ambiguity of the image with a fragmentary and hesitant line. Prefiguring the voices of *Out of Ireland*, the flapping of the shawl draped on the stone becomes the voice of the idol in whom both ends of the moral spectrum meet:

> with tongue flapping, *Agath, Kak,*
> and dropped to earth.
> (P [16], C 173 var.)[38]

Kinsella's exploration of origins and identity shifts from the mythic to the familial in the next three poems, '38 Phoenix Street', 'Minstrel' and 'His Father's Hands.' Yeats's image of a series of smaller chromosomes ranged around a larger, more central one emphasises the importance of the biological, and therefore familial, in the identity of the self. The crossing-over integral to the work of the chromosome has resonances which connect with both parts of *One*, since similar movements of crossing-over and intertwining are characteristic of the origin of the nation, and of the family, from which the speaker of the poem comes.[39] While the questing self with whom the sequence opens has proceeded into the depths of a mythical underworld which can also be understood as the realm of the self's unconscious, in these next three poems the speaker searches back through memory to understand the family from which he comes. '38 Phoenix Street' opens with a child's perspective, as the speaker is lifted up to greet a neighbour's child across the garden wall. The meticulous precision with which the child observes the insects below, 'a quick / wiry redgolden thing', figures again as the child observes the reflections of the flame on the surface of the lamp, 'On the glassy belly / little drawnout images quivered' (P [18], C 174). The movement of the gramophone needle (conveyed by the rhythmic 'liftfalling, liftfalling') which plays a record of the popular tenor John McCormack[40] is taken up by the 'wavering tip' of the oil-lamp. The title of the poem refers to the house of friend and next-door neighbour, Jimmy Cummins.[41] The poem is divided into four sections which deal with a child's observations of a child, a mother, a father and a religious icon. The life signified by the new baby in section one is mirrored by the figure of death in the third. While Kinsella's voyagers in the first part of the sequence come from the Land of the Dead, which is also the land of origin, 'Mister Cummins' of the second part comes from a land of the dead which is marked by the horrors of the First World War:

> Sealed in his sad cave. Hisshorror erecting
> slowly out of its rock nests, nosing the air.
> He was buried for three days under a hill of dead,
> the faces congested down all round him
> grinning *Dardanelles!* in the dark.
>
> (P [19], C 175)

The 'black rubbery scar' with which his near-death has marked him echoes the 'forehead torn crisscross' of the god in 'The Oldest Place.' The slaughter of war and of mactation are placed in unsettling proximity by the image of the beating heart which figures in the last two sections of the poem. Each heart signals life, whether it is through the 'thread of blood' pushed forth by the weakened heart of the soldier, or the 'Sacred Heart' with which another god, this time Christian rather than pagan, is identified. Both Mister Cummins and Christ are sacrificial victims: the one of politics, the other of religion. The 'mild mother' of 'Finistère' becomes the feminised Sacred Heart 'with his woman's black hair' and 'his women's fingers'. In a reference to human sacrifice which recalls 'The Oldest Place', and to which Kinsella will return in the poems of *Madonna*, the child of '38 Phoenix Street' is offered a heart which is both plaything and living thing:

> [. . .] He held out the Heart
> with his women's fingers, like a toy.
>
> The lamp-wick, with a tiny head
> of red fire, wriggled in its pool.
> The shadows flickered: the Heart beat!
>
> (P [19], C 175)

Though this life is an illusion of light and shadow the movement that causes it emulates the primordial life-forms with which *One* opens, '*everywhere alive with bits and pieces, / little hearts beating*' (P [5], C 165).

The animal appetite of the 'Prologue' is linked to the artistic appetite of 'Minstrel' which depicts the poet-protagonist at work:

> A dry teacup stained the oil cloth
> where I wrote, bent like a feeding thing
> over my own source.
>
> (P [19], C 175)

The detailed instance of the poet's efforts is set against the movements of creation linking the heavens and the earth through the 'little directionless instincts' which echo the opening of *One*. The different beating of the hearts in '38 Phoenix Street' become a single 'enormous black beat' of the universe in 'Minstrel', and echo as the 'last lovely heartbeat / of the whole world' with which *Her Vertical Smile* opens (P 7, C 247). The 'distant point of light' that 'winked at the edge of nothing' recalls the Tower of Bregon in the Land of the Dead (P [20], C 176). Into this reverie of aesthetic and cosmological generation interrupts the figure of the poet's father, a temporal instance of those 'claw marks, breasts, / ribs, feathery prints, / eyes shutting and opening' from which life originates (P [20], C 176 var.):

> A knock on the window
> and everything in fantasy fright
> flurried and disappeared.
> My father looked in from the dark,
> my face black-mirrored beside his.
>
> (P [20], C 176)

The doubled image of father and son emphasises the generation of which the poet is a part. Family and world meet in the 'black beat' of the heavens which becomes the 'black-mirrored' image of the two men. The window provides a passage for vision through which the father sees the son, and also a barrier for vision in which the poet's own image is returned to him.

'His Father's Hands' draws a portrait of the poet's father and grandfather with the same kind of observation and attention to detail found in '38 Phoenix Street'. Kinsella divides the poem into five sections which explore the relationship between father and son; the family's relationship to history; the individual's connection with pre-history; the transformation of generations; and the inexorable movement of life toward multiplicities. Through images of each father's hands Kinsella links the generations: 'I have watched / his father's hands before him' (P [22], C 177). The first section begins with father and son in conversation:

> His finger prodded and prodded,
> making his point. Emphas-
> emphasemphasis.
>
> (P [22], C 177 var.)

It then shifts to an observation of his grandfather as he prepares his pipe, mends shoes, and plays the fiddle. In the *Collected Poems* Kinsella has changed the word 'making' to 'marring', introducing a degree of belligerence to the conversation and further emphasising the constant shifting and re-evaluation indicative of family relationships. The section ends with the grandfather playing the air of 'The wind that shakes the barley':

> To his deaf, inclined head
> he hugged the fiddle's body,
> whispering with the tune
>
> (P [23], C 177)

This song comes from Wexford and tells of the 1898 rising in which Kinsella's family played some part. The second section of 'His Father's Hands' elaborates that history, drawing on a letter written by Kinsella's uncle Jack Brophy:[42]

> Your family, Thomas, met with and helped
> many of the Croppies in hiding from the Yeos
> or on their way home after the defeat
> in south Wexford. [. . .]
>
> (P [23], C 178)

Kinsella's decision to leave the text in prose, noted in his drafts of the poem, conveys the tone of the letter and the sense of a family history being passed down.[43] However beyond the narrative, 'Beyond that', lies another kind of history, one based on a visceral rather than conceptual memory. Here, in this land of 'Littered uplands. Dense grass. Rocks everywhere, / wet underneath, retaining memory of the long cold' the speaker connects with the first peoples and memories of the sacrifices necessary to keep the land fertile and the people alive:

> [. . .] It feels evil.
> Terrible things happened.
> I feel afraid here when I am on my own.
>
> (P [24], C 179)

From the different and various peoples whose successive invasions or 'takings' of Ireland give rise to the country today, the speaker returns to the fireside of family. By linking the individual with his family through the figure of the father; and then linking both with the family history through the centuries ('In the 18 / and late 1700s'), and into pre-history with memories of Partholón and the sons of Míl ('Dispersals or migrations'), Kinsella places the self in the context of a greater whole in which a sense of identity can be found:

> Dispersals or migrations.
> Through what evolutions or accidents
> toward that peace and patience
> by the fireside, that blocked gentleness . . .
>
> (P [24], C 179)

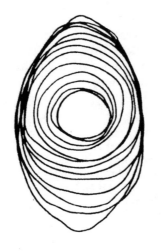

One [27]

(Drawings by Anne Yeats)

One [21]

The 'gentleness' of the grandfather has already been 'modulated twice' through son and grandson into the 'earnestness and iteration' (remember 'emphasemphasis'), of the former and the 'offhandedness, repressing various impulses' of the latter (P [25], C 179).

The poem closes with the powerful image of the block of wood, evidence of the grandfather's labour, the grandchildren's play, and of the connections which bind generations:

> Extraordinary. . . The big block – I found it
> years afterwards in a corner of the yard
> in sunlight after rain
> and stood it up, wet and black:
> it turned under my hands, an axis
> of light flashing down its length,
> and the wood's soft flesh broke open,
> countless little nails
> squirming and dropping out of it.
>
> (P [25], C 180)

The squirming nails recall the 'maggot of the possible' in 'Finistère', and the block of wood signals the numeral or letter 'I' which opens the poem. Juxtaposing the one against the many in their interdependence, Kinsella returns to the image of the snake with which the sequence opens and the numerical system which informs the work. In conversation with Daniel O'Hara, Kinsella emphasises the importance of the snake as a device through which 'the poems can organize their own behaviour'.[44] The snake is both zero and one. The movement of the poem involves 'the zero uncoiling and striking up' into the individual 'I' from where the poet speaks.

The final poem of *One*, untitled in the Peppercanister edition and titled 'Epilogue' in the *Collected Poems*, mirrors the opening poem of the volume through its italic typeface. The scene described is also of archetypal significance, but here it is the great Mother, combined with the Medusa or Hecate figure, who presents herself in all her terrible aspect. She combines with the image of the snake as her hair 'stiffened and moved / by itself, glistening on her shoulders'. This snake imagery also links her with the figure of Mercury or Hermes which is integral to the later volume *The Messenger* written in memory of Kinsella's father.[45] The 'cell of nightmare' recalls the realm the questing self delves into in order to seek understanding. Into this scene rises a 'suffused heart', which combines the creative and destructive aspects of the Christian and pagan symbols motivated by Kinsella in the preceding poems. In a description which vividly recalls the iconography of the Sacred Heart, 'the heart beat / and broke open, and sent a fierce beam / among our wriggling sheaves' (C 181). The elemental self, at first a primeval snake, then a gametic squirming nail, is now connected with notions of harvest. Contributing an even deeper resonance to Kinsella's imagery, Brian John notes the connection between the Medusa or Hecate figure and the *cailleach* who is associated in Irish folklore with the harvest, since 'the final stook in the harvest field was given particular attention and named the *cailleach*'.[46]

Yeats provides the volume with a closing image that encapsulates the idea of the coiled snake, the uroboros, the egg, and the universe. Yeats's dense and circular design conveys a sense of closure and spiral in which the elemental voice of the poem 'writhed and reversed'. The tone of the poem shifts as the speaker takes a more meditative perspective:

> Mostly the thing runs smoothly, the fall is cradled
> immediately in a motherly warmth, with nothing
> to disturb the dark urge, except from within
> – a tenseness, as it coils on itself, changing
> to obscure substance.

(P [28], C 181)

Here Kinsella describes the development of the self in a life which is designed to 'run smoothly' but within which there are disturbances which ought not be ignored. These 'anxieties' are acknowledged but often not recognised, consigned to 'incommunicable' dark where they exist as a 'private shadow.' It is this private shadow which Kinsella explores in *One*. The challenge for the poet is to find a way of writing which can speak of the incommunicable, to forge a language which explores rather than describes. Through the narratives of family history and pre-history, through images of self and subject, Kinsella sets out 'toward the dawn zone' in order to awaken that 'private shadow, not often called upon' (P [28], C 181).

A Technical Supplement

Where *One* moved from the zero of *Notes from the Land of the Dead* to a consideration of the one, the 'I' or singular identity, *A Technical Supplement* develops Kinsella's numerological system to its next stage: the division of the self into two. Speaking of the interrelationship between these three volumes Kinsella delineates the development:

In *Notes from the Land of the Dead*, the 0 manifested itself half-way through the book, but the patron numeral was clearly established in 'One', and – for what it's worth – the next book hovers on the notion of two, the divided unit.[47]

In the sixth Peppercanister Kinsella brings together the body of the poet and the body of poetry in a sequence which analyses the nature of inquiry through the science of anatomy and the art of poetry. With a twenty-four section structure which mirrors the twenty-four hours of the day, Kinsella constructs a series of observations and meditations which dispenses with narrative line, proceeding instead 'through a less organized or less limited sequence of states of mind.'[48]

A Technical Supplement was published in 1976, in deluxe, library and trade editions. Each volume contains twenty-four sections which are numbered with roman numerals. The first three sections of the work were published first as *A Short Sequence* by the University of Connecticut Library in 1975.[49] In the deluxe edition of the Peppercanister Kinsella added a handwritten poem which begins 'No one did anything at first'. Drafts of this poem, which becomes the 'Prologue' in the *Collected Poems* (C 183–4), are to be found among the drafts for the volume *One* and certainly the poem provides a bridge between the two volumes. The primeval mud and elementary movement, 'wriggling', recalls the snake-like figure in the prefatory poem of *One*, and the reference to 'backbone' reminds us of the earlier passage:

> A maggot of the possible
> wriggled out of the spine
> into the brain.

> (P [10], C 168)

In lines which convey quite viscerally the energy of procreation, and recall the voyage of the five kindred, Kinsella moves from the singular or individual figure that was the focus of *One* towards an exploration of a multiplicity which evokes origin both in a biological and mythical sense:

> *I started. There was one more after me*
> *then the whole world exploded behind us*
> *and a golden light blasted us out.*

> *We found each other afterwards,*
> *inert and stunned, but alive.*
> *Five.*

> (C 184)

This generative moment prefaces a sequence of poems in which the act of reading is described as 'closing a circuit' between the text and the mind, the 'eyes bridging the gap' (P [34], C 197). Kinsella develops this view of reading in conversation with John F. Deane, arguing that the Peppercanister books

> assume that the act of reading is a dynamic one, the completion of an act of communication, not an inert listening to something sweet or interesting or even informative. They are not meant to increase the supply of significant information but to embody a construct of significant elements.[50]

A *Technical Supplement* is such a construct. Through a combination of meditations, descriptions and inquiries Kinsella joins together twenty-four very different poems which probe the nature of understanding and the procedures of poetry.

The sequence begins with an entreaty to 'Blessed William Skullbullet' or William Petty, the seventeenth-century cartographer of Ireland.[51] With an irony which has much in common with Brian Friel's play *Translations*, Kinsella takes Petty's Down Survey of Ireland as an example of the difficulty encountered if a system or structure is imposed upon the details of experience rather than being elicited from them. Kinsella's choice of cartography as an example of systematised understanding which does not always correspond to the physical reality gains a greater resonance when we compare the attitude of the cartographer towards the landscape with the relationship between the people and the land expressed in *One*. In order to map, the cartographer must consider the land to be stable and inert; yet the very land which William Petty seeks to map is described in early mythology as something dynamic and interdependent with the people living on it: 'there was something in the way the land behaved: / [. . .] yet it surprised us more than once / with a firm life of its own, as if / it used us' (P [15], C 172). The political implications of Petty's cartography are clear when we understand that 'its purpose was to facilitate the distribution of the forfeited lands of the rebels of 1641, in equal moieties, among the soldiers of the Cromwellian army and those who had subscribed money for the army's support'.[52] In his treatise on *The Political Anatomy of Ireland*, Petty uses the body as a metaphor for society. Echoing Francis Bacon's parallel between the 'Body Natural' and the 'Body Politic', Petty underlines the importance of anatomy for proper maintenance of both bodies:

> And it is as reasonable, that as Anatomy *is the best foundation of one, so also of the other; and that to practice upon the* Politick, *without knowing the* Symmetry, Fabrick *and* Proportion *of it, is as casual as the practice of* Old-women *and* Empyricks.[53]

Through reference to Petty, Kinsella situates *A Technical Supplement* within a wider contextual framework in which the body of Ireland, the

corporeal body, and the poetic body become conflated as each are sub-
jected to the anatomical gaze of the poet. 'Blessed William Skullbullet'
voices the supplication which animates the entire sequence and can be
taken as emblematic of Kinsella's work as a whole:

> let our gaze blaze, we pray
> let us see how the whole thing
>   works
>   (P [9], C 184)

Kinsella uses anatomical inquiry as a metaphor for understanding in
poems two to six. The second poem of A Technical Supplement describes
in detail an anatomy lesson in which the individual parts of the body are
laid out for scrutiny. The flayed body is known through its individual
parts, 'even the eyes – dry staring buttons of muscle' (P [10], C 184). Yet
the cost of this knowledge is the destruction of the body itself. Under the
kind of scrutiny which demands atomisation, the scrutiny described as a
'violation', the body 'would rip into pieces and fly apart / with terrible
spasms' (P [10], C 184). Like a body of poetry which must be considered
in its totality in order for the parts to be understood, the physical body is
a coherent unity, which if examined in discrete parts, ceases to make
sense. The themes of death and sacrifice in One return here through the
image of an ambiguous figure lodged in the ground, which undergoes a
transfiguration akin to Moses or Jesus on Mount Calvary.[54] Figures such
as Mister Cummins of '38 Phoenix Street', buried alive during the First
World War, and the Greek marking stone – the herm – from which
Kinsella draws his images of Plato in The Good Fight, are incorporated
into the dominant image of the crucifix, 'that serene effigy / we have
copied so much / and set everywhere', which signals sacrifice and redemp-
tion through understanding (P [12], C 186).

The fourth and fifth poems of A Technical Supplement explore two
kinds of physical penetration. The first kind retains the integrity of the
body being probed which, though ruptured, vivifies the instrument until
instrument and flesh unite:

> Persist.
>   Beyond a certain depth
> it stands upright by itself
> and quivers with borrowed life.
>   (P [14], C 187)

The second kind of inquiry is closer to the vivisection described in the
sixth poem because it annihilates the body it cuts. Kinsella uses the meta-
phor of language to describe the relationship between the blade and the
severed flesh: 'A blade licks out and acts / with one tongue. / Jets of

blood respond / in diverse tongues' (P [15], C 187). But rather than a reciprocal conversation, these tongues engender a multiplicity of language which, like Babel, convey diversity and confusion rather than unity and understanding.[55] The sixth poem accepts Kinsella's invitation to 'enter this grove of beasts' and brings the reader on a detailed journey through a commercial slaughterhouse which may, as W. J. Mc Cormack points out, 'be an American abattoir belonging to the firm of Swift (meatpackers) or may be a composite site including Jonathan Swift's endowed hospital and one of the several knacker's yards in the same area of west Dublin.'[56] With exquisite particularity the poem details the different stages of butchery:

> Great bulks of pigs hung from dainty heels,
> the full sow-throats cut open the wrong way.
> Three negroes stood on a raised bench before them.
> One knifed the belly open upward to the tail
> until the knife and his hands disappeared
> into the fleshy vulva and broke some bone.

> (P [16], C 188)

The realistic descriptions of poem six contrast with the surreal images conjured up by poem seven: 'Play-blood / bursting everywhere out of / big chopped dolls' (P [18], C 189). The pragmatic approach of the former poem which concludes that 'At a certain point it is all merely meat', contrasts with the moral stance of the latter poem which poses a moral dilemma: 'Is it all right to do this? / Is it an offence against justice' (P [18], C 189). This ethical question is not so much answered as explored in the eighth poem through the idea of appetite. Through three separate observations Kinsella describes a lizard eating, 'a living thing swallowing another' (P [19], C 189). The 'unfulfillable' face of the sated lizard is mirrored in the faces of the underwater creatures of the ninth poem which takes place in an aquarium, 'The Stations of the Depths' (P [20], C 190). There the speaker observes a variety of aquatic animals including 'a herring-flock', 'Two morays', and 'Gross anemones' (P [20], C 190). Kinsella moves along a descending scale of sentience from the warm-blooded creatures butchered in 'Swift's slaughterhouse' – 'A flock of them [sheep] waited their turn / crowded into the furthest corner of the pen, / some looking back over their shoulders / at us, in our window (P 16, C 188) – to the cold-blooded reptile whose 'leather-granite face' is as impassive as the 'leopard shark' patrolling the artificial sea of the aquarium. The difference between the warm and the cold-blooded creatures provides a context for the dilemma posed in the eighth poem: under what conditions is it permissible for a living thing to swallow another? What hierarchy does our appetite impose upon living things?

With the tenth poem Kinsella links questions of appetite with the artistic process. Situating the poem in the newly acquired Percy Place house, he outlines a scene of renewal and renovation which parallels his own approach to poetry:

> We have to dig down;
> sieve, scour and roughen;
> make it all fertile and vigorous
> – get the fresh rain down!
>
> (P [23], C 192 var.)

Kinsella describes the poetic act as a 'process whereby one's experience is ingested, processed, deposited, prepared for use, made ready – brought to a condition where it can be "set off" by a new significant experience striking it.'[57] Though deemed repugnant by the woman who 'stumbles away helplessly / and has to sit down / until her sobbing stops' (P [18], C 189), the violence of the abattoir is part of the experience which must be ingested and processed. No aspect of experience can be deemed outside the remit of poetry, if that poetry is to remain true to life as it is lived. In a moment of release signalled by the end of a rain-shower and the reappearance of the sun, the eleventh poem celebrates the small realm of order achieved by art:

> We have shaped and polished.
> We have put a little darkness behind us,
> we are out of that soup.
> Into a little brightness.
>
> (P [24], C 192)

Through metaphors of anatomy, appetite and fertility the first half of *A Technical Supplement* examines the conditions and attitude necessary for poetry, closing with an assessment of poetic development which criticises those who rush to judgment:

> There isn't a day passes but I thank God
> some others I know – I can see them, mounting up
> with grim pleasure to the judgment seat –
> didn't 'fulfil their promise'.
>
> (P [25], C 193)

This twelfth poem characterises the poet's development in terms of 'An arrogant beginning, *then* / the hard attrition' (P [25], C 193). Poetry, celebrated as a 'little brightness' in the eleventh poem, is cherished as 'a small excellence – very valuable' in the twelfth. Here Kinsella describes his own trajectory as a poet from the lyric cadences of his early work to the formally experimental sequences of the later poetry which mark his position 'at the unrewarding outer reaches' of poetic endeavour.

The second half of *A Technical Supplement* focuses on the poet's own attitude towards his work. Beginning with a meditation in the form of call and response in the thirteenth poem, the poet describes writing in terms of an inward journey which is both liberating and threatening. The grotesque dream of the fourteenth poem, '*a dish of ripe eyes gaped up / at the groaning iron press descending*', is transformed by poetry into something beautiful – 'a sheet of brilliant colour' (P [27], C 194) – yet the actions of the muse are described in the fifteenth poem in antagonistic terms as 'sudden and / peremptory incursions' (P [30], C 194). Rather than relying on inspiration, the speaker describes the work of poetry in terms of the patient transformation of everyday experience which involves an element of distanciation, or 'getting separated from one's habits / and stumbling onto another way' (P [31], C 195). The sixteenth and seventeenth poems give examples of such experience – the 'detailed warmth, the touch under the shirt', the 'smell of hot home-made loaves' from the kitchen' (P [31–2], C 195). Using a metaphor of industrial production, Kinsella describes the craft of writing in terms of a finely judged balance of elements within a system:

> tinker and trim, empty your oil-can
> into the hissing navels, tap the flickering dials,
> study the massive shimmering accurate flywheels.

(P [33], C 196)

From this point, Kinsella moves into a closer analysis of the practice of writing. He begins, in the nineteenth poem, with an analysis of reading which contrasts 'a romance devoured / at one stroke' with 'a *serious* read' that entails a real communication between reader and writer, 'a mingling of lives' in which the reader assumes another's experience (P [34], C 197). Kinsella ends the poem with an *aisling* in which a 'fair maid' appears to the poet and speaks to him of the dark aspect of the self from which poetry comes:

> *My heart is a black fruit.*
> *It is a piece of black coal.*
> *When I laugh a black thing hovers.*

(P [35], C 198)

The next two poems detail the mechanics of writing, and the choices the poet makes in his work. Kinsella give us an example of revision. The line 'And so the years propel themselves onward / toward that tunnel, and the stink of fear' is changed to 'And so the years propel themselves / onward on thickening scars, toward / new efforts of propulsion', with the remark that 'Time permits / a certain latitude' (P [36], C 198).

Through an image of language as sustenance the poet contrasts concrete words with abstract terms, choosing the former over the latter:

> The words 'water' or 'root'
> offered in real refreshment. The words
> 'Love', 'Truth', etc., offered with force
> but self-serving, therefore ineffective.

(P [37], C 198)

The final three poems of *A Technical Supplement* draw back from the art of poetry to examine the person of the poet. The self-reflexive gaze of the speaker reveals a self which is dividing, 'the forehead opened down the centre' (P [39], C 199). This split is a symptom of the inward journey the poet must make, the 'split id' and the 'knifed nous' reflecting the internal fissure already implicated in the idea of the self:

> Two faces now returned my stare
> each whole yet neither quite 'itself'.
> (But then the original could not
> have been called 'itself' either.
> What but some uneasiness made it divide?)

(P [39], C 200)

A Technical Supplement ends with the split self which signals Kinsella's move into the third stage of his numerological system in which the consciousness becomes aware of itself.

The manner in which the twenty-four poems of *A Technical Supplement* weave together to form a fabric of inquiry into the nature of the self and the nature of the poetic process is emblematic of the modern poetic sequence, defined as

> a grouping of mainly lyric poems and passages, rarely uniform in pattern, which tend to interact as an organic whole. It usually includes narrative and dramatic elements, and ratiocinative ones as well, but its structure is finally lyrical.[58]

A vital component of the sequence are the illustrations from Denis Diderot's *Encyclopédie* that Kinsella includes in the Peppercanister edition of *A Technical Supplement*. Unlike *One*, in which the text and the image complement each other but are not interdependent, the engravings which illustrate *A Technical Supplement* are integral to an understanding of the poetry. Kinsella has chosen six illustrations from the eleven volumes of plates entitled *Recueil de Planches sur les Sciences, les Arts Libéraux, et les Arts Méchaniques, avec leur explication*, published between 1762 and 1772. These volumes were produced to accompany and illuminate the seventeen volumes of text prepared over the period 1751 to 1772, which together form the *Encyclopédie* or *Dictionnaire raisonné des sciences, des arts, et des métiers* edited principally by Denis Diderot.[59] This encyclopaedia was intended, at the outset, to be a translation of the English Chamber's *Cyclopaedia*. However, it developed into a project which sought to bring together all the diverse knowledge of the eighteenth century, stressing the interconnections between disciplines, and exploring the applications and principles of each. The definition of the word 'encyclopédie' provided by the *Encyclopédie* outlines the three primary goals of an encyclopaedia: the accumulation of disparate forms of knowledge, the exposure of the underlying system or structure of this knowledge, and the transmission of this knowledge to succeeding generations.[60] This definition of the encyclopaedia can be used to understand Kinsella's view of poetry as a means by which the underlying structure of understanding may be apprehended.

Kinsella provides a commentary on Diderot's illustrations, which is taken from the 1923 edition of John Viscount Morley's *Diderot and the Encyclopaedists*. Morley emphasises the ability of the illustration to move from the particular to the general and to present specific individual data while giving a 'splendid panorama of all the busy life of the time'.[61] This co-existence of the particular and the general is further emphasised by Morley when he describes how the plates 'strike us even more by the semi poetic feeling that transforms the mere representation of a process into an animated scene of human life, stirring the sympathy and touching the imagination of the onlooker as by something dramatic'.[62]

The illustrations of *A Technical Supplement* are drawn from the first three of the eleven volumes of engraved plates issued with Diderot's *Encyclopédie*. Kinsella has chosen two details from plates illustrating the Art of Writing, one from Drawing, one from Anatomy and two from Surgery. He has placed these images throughout the poem in such a way as to form a symmetry of location through which the sense of one group of images overlaps onto another, informing the work as a whole. The first two images of *A Technical Supplement* are of a penknife, and of the correct manner in which to hold the pen. Located on the cover of the Peppercanister edition, this first image has been confused with that of a scalpel.[63] However, according to the explanation provided, it represents a penknife, 'le canif fermant', one of the 'trois instrumens convenables à l'art d'Écrire' [*sic*].[64] The second image appears on the title page of *A Technical Supplement*. It comes from the same plate as the image of the penknife and illustrates an explanation of the correct way to hold the pen: 'Sur la représentation d'une main qui tient la plume' (Écritures, p. 2). This image, which shows a man's right hand holding a pen in preparation to write, illustrates the delicate balance of stress, weight and control needed in order to write properly.[65] The image of a right hand firmly but

Denis Diderot, *Encyclopédie, Recueil de Planches* vol. 23. *Dessein.*
A Technical Supplement [13].

Denis Diderot, *Encyclopédie, Recueil de Planches* vol. 22.
Art d'écrire. A Technical Supplement [4–5].

delicately holding a pen mirrors almost exactly the hand of the fifth illustration, the first of two details taken from the plates illustrating the subject 'Surgery'. The fifth illustration shows a man's right hand holding a surgical probe, which pierces the eye of another as it is being restrained by the man's left hand.[66] This image brings to mind the striking opening scene of Dali and Buñuel's film *Un Chien Andalou*, but whereas their image is one of destruction – the slitting of the eyeball with a razor blade – the image chosen by Kinsella is one of construction in that it depicts the 'Attitudes pour l'ancienne méthode de faire l'operation de la cataracte' (Chirurgie, p. 3). The aim of the cataract operation is to remove the cloudy crystalline lens from the pupillary opening in order to enable light rays to strike the retina unimpeded, and was revolutionised in the early eighteenth century when Jacques Daviel of France extracted the first total cataract from a patient's eye through an incision in the cornea.[67] The importance of vision for understanding, whether it is a matter of internal or external scrutiny, is emphasised by Kinsella in the third section: 'lenses, letting the light pass easily / in either direction' then 'grew opaque, and began to glow' (P [11–12], C 185–6).

The parallel between the second and the fifth illustration, the confusion of the penknife with a scalpel, and the symmetry of placing the details from the art of writing as the first two illustrations of the poem, and the details from surgery as the last two, all provide a resonance which emphasises Kinsella's central metaphor of *A Technical Supplement*, that of poetry as self surgery. Images of blades – scalpel, razor-sharp divider, knife, shark teeth – occur throughout the poem, interchanging at times with images of the pen. In section xv, which comes directly after the fifth illustration, Kinsella draws a parallel between the pen and the probe in the act of writing poetry as he senses the approach of the Muse:

> The pen writhed. It moved
> under my thumb!
> It has sensed
> that sad prowler on our landing again.
>
> (P [30], C 194)

The speaker vows 'If she dares come nearer' to 'pierce her like / a soft fruit, a soft big seed!' (P [30], C 194).[68] Both penetrations, of the eye by the probe, and of the Muse by the pen, let in 'a little brightness' which allows for artistic possibility (P [24], C 192). Writing poetry is described in vibrant terms as the ability momentarily to pull 'a sheet of brilliant colour / free from the dark' (P [27], C 194). The obligation to destroy in order to create is recognised by Kinsella in section iv of *A Technical Supplement*. Like the pen piercing the soft fruit, and the probe piercing the eye, here Kinsella traces the passage of 'the point' as it pierces the skin, penetrating the tissue and nerves to the very core of the body where:

> it stands upright by itself
> and quivers with borrowed life.
>
> (P [14], C 187)

This 'borrowed life' is what nourishes the poetic process just as the lizards are nourished by their prey:

> Again. The head inside the mouth
> and the little hands and feet and the tail
> and the suddenly soft round belly
> hanging down outside.
>
> (P [19], C 190)

Kinsella introduces an ethical dimension with the question 'is it all right to do this' (P [18], C 189), to be implicated in the 'dripping groves' where the carcasses of animals hang like 'Huge horned fruit not quite dead' (P [16], C 187)? Or is all this experience valuable grist for the artistic mill:

> Ah well. . .
>   Grind it up, wash it down,
> stoke the blind muscular furnace,
> keep the waste volatile
>
> (P [33], C 196)

This view echoes succinctly the general formula of life which Diderot expounds in 'Le Rêve d'Alembert' – eat, digest and distil – where man moves along a series of successive stages in the life cycle as 'an inert being, a sentient being, a thinking being, a being solving the problem of the precession of the equinoxes, a sublime being, a marvellous being, a being ageing, degenerating, dying, passing through dissolution, and returning finally to humus'.[69] Kinsella distrusts the easy inevitability of this mechanical view of life, seeing instead a world which is 'penetrated by squalor, disorder and the insignificant'.[70] His impulse is to make sense of this world digging deep until:

> A few times in a lifetime, with luck,
> the actual *substance* alters: fills with
> expectation, beats with a molten glow
> as change occurs; grows cool; resumes.
>
> (P [31], C 195)

Though Diderot's assertion that 'flesh can be made into marble, and marble into flesh' is more radical than Kinsella's statement; the French philosopher's investigation into the connection between art and life, (between the 'inactive sentience' of art and the 'active sentience' of life), prefigures Kinsella's exploration of the contrast between the ideal proportions of a work of art and the confusion of life from which it arises.[71]

Kinsella juxtaposes an engraving of the ideal proportions of the statue of Laocoön with the subsequent sections dealing with the 'Vital spatterings' of life (P [18], C 189), the 'hot confusion'(P [16], C 187) of the slaughterhouse, probing the discrepancy between appearance and reality, the same discrepancy which forms the main theme of Virgil's tale in the *Aeneid* which recounts the destruction of Laocoön and his sons by two enormous sea-serpents.[72] The discrepancy between appearance and reality emphasised by the legend is reiterated in the engraving printed in the *Encyclopédie* (and consequently its reproduction in *A Technical Supplement*) which gives us an image of Laocoön's agony in reverse.[73] It is the right arm of the statue which reaches upwards, whereas in the engraving it is his left. This reversal is due to the process of engraving whereby the engraver traces the image of the statue of Laocoön onto the copper plate. Thus the printed image is the reverse of the actual image of the statue. This reversal shows that the importance of this image as part of the *Encyclopédie* lies in the relation between the various parts of this statue, the proportion and measure of the parts of the body rather than the agony that it expresses:

> Or half a dozen outward howls of glory
> and noble despair. Borrowed glory,
> his own despair. For the rest, energy wasted
> grimacing facetiously inward. And yet
> a vivid and lasting image: the racked outcast.

(P [37], C 198)

Kinsella's assertion that 'the artistic act has to do with the eliciting of order from significant experience, so as to come to terms with that experience'[74] emphasises his insistence throughout *A Technical Supplement* that structure and order must be forged from within, that 'We have to dig down; / sieve, scour and roughen; / make it all fertile and vigorous / – get the fresh rain down!'(P [23], C 192). Kinsella also recognises that in order to understand experience one must take it exactly on its own terms, that 'a good work of art embodies the capacity to grow, to keep the potential for enlarged relevance' just as the poet's own work – the long poems and the sequences – enlarge their own terms of reference.[75] As Floyd Skloot points out, Kinsella never deludes himself about the role of reason or the ability of human rationality to order or understand the universe, 'our victories over disorder are always temporary, our structures bound to erode or dissolve before us to demand new struggles toward order.'[76]

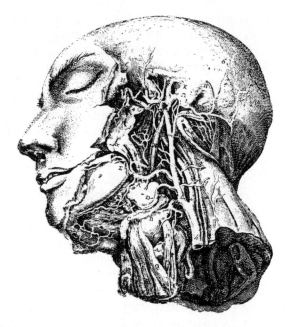

Denis Diderot, *Encyclopédie, Recueil de Planches* vol. 21. *Anatomie. A Technical Supplement* [21].

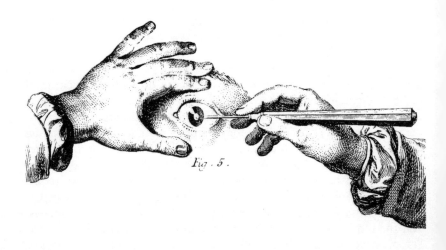

Denis Diderot, *Encyclopédie, Recueil de Planches* vol. 23. *Chirurgie. A Technical Supplement* [28–29].

By prefacing *A Technical Supplement* with Diderot's letter to Voltaire, Kinsella makes explicit the connection between his own twenty-four poem sequence and Diderot's *Encyclopédie*, to which his own work may be seen as a technical supplement. Similar concerns inform both Diderot's and Kinsella's projects:

> [The *Encyclopédie*] seemed to gather up into a single great reservoir all that men knew, and this fact of mere mechanical collocation was a sort of substitute for a philosophic synthesis. [. . .] it furnished a provisional rallying point for efforts the most divergent, without requiring the sacrifice of any points of essential independence, in such a way as to secure for a body of incoherent speculation an external look of system.[77]

But whereas Diderot's *Encyclopédie* is described as having 'an external look of system', Kinsella's poetic project seeks to establish a coherence between each poem or sequence which operates at every level, not just on the surface. That this great eighteenth-century enterprise, the gathering together in one publication all the knowledge of the time, from theoretical dissertations to detailed practical explanations, should be seen as a sort of substitute for a philosophical synthesis, that this concerted effort to see at last how the whole thing works should be viewed as securing for a body of incoherent speculation an external look of system, is intimated by Diderot in his letter to Voltaire which Kinsella quotes in *A Technical Supplement:*

> *Be useful to men! Is it quite clear that one does more than amuse them, and that there is much difference between the philosopher and the flute-player? They listen to one and the other with pleasure or disdain, and remain what they were.*
>
> (P [7], C 183)[78]

Diderot resists the temptation to abandon his work on the *Encyclopédie* for a life of peaceful obscurity and, even though he recognises that his work may have no significant effect on the world: '*There comes a time when all ashes are mingled. Then what will it boot me to have been Voltaire or Diderot, or whether it is your three syllables or my three syllables that survive?*' (P [7], C 183).[79] Kinsella's comment on his own work as having 'An arrogant beginning, *then /* the hard attrition' (P [25], C 193) is testament to a vision of art as a process of endurance the rewards of which are unknown. Yet the poet's command intimates reward:

> Persist.
>   And you may find
> the buried well. And take on
> the stillness of a root.
>
>   (P [14], C 187)

Kinsella's hard attrition takes him in the opposite direction to Diderot. He turns inward, stripping away, layer by layer, the constructs of fiction which form the self, 'scraping and scraping / down to the wood, / making it good' (P[22], C 191). Kinsella speaks from the vulnerable centre of his self, from his own 'nervous nakedness' (P [35], C 197). He is 'the split id', 'the knifed nous' (P [40], C 201) who attempts 'to peel the body asunder, / to pick off the muscles and let them / drop away one by one writhing' (P [10], C 184). 'The mind flexes. / The heart encloses' (P [24], C 192) as Kinsella considers how best to 'ply the knife, the merits of alternative incision strategies, the best way to get in at what lies tangled beneath the surface',[80] and it is perhaps the poet himself who is 'the wretch about to undergo the most dangerous operation in surgery'.[81] Underneath the surface lie '"contained" muscles':

> – separate entities, interwound and overlaid,
> firm, as if made of fish-meat or some
> stretched blend of fibre and fat.
>
> (P [10], C 184)

Kinsella explores the 'blind muscular furnace' of the second poem through a description of anatomy the detail of which equals that of two plates of the *Encyclopédie* which illustrate the flayed body (*l'écorché*), an anatomically precise diagram of the subcutaneous layers of the body:[82]

> This one, for example, containing – functioning as –
> a shoulderblade; or this one like a strap
> reaching underneath it, its tail
> melting into a lower rib; [. . .]
>
> (P [10], C 184)

In *Le Regard dans le Texte* Claude Gandelman traces the theme of the flayed body in art and literature to the myth of the satyr Marsyas, the inventor of the flute who challenged Apollo to a musical contest when he had already been (musically) defeated by the god, and was therefore skinned alive by Apollo. Gandelman transposes this myth to the realm of art where, by drawing a parallel between Apollo and and art, and Marsyas and the artist, he suggests that in order to produce a work of art, the artist must let himself be torn from himself by art.[83] Marsyas's anguished cry, 'Why do you tear me from myself' contrasts with Kinsella's self control as he looks in the mirror and sees his face begin to separate 'the head opening / like a rubbery fan' (P [39], C 199). This is a visual echo of the image which follows section ix of a serene face whose skin has been peeled back and the muscles stripped to reveal the arteries and the fine web of veins clustered in the hollow of the head. This image 'crusted with black detail' (P [20], C 190) is one of Diderot's illustrations of 'Une partie de la distribution de la carotide externe d'après Haller.'[84] The 'unfolded pale new detail' (P [39], C 199) of the exposed blood vessels in the severed head parallel the black detail of the crayfish dreaming on twig tips, and the unfolding anemones 'flesh-brilliant on slopes of rock' (P [20], C 190).

The tranquil underwater scene of 'bird-beaked heads / peering up at a far off music of slaughter' (P [20], C 190) finds its echo in the final illustration of A *Technical Supplement*, 'l'operation du trépan' (Chirurgie' p. 2), where the right temple of a head, the eyes of which are open but not alarmed, is delicately drilled while being gently restrained.[85] These two images show us the self in a state of violation, and their anaesthetised inertia belies Kinsella's assertion that:

> It would seem possible to peel the body asunder,
> to pick off the muscles and let them
> drop away one by one writhing
> until you have laid bare
> four or five simple bones at most.
>
> (P [10], C 184)

Except that under such examination the body is ripped asunder. The self, however, is made of sterner stuff. The 'private blade' is planted deep 'from bowels to brain' (P [40], C 200) tearing the self from itself:

> The eyes moved wider apart
> and another eye surfaced between them and divided.
> The nose divided and doubled and moved out
> one to right and left.
> The mouth stretched in a snarl
> then split into two mouths, pursed.
>
> (P [39], C 199)

The speaker sees himself 'twinned, glaring and growing' in a process of division (P [41], C 201). Like Diderot's *Encyclopédie*, A *Technical Supplement* brings together encounters from the flux of life, searching for 'a nexus' (P [34], C 197) which will make sense of that life, revealing an underlying order or structure which can provide the foundation for 'a meaningful model for the life lived'.[86] In order to construct this model, the poet does not look to the definitions of the *Encyclopédie*, those 'insane nets' which can only 'plunge and convulse to hold thy furious catch' (P [9], C 184). He looks instead to the illustrations of the *Encyclopédie*. These engraved plates form a visual framework for A *Technical Supplement* in which Kinsella explores the ideals of art (Dessin) and the bloodied confusion of life (Anatomie), providing a point of departure for his inward turn, his descent into the 'violent zone'[87] of

Denis Diderot, *Encyclopédie, Recueil de Planches* vol. 23. *Chirurgie.*
A Technical Supplement [38].

poetry and of the self, where the pen (l'Art d'Écrire) approximates the scalpel (Chirurgie) and where:

> The divider waits, shaped
> razor sharp to my dream print.
>
> (P [41], C 201)

The epistolary address with which *A Technical Supplement* opens echoes a similar address in the 1966 volume *Wormwood*. In the earlier work the speaker addresses his beloved with a meditation on the necessity of a search for self knowledge which he describes as an ordeal, but one which carries with it the possibilities of transmutation:

> We reach out after each new beginning, penetrating our context to know ourselves, and our knowledge increases until we recognise again (more profoundly each time) our pain, indignity and triviality.[88]

Ten years later, in *A Technical Supplement*, Kinsella revisits that inward turn, reiterating that 'The beginning / must be inward' (P [31], C 195). The poet is not content just to recognise the pain, indignity and triviality of the self, now he must strive, 'Emotion expelled, to free the structure of a thing, / or indulged, to free the structure of an idea' (P [37], C 199). Structure, whether it is corporeal or noetic, is a central concern of *A Technical Supplement*. The need to focus upon the concrete and the specific in order to come to an understanding of abstract or general concerns is the governing perspective of Kinsella's work:

> The entirety of one's being
> crowded for everlasting shelter
> into the memory of one crust of bread.
>
> (P [37], C 199)

In a conversation with the poet in 1986, John F. Deane characterises Kinsella's poetic process as beginning from particularities. Kinsella affirms this, replying: 'Yes. And every generalisation that I nerve myself to make will have been earned by the behaviour of the poem.'[89] However, Kinsella also understands that concentration on the individual encounter transmutes that encounter as it is stopped 'in flux, living', and held 'out from / the streaming away of lifeblood, timeblood' (P [34], C 197). In order to see how it works, to find (or forge) the structure of the thing, one must make the habitual inhabitual. One must stumble 'onto another way' – away from 'all these things, they cling, they delight, / they hold us back' (P [31], C 195) – towards the 'unrewarding outer reaches' where 'the integrity of the whole thing is tested' (P [25], C 193).

Song of the Night and Other Poems

In his essay on Kinsella's poetry of the 1970s and 1980s Maurice Harmon opens with a consideration that the 'Taoist idea of nature might serve as an allegory for Thomas Kinsella's idea of a poem.'[90] Taking his lead from the title of one of the poems in the collection *Song of the Night and Other Poems*, 'Tao and Unfitness at Inistiogue on the River Nore', Harmon sees a correspondence between Taoist perception and Kinsella's creation:

> The subject is delicate, the means recalcitrant. One constant is the distinction made between ordinary observation and intuitive communion. The attractive casualness of the former, a relaxed noting of place and people, is subtly offset by the gentle quietism of the latter.[91]

In the two years between *A Technical Supplement* and *Song of the Night and Other Poems* Kinsella has moved from the visceral and numeric concerns of the former towards an evaluation of love and the nature of understanding. 'Gentle quietism' well describes the change in tone from the vigorous interrogative of *A Technical Supplement* to the considered meditation of the subsequent volume.

Song of the Night and Other Poems was published in tandem with *The Messenger* in 1978, numbered 7 and 8 of the ongoing Peppercanister series. Three of the poems in the volume made their first appearance in journals: 'C.G. Jung's "First Years"' in *Tracks*, Philadelphia; 'Anniversaries' in *The Chowder Review*, Madison, Wisconsin; and 'Tao and Unfitness' in *The Sewanee Review* of June 1978. Like the previous two Peppercanisters, and its companion, *The Messenger*, *Song of the Night* was issued in the deluxe, library and trade editions that had become customary for the Peppercanister Press from 1974 to 1987. Similarly to other Peppercanisters, Kinsella added a handwritten verse to the deluxe edition which becomes the italicised first verse in the *Collected Poems*, with the addition of the phrase 'blue-white' to describe the gaslight.

This first verse reaches back to childhood memory of a father carrying the poet-child through the night. A heightened sensory perception characterises this verse as the scent of the father's '*night-smelling overcoat*' gives way to the rhythm of walking and to observation: '*Sticks in a black hedge / went flickering past. Frosty twinkles / danced along in the granite'* (C 203). The poem is built on a series of opposites or contradictions which are anticipated by the distinction between light and dark as man and child move between the street-lamps; and find their focus in the final lines:

> as he carried me, warm and chill,
> homeward, abandoned, onward to the next shadow.
>
> (C 203)

In a movement which connects this volume with the earlier *One*, Kinsella rewrites childhood in terms of 'C. G. Jung's "First Years"'. Drawing directly from Jung's autobiography *Memories, Dreams, Reflections* the poet focuses on certain key dreams or visions in Jung's early life.[92] The poem has two numbered sections, the second of which is also divided into two, and it opens with an image of water which recalls Amairgin's difficult landing from *One*: 'Dark waters churn amongst us / and whiten against troublesome obstacles:' (P 5, C 203). The word 'amongst' takes the place of the expected 'around', transforming the water which has previously had primordial significance into an image of the unconscious which only gains form or visibility through certain key moments or 'obstacles'. In the drafts to the poem Kinsella signals more clearly the parallel he draws between his own exploration of the self and that of Jung when he writes, perhaps alluding to the italicised previous verse, 'I, also, rest a good deal on a certain particular scrap of memory.'[93] The role of memory in the formation of the self operates in terms of both the individual and of community. Kinsella has used myth (which in Jungian terms can be considered a kind of communal memory) and his individual memories of family members and events to provide a framework through which an understanding of the self can be reached. By using Jung's memories in 'C.G. Jung's "First Years"', Kinsella distances himself from the operation at hand, allowing him to focus more clearly on the form of his inquiry.

The first of Jung's memories used is that of a woman, not his mother, who looked after him:

> A nurse's intimate warm ear
> far in the past; the sallow loin of her throat;
>
> (P 5, C 203)

The connection that Jung makes between the strongly physical memory of the woman and the development of his unconscious ('this type of girl later became a component of my anima'[94]) is rewritten by Kinsella in specifically visceral terms:

> combined in her entrails
> memories of womanly manipulations
> with further detailed plans for the living flesh.

> (P 5, C 203)

As the last line makes clear, the connection between the individual and the larger community takes place, not so much on the level of an abstract unconscious, but rather on a specifically corporeal level through pro-creation. The second section of the poem opens with three scenes from Jung which relate to an early explanation of death, anxieties regarding gender uncertainty, and concerns about the power of the phallus:[95] 'Jesus, and his graves eating the dead . . . / A Jesuit – a witchbat –' and 'A pillar of skin' (P 5, C 204 var.).[96] These traumatic moments are figured as waves of the 'dark waters' with which the poem opens. They approach, climax and retreat with the constant possibility of return:

> The dreams broke in succession and ran back
> whispering with disappearing particulars.

> (P 5, C 204)

With a symmetry that cancels out what went before, Kinsella closes the poem in a mood of absolute control. The terrors which haunt the young child are confronted and banished. Jesus is eaten, and the 'sleeve-winged terror' shrinks away (P 5, C 204). In a turn which would do Lacan proud, the speaker assumes the phallic throne.

Jung's memories give way to Kinsella's own in the second poem 'Anniversaries'. He divides the poem into four temporal units which mark significant moments in his life. The first, 1955, remembers the poet's wedding on the 28 December of that year. In his drafts Kinsella names the place as Enniscorthy Cathedral, but the final poem speaks only of 'a cage / of flowering arches full of light' (P 6, C 204), which echoes a scene of love described in the earlier poem, 'Midsummer', from his 1956 collection:[97]

> Grown silent and,
> Under beech and sacred larch,
> Watched as though it were an arch
> That heart expand.

> (C 7)

While the natural setting of 'Midsummer' contrasts with the man-made space of this first stanza of 'Anniversaries', it is into the hands of 'Nature' that this couple place themselves through their union. The third-person perspective of this first section of '1955', which sees the lovers as 'creatures to catch / Nature's attention', becomes first-person plural in the second section as they see themselves as ones 'on whom / Nature had as yet / worked so little' (P 6–7, C 204–5). Drawing together the winged image on the cover of the Peppercanister, and the fearsome 'witchbat' of 'C. G. Jung's "First Years"', both lover and beloved are described in chiropteric terms:

> We preened and shivered
> among pale stems
> under nodding grain. Breezes nibbled
> and fingered at our fur.
>
> (P 6, C 205)

The natural and the elemental find focus in the two lovers as 'sunlight passed direct / into our blood' and 'Mercury // glittered / in the needle-nails we / sank' (P 6–7, C 205). However, the mention of mercury, here given the status of a proper name, reaches us back to *One* and forward to *The Messenger*. The Roman god Mercury, who has his counterpart in the Greek Hermes, has also a counterpart in Celtic mythology in the figure of the god Lug. Drawing on 'De Bello Gallico' de Jubainville notes that:

> Lug is none other than the Gaulish god whom Caesar describes as the inventor of all the arts: *omnium inventorem artium*. Caesar calls him Mercury.[98]

Lug, or Mercury, is also the guide who directs the traveller, and one who has great influence in the acquisition of riches.[99] Empowered by this quicksilver god, the couple look to a future blessed by invention in the arts, safety in travel, and success in commerce. All this is possible for:

> (The three qualities that are necessary
> She has, namely: patience,
> deliberation,
> and skill with the instruments.)
>
> (P 6, C 205)

Here, Kinsella recalls his early work of translation in *Thirty Three Triads*, published by Dolmen in 1957, in which virtues, and vices, have a three-fold nature:

> Three excellent qualities in narration: a good flow, depth of thought,
> conciseness.
> Three dislikable qualities in the same: stiffness, obscurity, bad delivery.[100]

This reference to Kinsella's early work brings us directly to the next section of 'Anniversaries': '1956'. Taking place the year when Kinsella's first book *Poems* was published, the section describes the act of writing in orgiastic terms: ' – elephant into orgasm – / and I was about ready. // I crooked my foot / around the chair-leg / and my fingers around / the pen [. . .]' (P 7, C 205–6). Before he sets to writing, there is some preparation: 'Fifteen minutes or thereabouts / of Prelude and Liebestod' (P 7, C 205).

Here Kinsella refers to Wagner's opera *Tristan und Isolde*, the prelude and final aria of which are often performed, or recorded, together. The surreal vision of Kinsella's workplace, the finance files dreaming and the desk moving 'infinitesimally. / Over the entire country', joins with a meditation on the 'emanations of government' which were the poet's business, and a memory of the emigration which was endemic in 1950s Ireland (P 7–8, C 206). As Kinsella notes in the drafts of the poem: 'in the grim years, the whole country was an empty pocket'.[101] All of these observations go to form the speaker's first book of poetry, which is figured in terms of the flight emblematic of *Song of the Night and Other Poems*:

> A book came
> fluttering out of the dark
> and flapped
> at the window.
>
> (P 8, C 206)

The final two sections of 'Anniversaries' give us two versions of a scene set in 1975. Both sections are placed in quotation marks, distancing the voice, and the writer, from what is being said. The speaker is once again the lover from the second part of '1955', who speaks of the couple in their winged form, now as birds of prey: 'We flew down / and our claws curled, as one, / around the same outer branch' (P 8, C 207). In both versions the attention is firmly on the thrill of the hunt, whether it is the excitement of seeing 'stems dipped everywhere / under mouse-fruit' or the 'stubble / sprinkled with eyepoints of fierce fright and malice' (P 9, C 207). Either way, the urge is always 'to strangle at them with our feet!' (P 9, C 207).

In notes towards *Song of the Night and Other Poems* Kinsella divides the collection into two parts. The first three poems of the collection come under the heading 'Sex Poems', and the last three under the heading 'Three Occasional Poems'.[102] The final poem of this first part writes of love through a framework of love-letters. The title 'Artist's Letters' lends the poem a distinctively autobiographical attitude which is in keeping with all the poems of the collection. Written with little revision, Kinsella envisaged the poem as a prose poem. The search 'for something, / confirmation of something' leads the speaker to 'fat packets of love letters' (P 10, C 208). In a return which brings us back to the time before 1955, the speaker meditates on the nature of love, and the relationship between romance, writing and desire. Love is unique: 'There is one throw, no more. One / offering: make it' (P 10, C 208), but the orthographic evidence of that love gives rise to embarrassment and exposure:

What is it about such letters,
torn free ignominiously
in love? Character stripped off
our pens plunge repeatedly
at the unique cliché, [. . .]

(P 11, C 209)

In an image which returns us to the primordial world depicted in the opening of *One*, Kinsella rewrites the marriage scene of 'Anniversaries' in terms of a psychic and physical union of love. The two figures, artist and beloved, are 'nicely eaten' by a 'toothless mouth' which recalls the Great Mother image of Jungian thought. The instinctive nature of this desire is neatly conveyed by the lines: 'and we throw ourselves, enthralled, against our bonds / and thrash toward her' (P 11, C 09). Union between the two lovers is effected as 'our parts' are 'spat out whole and have become / "one"' (P 11, C 209). With a wry irony Kinsella juxtaposes the private life of desire and the public life of the mind as he concludes: '*then* we can settle our cuffs / and our Germanic collar / and turn back calmly toward distinguished things' (P 11, C 209).

Though it is titled *Song of the Night and Other Poems*, this collection has a unity and coherence which its title disavows. The penultimate poem, 'Tao and Unfitness at Inistiogue on the River Nore', gives us a wider perspective on some of the scenes in 'Anniversaries', especially the scenes from '1975'. When it was first published separately in 1978 the title Kinsella gave it was 'Tao and Unfitness at Inistiogue on the River Barrow'.[103] The scene is the Kinsella family's visit to the town of Inistiogue around June 1974.[104] The poem takes place between noon and nightfall, dividing time into three parts marked by the strength of the sun. Kinsella weaves observation and analysis of the river, town and the ruined house with a varied refrain which takes its lead from the 'Tao' of the title. These gentle exhortations provide an indirect commentary on the situation and provide a glimpse of the attitude necessary to deal with the historical material presented in the poem. The first, 'Move, if you move, like water', evokes the contrast, and interconnection, between movement and stasis; and the relationship between the part and the whole. The 'volumes of water' which constantly flow form also the 'river curve' which is a constant, static, presence. The mayflies which form the 'insect haze' lose their individuality in the ever moving cloud which hovers above the river. The second, 'Respond. Do not interfere. Echo', works from the two-way description of the river as a 'deep mirror.' The injunction to 'Respond' is immediately qualified by 'Do not interfere', as the mirror aspect of the river which reflects the viewer while also allowing vision beyond the surface is taken up by the less engaged 'Echo' (P 12, C 210).

The noontime section closes with a moment of alliteration and assonance which breaks the mostly plain diction of Kinsella's writing as the:

> Thick green woods along the opposite bank
> climbed up from a root-dark recess
> eaved with mud-whitened leaves.
>
> (P 12, C 210)

The 'Afternoon' describes the town of Inistiogue in a way which draws our attention to the intersection between history, politics and religion. Kinsella casts his critical, and somewhat distainful, eye over the 'typical English village' with its '"village green"' and picturesque water pump placed 'with an eye to the effect' (P 13, C 211–12). A harshly judged moment colours the scene:

> The Protestant church was guarded by a woman
> of about forty, a retainer, spastic
> and indistinct, who drove us out.
>
> (P 13, C 211)

The sentiments expressed here have a greater affinity with a time past, a time of the Baron of Brownsfoord of 1621, and later, in 1879, of Louisa M. Tighe, born a Lennox and subsequently a widow of William Frederick Tighe. The Tighe family were of Woodstock, Inistiogue, County Kilkenny and Rosanna, Ashford, County Wicklow, controlling parliamentary boroughs in both areas.[105] Monuments to these two families mark the centre of the town:[106]

> An obelisk to the Brownsfoords and a Victorian
> Celto-Gothic drinking fountain, erected
> by a Tighe widow for the villagers,
>
> (P 13, C 211)

The ruin which the Kinsella family visits is 'Woodstock, once home of the Tighes' (P 13, C 211). The distinction between inside and out is complicated by the dilapidation of the structure: 'Deserted spaces, complicated / by door-openings everywhere' (P 14, C 211). The 'brick-red stillness' of the house is drawn out to form the third taoist advocation (P 13, C 211): 'Be still, as though pure. // A brick, and its dust, fell' (P 14, C 212). The previous three precepts find their focus in the scenes that occur in the 'Nightfall' section of 'Tao and Unfitness at Inistiogue on the river Nore'. Here, as the family return to their lodgings, the speaker sheds light on the 'ragged feeling, old angers and rumours' that have tainted the previous section of the poem. It is a question of history and of how much incidents of the past influence attitudes of the present:

Black and Tan ghosts up there at home
on the Woodstock heights: an iron mouth
scanning the Kilkenny road: the house
gutted by the townspeople and burned to ruins . . .

(P 14, C 212 var.)

In his earlier *Sewanee Review* version of the poem Kinsella is more direct:

The Black and Tans
given use of the Woodstock heights for a big gun
overlooking the Kilkenny road. The big house locked,
plundered by the local people and burned to ruins.[107]

This story from the Irish War of Independence points up the particular
cultural tensions which, though named by religion, have their origin in
the politics of colonialism. Against this scene of unresolved antagonism
Kinsella contrasts the calm world of the river, the current cancelled out
by the incoming tide. A sense of balance is restored by the 'gleaming
calm' of the river, with fish below and mayfly above. Using the word
'imago' which, as Brian John draws to our attention, means both the
'final and perfect stage or form of an insect after it has undergone all its
metamorphoses' (OED) and, in Jungian terms, a version of the anima
which is one of the necessary links to creative possibility, Kinsella links
the events of history with those of the individual's psychic development:[108]

Down on the water . . . at eye level . . . in the little light
remaining overhead . . . the mayfly passed in a loose drift,
thick and frail, a hatch slow with sex,
separate morsels trailing their slack filaments,
olive, pale evening dun, imagoes, unseen eggs
dropping from the air, subimagoes, the river filled
with their nymphs ascending and excited trout.

(P 15, C 213)

Appetite is the impulse which breaks the silver surface of the water. The
sexual activity in the air above is matched by the hunger in the water
below. Between the contrary flows of the river which cancel each other
out, and the opposite drives of life and death which join the air and the
water, lies the speaker: 'We drifted, but stayed almost still' (P 15, C 212).
The calm and stasis evoked by this image is echoed in the last Taoist
phrase: 'Be subtle, as though not there' (P 15, C 213). But the problem,
surely, is that one is there. The speaker is part of a present which is
contaminated by the divisions of the past. If, as Jung suggests, Tao 'is the
method or conscious way by which to unite what is separated' the chal-
lenge for the speaker, and the reader, is to find a way or means by which
this unity can be effected.[109] Does the burning of Woodstock cancel out
the betrayal of the Tighes through their cooperation with the Black and

Tans? Or does each injustice endure in a cycle of suspicion and resentment which finds voice in the bitter lines describing the retainer of the local Protestant church? The poem closes with an ambiguous image which reminds us of the earlier salmon poachers, and suggests the figures of shades or shadows which represent the dark side of the self:

> We were near the island – no more than a dark mass
> on a sheet of silver – when a man appeared in midriver
> quickly and with scarcely a sound, his paddle touching
> left and right of the prow, with a sack behind him.
> The flat cot's long body slid past effortless
> as a fish, sinewing from side to side,
> as he passed us and vanished.
>
> (P 15, C 213 var.)[110]

In the light of this passage, the title of the poem comes into focus. It concerns Tao and unfitness: the search for unity and understanding, and the unfitness of the individual to achieve either. However the next, and final, poem of the volume introduces a moment of epiphany in which darkness is balanced by light.

'Song of the Night', the title poem, speaks of the dark side of the human psyche and of history, but also of the power of love as an enabling force. It recalls the 'Prelude and Liebestod' of 'Anniversaries' and Wagner's *Tristan und Isolde*, in which the lovers sing of a passion which can only flourish at night.[111] The night of Wagner's opera is not simply the time of rest and dreams, it is also 'a realm of direct contact with being; a realm that surrounds and underlies life, and is known in deep, dreamless sleep, in the experience of love, and especially in death, when human love is superceded by the bliss of union with the universe.'[112] Wagner's opera has relevance historically, in the context of the 'Afternoon' section of 'Tao and Unfitness at Inistiogue on the River Nore', when we learn that the story of the *Tristan und Isolde* takes place at a time of emnity between Ireland and Cornwall which is only overcome through love and death. This nocturnal poem opens between Philadelphia and Carraroe with a powerful evocation of the ocean mingling with the sounds of the city we have already heard in *Vertical Man*:

> A compound bass roar
> an ocean voice
> Metropolis in the ear
> soft-thundered among the towers below
>
> (P 16, C 213)

From the pages of a 'great atlas', the Atlantic is seen joinging the poet's two homes: the U.S. with Ireland, and Philadelphia with Carraroe, the place of work with that of vacation. These two locations can also be read as the two aspects of the self, the one 'without wave-rhythm / without breath-rhythm / exhalation without cease' (P 16, C 213), the other a rhythmic alliterative movement as:

> Films of liquid light run
> shimmering, cut by shell-points, over
> stone inclines and clotted buds of anemones.

> (P 17, C 214)

Gorumna Island reminds us of the island at the close of 'Tao and Unfitness at Inistiogue on the River Nore', and the upright boulder on the shore of Carraroe recalls the opening lines of 'C. G. Jung's "First Years"' (P 5, C 203). The dark waters of the self join with the 'dark masses' of the Atlantic which both whiten against an obstacle to understanding or passage:

> On our shore, among a tumble of boulders
> on the minced coral, there was one
> balanced with rugged edge upward,
> stuck with limpets. Over it,
> with the incoming tide, the waters
>
> wash back and forth irregularly
> and cover and uncover the brown angles.

> (P 16–17, C 214)

Moments of clarity follow as the water 'withdrew rustling down the invisible grains' (P 17, C 214). With the retreat of the ocean comes a release effected through love.

Three remarkable scenes, which bring together sea, sky and earth in a movement of renewal and release, close the volume. The first recalls the primordial scene of the serpent with which *One* opens. This time, however, the first stirrings of life are symbolised by the sand-eels which, through alliteration and accumulative rhythm, seem to merge with both sand and sea:

> Silvery sand-eels seethed everywhere we stepped:
> shivered and panicked through the shallows,
> vanished – became sand – were discovered,
> picked up with exclamations,
> held out damp and deathly,
> little whips fainted away
> in wet small palms, an iodine smell.

> (P 18, C 215)

The second scene takes place in the sky and recalls the Faustian theatre of *One*. Artifice gives way to the sublime as the speaker's wife, 'urgent and quiet' exhorts: 'Look back'. Looking back is what the speaker has been engaged with throughout the volume, whether it is the individual events of his own life, or those of his country. But this backward glance provides the possibility of looking forward:

> The great theatre of Connemara,
> dark. A cloud bank stretched in folds
> across the sky, luminous
> with inner activity.
>
> (P 18, C 215)

The veiled light of the heavens joins that of the earth as the spotlight falls again on the children on the shore who provide the possibility of future as their 'crystalline laughter escaped upward, / their shadows huge' (P 18, C 216). The sounds of the night become the 'Song of the Night', a song which can be understood in Schopenhauerian terms as that music which expresses the innermost essence of the world, and which prefigures the music of 'the great Harp of Life' in *Her Vertical Smile* (P 7, C 247). Joined in love, the speaker and his beloved become part of 'That old / body music' which joins man and nature (P 19, C 216). The music is '(– "darkly expressive, / coming from innermost depths . . ."' and coming also from the dark or shadowy aspects of the self, and of history, with which the speaker strives to come to terms: '*Schattenhaft*. SONG OF THE NIGHT . . .' (P 19, C 216 var.). The final scene plays out, in full harmonies, the last phrases of Isolde's *Liebestod*. This aria echoes the ebb and flow of ocean which underpins *Song of the Night and Other Poems*.[113] The 'string sounds', and 'persistent / tympanum double-beat' join with the 'long horn call' to describe the closing bars of Wagner's opera.[114] But rather than an ecstatic union in death, Kinsella's poem gives a reply to those lingering notes:

> Overhead a curlew – God in Heaven! –
> responded!
>   'poignant . . .' Yes.
> 'hauntingly beautiful . . .' Yes!
>
> (P 19, C 216 var.)[115]

The 'dark waters' with which Kinsella opens *Song of the Night and Other Poems* gives way to the iridescence of understanding as 'The bay – every inlet – lifted / and glittered towards us in articulated light' (P 19, C 216). The dark aspect which has shadowed the poet in *Song of the Night and Other Poems*, depicted in Kinsella's ink drawings of the cover and on the last page of the volume, moves in a moment of release:[116]

A part of the mass
grated and tore, cranking harshly,
and detached and struggled upward
and beat past us along the rocks,
bat-black, heron-slow.

(P 19, C 216)

Articulation is Kinsella's concern in this volume. Continuing the process initiated in *Notes from the Land of the Dead*, the poet draws from the simple events of a town visited, dishes washed, a hand held, to create a complex meditation on the nature of love and responsibility in the context of the personal and the public. Every element in the poem is put to work in a way which reflects Wagner's idea of 'infinite melody' in which every note is significant, and every momement has specific relevance to the scene at hand, while also being intrinsically linked to the other moments of the work.[117] The music of *Song of the Night and Other Poems* is just such a melody.

The Messenger

In a note to the *Poetry Book Society Bulletin* in 1958 Kinsella described his father and grandfather in these terms:

> My grandfather came to Dublin, eighty years ago, from desolate hill country near Tinahely in County Wicklow. He worked for most of his life in Guinness's Brewery and became eventually captain of a Liffey barge. [. . .] My father, who surrounded my childhood with books and music, continues the association with Guinness's. He is a man of high and punishing ideals.[118]

It is in memory of his father John Paul Kinsella, who died in May of 1976, that Kinsella writes the *The Messenger*. Unlike Kinsella's other elegies, the subjects of which are connected with the poet through politics, culture or friendship, *The Messenger* looks to the connections of blood and family from which the poet, and his father, have come.

The cover of *The Messenger* is striking. On a blood-red background Jarlath Hayes has redrawn the emblems and motifs of the devotional magazine, *The Irish Messenger of the Sacred Heart: organ of the apostleship of prayer*. In place of Christ there is an image of the winged god Mercury / Hermes carrying a caduceus, the staff entwined by two snakes and bearing two wings on top which is symbolic of the herald. It is used to symbolise the physician, and is also associated with the alchemical symbol for *coniunctio* which means the marrying of opposites. The figure of Mercury on the refashioned cover of the *Messenger* does not so much banish Christ as incorporate him since Mercury, or in alchemical texts, Mercurius, is the analogue of Christ.[119] Twin snakes encircle

On a blood-red background Jarlath Hayes has redrawn the emblems and motifs of the devotional magazine *The Irish Messenger of the Sacred Heart: organ of the apostleship of prayer* for the cover of Kinsella's eighth Peppercanister volume, *The Messenger*.

Mercury, drawn in the interlaced style of old Irish illuminations, illustrating the circularity of the uroboros dragon with which Mercury is associated, and alluding once again to the Christ figure:

> As the uroboros dragon, he impregnates, begets, bears, devours, and slays himself, and "himself lifts himself on high," [. . .] so paraphrasing the mystery of God's sacrificial death.[120]

To the left of the figure, the image of the papal crown featured on the *Messenger of the Sacred Heart* is replaced by a label for Guinness Extra Stout. To the right, the image of an Irish harp featured on the devotional magazine is replaced by an emblem of the Irish labour movement, the plough and the stars. Religion gives way to business, and patriotic idealism to social realism.

The poem opens with a portrait of late-awakening grief:

> For days I have wakened and felt immediately
> half sick at something. Hour follows hour
> but my shoulders are chilled with expectation.
>
> (P 5, C 217)

The speaker widens his concerns from the immediate pain of grief – 'It is more than mere Loss' – or the recollection of events no longer shared – 'or "what you missed"' – to a consideration of the mortality that must be faced when the generations no longer precede you. Mortality is envisioned in material and moral terms; a dissolution into 'filth' which can be understood as both the earth to which the body is consigned, and the depravity to which the self can descend:

> Deeper. A suspicion in the bones
> as though they too could melt in filth.
>
> Something to discourage goodness.
>
> (P 5, C 217)

The contrast between goodness and the filth is refigured in the subsequent lines which recall the primordial sensibilities of *A Technical Supplement*: '*A moist movement within. / A worm winds on its hoard*', and the 'planetary pearl-blue' of the Land of the Dead in *One*: '*A dead egg glimmers – a pearl in muck*' (P 5, C 217). In his revision of the poem for the *Collected Poems* edition, Kinsella removes the lines in this passage which make overt reference to a less primordial body, and which return our attention to the 'half sick' speaker: '*A rim of hide lifts like a lip. // The belly settles and crawls tighter*' (P 5). Kinsella describes the link between father and son, not in terms of intangible memory, but as a

visceral rootedness which continues beyond death: '(your tomb-image /
drips and blackens, my leaden root / curled on your lap)' (P 5, C 217).
The movement of this prefatory poem is inwards, 'Deeper', to a point of
birth or generation which is psychic, though imaged in specifically
somatic terms. Through the figure of Mercury, or Mercurius, Kinsella
explores the development of both an interior and exterior life. Developing
on the elements of Jungian Taoism in *Song of the Night and Other
Poems*, Kinsella draws on Jung's work on how alchemical processes can
be understood as parallels for the evolution of the psyche in *The
Messenger*. The '*dead egg*' echoes the falling egg of 'Hen Woman', and it
can be understood as the 'philosopher's egg' which is an alchemical
symbol of creation.[121] From this image of potentiality buried in blindness,
'*a pearl in muck*', Kinsella explores his father's life. The first part of the
poem outlines John Kinsella's achievements, but also points to his
limitations; a life of social and political development is not matched by
self realisation. The second part enacts the development and exploration
of the psyche or 'Self' left undone by the father. The poem closes in the
third part with a moment of release and regeneration.

The first part of *The Messenger* combines closely observed sketches of
the father's character, memories of the death and funeral, and a recol-
lection of his life's achievements. Kinsella opens with a description of
death as the conflation of gender and generation, bringing to mind the
powerful grandmother figures of poems like 'A Hand of Solo', 'Ancestor'
and 'Tear':

> His mother's image settled on him
> out of the dark, at the last,
> and the Self sagged, unmanned.
>
> (P 6, C, 218)

With wit and compassion the poem recalls John Kinsella's old age: his
frustration at losing his hearing, 'he glared from his rocker / at people
whispering on television', and the enthusiastic reiteration of 'His last
battle' to his elderly companions even as, 'All about him, open mouthed,
/ they expired in ones and twos' (P 6, C 218). Here Kinsella makes refer-
ence to his father's lifelong political activism. The battle referred to is the
fight for an index-linked pension from Guinness in pursuit of which
John Kinsella formed a pensioners' union.[122] Kinsella interleaves these
memories with a recollection from his father's funeral in which the
significance of the individual is contrasted with the importance of family:

A thoughtful delegated word or two:

'His father before him. . . Ah, the barge captain . . .
A valued connection. He will be well remembered . . .
He lived in his two sons.'

In his own half fierce force
he lived! [. . .]

(P 7, C 218)

Evidence of this 'fierce force' comes in a number of scenes throughout the poem. John Kinsella's efforts to form a union in Guinness brought him into conflict with the established powers of secret and not so secret societies, 'Mason and Knight', 'manager and priest', which resulted in his temporary dismissal at the age of twenty-one. The lugubrious rhythm of the hymn *Faith of our Fathers* becomes a ridiculous 'jigtime' as the complicity between politics, economics and religion is exposed:

Mason and Knight

gave ground in twostep,
manager and priest
disappeared

and reappeared under each other's hats;
the lumpenproletariat
stirred truculently and settled;

(P 7, C 219 var.)

Kinsella questions the value of struggling against such an establishment when he counterpoints the risks of political engagement with the physical bravado displayed by his father as he 'traversed a steel beam in the Racking Shed / and dared with outstretched arms / what might befall' (P 8, C 219). The young man who was left 'high and dry' by Guinness is eventually 'well remembered' in death, for on his return from Manchester with a young family to support, he obtains another post in Guinness: 'florid and with scorn, // [. . .] he stomached it' (P 7, C 219). The ambivalence of his acceptance is neatly caught in the parenthetical phrases: '(I care) (But accept) (I reject) (I do not)' (P 7). Within the 'full vigour' of life, the first movements towards death begin as 'the muffled inner / heartstopping little / heartblows began' (P 8, C 219). Kinsella's arrested diction culminates in a concrete poem which mimes the shape of the heart and, with its archaic heraldic diction, parodies 'a family crest, with motto'.[123] This poem gathers together all the aspects of John Kinsella that have gone before. The 'bright prospects' of the young employee are shadowed by 'sable' and 'a slammed door'. The proud vitality of the young man is put in 'check'. His course is run

    A brave leap   On bright prospects
    in full heart   sable: a
    into full stop   slammed door.

              Vaunt and check
              Cursus inter-
                 ruptus.

                    (P 8, C 220)

the final disjointed words conveying the interruption of life, the transi-
tion from life to death, and the rupture of muscle and membrane which
is its cause.

   Kinsella now turns from the father's public persona to his private one.
The focus is on the 'Self' which is depicted as 'islanded in fog'. In an
image reminiscent of Shakespeare's *The Tempest* Kinsella describes a
subject which has banished those aspects of itself which it will not, or
cannot, come to terms with: 'Every positive matter / that might endanger –
but also enrich – / is banished' (P 9, C 220). The metaphor for these
repressed elements is that of a sleeping dragon, monster or beast. The
unfulfilled aspirations and unforgotten disappointments of life are con-
tained within, but kept separate from, the body in a benign but painful
'cyst'. The postcolonial references contained in this allusion to *The
Tempest* introduce a larger social and political framework to the elegy,
paralleling the individual's quest for wholeness and self-recognition with
that of a nation. In lines which evoke Caliban's furious ignorance,
Kinsella writes of the unconscious:[124]

              Somewhere on the island, Cannibal
              lifts his halved head and bellows
              with incompleteness . . .   [. . .]

                    (P 9, C 220 var.)

In the *Collected Poems* Kinsella combines the last two tercets of this part
into a tighter and less allusive stanza:

              A dragon slashes its lizard wings
              as it looks out, with halved head,
              and bellows with incompleteness.

                    (P 9 var., C 220)

This beast comes between father and son, asking uncomfortable questions
which sound like riddles, in a tone which recalls the odd animosity
between parent and child: '"Who flings off in a huff / and never counts
the cost / as long as there's a bitter phrase / to roll around on the
tongue?"' (P 10, C 221). The beast's last question, spoken in a tone of

playful indulgence, '"Who'd like to see what *I* have?"', elicits a response which makes clear the purpose of *The Messenger*:

> *I* would . . .

> And have followed
> the pewtery heave of hindquarters
> into the fog, the wings down at heel.
>   (P 10, C 221 var.)

The alliterative image captures the scale and perspective of a child's point of view, and links the father with an out-of-sorts Mercurius who is also the self.[125] Mercurius is a herald or messenger, but he is also quicksilver or *aqua vitae* – a connection which recalls the 'lifewater' or *uisce beatha* that the father lifts 'to his lips' in the opening scenes of the poem. A play on the whiskey's brand name 'Power' underlines the regenerative properties ascribed to both waters. The speaker's quest ends at the point of total darkness, out of which emerges an image of the father 'supine, jutjawed and / incommunicable' (P 11, C 222). In a move linking life with death, the speaker reaches into the dissolving form of his father to find the essential part of him that will endure:

> The eggseed Goodness
> that is also called
> Decency.
>   (P 11, C 222).

This 'Goodness' is characterised as something 'Abnormal'. It is both the 'cyst' of the father's earlier disappointments, and a pearl, 'A milkblue / blind orb', which recalls the fog of the previous stanzas and the 'dead egg' which 'glimmers' in the prefatory poem. From this obscure globe are conjured scenes in which the essential goodness and decency of John Kinsella can be clearly apprehended. In this part of *The Messenger* Kinsella draws us backward in time, from childhood memories, to scenes of his father's and grandfather's life, as if completing the journey of individuation left unresolved by the father.

The first two scenes detail John Kinsella's keen sense of social justice. Here, the father's activism against the prejudice of politics and religion are described from the young son's perspective. In the first scene the son watches his father rail against the Blueshirts (a fascist organisation of the early 1930s called the Army Comrades Association headed by Eoin O'Duffy). Referring to himself as a 'blackvelvet-eyed jew-child' this scene can be read in the context of the holocaust to which Kinsella has referred before in his 1968 poem 'Nightwalker': 'A red glare plays on their faces, / Livid with little splashes of blazing fat. / The oven door closes' (C 78).

This connection gives the scene a significance beyond that of local politics, and places John Kinsella's activism within a larger European context. Through an echo with the word 'jewel', the description 'jew-child' connects with the symbol of the pearl which links the first and second parts of *The Messenger*.[126] The pearl, or jewel, stands for the philosopher's stone which is a metaphor for the goal of alchemy: the differentiation of psyche and matter or, to put it more plainly, self-realisation.[127] Contained within this scene of vigorous protest are signs of debilitation:

> He is shouting about the Blueshirts
> but his voice is hoarse.
>
> (P 13, C 222)

The 'hoarse voice' is an early indication of the 'bronchi' that 'wrecked him with coughs' in his last years. In the second scene the child recalls his father walking out of Mass in protest at the anti-communist rhetoric of the priest. The perspective of the child is closely observed: 'I made faces at my ghost in the brawn marble / The round shaft went up shining / into a mouth of stone flowers' (P 13, C 223). Within this elevated architecture religion and politics combine:

> and the angry words echoed among
> the hanging lamps, off the dark golden walls,
> telling every Catholic how to vote.
>
> (P 13, C 223 var.)

In his revisions for the *Collected Poems* Kinsella has lessened the political focus of the stanza, moving 'off the dark golden walls' to substitute for the last line (C 223). The 'solid body' of John Kinsella's indignation is set against the anger contained in Father Collier's 'muscular black soutane' as he 'grabbed the crimson velvet ledge' of the pulpit. As father and son leave the crowded church the final image provides a chromatic symmetry between the Oblate father's actions and his appearance:

> – thick white hair, glasses
> a red face, a black mouth –
> shouting Godless Russia at us.
>
> (P 14, C 223 var.)

In his notes to the poem Kinsella writes that 'indignation is an index to goodness.' This indignation is the 'half fierce force' to which Kinsella alludes in the opening of *The Messenger*, and it is in these two scenes of protest that this force is felt.[128]

From these remembered scenes the poet moves back to the point of his own conception and beyond, through three generations of Kinsella men. The scene of love between 'a woman and her secret husband' announces the speaker's own arrival, 'I *think* this is where I come in', and alludes to a larger family history which is mentioned later in *St Catherine's Clock*: 'she took the certificate / and slapped it down on the table. / It took that to shut them up' (P 21, C 278). The anthropomorphic 'great womb-whisper' answers the *logos spermatikos*,[129] characterised as a dragon-fly, which recalls the primordial figures of *One* and *A Technical Supplement*. From this moment of primary division and generation which is psychic as well as corporeal, the poem moves backward to trace the origin and development of the self. The movement of the second section here is from darkness into light. The 'cobbler's shop' where we find the father as a young man, 'almost still a boy', is dim, overcast and diffuse (P 16, C 224). The boy's awkwardness, (he is 'ill at ease // in the odour-bearing light') contrasts with the grandfather's ease at his work (P 16, C 224 var.). The grandfather has what the speaker's beloved has in *Song of the Night*, 'namely: patience, / deliberation, / and skill with the instruments' (P 6, C 205). Set against this scene of quiet craftsmanship is a memory of the grandfather's days as a barge-pilot, negotiating the bridges of the Liffey:

> The tide is rising and the river runs fast
>
> into the middle span of the last bridge.
> He touches the funnel on a nerve at the base
> and doffs it on its hinge at the last instant
>
> (P 16, C 225)

Kinsella contrasts the interior, near solitary, work of the cobbler with the outdoor, convivial work of the barge captain: 'Here and there along the Liffey wall // he is acclaimed in friendly mockery' (P 16–17, C 225). The tools with which the father will find his purpose in life are not the 'knife-blades, / the hammers and pincers, the rasps and punches' of the cobbler for 'He will not stick at this' (P 17, C 225). Instead, his future is envisaged within a larger political and historical framework of the Irish labour movement:

> He reaches for a hammer,
> his jaw jutting as best it can
> with Marx, Engels, Larkin
>
> howling with upstretched arms into the teeth
> of Martin Murphy and the Church
> and a flourish of police batons,
>
> (P 17, C 226)

The scene referred to here is the Dublin lockout of 1913 where the labour leader, Jim Larkin, was pitted against the Cork-born capitalist, William Martin Murphy. This was a watershed in Irish labour politics.

The strike which Larkin's Irish Transport and General Workers' Union, founded in 1908, called against Murphy's Dublin United Tramways Company was countered by a lockout of union members. Murphy's action was imitated by other businesses and merchants. By the end of September, almost 25,000 men were off work.[130] The result was violence. As Larkin was arrested for seditious libel and conspiracy,

> scuffles broke out and the police, who had already been in frequent collision with pickets from Larkin's unions, turned on the crowd with savage baton charges. These in turn provoked mob rioting and at the end of it all two people had been killed and many hundreds wounded, including two hundred policemen.[131]

The lockout of 1913 saw the twin aims of nationalism and labour reform come into conflict. Labour reform lost to nationalism. In 1916 James Connolly, another key labour figure, was executed for his part in the Easter Rising in Dublin:

> Connolly strapped in a chair
> regarding the guns
> that shall pronounce his name for ever.
>
> (P 17, C 226)

This last line echoes Pádraig Pearse's conviction, parodied effectively in Seán O'Casey's *The Plough and the Stars*, that political execution creates martyrs and heroes. In this short section Kinsella parallels the development of an individual with the development of a nation. He probes the tensions between the twin aspirations of political and social justice, pointing to the success of the former at the expense of the latter. Regardless of sovereignty, capitalism endures: 'Baton struck, / gun spat, / and Martin Murphy shall change his hat' (P 17, C 226). Against these scenes of violence and turmoil is set the quiet unity of father and son, the cobbler's thread a metaphor for familial and historical continuity:

> Son and father, upright, right arms raised.
> Stretching a thread.
> Trying to strike right.
>
> (P 17, C 226)

The upright movement with which this passage closes is carried on to the next scene in which the young John Paul Kinsella is portrayed as the mischievous Mercury, messenger of the gods.

Bringing us 'Deeper' into the centre of family life, and into the centre of the self, Kinsella describes the excited preparations for the young man's first day as a messenger for the Post Office:

A new messenger boy
stands there in uniform, with shining belt!

He is all excitement: arms akimbo,
a thumb crooked by the telegram pouch,
shoes polished, and a way to make in the world.

(P 18, C 226)

The openness and vitality of this scene stands in marked contrast with the
darkness and obscurity of the previous one. The poem reaches a moment
of release which finds its focus in the Mercurial figure of the young Kinsella,
emerging from the dark room 'behind the shop' and setting off uphill:

[. . .] The urchin mounts. I see
a flash of pedals! And a clean pair of heels!

(P 18, C 227)

The upward movement of the messenger boy echoes the upright arms of
father and son mentioned earlier, and recalls the importance of the
Vertical Man in Kinsella's poem of that name. It contrasts with the
'supine' position of the father earlier, even as the tyres of 'the great Post
Office bicycle' prefigure the 'rubber tyres' on which the father's coffin
will be carried. The boy's 'clean pair of heels' works both literally and
metaphorically as it recalls the earlier manifestation of Mercury with
'pewtery heave of hindquarters' and 'wings down at heel' (P 10, C 221).
The movement of these heels is a transformation of the 'black stumps of
heelball' which occupied the boy formerly (P 17, C 225). The cobbler's
tools are replaced by 'a few of the Gentlemen's Sixpenny Library' (P 18,
C 226). The father's intellectual development is framed by works which
combine a vital imaginative engagement with an acute moral sensibility.
Thomas Carlyle's *Sartor Resartus*,[132] Dante's *The Divine Comedy* and
Shelley's *Prometheus Unbound*, works which explore the development of
the individual in the face of difficult social and moral circumstances, are
balanced by the power of love and art in Shakespeare's *A Midsummer
Night's Dream* and the traditional Irish songs of Moore's *Melodies*.[133]

As Kinsella returns to the scene of the funeral with which *The
Messenger* opens, the enduring nature of the goodness and decency
which distinguishes the father is juxtaposed against the transient nature
of the body. In a line which does not appear in the *Collected Poems*,
Kinsella brings 'membrane and mineral' into 'precious combination'.
The metaphor of the pearl underlies this italicised section:

> *A cross grain of impotent anger. About it*
> *the iridescent, untouchable secretions*
> *collect. It is a miracle:*
>
> *membrane and mineral in precious combination.*
> *An eye, pale with strain, forms in the dark.*
> *The oddity nestles in slime*
>
> *functionless, in all its rarity,*
> *purifying nothing. But nothing can befoul it*
> *– which ought probably to console.*
>
> (P 20, C 227 var.)

Anger and frustration, the 'many disappointments', are the irritants which produce the 'eggseed Goodness' for which John Paul Kinsella will be remembered. The tension between membrane and mineral echoes the contrast between pearl and muck with which the poem began. The pearl is associated with the generative properties of the egg, and also with the eye which makes insight and understanding possible. But this pearl, like the philosopher's stone, cannot transform the base material into mercurial lifewater. It is an '*oddity*', '*functionless*', '*purifying nothing*' (P 20, C 227). But yet '*nothing can befoul it*' (P 20, C 227). Endurance and transformation connect the mineral with the membrane, and point to a continuation of the self through blood and family in the form of the successive generations:

> By their own lightness
> four girls and three boys separated themselves
> in a ragged band out from our dull custom
>
> and moved up close after it, in front,
> all shapes and sizes,
> grandchildren, colourful and silent.
>
> (P 20, C 227 var.)

In the four volumes of this chapter Kinsella returns to the numerological system which provides a working structure for his poetry but which, he admits, ceased to become a determining system in the work, and more an enabling structure.[134] Kinsella summarises the schema as an approach towards the material of poetry on a 'simple numerical basis':

> Zero, I was not there. One, I exist. Two, I am aware. Three, I am involved. Four, it exists. Five, it is over. But before it vanishes we are back with Zero again.[135]

The volumes of this chapter do not adhere strictly to this system, yet they do move from an awareness of the self as a unity in *One* to an understanding of the self as split in *A Technical Supplement*. Combined with this is an exploration of the self in the context of the other or the beloved, which includes the children of that union, in *Song of the Night and Other Poems*. Finally, in *The Messenger*, the self is scrutinised in the context of previous generations, and looks to the assorted grandchildren as the continuation of the self into the future. The self, here, only makes sense in the larger framework of the successive generations. But these volumes are not simply about an exploration of subjectivity and its various relationships. Underpinning this writing is a subtle and attentive examination of the development of Ireland. Kinsella begins, in *One*, with a story of Ireland's origins based on a mythology which celebrates multiplicity and diversity. He continues, in *A Technical Supplement*, with a division into two which is contextualised by William Petty's Down Survey, and *Political Anatomy of Ireland*. Through a tale of love and conflict between Cornwall and Ireland in *Song of the Night and Other Poems* (see Wagner's *Tristan und Isolde*), Kinsella points to moments of conflict and resistance which result from the division between people, located particularly in the burnt-out home of the Tighes. Yet the moment of release through articulated light with which the poem ends suggests a need both to acknowledge points of conflict and to clarify lines of dialogue through which resolution can be achieved. The duality of *The Messenger* lies in the tension between the ideals of socialism and nationalism understood through the individual actions of the speaker's father and grandfather. Here Kinsella draws out the implications of two powerful ideologies within the context of a specific family history. The movement of these four volumes is from the unattributed narratives of pre-history to the living memories of the contemporary world, and in each the speaker and his society are brought to a new, and sometimes unsettling, understanding.

3

HISTORICAL
PARTICULARS

The seven years between the publication of *The Messenger* and *Songs of the Psyche* are the longest break in the publication of Peppercanister editions. During this period Kinsella embarked on two editing and translation projects. The first, with Seán Ó Tuama, is an anthology of Irish poems in the original and in translation called *An Duanaire: 1600–1900, Poems of the Dispossessed*. Published by the Dolmen Press in 1981, in conjunction with Bord na Gaeilge, it makes available to a wide audience the Irish language poetry of the period. The second was *The New Oxford Book of Irish Verse*, published in 1986, which includes poetry from the Irish and the English, and seeks to 'present an idea of these two bodies of poetry and of the relationships between them'.[1]

During this period Kinsella embarked on two projects which might have become Peppercanister 9. The first was a collaboration with the Irish artist Cecil King published in a limited edition by Editions Monika Beck of Saar, Germany.[2] Kinsella was in correspondence with Beck around August 1981. The project was titled *King and Kinsella* and contains a series of Kinsella's poems illustrated with four screenprints by King. Among the poems for the edition were 'Percy Lane: A Gloss', 'Wyncote, PA: A Gloss' (a version of which had already been published in *New Poems 1973*). The Peppercanister edition of these poems was to be titled *From My Desk, May 1981*.[3] Two of these poems echo the form of the glosses written by the medieval scribes on the margins of their transcriptions, glosses which Kinsella will have been translating for *The New Oxford Book of Irish Verse*. The idea of the additional poem or comment on an earlier text is evident in earlier works such as *A Technical Supplement*, which is both a supplement to Diderot's *Encyclopédie* and to Kinsella's own oeuvre. In a commentary on 'From my Desk' Kinsella explains the gloss:

Old Irish literature is rich in such short lyrics of immediate response to natural phenomena – details of animal and bird life or the weather or the changing seasons. Many of these lyrics survive in the margins of old manuscripts, and are clearly the impromptu writings of scribes interrupted at their work by sudden perceptions of the natural beauty surrounding them in their woodland workplaces. And many of these 'glosses', despite their obvious immediacy, are remarkable for their linguistic and metrical skills, giving us intimate access, for brief moments, into minds intensely occupied with artistic and sensual detail.[4]

The poems on which Kinsella appends a gloss in 'Wyncote, PA: A Gloss' are 'five separate lyrics from the Old Irish, dating from 9th and 11th centuries'.[5] The gloss that Kinsella puts on these lyrics concern the art of poetry and the nature of expression. The lyrics are in plain text, Kinsella's words underlined:

> The cuckoo sings clear, in lovely voice
> in his grey cloak, from a bushy fort.
> I swear it now, but God is good!
> It is lovely writing out in the wood.[6]

> That's it. The place fixed, and that 'other'
> element. A little more work . . . but enough
> for the moment.

> How lovely it is today!
> the sun breaks and flickers
> on the margin of my book.[7]

The second possible Peppercanister 9 was a collaboration, on the theme of love, with the artist Pauline Bewick called 'Men and Women'. Kinsella notes plans for the book: 'possible P/C with Pauline Bewick (from NOBIV)'.[8] On 29 May, 1978, just before *Song of the Night and Other Poems* and *The Messenger* came out, Bewick sent Kinsella an invitation to a private view of her works at the Cork Arts Society Gallery, enclosing a note: 'I haven't forgotten Cúchulainn's dream, have you written it yet? if so I'd love to see it to see if I could illustrate it – Pauline.'[9] The poems for this Peppercanister were a selection of thirty poems from Kinsella's *New Oxford Book of Irish Verse*.[10] Neither of these projects came to fruition.

The papers relating to *Songs of the Psyche* are distinctive among Kinsella's papers because they contain segments of poems which read like drafts of later Peppercanister poems, such as *Out of Ireland*, *Poems from Centre City*, and *Madonna and Other Poems*. A poem called 'Man's Love', with its focus on grief in a rural setting and reference to 'the warm devil grinning / cross legged over the exit arch', recalls the second poem of *Out of Ireland*, 'Native Wisdom'.

[. . .]
To the impact and the brutal tears
let the sacred litter
stand witness:

in the shimmering spring water guided
by the holy gutter out among the fat
christian stones into the air

and the pieces of bone and the knives
and the little pieces of mirror
in there on the sheep in the half dark,[11]
[. . .]

A poem called 'Departure' becomes, with very little revision, 'Departure Platforms' in the Oxford editions *From Centre City* and *Collected Poems*:

People were crowding the platform.
A woman stood among them in middle age,
both legs wrapped in reddened bandages.
She looked down in knowledge and tiredness.
'Look,' I whispered. 'They are still bleeding.'
'Now, now, Thomas,' he chided, smiling.[12]

There are also notes and drafts for a poem which becomes the first four stanzas of 'Morning Coffee' in *Madonna and Other Poems*. This draft also includes a verse which becomes the prologue to the *Collected Poems* version of *One*, and the short handwritten poem included in the deluxe Peppercanister edition of *One*:

A storyteller with his face in the shadow
hones his flickering blade near the fire
for the voyage of the first kindreds[13]

Songs of the Psyche

The nature of the papers contained in the folder for *Songs of the Psyche* suggest that the seven-year period between *The Messenger* and this volume was one of gestation and exploration for Kinsella. The journey of self-interrogation which began with *One* and found its most visceral expression in *A Technical Supplement* moves out of the darkness. The 'racked outcast' of the latter poem, who characterises his work, and himself, in terms of

> [. . .] half a dozen outward howls of glory
> and noble despair. Borrowed glory,
> his own despair. For the rest, energy wasted
> grimacing facetiously inward. [. . .]
>
> (P [37], C 198)

becomes the 'graceless' and 'unsightly' character of *Songs of the Psyche* who can at last 'see // through those clear eyes I had once' (P 21, C 233). And the excruciating and unavoidable division that splits self from itself in the downward fall of the psyche so powerfully presented in *A Technical Supplement* finds a means of resolution in *Songs of the Psyche*, even if 'it *is* / a matter of / negative release: // of being thrown / up out of a state of storm / into a state of peace // or sleep' (P 34, C 240 var.).

Out of this period of silence comes a complex sequence of poems which give voice to the songs of the psyche. The songs themselves are prefaced by three poems which are grouped under the rubric 'Settings'. Then comes an 'Invocation', followed by the thirteen part 'Songs of the psyche'. The volume closes with eight poems grouped under the title 'Notes'. *Songs of the Psyche* draws substantially on the poet's biography. The volume opens with scenes from early days in the 'Model School, Inchicore': playing with plasticine, learning addition tables, finding out about history and religion. Kinsella's use of the word 'marla' (which means plasticine) indicates the way in which the Irish language was part of the vocabulary of education in Ireland in the 1930s. We see this also when the speaker comes to learn his five-times tables: 'We always tittered at each other / when we said the adding-up table in Irish / and came to her name' (P 11, C 229). Run together, the words four and nine in Irish sound just like 'Carney' to the young boys' ears:

> Cúig is a náid, Cúig.
> Cúig is a haon, Sé
> Cúig is a dó, Seacht
> Cúig is a trí, Oct
> Cúig is a CE'AR, NAOI![14]

Appropriately for Kinsella's interest in sequences of five, and in the figure of the quincunx, the number five provides the pivot point around which this scenes revolves. The snake, emblematic of Kinsella's concerns with destruction and regeneration, and containing mythic and psychological resonances, is writ small in the hands of the child:

> You started with a ball of it
> and rolled it into a snake curling
> around your hand, and kept rolling it
> in one place until it wore down into two
> with a stain on the paper.
>
> (P 11, C 229)

The language in this poem is the clear diction of a child: the next teacher, Mr Browne, has 'white teeth in his brown man's face' (P 11, C 229).[15] It is he who introduces the students to decimals (the 'white dot' echoing the zero in 'Notes from the Land of the Dead' and the one of *One*) and teaches them the history of themselves and their country. In his drafts Kinsella makes more specific the kind of history he has in mind:

> Most of the things he told us were like fairy tales. About giants and Firbolgs and one-eyed Balor and wars with showers of boulders. [. . .] There is a whole Book of Invasions.[16]

The playful images of schoolboys playing in the Autumn leaves give way to solitary self-assesment as the speaker recalls the catechism learned in preparation for his confirmation. The question and answer format repeats exactly the rote learning through which religion was conveyed in school, but it also points to the process of self-interrogation which is integral to the poet's project. Drawing on Matthew 12: 36, the speaker recites to himself:

> Will God judge
>   our most secret thoughts and actions?
> God will judge
>   our most secret thoughts and actions
> and every idle word that man shall speak
> he shall render an account of it
> on the Day of Judgment.
>
> (P 12, C 230)

The biblical language of this passage contrasts with the simple words of the child's own expression. Judgment is inextricable from knowledge, whether it is the self-knowledge of one's 'most secret thoughts and actions' or the knowledge gained in school. Knowledge is imaged in terms of consumption and repulsion: 'The taste / of ink off / the nib shrank your / mouth' (P 13, C 231). The figuration of knowledge in corporeal terms appears again under more extreme circumstances in *Out of Ireland* in which the Eriugena is stabbed by his students' pens because he makes them think. The connection between religion and knowledge with which this poem closes has a wider social resonance when we understand the history of the Model Schools in Ireland. Established in 1811 by the Kildare Place Society as multi-denominational Christian schools for the education of the poor, the Model Schools came up against opposition from the Catholic hierarchy for the way in which the Bible was being taught: 'it was felt increasingly by Catholic interests that the Society was not abiding strictly by its own rules: that teachers who wished to do so were interpreting the Bible after their own fashion, in some cases as a weapon against the Catholic faith'.[17] Support from the Government was subsequently withdrawn in 1831 and a National Board of Education on which Catholics and Protestants were represented was set up.

From the school scene of 'Model School, Inchicore' where issues of knowledge, religion and society come together under the gaze of the young poet, Kinsella turns to 'Phoenix Street' and 'Bow Lane', the homes of his own family, and that of his paternal grandparents. In both of these poems the speaker investigates the dark recesses of the house to find evidence of where he comes from. 'Phoenix Street' connects with *The Messenger* as the speaker plunders his father's 'dark nest' which 'stirred with promises' to find books of politics and literature, 'Ruskin and Engels and Carlyle; / Shakespeare in tiny print', and evidence also of business and pleasure:

> the insurance collection book
> in a fat elastic band;
> a brown photograph
>
> with four young men
> dressed up together
> and leaning together in laughter.
>
> (P 14, C 231)

The 'triangular / press' of 'Phoenix Street' cedes to the 'back corner / of the wardrobe' in 'Bow Lane' as the starting point for the boy's search (P 14–15, C 231–2). The importance of these closed spaces is underlined by Maurice Harmon:

> The interconnecting imagery of [Kinsella's] work is closely linked with his openness to these half-understood but meaningful experiences. References to shadows, darknesses, hidden rooms, pits, recesses indicate the unconscious within which frightening and potentially significant experience may be encountered.[18]

The comparison made between the rustling of the blind and a trapped bat recalls the dark bird-like figures emblematic of the self's shadow of *Songs of the Night and Other Poems*. In a resonant conjunction of dates and images, the death of the speaker's uncle, and the poet's namesake, in 1916, is recollected through his painting of a steamer which recalls his grandfather's skill with funnels as a barge captain for Guinness in *The Messenger* (P 16, C 225). The date 1916 is unmistakably linked to the

Easter Rising and ideas of martyrdom. Here, however, the suffering is personal and private, and unrelieved by an early death:

> He died in here in 1916
> of cancer of the colon. My father heard him
> whispering to himself: 'Jesus,
> Jesus, let me off.' But nothing worked.

> (P 15, C 232)

Like the previous two poems, the tone is calmly descriptive, and the setting out of memories and recollections contains the same reliance on local detail for which Kinsella praised Pound's *Cantos*.[19] Another memory emerges which concerns knowledge and origin rather than death. The 'grey animal book' with its pictures of Capuchin monkeys (resonant of both Darwinian theory and of the Capuchin religious order) refuses to yield up its text. The visible and the lisible are counterpointed in a scene in which the conditions for fulfilling the demand undo the need for the demand:

> I asked Tom Ryan once: 'Tell me the print!'
> but he only grinned and said
> 'I will if you can spell Wednesday.'

> (P 15, C 232)

The grandmother, whose clear voice at the close of 'Bow Lane' interrupts the speaker's quiet perusal, is transformed into the 'Sweet mother' to which the poet sends an 'Invocation'. The connection between the grandmother and the Great Mother of mythic renown underlines the importance of the relationship between grandparent and child, as Kinsella emphasises: 'I believe that the relationship between grandparent and child is the potent one. That is where the handing on takes place.'[20] The speaker's invocation is to the three aspects of the Great Mother; she who is 'at the same time maternal ("Sweet mother"), sexual ("sweet muscle"), and destructive ("predatrix")'.[21] In the Peppercanister edition the voices who make this invocation are the primordial energies familiar to *One* and *A Technical Supplement*: 'as we bob and strike / with a wriggle of our tails // in the glum-green shallows / for our mud-green feed' (P 17). While the entreaty to 'Judge not. / But judge' is directed at the 'Sweet mother' who represents the universe and nature, it is also directed at the self who must, surely, be the final arbiter (P 17, C 233). Universe and self are united in the 'psyche' which is identified with breath, life, soul, or spirit. It is the animating principle in animals, including man. As the *anima mundi* it is the animating principle of the universe.

This self comes into clearer focus in the subsequent set of thirteen verses gathered under the title 'Songs of the Psyche'. The poem enacts the process of understanding by which the individual accesses the *anima mundi* and, by corollary, understanding of his own spirit or soul. This process is based on the Celtic mantic tradition of *imbas forosnai* or 'the knowledge which illuminates'.[22] This knowledge comes from 'a process of revelation brought on by mantic sleep'.[23] Recalling the Faustian figure of 'The Entire Fabric' in *One*, the speaker of 'Songs of the Psyche' is introduced as 'a character, indistinct' (P 21, C 233). This self-deprecating speaker, reminiscent, as Brian John points out, of Eliot's Prufrock,[24] bemoans his lack of wisdom and insight, asking:

> Why had I to wait until I am graceless,
> unsightly, and a little nervous of stooping
> until I could see
>
> through those clear eyes I had once?
>
> (P 21, C 233)

It is not an outward vision that the speaker seeks. Rather it is an inner wisdom or knowledge that is only obtained by means of a specific ritual:

> The poet chews a piece of the red flesh of a pig, dog, or cat, and then puts it on a flagstone near the door and chants an invocation over it to unnamed gods. He chants over his two palms and asks that his sleep not be disturbed, and then puts his two palms on his cheeks and sleeps. Men guard him that he may not be disturbed or turned over. At the end of three days and nights the poet may judge whether imbas forosnai has come to him.[25]

The 'Invocation' which announces 'Songs of the Psyche' is also the poet's own prayer seeking a wisdom beyond the limited understanding of the individual. Evidence of internal turmoil and distress are succinctly conveyed by the image of the speaker 'taken away / teeth grinding / and eyes alight' (P 22, C 234). But this image may also indicate the outward signs of an inward journey on which the speaker prepares to embark by reenacting the ritual which may lead to *imbas forosnai*. The speaker prepares the flesh as an offering to the gods, 'Chew nine times / on the chosen meat / and set it down / outside her door' (P 23, C 234), and utters the invocation which may give him access to the 'sweet mother' before retiring, palms on cheeks, to sleep and wait:

> An unholy muttering
> lingered on my palms
> as I laid them to my cheeks
> and slept.
>
> (P 22, C 234)

The 'spirits // that cower close / on innermost knowledge' are 'ill-chosen' perhaps because, as Kinsella notes in his drafts, they come from a pagan system which was banished with the advent of Christianity (P 24, C 234–5).[26] The sections which follow describe the visions or visitations experienced by the speaker during his 'inward turn'. Like the fifty-year-old father figure in *The Messenger*, the speaker of 'Songs of the Psyche' is also in middle age. As he descends on his journey towards knowledge, the recognition of horror distinctive to Kinsella's poetry is evidenced by the acknowledgement that 'A monster bore me / and I bear / a monster with me' (P 25, C 235). The difficulty of passage from the world of every-day knowledge to the world of esoteric understanding is conveyed through the images of 'a crack in the dirt' (P 22, C 234) and 'the grin of stone upon stone' (P 26, C 235) through which the speaker must pass. This 'grin' and the 'beaten smile' prefigure the 'Vertical Smile' of the next Peppercanister volume, and allude to the great mother or eternal feminine whose *imbas* or great knowledge the speaker of 'Songs of the Psyche' strives to gain.

The visions the speaker receives concern love, family, and the develop-ment of the self. In the seventh and eleventh songs courtship is described in a style reminiscent of folk poetry.[27] A demure vision of nature in the eleventh song sets the scene for love:

> Come with me
> o'er the crystal stream
> where eyelids dart
> in the dappled shallows
>
> (P 32, C 238)

But menacing this idyll is an intimation of destruction: 'and leeches wrinkle / black in the water, / willow leaves / that have fed on blood' (P 32, C 239). The lover's gesture: 'She offered me her hands' (which prefigures the line '*Tabhair dom do lámh*' in *Out of Ireland*) is received by a reluc-tant speaker: 'I took them in mine / – averse' (P 27, C 236). In a passage which recalls Ariel's predicament in *The Tempest*, and quotes from his earlier poem 'Wormwood', Kinsella describes the lovers as 'A tree with a twisted trunk; / two trees grown into one' (P 28, C 236). In a litany which pairs colours with emotions Kinsella outlines the successive stages of love:

> gold for the first blaze,
> red for the rough response,
> dark blue for misunderstanding,
> jet black for rue,
>
> pale for the
> unfinished children
> that are
> waiting everywhere
>
> (P 28, C 236–7)

Kinsella's ability to see 'through those clear eyes' is evident throughout 'Songs of the Psyche' in which the conventional vocabulary of romance is overturned in favour of a recognition of the difficulty and trials of love. As 'Night foxes' the lovers are predatory animals (albeit in city guise) but also embody the darker side of the self in the form of the Jungian shadow. The relationship between the lovers in these songs is that of one with another, but also that of one with itself. This self is evident again in the tenth song as 'A moth fumbled / with its fragile blur up / the tobacco-smelling chimney-corner' (P 30, C 237).[28] Psyche is usually identified with the butterfly, but it is also 'a genus of day-flying bombycid moths typical of the family *Psychidae*' (OED). The connection is made more explicit in the second section of this song as the 'great delicate self' is identified with 'a great moth of prey' (P 30–31, C 238). Contrasted with the predatory moth is the delicate 'silk maggot' emblematic of origin and potentiality.

The speaker's nocturnal journey toward knowledge or *imbas* comes to a close with an echo of the phrase 'it is time' from the first song of the psyche: 'It is time, the night / gone, first light / fidgetting under the leaves' (P 33, C 239 var.). His reveille takes a number of stages:

> *I woke suffocating,*
> > *slipped through a time fault*
> *into total dark.*

No.

> *I came to myself*
> > *in the middle of a dark wood,*
> *electric with hope.*

Please . . .

(P 34, C 239)

Kinsella's excision of the word 'time' in his revisions for the *Collected Poems* removes the somewhat science-fiction associations of 'time-fault',[29] but the phrase 'dark wood' retains its Dantean allusion, creating a parallel between Kinsella's fifty-year-old poet-speaker and Dante's protagonist: 'Midway in the journey of our life I found myself in a dark wood, for the straight way was lost.'[30] The entreaty 'Please . . .' echoes the invocation which prefaces 'Songs of the Psyche'. It is a request, not only for poetic talent or inspiration gained through *imbas forosnai*, but also for the wisdom and illumination which comes with self-knowledge. It is also, as Kinseella points out, a self-deprecating 'protest at the obviousness' of his poetic stance.[31] Lines from the Peppercanister, omitted from the *Collected Poems*, give a distinctively Jungian turn to this self-knowledge:

> By normal process
>   organic darkness,
> *in potentia* all things,
>
> would summon
>   Self firstly into being,
> a Shadow *in actu*,

(P 34)

The understanding achieved by Kinsella's speaker through the 'Songs of the Psyche' is described in terms of Celtic and Christian mythology. In tercets which rewrite the narrative of the *Book of Invasions* used in *One*, Kinsella traces the ways in which existence has been understood, culminating in:

> [. . .] stealers of fire;
>   dragon slayers; helpful animals;
> and ultimately the Cross.

(P 35, C 240)

But there is an alternative to these traditional world-views. Kinsella strips away the narratives which make sense of our world and posits instead an understanding based on basic (yet all embracing) animal impulses:

> Unless the thing were to be based
>   on sexuality
> or power.

(P 35, C 240)

The third section of *Songs of the Psyche* takes the form of 'Notes' which retrace the themes of love, friendship and family explored earlier. 'A New Beginning' re-enacts the originary word of the Book of Genesis, but points to the necessary conjunction between the incorporeal word and physical matter (the former male, the latter female) for the generation of life and langage. God must 'lean Himself / over the mothering pit' in order that 'the ache / of I am' can be given voice (P 39, C 240–1 var.). 'Opposites' continues this theme in the context of love, re-enacting the kiss between God and nature on a human scale: 'Our mouths locked in privacy. / The shadow pattern shifted' (P 40, C 241). From this love between two comes a third, and more. 'The Little Children' (which incorporates earlier drafts titled 'Girl Child' and 'Boy Child') describes the development of children in terms of 'breaking and renewing / energies' which find their release 'in laughter and panic / into darkness and fire' (P 41, C 241 var.). The conflicts which the speaker of these poems seeks to resolve, or understand, is already evident in the combination of 'feathery touches / and brutal fumblings, / in stupefying waste, /

brooding and light' which characterise the child's 'series of beginnings'
(P 41, C 242 var.). 'Brotherhood' looks at the darker side of familial
relationships as siblings come into adulthood and the bonds of trust and
love are broken:

> I stretched out
> my hand to you. Brother.
>
> The reason for the impulse
> was unclear:
>
> your behaviour and your work
> are incomprehensible to me.
>
> (P 42, C 242 var.)

There is no easy reconciliation or forgiveness. The concept of personal
responsibility so important to Kinsella's view of human behaviour deter-
mines the closing lines: 'We must bear in mind / the quality of the Fall. //
I dropped your hand' (P 42, C 242 var.). The theme of responsibility is
continued in 'Talent and Friendship'. Both of these attributes, or gifts,
must be nurtured and developed for 'Either persisted in without change /
grows ridiculous // and either at any time / may fail' (P 43, C 242). In
lines edited from the *Collected Poems* this failure is depicted as a figure
similar to the síle-na-gig of *Out of Ireland*:

> that fig-bodied stone devil
> on your sanctuary wall
>
> gross mouth open
> to all comers
>
> (P 43, cf. C 243)

The echo of Ó Riada contained in the reference to *Out of Ireland*, which
is a final farewell to the composer, joins with the rememberence of 'the
graves and the young men' and the 'Loss' of *The Messenger* to
contextualise the scene of the 'still youthful witch' 'in sharp argument
with her pale son' (P 43, C 243). It is to one's own talents and friendships
that one must look. Inheritance cannot be relied upon, for 'There is no
mantle / and it does not descend' (P 43, C 243).

The final three poems of *Song of the Psyche* explore the self through
processes of scrutiny, release and renewal. With a vocabulary that recalls
A Technical Supplement, Kinsella describes mental evisceration in speci-
fically corporeal terms. The 'threadbare body' in 'Self-Scrutiny' 'grows
conscious / of its composite parts' as eyes, ears, tongue and fingers take
on a heightened aspect (P 44, C 243). Through these senses the seeds of
distress are sown. The 'snarl / of mutabilitie' is admitted through the ear

'direct to the brain' as the tongue, though cleaving to the palate, utters the 'curse made flesh' (P 44, C 243–4). The speaker's distress is make manifest in 'Self-Release'. The corporeal curses of the previous poem become 'gutteral Christ curses' uttered as the speaker presents his interlocutor with a choice between the outward demonstrations of anguish, 'destroying my nails down the wall / or dashing myself to pieces', or the artificial calm induced by self-surgery:

> I will ease it somehow.
> I could pull down a clean knife-shaft
> two-handed into the brain and worry it
> minutely about until there is
> glaze and numbness in 'that' area . . .
>
> (P 45, C 244)

The results of this proposed lobotomy would be the adoption of a behaviour and attitude deemed acceptable by society. Here Kinsella cuts quite close to the bone as he comments acerbically on the conflation of personality and poetry often found in critical and popular assessment:

> Then you would see how charming
> it is possible to be,
> how recklessly fluent and fascinating,
> a startlement to all,
> internationally, and beyond.
>
> (P 45, C 244 var.)

'Self-Renewal' turns from the concern with others to a meditation on the self which is reflected in the three planes of a dressing-mirror. The tripartite image in the glass echoes the three sides of the deity in 'Invocation' Through a process of self-scrutiny which recalls section twenty-two of *A Technical Supplement*, the speaker sees his 'shame' shared by 'all / the lonely' (P 46, C 245). In a tone that is both optimistic and resigned, Kinsella closes the poem with an image of acceptance, as 'they felt more able / to slip off about their business' (P 46, C 245). But the clarity of vision, and understanding, sought is still out of reach:

> and the glass clouding over
>
> the memory of a couple
> of fading eye diagrams.
>
> (P 46, C 245 var.)

The cover image of a circular flower-like pattern on the cover of *Songs of the Psyche* mirrors the 'pale secrets' of the speaker's iris reflected in the clouding glass (P 46, C 245). Taken from P. W. Joyce's *A Smaller Social History of Ireland*, the cover image is of an ornament comprising 'a flat circular disk, half-inch thick, the body of dark blue glass, with a wavy pattern of white enamel, like an open flower, on the surface.'[32] Evidence, as Joyce points out, of a high level of artistic skill in the manipulation of molten glass, the ornament can also be read as a form of the mandala or 'magic circle' which Jung interpreted as an expression of the psyche or self. This image also links back overtly to Kinsella's concerns in *Song of the Night and Other Poems*, in particular to 'Tao and Unfitness at Inistiogue on the River Nore' but also to the previous Peppercanisters in which an exploration of the self is fundamental, through its connection with the taoist approach to self-knowledge:

> [Mandalas] are all symbolic images of that 'middle way' which the Orient called 'TAO' and which for the Occidental consists in the task of finding a unification of the opposites of inner and outer reality, of consciously shaping his personality in knowledge of the forces of his primal nature and in the direction of structural totality.[33]

Gaining knowledge of these forces is an integral part of Kinsella's project. The ironic single eye 'cocked at itself' with which *Songs of the Psyche* ends marks a turning away from the intimately self-aware poetry of the 1970s (of which this volume forms a part through its gestation if not the date of its publication) toward a poetry in which art, politics and history play a more prominent part.

Though it was published in tandem with *Songs of the Psyche* in 1985, *Her Vertical Smile* moves away from a consideration of the inner processes of the psyche and towards an examination of how the actions of the individual and of society combine to write a history in which all are implicated. It also explores art and politics as systems through which we make sense of experience. *Out of Ireland* continues the themes developed in the former volume, expanding them to include an examination of notions of national identity in the context of history and culture. *St Catherine's Clock* focuses on the writing of history itself. By questioning the possibility of writing one single history out of the multiple narratives that arise from an event, Kinsella once again emphasises the importance of place for an understanding of society, and cautions us on the uncertainties of historical positioning.

Her Vertical Smile

Her Vertical Smile takes us to middle Europe at the beginning of the twentieth century. Kinsella chooses Vienna, heart of the Austrian Empire, as a place where music and war exemplify the extremes of good and evil possible in mankind. The scene which Kinsella sets for us is the première of Mahler's Eighth Symphony, a magnificent and overwhelming piece which, because of the numbers of vocalists and musicians involved, is dubbed 'The Symphony of a Thousand'. Against the background of high society and artistic achievement, Kinsella contrasts the battlefields of the First World War. The horror of that war betrayed the glorious intentions of those who believed in the purification of society through bloodshed, and exposed the motivation behind the patriotic rhetoric as grudging national antagonisms.

The disharmony and waste of war are overcome temporarily by Mahler's music. The 'Music Master', as Kinsella calls him, is projected as the one who can establish order on the chaos all around. However, underlying the images of war and of music which Kinsella sets out for us in this poem is a force which lies at the heart of both. This force is conceived of as a coming together of the natural and of the divine and is expressed in the poem variously through the figures of the Mater Gloriosa of Goethe's *Faust*, the Great Mother of Jungian archetype, and Mahler's wife Alma. Kinsella writes *Her Vertical Smile* in tercets grouped into five parts. The structure of the poem emulates the structure of music. The poem is introduced by an *Overture*. The *Intermezzo* divides part I from part II, and the poem closes with a *Coda*. Music informs this volume throughout, as both an organisational and a thematic structure. In conversation with Dennis O'Driscoll, Kinsella emphasises the importance of music in his poetry:

> The music of poetry, however understood, is of primary importance. Rhythms and rhythmical structures and the rhythm of form – not merely the audible rhythm line by line but the achievements of a totality and the thematic connections amongst one's material – all of that is absolutely primary.[34]

In *Her Vertical Smile* Kinsella takes the structure of music and weds it to that of history as a means of coming to some understanding of the interrelationship between creation and destruction and the position of the self between these opposing forces. Kinsella explores the theme of his poem by drawing together a number of scenes such as Mahler's presentation of his Eighth Symphony, Michelangelo's depiction of the creation of Man, Thomas Mann's patriotic anxieties, the brutality of the First World War, and Gustav and Alma Mahler taking the air by the seaside, and setting them in counterpoint with one another. The following reading of the poem explores the source and the positioning of these scenes as a means through which we can understand more fully what Kinsella means when he describes *Her Vertical Smile* as 'a poem of four hundred lines on a theme of violence, order and music'.[35]

Her Vertical Smile opens with an epigraph drawn from Kinsella's commentary on the second and third Peppercanister volumes, *A Selected Life* and *Vertical Man*, which is included in the Dolmen edition *Fifteen Dead*.[36] It sketches the scene of Kinsella and Ó Riada sitting in the latter's small flat, listening to Richard Strauss's *Der Rosenkavalier* with an intensity which mirrors both poet's and composer's work. Once again Ó Riada's presence is felt strongly in Kinsella's writing as the title *Her Vertical Smile* echoes directly the earlier *Vertical Man*. Even the pale green of the cover recalls a similar shade of *A Selected Life*. The poem begins with an *Overture* in which Kinsella gives us the closing passage of Mahler's Eighth Symphony. The contralto joins the massed choir in a passage which opens with a gentle meditation on the transitory nature of existence and rises to a climactic exultation which describes a feminine god withdrawing into the heavens as the choir sings: 'the Ever-Feminine draws us higher'.[37] The opening line of *Her Vertical Smile* 'For ever and ever' (P 7, C 247) is a translation of the closing line of the first part of the Eighth Symphony: 'In saeculorum saecula.' With this line Kinsella links the Eighth Symphony with Mahler's subsequent composition, *Das Lied von der Erde* (already referred to by Kinsella in *Vertical Man*) in which the final song, 'Der Abschied', describes a farewell between friends and ends with these words of parting: 'forever . . . forever'.[38] The opening line of *Her Vertical Smile* also anticipates the close of the poem in which *Das Lied von Der Erde* is invoked again with the words:

> in a distance turning to pure light
> shining blue
> for ever and for ever.

(P 24, C 260)

The theme of parting from friends is transformed in *Her Vertical Smile* into the much larger theme of the division between heaven and earth and the relationship between the material and the spiritual. The female voice of the contralto becomes, in Kinsella's poem, the voice of a feminine god who is 'drawing back // through the luxuriant heavens / into the light / from whence she came' (P 7, C 247).[39]

Kinsella draws together details from the close of the Eighth Symphony, 'a low terrible string plucked', 'a major triad of strings', and emphasises the connection between the music and the otherworldly when he describes how the music of Mahler's work is 'released from all earthbound tonalities' (P 7, C 247). Mahler expressed a similar opinion of the Eighth in a letter written one month before the Symphony's première in which he compares his work to the music of the spheres. Writing to Willem Mengelberg, Mahler describes how the music of the Eighth Symphony would reach out beyond the stars:

> All nature is endowed with a voice in it . . . it is the biggest thing I have done so far . . . Imagine the universe beginning to ring and resound. It is no longer human voices. It is planets and suns revolving in their orbits.[40]

These planets and suns become the '"celestial companions" / shivering all about us in the night' which Kinsella describes in part I (P 13, C 252). They also recall the astronomical image which Kinsella chooses for the cover of the Peppercanister volume of *Her Vertical Smile*. The image depicts two spheres, one in orbit around the other. Kinsella notes in the colophon of the volume that:

> the design on the title page, taken from P.W. Joyce's *Smaller Social History of Ancient Ireland*, is a diagram in an astronomical tract of about 1400 AD in the Royal Irish Academy. The lower circle is the Sun (sol); the middle circle is the Earth (*terra*), throwing its shadow among the stars.

Here, Kinsella brings music and astronomy together here as examples of how order is elicited from the living world. This early Irish astronomical diagram depicts the earth at the centre of orbit, with the sun circling around it on a fixed path. The mass of the earth throws a shadow over the stars. The earth is divided into one area of illumination and one of darkness. This division into light and dark brings to mind the significance of the shadow in Jungian archetype which represents the impulsive and destructive part of the psyche. The cover image of *Her Vertical Smile* emphasises the inevitable duality contained in a world in which there is both good and evil. In a poem which is situated during the lead up to a war which one could argue was the result of misrepresentation and misunderstanding, this pre-Copernican image of the universe emphasises how our perspective on an event can radically alter our understanding of that event, sometimes with far-reaching consequences.

Part I of *Her Vertical Smile* is divided into four sections. The first section takes place during the première of Mahler's Eighth Symphony on 12 September 1910 in Munich, which the composer conducted. In *Her Vertical Smile* Kinsella transposes the location of the performance from Munich to 'old Vienna' where Mahler had been the conductor of the Vienna Philharmonic before moving to the United States to lead the Metropolitan Opera. Mahler's emigration from Austria parallels Kinsella's own move from Ireland in the late 1960s. Mahler's return to Europe for the première of the symphony can be seen as a kind of homecoming, but it also emphasises the loss of home which would result from the destruction of the First World War. The second section of part I focuses on the transition period in Vienna just before the outbreak of the First World War. The third section considers the orders and systems through which existence originates, before introducing Michelangelo's representation of the creation of man. The fourth section moves the poem from creation to destruction as it questions the waste and futility of war, and points to the enduring power of love.

Kinsella gives us a very particular vision of Mahler conducting the première of his Eighth Symphony. He stands 'Arms uplifted on the podium, / the left hand dangling tyrannical' (P 9, C 248).[41] Though the conductor is rooted firmly on the ground – 'the stance flat footed' – the stability of his form is undercut by the oxymoronic description: 'the face a fragile axe, / hard and acid, rapt' (P 9, C 248). Through the figure of Mahler, Kinsella develops the notion of the artist whose achievement is a result of perseverance and determination. As Brian John perceptively remarks, the idea of the will is 'always crucial on Kinsella's path to understanding'.[42] Mahler's 'force of will' enables him to 'embrace risk, // tedium, the ignoble' in order to write his music (P 9, C 248–9).[43] The idea of the artist that Kinsella is developing here is not a Keatsian one for whom poetry comes as easily as leaves to a tree. For Kinsella, the artist is one who endures and perseveres, who will 'try anything ten times' in order to achieve his or her vision (P 9, C 249). The 'ten times' of the poem refers to Mahler's ten symphonies,[44] the last left unfinished at his death; but it also refers to Kinsella's own work, since *Her Vertical Smile* is the poet's tenth Peppercanister volume. The image of the composer bringing together and ordering the multitude of sounds which make up the Eighth Symphony is used by Kinsella to explore the relationship between the individual and the larger forces which surround him. The feminine force or Mater Gloriosa alluded to in the *Overture* is recast here in specifically sexual terms as the composer draws forth a sonorous re-enactment of the Pentecost:

There is an overpowering tinkle;

a pregnant hush.
Masterful yet sensitive

his baton explores
        Her core of peace,
every rhythm drained

(P 10, C 249 var.)

The poem turns back again to the scene of the performance. The symphony is over and the audience are suspended in a rapturous silence. Here Kinsella incorporates accounts by Alma Mahler and Bruno Walter who were present at the performance. Alma Mahler reports that the 'breathless silence' which followed the close of the symphony 'was the most impressive homage an artist could be paid'.[45] And Bruno Walter describes how Mahler shook the hand of almost every member of the children's choir immediately after the performance in 'a symbolical greeting to youth'.[46]

    The closing line 'there at the heart of old Vienna' both reminds us of Kinsella's transposition of the scene from Munich to Vienna, and introduces us to high society in which the pulse of political manoeuvres beats time to the Viennese waltz:

Overtures and alliances.
        White gloves advance,
decorated bellies retire

down mirrored halls.

(P 11, C 250)

The simple alliance of dancing partners becomes an 'Entente' (P 11, C 250). Here Kinsella brings art and politics together with his play on the word 'entente', which means an agreement between governments or powers for co-operative action or policy. But the political powers which Kinsella evokes with these lines are capable of a swift volte-face if the situation demands. The term 'Entente' includes in its meaning ideas of listening and understanding. With this word, Kinsella weaves Mahler's music into a consideration of historical process and emphasises the structure underlying music and politics.

    The tone of the poem changes swiftly to acerbic irony as the rhythm of the waltz becomes that of marching soldiers who are 'off to the mutton-chop slaughter' (P 11, C 250). The glory anticipated by the participants of the war is conferred not onto their 'tangled woebegone' remains, but instead to the place on which they fell, the 'field that will live for ever in glory' (P 11, C 250). It is to the ground on which the killings took place that the poet looks in order to comprehend the carnage. Understanding is figured here in musical terms: 'We might search for harmony there' (P 11, C 250). And it is the ear rather than the eye which is the organ of perception:

> Or we might choose to listen
> down echoing and mirrored walls,
> chandelier after trembling chandelier

> to the vanishing point,
>
>   (P 11, C 250)

The vanishing point normally accorded to visual perspective is now located in 'that infinite / imperial Ear' (P 11, C 250). By locating the vanishing point of this aural scene in a specifically imperial ear, the poet questions the possibility of balanced perspective at this point in history when the Austrian empire is on the verge of war. The 'ominous drumrolls' and 'blaze of trumpets' of Mahler's symphony are now no longer in the service of spiritual redemption (P 12, C 251). Instead they announce the impending mobilisations of troops and warships. The 'great iron entities / afloat like towns erect on the water / with new murderous skills' allude to the two warships of the Austrian navy, which were dispatched by Franz Josef as a warning to Serbia and Italy that Austria would not be challenged with impunity, but they also recall the proliferation of nuclear submarines in the poet's own time (P 12, C 251).[47] The 'logic of majesty' is made bitterly clear here as, through misunderstandings and misrepresentations, Europe is brought to war (P 12, C 251). The creative and redemptive mother figures of Mahler's symphony and the poem's *Overture* are overturned now as 'the Empire / turns once more toward its farrow' (P 12, C 251).

The third section of part I returns to the figure of Mahler, introducing biographical detail regarding his last performance and his death six months later in 1911. The endurance of hope is evoked by the reformulated adage: 'Was there ever one chasm closed / but another opened' (P 12, C 251). The possibility of creative order providing a bulwark against, or a remedy for, the chaos and disorder to which the world inevitably seems to return is suggested by the image of a curse being folded back upon itself through the power of music. The redemptive powers of the creative act are emphasised as the conductor transforms sound into music. He traces his music:

> in sensible figures in the air
> so the blood might beat at our temples
> with the pulse of order
>
>   (P 13, C 251)

That the blood will beat there is no doubt, but the choice Kinsella underlines here is one between order and chaos. The material of life will always be the same. What we have control over is the shape we form it into.

Kinsella links the notion of order in music with order in astronomy as he describes how we read the stars or 'celestial companions' in terms of western mythical figures. We see here how Kinsella reinforces the idea that we understand experience only by giving it shape. The night sky cannot be simply apprehended as a collection of stars, it must be divided and ordered according to a preordained system such as the shape of the gods of mythology. Kinsella joins the human with the celestial through a mythic conjunction in which man and woman, here capitalised to include all humankind, unite to form 'a single figure: The Elect'.[48] Here Kinsella alludes to the figures of Alma and Gustav Mahler, to whom he will return in the second part of the poem through an exploration of the responsibility one individual has for another and the extrapolation of that responsibility to include social and political responsibility.

In ironic counterpoint to his vision of The Elect, Kinsella gives us Michelangelo's representation of the beginning of the world, painted on the roof of the Sistine Chapel, as God the Father gives life to Adam through the touch of a finger:

> patented on his Chapel ceiling
>   propped on an elbow,
> a languid and burly young man
>
> with everything limply on show,
>   and a little out of condition,
> finger to finger with God the Father,
>
>   (P 13, C 252)

The glory of this moment is undercut by the poet's remarks on how far Adam's physical condition departs from the ideal. Kinsella also emphasises the iconic power of this image for the Western world as he replaces the word 'painted' with 'patented' thereby suggesting that society has validated this explanation of the beginning of the world over many possible others. Against this ideal image of creation is contrasted another less elegant one. which involves 'outrageous rummaging, / breath stopped, pulse paused' (P 14, C 253). This wryly humorous observation on human sexual behaviour nonetheless acknowledges its efficiency as, 'with forces narrowed / in each chosen other', two become one (P 14, C 253).

Her Vertical Smile is a poem of contrasts and counterpoints. An image of Viennese ballrooms and symphony performances is juxtaposed with scenes of slaughter from the battlefields of the First World War. As part I of the poem closes Kinsella asks 'For what shall it profit a white gloved /

and glittering bellied elder' that 'bannerets of our own selves / dangle on wires along / irregular rivers of our own making' (P 14–15, C 253). The biblical echo of 'for what shall it profit a man if he gain the whole world yet lose his soul', contained in the lines, gives it a resonance beyond the particular events depicted. The cost of war is balanced against its results. And the photographs of 'the late enemies together like family groups' question the enmity which has fuelled the slaughter (P 15, C 254). However, the serenity of this scene of reconciliation is grotesquely under-cut by the observation:

> There is a heavy boot in one
> actually standing on a fallen hand.
>
> (P 15, C 254)

Part I and part II of the poem are divided by an *Intermezzo* in which Kinsella rewrites a letter from Thomas Mann to Richard Dehmel of 14 December 1914.[49] In this letter Mann expresses his admiration for the Berlin poet many years his senior who has volunteered to serve in the war. Mann himself was excused from service because of his literary standing and, although he expresses frustration in this letter at not being able to serve on the front, he seemed content to focus his energies writing in support of the war in essays such as 'Thoughts in the War'. These essays hold what was then the conventional patriotic line in which war is hailed as a purification of and a liberation from what was seen by many as the corruption of peacetime civilisation.[50] The patriotic, and strongly Nietzschean, sentiments expressed in these writings are contained also in the letter which in Kinsella's rewriting describes how 'all things will be made new / by this profound and powerful event' (P 17, C 255).

The notion of purification and renewal through struggle and blood-shed parallels the idea which Kinsella has been developing in the poem: that of the transformation of brute materiality through the ordering power of music. By introducing this letter as a pause in the poem, Kinsella cautions us that the costs of transformation or renewal can be high, sometimes too high. And that the medium of transformation, be it war or art, cannot in itself be made responsible for the results produced. That responsibility lies with those who control the process. Through Thomas Mann's letter, Kinsella makes a number of connections, both within the poem and within his work as a whole. We have already noted how *Her Vertical Smile* picks up some threads from *Vertical Man*. This letter of this *Intermezzo* introduces another link which reinforces the themes of *Her Vertical Smile*. The title of the poem *Vertical Man* was taken from the title of one of Seán Ó Riada's recordings which was in its turn taken from a line in a poem by W. H. Auden. This poem refers to

Christopher Isherwood as a vertical man, a man of honour. An example of Isherwood's moral position and willingness to help others is his role in enabling Thomas Mann's daughter to obtain a British passport when she was about to be stripped of her German citizenship in 1935.[51] Through Mann, Kinsella brings the concerns of Goethe's *Faust*, which are explored again in Mahler's Eight Symphony, into the twentieth century as music and politics, risk and redemption are explored analogously in Mann's *Dr Faustus: The Life of the German Composer Adrian Leverkühn as Told by a Friend*, 1948. Here also Mann's theme of national crisis paralleling artistic crisis underscores Kinsella's own work. Another way in which we can understand how Thomas Mann's letter works in *Her Vertical Smile* is to look at how, in a very direct way, Kinsella is using Mann to explain and to exemplify his working method. Kinsella is drawn to Mann's writing because of what he calls 'the comprehensiveness and reach of his ideas, his minute control over detail'.[52]

Kinsella's approach to writing is similar to Mann's in that both use montage techniques as a working method.[53] In his writing Mann would blend fact with fiction and incorporate passages from a variety of literary sources. He would also introduce real people, both living and dead, into the plot of his writing and use people he knew as models for his characters.[54] By including this version of Mann's letter in his poem, Kinsella refers directly to his own use of montage in his writing: the way in which he appropriates and incorporates foreign material into the poetry and, as we shall see in such Peppercanisters as *The Good Fight*, *St Catherine's Clock* and *One Fond Embrace*, how he also introduces real figures from history and the contemporary world into his writing. But perhaps most significant for our reading of Kinsella's poetry is the way in which he brings in details and passages from earlier works into his later writing to create a poetry which is constantly rewriting previous work by giving it a new angle in the context of the present work. Thus the reader of Kinsella's poetry must work both backwards and forwards. The means of understanding the poem does not always lie simply in the poem itself.

Part II of *Her Vertical Smile* is divided into three sections. The first returns us again to the performance of the Eighth Symphony, but the music brings us into the landscape of the psyche where, in the second section of part II, Kinsella explores the origin of the self at its point of creation. The poem then shifts to a consideration of the destruction of war before, in the third section, bringing us back to Mahler, this time in the company of his wife, Alma. Through this couple Kinsella raises questions of responsibility, linking the responsibility of society for the individual to the responsibility of one spouse for the other. Part II ends with an evocation of Mahler's *Das Lied von der Erde* and a meditation on the origin of the order through which music and violence comes.

Part II opens with Mahler once again in the throes of conducting the Eighth Symphony, summoning forth '"Glockenspiel!"' and '"Tuba! Double basses!"' (P 19, C 255). Kinsella describes Mahler's work in terms of getting to the heart of the matter. With the sounds of the tuba and the double basses 'There is a prolonged emptying / of the writhing contents' (P 19, C 255). And again, to the sound the the trumpet and strings Kinsella asks: 'Is there anything like quite like / getting to the root?' (P 19, C 255). With this question Kinsella returns to the landscape of his earlier works such as *One*, *Notes from the Land of the Dead* and *Wormwood*. The themes of ordeal, endurance and death join with an exploration of the nature of the union between two people and the responsibilities which that entails. The compound adjective 'fishchill' recalls the 'Snapdelicious' and 'Throbflutter' of *One*'s opening sequence as the poem plumbs 'the depths' reminiscent of the Faustian underworld in *Notes from the Land of the Dead*:

> Falling. Mind darkening.
>   Toward a ring of mouths.
>
> Flushed.
>   Time, distance,
>   Meaning nothing.
>   No matter.
>
>   (C 96)

From this place in which there is neither body nor significance, this 'lower cold // where the senses have no function' comes a single move-ment of life (P 20, C 256). Kinsella's description of union, the 'entities that made it possible // are locked together still' (P 19, C 256) returns us to the intertwined tree-trunks of 'Wormwood' in which 'their join' becomes 'A slowly twisted scar' (C 63).

Kinsella approaches the responsibilities of love on two levels – the first is procreative, the second personal – but both are linked in his larger meditation on the responsibilities of the individual towards others. He links the procreative power of sexual union with the figures of creation, both male and female, in a meditation on the transformative power of love in which two become one, and in that union produce others, who are:

> – teeming everywhere
> with your aches and needs
>
> along our bloody passageways,
>   knocking against one another
> in never ending fuss
>
>   (P 20–1, C 257 var.)

The resigned humour of these lines gathers into a consideration of the nature of life itself which Kinsella sees as a process of 'unsureness or error.' However the pessimism indicated by this phrase is undercut by a certain limited optimism in which it is made clear that error and existence are concomitant:

> waste
>   a part of the process,
>   implying life):
>
>   (P 21, C 257)

The subsequent stanzas outline a vision of life which is horrible. But even from this appalling and savage existence a thing of order and beauty might yet be made. The circling of the 'outer carrion' may yet be transformed into that dance of order and precision, the gavotte.

The closing section of part II of *Her Vertical Smile* introduces the image of Alma and Gustav Mahler taking a walk together. The idyllic image of contented union between two people recalls the earlier appearance of the couple universalised as 'a Man and a Woman' in part I. The 'hatchet face' (P 13, C 252) of this figure repeats Kinsella's previous description of Mahler's face as a 'fragile axe' (P 9, C 248). The universalised man and woman are drawn together in what is described as 'a happy ending' and this optimism would seem to be borne out by the scene which Kinsella describes:

> Our couple are taking the air
>   by the sea side,
>   content in their own sweet silence
>
>   (P 22, C 258)

However, the happy ending and the sweet silence are qualified by the 'arm's length' at which the one holds the other (P 22, C 258). Instead of man touching woman, 'it is ocean and earth / that are touching' (P 22, C 258). Kinsella takes this scene from biography: it is drawn from a 'faded photo' which depicts Alma in a 'broad-brimmed hat' and Gustav 'in his tight trousers' (P 22–3, C 258–9).[55] But biography tells a story which is very different from the 'sweet silence' of the seaside scene.[56]

Kinsella contrasts two views of Mahler: Mahler as an exemplar of the 'Music Master' who elicits order from chaos, and Mahler who nurtures his own creative powers at the expense of those of his wife. The universal is reduced to the particular as the speaker asks a question which reverberates throughout the whole poem: 'how to respond, // how to admire the solid beloved' (P 23, C 259). *Her Vertical Smile* opens with a meditation on issues of universal concern which involved collective responsibility. The poem closes with a focus on individual responsibility in a vision of life being lived in response to another. Through the figures of Alma and Gustav Mahler Kinsella particularises the themes of the Eighth Symphony. Redemption through love is explored in the texts of both parts of the Symphony. The first part uses the Latin text of 'Veni, Creator Spiritus' by Hrabanus Magnentius Maurus, which is an invocation written for the feast of the Pentecost celebrating the descent of the Holy Spirit into the world. The second part comes from Goethe's nineteenth century verse drama, *Faust*, in which the direction of the relationship between spirit and matter is reversed as the Everyman figure of Faust is finally redeemed and drawn into the heavens by 'the intervention of the Eternal Feminine, the creative power of love which subsumes all'.[57] Both parts of the symphony close with a hymn to love: the first celebrates 'The Birth of Love, and the second 'Creation through Love'.

It is interesting that in *Her Vertical Smile* Kinsella gives far greater prominence, and power, to the female force of creation than to the male. From the Mater Gloriosa or Ever-Feminine evoked in Mahler's setting of Goethe's *Faust* to what Brian John terms the 'Muse-Mother' explored by Mahler's baton[58] with its echoes of the Jungian Great-Mother, the figure to whom Kinsella attributes the power of life and death is most frequently feminine. A masculine god makes a single, somewhat humorous appearance in the person of God the Father as painted on the Sistine chapel, but here the focus of his power is somewhat off the mark:

> with the nub of the matter displaced
> in a fold of His purple shift.
>
> (P 13, C 252)

Kinsella conceives of that figure to whom we all return as unequivocally feminine. She is accorded the tone and trappings of a conventional deity as the catechetical inflection of the following stanza shows:

> now, before we suffer Her
> to gather us once more
> into Her farewell and for ever,
>
> (P 21, C 257)

Indeed, this is not the first time in Kinsella's poetry that God has been figured as a woman. Comparing the text of the second chapter of Genesis with Kinsella's rewriting of that story in his early poem 'Nuchal' from *Notes from the Land of the Dead*, Carol Tattersall points out that: 'the implication of Kinsella's account, since the woman divides the waters, is that either she has always co-existed with God, or else she *is* God'.[59]

Kinsella joins these images of the feminine as human and as divine when he returns, in the close of part II, to *Das Lied von der Erde*. The echoes of the song which we heard at the opening of the poem – 'For

ever and ever' – are taken up by 'a single throat / thrown wide // in a
gasp of / alarm and praise –' (P 23, C 259). Though the song on which
this section of the poem is modelled is called 'Der Abschied' or 'The
Farewell', it seems as if we are only at the beginning:

> Let the Fall begin,
> the whole wide
> landscape descend gently

> (P 23, C 259)

The capitalised 'Fall' evokes the fall from paradise into the sinfulness of
the world, a world which, as Kinsella notes in the preparatory drafts of
the poem, is divided into good and evil.[60] Kinsella transforms the indi-
vidual leavetaking of a friend, which is the subject of 'Der Abschied',
into the universal leavetaking of mankind from paradise:

> and a portal close.

> And there ought to be
> a good deal of wandering
> and seeking for peace.

> (P 23, C 259)

Though the details of 'Der Abschied' are evoked in the lines: 'forest
murmurs; a tired horseman / drinking in friendship and farewell', Kinsella
takes the subject of the Eighth Symphony as an example of how humanity
comes to terms with this fall from grace, for it is through the power of
art that the contingent condition of man is transformed into something
enduring and the universal. It is the 'simplest poetry' made from 'Good
man-made matter' which makes possible the transformation through
which love, and war, can be understood. Poetry forms a bridge between
the material and the ideal.

The redemptive power of art echoes the redemptive powers of the
female deities who, in each of the texts which inform this poem, act
as figures of salvation. As *Her Vertical Smile* draws to a close, music
approaches the condition of the divine with the near conflation of the
mezzo-soprano singing *Der Abschied* and the figure of God herself.
However it is the 'Song' rather than the singer which is the eternal force.
But this is a force which, as Kinsella makes very clear, is rooted in the
materiality of the body:

> And central to the Song's force
> an awareness
> (in the actual motions of the mouth,

the intimacy of
    its necessary movements)
of her two nutrient smiles:

(P 24, C 260)

The 'two nutrient smiles' through which the Song gains its force are the smile which gives voice and the smile which gives life. Here creation and procreation are not opposed as radically different spheres of life. Instead, Kinsella recognises the inevitable and necessary link between the two. In *Her Vertical Smile* the body is seen as the source of life and of art. And the responsibility for both lies with the self.

In this poem Kinsella presents us with the dilemma which has become emblematic of twentieth-century literature. How to respond in a rapidly changing world in which the old orders of understanding have given way to a new chaos? The First World War stands as a significant marker in this change because of the way in which it announced new and unimaginable destruction. Against this vision of destruction Kinsella places his faith in the creative, and procreative, powers of the individual. Significantly, however, he does not portray this individual in splendid isolation. Instead, Kinsella argues that it is only in communion with the other that the powers of the individual can be fully realised. His is not a solipsistic world.

In *Her Vertical Smile* Kinsella takes music as an example of the systems of order through which understanding can occur. The artist, be it poet or composer, searches to construct an order in the material at hand. This search draws on the past as much as the present in its efforts to produce a system, however flawed, through which life can be lived. As Kinsella makes clear in the drafts to this poem:

> my system clear at last
>   in its great weaknesses and strengths,
> by pulse beating with a private possible;
>
> of known things in their known order
>   taking a bare and lonely light
> from the ancient measured erratic,[61]

Kinsella describes *Her Vertical Smile* as a poem which explores the themes of violence, order and music. This triumvirate can be seen in terms of division and union. Violence and music are set against each other as ways through which experience is dealt with. Order stands apart as an ideal towards which we struggle. It is only in 'her vertical smile' that the completeness of an order 'dwelling upon itself for ever' is to be found (P 24, C 260). But, as Goethe's *Faust* makes clear, for that we need divine intervention. *Her Vertical Smile* ends with a *Coda*, which wryly undercuts any glory which might be attributed to the artist. At the heart of this struggle for order is not the searing intellect of the artist, but rather that most capricious of elements: 'Luck'. In a move reminiscent of Beckett's *Waiting for Godot*, Kinsella sets himself up:

> I lift my
>   baton and my
> trousers fall.
>
> (P 25, C 260)

Out of Ireland

The concern with place and passage finds its most concentrated exploration in Thomas Kinsella's eleventh Peppercanister, *Out of Ireland*, published in 1987 in tandem with the twelfth volume, *St Catherine's Clock*. The title evokes Yeats's poem 'Remorse for Intemperate Speech' in which he writes 'Out of Ireland have we come. / Great hatred, little room, / Maimed us at the start.'[62] Issues of origin and influence are explored in both Yeats's and Kinsella's poems, but it is *Out of Ireland* which juxtaposes contemporary identity with cultural history as it asks some unsettling questions. What does it mean to come out of Ireland? How do we constitute the place, or space, called Ireland? Where does one go, once one is out of Ireland? The phrase 'Out of Ireland' suggests a movement or passage which is defined by its origin. But this origin can only be understood from the distance of departure. It is in this reciprocal space between place and passage that Thomas Kinsella's poetry is written.

Out of Ireland is made up of seven poems, entitled 'Entrance', 'Native Wisdom', 'Harmonies', 'The Furnace', 'The Dance', 'The Land of Loss' and 'Exit' respectively. The poems take place in the graveyard of St Gobnait's church in Ballyvourney in County Cork. The occasion is a memorial service for the renowned Irish composer Seán Ó Riada whose death is commemorated by Kinsella in the earlier Peppercanister volumes, *A Selected Life* and *Vertical Man*. *Out of Ireland* has been described by Kinsella as 'a final farewell to Ó Riada'.[63] Ó Riada embodies a particular moment in the emerging identity of the newly founded Irish republic in which the native culture and language were being reclaimed. Seán

Ó Riada grew up as John Reidy, and is referred to by both names in Thomas Kinsella's poetry.[64] The decision to name himself in the tongue of his forebears, and to adopt this tongue for himself, abandoning the English language in favour of Irish, was a decision taken by many of Ó Riada's, and Kinsella's, contemporaries. These are the two languages of which Kinsella writes in the opening lines of *Out of Ireland:* 'Crows scoured the wet evening clean / above our heads. // Two languages interchanged' (P 9, C 261).

These are also the languages which conflict within 'Seamus of the Smart Suit' as 'he struggled in his nose with English' (P 12, C 263). But these two languages can also be understood as the Irish and Latin which were the working languages of the 'long library bodies, their pens / distinct against the sinking sun' (P 9, C 261). Irish, English and Latin come together at the close of the poem 'Exit' in the line '*Give me your hand*' (P 17 var., C 267). This line is written in Irish, '*Tabhair dom do lámh*', in the Peppercanister volume, and in English in the Oxford University Press editions, *Blood and Family* and *Collected Poems* (P 17, C 267 var.). The notes to the first two editions explain that it is 'the title of an early seventeenth-century Irish air – often given in the Latin, Da mihi manum' (P 28).[65] With this note Kinsella emphasises the level of scholarship in seventeenth-century Ireland, and points to the demise of Gaelic culture at the end of that century, a century which, in Kinsella's words, 'ends in darkness, with the Gaelic aristocracy ruined and the death-blow already delivered to the Irish language'.[66]

Kinsella is acutely aware of the tension between the two languages of Ireland, and of the implications of his own decision to write in English rather than Irish. In his 1966 address to the Modern Language Association Kinsella explored the relationship between the writer, and the language and tradition in which he writes. He asked what it means to be an Irish writer, and makes explicit the dilemma facing the contemporary Irish writer with the question:

> Why can I not make living contact with [my literary] inheritance, my own past? Others have. It is because I believe I would have to make a commitment to the Irish language; to write in Irish instead of English. And that would mean loss of contact with my own present [. . .]. But in the end it is really not a matter of choice; for my own part I simply recognize that I stand on one side of a great rift, and can feel the discontinuity in myself.[67]

This great rift is one of the consequence of being out of Ireland, of being from a country in which the language of one's tradition has almost been silenced, and being faced with a choice between the present and the past.

Between these poles lie the 'half-certainties' which bring the poet 'to a halt' (P 9, C 261). What interjects after this truncated line in the first poem of the series is a voice of a different kind. It is the voice of the poet's own past as Kinsella grafts a quotation from his earlier poem 'Phoenix Park', written in 1968, into the body of the poem:

> that love is
> to clasp simply,
> question fiercely;

> (P 9, C 261var.)

The stanza from which these lines are taken places love between the limitations of the material and the immaterial. Kinsella names love as the means by which these limitations may be transcended:

> – That flesh is finite, so in love we persist;
> That love is to clasp simply, question fiercely;
> That getting life we eat pain in each other.
> But mental, in my fever – mere idea.

> (C 91)

Here, Kinsella refigures the relationship between flesh and idea explored in 'Phoenix Park' according to the philosophy of the ninth-century scholar, John Scotus Eriugena, whose very name provides the title of *Out of Ireland*.

Eriugena came to prominence in the court of Charles the Bald during the second Carolingian Renaissance of the mid eighth and early ninth century. He joined other Irish scholars, who were also working in the cultural centres of the Continent, to create an intellectual community of 'free speech, worldly science, and intellectual audacity'[68] until it seemed as if, in the eyes of one chronicler, 'nearly the whole of Hibernia has emigrated to our coasts in a hoard of philosophers'.[69] Eriugena's most renowned work, called *The Division of Nature*, takes the form of a catechetical dialogue in which Nature is defined as that which is and that which is not, as well as that which can be known and that which cannot. Kinsella outlines Eriugena's thought in the notes he provides for *Out of Ireland*. He emphasises the cycle of procession from God and return to God in which all Nature takes part. Nature includes contraries and impossibilities; it incorporates the paradoxical movement which is 'static in a dance of return' (P 12, C 263). Most importantly for a reading of *Out of Ireland*, Eriugena's philosophy maintains that 'corporeal things come from incorporeal things and return to incorporeal things'[70] and that 'the body can, therefore, simply pass into soul, and soul into intellect, and intellect into God: there is no transmutation of properties or confusion or destruction of essences or substances.'[71] Thus, the 'Imperishable creatures' of which Kinsella writes in 'The Furnace' are intensified 'into flowing fire' (P 13, C 264). The multiple becomes singular:

and will turn again toward the same furnace
that melted the union of our will
to ineffable zero

(P 13, C 264)

This 'ineffable zero' is both the beginning and the end. It marks a
'resurrection, not a vanishing' (P 13, C 264) and completes the cycles of
procession and return mentioned above. As Kinsella remarks in the
drafts towards this poem, 'In this return the substance of things does not
perish but moves upwards [. . .] it is not a change of corporeal to
incorporeal but an ineffable unity of substances. Molten iron does not
"cease" in fire, but is further on the way of return.'[72]

Once again Kinsella inserts a quotation from the earlier poem
'Phoenix Park' into *Out of Ireland*. The tense of the quotation changes
from present to past, from *'consign'* to *'consigned'*, as if to acknowledge
the temporal discontinuity of the insertion. In 'Phoenix Park' the poet
addresses his loved one, the 'Fair Ellinor' (C 91), saying:

> *You approach the centre by its own sweet light.*
> *I consign my designing will stonily*
> *To your flames. Wrapped in that rosy fleece, two lives*
> *Burn down around one love, one flickering-eyed*
> *Stone self becomes more patient than its own stone.*

(C 92)

It is love which makes two into one, and transforms the conflagration
to stone. Love reconciles opposites and places unity where there once
was division. By quoting from 'Phoenix Park' in *Out of Ireland* Kinsella
draws the reader into the accumulating unity of his poetic project. He
creates a dialogue between the past and the present in the form of a
citation which:

> breaks the continuity or the linearity of the discourse and leads necessarily
> to a double reading: that of the fragment perceived in relation to its text
> of origin; that of the same fragment as incorporated into a new whole, a
> different totality.[73]

This new whole into which the citation is inserted rewrites the power of
love in terms of the unity which is sundered into the two genders, 'Male
and Female' (P 13, C 264). Gender is the post-lapsarian condition of Man
occasioned by his will. Eriugena explains that 'oppressed by the guilt of
his disobedience, [Man] suffered the division of his nature into male and
female'.[74] In Kinsella's words:

Male and Female
in punishment for Man's will
and reminded of our Fall.

(P 13, C 264)

The will which occasioned the division of humanity into the sexes and distanced it from 'the Union and the Light' is the same will which Kinsella consigns '*stonily / to your flames*', to be melted to 'ineffable zero', momentarily ('for a minute or two') before recommencing the cycle of division and union: 'Until gender returned / and we were made two again' (P 13, C 264). The will of which Kinsella writes is a will to a knowledge which encompasses both the visceral and the conceptual.

Kinsella compares his poetic project to Eriugena's philosophical one when he writes: 'Eriugena's notion matching / my half-baked, bodily own', (P 13, C 264). The limitation contained in 'half-baked' suggests the incompletion of Kinsella's poetic project which is the need to 'see how the whole thing / works' (P [9], C 184). The 'whole thing' of which Kinsella writes in *A Technical Supplement* encompasses both ontology and epistemology. It joins the word and world in a search for understanding which will dispense with both. Kinsella asks:

> how many times in its radiant clasp
> (a cancellation
> certainly speechless for a minute or two)
>
> in token of the Union and the Light.
>
> (P 13, C 264)

How many times will the cycle of ignorance and understanding be turned? How many times will the 'ineffable zero' be reached only to be lost? As Mary Anderson emphasises: 'the repeating nature of the image of the zero, circle, coil, hole, darkness and void [. . .] represents the beginning of knowledge' in Kinsella's work.[75]

This is the knowledge which is peddled by the voices in the second poem of *Out of Ireland* called 'Native Wisdom'. These voices hark back to Kinsella's quotations of his own voice in the poem. To emphasise the difference between the words of the past and and those of the present these quotations are printed in italics. The textual differentiation makes these lines speak more urgently, lifting them from the surrounding poetry. The first speaker is a crow who declares from the parapet of the church:

> *I am native born in this place.*
>
> *I have knowledge*
> *of flesh and blood.*
> *Come and buy.*
>
> (P 10, C 262 var.)

The second is the voice of the Black Robber which, as Brian John notes, is 'the local name given to a stone carving of a human head in the wall

above the chancel arch at Ballyvourney'.[76] This voice repudiates the voice
of the crow, crying:

> *Give ear to him and he will fill it*
> *with nothing but white rubbish.*
> *I am native born*
>
> *in your foul deeds.*
> *Good and evil*
> *come and buy.*
>
> (P 10–11, C 262 var.)

Both speakers rest the authority of their words on the place of their
birth. Each takes up the cry of the ninth-century Irish scholars who
announced: 'If anyone desires wisdom, let him come to us and receive it,
for we are here to sell it'.[77] The carnal knowledge of the first speaker is
contrasted with the noetic knowledge of the second.

In a clash of the contingent and the abstract, flesh and body are
ranged against good and evil. These seeming opposites are brought
together by the third speaker, the *síle-na-gig*, who represents either a pre-
christian fertility figure or a Christian warning against the sin of lust.
This figure 'opened her offered self' (P 11) – 'offers her opened self'
(C 262) – saying:

> *This swallows them both*
> *and all the questions.*
>
> *Here you are native born.*
> *Yes and no*
> *Come here and buy.*
>
> (P 11, C 262)

The *síle-na-gig*'s speech emphasises the primacy of the somatic over the
symbolic. Her own sex is the point of origin and end for all questions
and all dualities. She avoids the marker of subjectivity by not saying 'I',
substituting instead the second person and therefore implicating the
reader. She places herself anterior to the previous two speakers when she
says '*Here you are native born*' (P 11, C 262). Here opposites converge
but do not cancel for her knowledge is of a different order.

The voice of the fourth speaker emerges from a half-dug grave.
Though it speaks from the soil this voice speaks of the spirit, saying:

> *I am born again in the spirit.*
> *So shall you be. Love is all*
> *or nothing. Come and buy.*
>
> (P 11, C 263 var.)

This speaker has completed the cycle of procession and return whereby the material returns to the spiritual by following the seven steps of contemplation described by Eriugena.[78] However Kinsella provides no sense of finality. This voice does not bring the poem to a close, but points towards the more immediate voice of a following poem, 'The Dance', which speaks from the shadow of Seán Ó Riada. It is in memory of this 'forgotten young hero' that 'Grieving solos fade / and twine on echoes of each other' (P 14, C 265). This 'music of memory' is turned to dance by the spirit of Ó Riada who takes his leave of the congregation with the invitation:

> *come and buy*
> *my terrible new capabilities . . .*
>
> (P 14, C 265)

These lines echo the call of the previous, more ancient, voices, but now the knowledge that they offer is a means of destruction rather than redemption. The words 'terrible new capabilities' recall the 'terrible beauty' of Yeats's poem 'Easter 1916' and the nuclear capabilities which fuelled the cold war of this century.

Each of these voices joins with the quotations, notes and references through which *Out of Ireland* is constructed to create an intertextuality which, as Kinsella implicitly suggests, is best understood in terms of polyphony; 'the simultaneous sounding of several notes forming a chord'.[79] Kinsella looks once again to Eriugena whose writing seeks to explain the possibility of unity in dissonance through an analogy with musical form:

> For as instrumental music is composed of notes of different length and quality (pitch), which, heard in isolation, differ considerably according to tension, but if they are combined variously in certain relations according to the rules of musical theory result in sounds of a natural sweetness, [. . .][80]

This analogy works not only with *Out of Ireland*, but also with the greater whole of Kinsella's writing for, as W. J. Mc Cormack points out:

> the Peppercanister publications draw attention repeatedly to their structural multiplicity, by means of all those epigraphs, prologues, italicised preliminaries, drawings, quotations backwards and forwards, marginalised commentary [. . .] which insist that the poem has no identity *with* its subject, but works at once on top of other, anterior writings and towards as yet unknowable formulations.[81]

The movement towards union which Kinsella has articulated in *Out of Ireland*, culminating in 'The Furnace', turns now towards dissolution in 'The Land of Loss'. Kinsella places the responsibility for experience firmly with the self when he writes: 'Nothing certain of this world / [. . .] / except for certain impediments / we might carry with ourselves' (P 16,

C 266). Kinsella does not look for some grand design through which to make sense of experience. Instead he adopts what Daniel O'Hara calls 'a stance of openness that takes experience on its own terms, amidst all its rigours and wastes, and elicits order from its complexities'.[82] However there are always risks involved in this immediate approach as Kinsella makes clear at the end of the poem when he describes how Eriugena, whose philosophic project underwrites Kinsella's poetic project, was driven from France under charges of heresy, and died at the hands of his students who 'stabbed him / with their pens / because he made them think' (P 16, C 266 var.).[83] That the instrument of one's creation becomes also the instrument of one's destruction is an irony not lost on Kinsella, who has already equated the writing of poetry with self-surgery in his earlier volume *A Technical Supplement*. But the risks are not all his own.

Kinsella describes his poetry in term of an artistic response to experience: 'If an artistic response is called into existence, that itself modifies the situation: it's a positive response even if we never solve anything.'[84] Kinsella's 'artistic response' can be understood in terms of Jean-François Lyotard's notion of the differend which emphasises the absolute necessity of response, even if that response is silence.[85] This notion of response extends also to the reader of Kinsella's poetry. Kinsella offers a challenge to his readers in the quotation which prefaces *Out of Ireland*:

> Hence it happens that the very things that afford unspeakable delight to the minds of those who have a fine perception and can penetrate carefully to the secrets of the art, bore, rather than delight, those who have no such perception – who look without seeing, and hear without being able to understand. When the audience is unsympathetic they succeed only in causing boredom with what appears to be but confused and disordered noise . . .
>
> (P 6, C 261).

Kinsella himself has often been charged with writing a confused and disordered poetry, a poetry which 'vacillates between a measured eloquence and a mutilated incoherence',[86] but, as the preface to *Out of Ireland* emphasises, art is a two-way communication which demands as much from those to whom it is addressed as it does from those by whom it is created. Eriugena's untimely end underlines the risk that Kinsella consciously assumes when he writes a poetry which reveals a face of Ireland that his readers would prefer not to recognise. Yet it is because Kinsella himself is out of Ireland, both in the sense of origin and of departure, that he can write a poetry which so rigorously interrogates the development of contemporary Ireland. In 1931 Yeats expressed some 'remorse for intemperate speech', but as Kinsella moves into the last decades of the century, his writing shows little sign of compromise with what is considered acceptable in terms of language and subject matter. Indeed, the very honesty and vigour with which Kinsella writes of Ireland ensures that his poetry does not sit easily with the notion of the Irish poet.[87] But it is this very unease which makes Kinsella's voice remarkable.

St Catherine's Clock

The sacrifice integral to art and learning in *Out of Ireland* becomes the sacrifice necessary for history and politics in *St Catherine's Clock*. Kinsella's twelfth Peppercanister volume explores the relationship between public and private histories and questions the choices involved in writing about each. Kinsella juxtaposes images from Irish history with images from his family history and, through an analysis of both, the poet destabilises the certainties upon which they stand. Once again Kinsella gathers around him public figures – Robert Emmet, Lord Kilwarden and Jonathan Swift – who each provide him with a different point of entry for his poetic purpose. Time lies at the heart of this volume, as the poet asks how the individual constructs him or herself through the intertwined strands of historical and personal time. Jarlath Hayes's stark and elegant design for the front cover of the Peppercanister volume depicts an historical marker of time: the hands of St Catherine's clock. These hands are linked, in Hayes's design, with an emblem of the sacrifice which time demands: the image of a single red drop of blood. Both life and time are insubstantial elements which by their very nature only make sense in their passing. History is the means by which each leave their mark on our understanding.

St Catherine's Clock moves backward and forward in time, taking in scenes from the eighteenth century to the present day. As with most of Kinsella's later work, the organisation of the volume does not conform to conventional stanza or even section division. In its first two editions *St Catherine's Clock* is organised according to the spatial layout of the page. Divisions in the poem are indicated either by a heading for a particular section, or by placing that section on a separate page. The *Collected Poems 1956–1994* presents us with a somewhat different poem, since the spatial division is absent and each section runs on from the other unless it is differentiated by a heading. In this reading of the poem I shall use as a guide the divisions indicated by the 1987 Peppercanister edition, which are also replicated in the 1988 collection *Blood and Family*. The poem is introduced by an epigraph, and begins with a section which can be considered a gloss or commentary on the poem as a whole.[88] The subsequent sections are divided by the three stanzas which mark the three hours during which the poem takes place. This orders the poem into two primary sections which are then subdivided. The poem ends with a short section which mirrors the gloss at the beginning. Kinsella structures *St Catherine's Clock* in layers which comment upon the other parts of the poem. He moves the reader from one location to another, and from one time period to another, so that space and time become integral elements through which we understand the poem.

The epigraph which opens the poem is differentiated from the rest of the text by the use of italics, and is presented as a quotation:

> *'. . . chosen and lifted up against the light*
> *for the Fisherman's thumb*
> *and the bowel-piercing hook.'*
>
> (P 6)89

This voice, appropriated from the past, presents an image which combines the base worm used as fishing bait with the elevated figure of the political martyr personified later in the poem in the figure of Robert Emmet. This incongruous conjunction sets the tone of the poem in which Kinsella questions the forms into which historical representations are placed and, in effect, prises them open to see what lies at their foundations. Reading backwards, in the light of what we will learn of Robert Emmet in the poem, the epigraph presents Emmet, not as the heroic instigator of revolution, but rather as the unlucky pawn in a larger political game.

In an urban echo of the opening of 'A Country Walk', *St Catherine's Clock* begins with the poet's impatient departure from home: 'The whole terrace / slammed shut', as he reclaims his old role of nightwalker or 'prowler' pacing the streets of Dublin by lamplight (P 7, C 269). Both the epigraph and this first part of the poem recall the atmosphere of Kinsella's 1968 poem 'Nightwalker':

> My shadow twists about my feet in the light
> Of every passing street lamp. Window after window
> Pale entities, motionless in their cells like grubs,
> Wait in a blue trance:
>
> (C 76)

The 'pale entities' of 'Nightwalker' combine to become, in *St Catherine's Clock*, the single 'stooped image' of a drug addict intent on the next fix

(P 7, C 269). Kinsella draws strong parallels between the addict and the writer as he compares the way in which the pen is held with the position of the needle: 'The fingers of the right hand are set / in a scribal act on the skin' (P 7, C 269). The injection itself is seen in terms of understanding and enlightenment. It is a 'gloss, simple and swift as thought' which is 'planted' into the flesh (P 7, C 269). The phrase 'scribal act' recalls the 'long library bodies' of *Out of Ireland* (P 9, C 261). But here, it is darkness rather than illumination which is being transmitted.

The last line of the opening gloss indicates the perspective of the poem as a whole. Kinsella's 'I see' brings together ideas of the visual and the intellectual as means of understanding (P 7, C 269). Both of these means of understanding are at work in the poem which analyses visual representations of places and events in the form of engravings, and works to order them within an historical narrative in which the self has a place. Kinsella has always shown an astute eye for the visual, whether it is through visual imagery in the texts themselves – the placing of visual material between the poems of a volume such as *One* or *A Technical Supplement* – or the choice of imagery for the covers of the Peppercanister editions. In *St Catherine's Clock*, Kinsella makes a fourth use of visual imagery by taking engravings of historical scenes as his point of departure for an examination of how we arrive at the perspective through which we understand history. However, it is not just history in the general or social sense that is under consideration here. The history of the individual is linked with the history of place and of nation.

If we wish to talk about history, then we must also talk about time. *St Catherine's Clock* uses time as an organisational structure. The poem takes place within the three hours determined by St Catherine's Clock:

> The clock
> on the squat front of St Catherine's
> settled a gilded point
> up soundless into place

(P 8, C 269)

The impassive face of the clock looks down on scenes of the everyday and scenes of the extraordinary. The three hours during which the poem takes place recall the three hours of darkness during the Easter passion, and this theme of sacrifice and death is revisited through two scenes of bloodshed, the death of Lord Kilwarden and the death of Robert Emmet. The first hour takes place in Thomas Street. The first scene of this hour is dated '1803' and is titled '*After the engraving by George Cruikshank*' (P 9, C 270). It takes place during Robert Emmet's failed insurrection of 1803 and depicts the killing of Lord Kilwarden, Chief Justice of the

King's Bench, outside his carriage. Kinsella includes historical matter not referred to directly in the engraving when he adds: 'Somewhere a nephew, / Mr Richard Wolfe, is fallen / and spilling his share of blood and matter' (P 9, C 270). The second scene also takes place in 1803 and is titled '*From a non-contemporary nationalist artist's impression*' (P 9, C 270). It depicts the execution of Robert Emmet on 20 September 1803 during which Emmet was first hanged then beheaded:

> The pasty head is separated and brandished aloft,
> the dead forehead with black wet lock
> turned toward the Fountain.
>
> (P 10, C 271)

Both of these events take place under the gaze of St Catherine's clock on Thomas Street, as Kinsella makes clear when he describes Robert Emmet standing on the scaffold which is 'as close as possible to the site of the outrage' of Kilwarden's murder (P 9, C 270).

Each of these engravings has its individual history. Though very little is known about the anonymous second engraving which comes from the National Library of Ireland collection,[90] the first is a print after the engraving by George Cruikshank which appeared in an edition of W. H. Maxwell's *History of the Irish Rebellion of 1798* in 1845.[91] However, what is interesting about both of these engravings in the context of *St Catherine's Clock* is that Kinsella has taken them from an educational pack produced by the Public Record Office of Northern Ireland called *Robert Emmet: The Insurrection of July 1803*. This pack, edited and introduced by Geraldine Hume and Anthony Malcomson, reproduces facsimiles of historical documents through which it aims to tell a story of 'conflict, honestly maintained on both sides, between one concept of duty, loyalty and nationality, and another'.[92] Rather than constructing a narrative about a certain event, the education pack presents readers with a series of facsimile documents through which they write their own history. The facsimile documents are presented as a means by which the inevitable bias inherent in written history can be circumvented. As the introduction emphasises:

> One of the more important functions of history, particularly in the Irish context, is to teach people to recognise bias and apply a corrective to it.[93]

However, one of the problems that Kinsella picks up in this regard, and develops throughout *St Catherine's Clock* is the difficulty of establishing the norm from which the bias diverges. What standards do we apply in order to figure out when a representation of an event is biased? Who decides what is the norm and what is the bias? Surely what is biased from one perspective is normal to another? How can history negotiate its way through these dilemmas?

Kinsella's approach to these question is to give us a reading of these two engravings which depict scenes around a particular event from very different political perspectives. The first concentrates on the way in which Kilwarden's death is represented. Kilwarden's stance has religious overtones as he 'genuflected / prim and upset outside his carriage door' (P 9, C 270). The drama of the scene is emphasised as the carriage door is described 'thrown back rhetorical' (P 9, C 270). In a visual echo of the cries of 'inhuman' and 'bestial' which accompany most atrocities even to the present day, the attackers in this scene are grouped together into a 'pack of hatted simians' who contrast directly with the refined features of Kilwarden's coachmen, 'picked, like his horses, from a finer breed' (P 9, C 270). Kinsella's description of this engraving points up the stereotypes through which politics is viewed. The title that Kinsella gives to his description of Robert Emmet's execution, '*From a non-contemporary nationalist artist's impression*', is taken from the heading given to a reproduction of an engraving contained in the facsimile pack.[94] It is interesting that no evidence is given in the facsimile pack as to why the engraving is deemed 'nationalist', however the manner in which the scene of Emmet's execution is portrayed does, in the eyes of the editors of the pack, indicate a particular political perspective. The caption which follows the reproduction of this image in the facsimile pack emphasises the accuracy of the historical detail regarding location and execution, but takes issue with the representation of how the crowds watching reacted to the execution, commenting that 'the rest of the picture is a figment of [the artist's] imagination as the crowd remained silent and passive, and there was no scene of riot and slaughter'.[95]

The scene of 'riot and slaughter' (a somewhat exaggerated description of what is depicted in the engraving) becomes the 'horrified populace' of Kinsella's poem as Robert Emmet:

> is dropped from his brief height
>
> into a grove of redcoats
> mounted with their rumps
> toward a horrified populace.
>
> (P 9, C 270)

The gulf between the forces of law and the general public is emphasised by the positioning of the mounted redcoats with swords drawn. The figure of Emmet himself is not prominent in the engraving. His body lies decapitated and bleeding on the dais as the executioner holds his head aloft. Rather, the focus of engraver's attention lies with the reaction of the massed crowd who occupy the foreground of the image. Kinsella intersperses details from this engraving with fragments from Robert Emmet's speech from the dock in the various forms in which it entered the public domain. Once again, questions of perspective arise as the versions of the speech differ according to the source from which they came. As Hume and Malcomson emphasise, Emmet's speech 'was so distorted by contemporary propagandists that it is now impossible to ascertain what precisely he said'.[96] There are four main versions of Emmet's speech: the text produced by Emmet's friends,[97] one sponsored by loyalist or government interests,[98] the State Trials version and the text printed in the French newspaper *Le Moniteur*.

In this section of *St Catherine's Clock* Kinsella weaves phrases from the loyalist or government sponsored broadsheet version of Emmet's speech and the *State Trials* report into his poetry. The third and fourth stanzas of this section use phrases drawn from the government sponsored version rather than the one produced by Emmet's friends, which is also included in the facsimile pack:

> As to me, my Lords, I have been sacrificed on the altar of truth and liberty. There have I extinguished the torch of friendship and offered up the idol of my soul. The object of my affections. There have I parted with all, that could be dear to me in this life, and nothing now remains to me, but the cold honors of the grave. My lamp of light is nearly extinguished. My race is finished, and the grave opens to receive me. All I request at my departure from this world, is the charity of silence.[99]

The fifth stanza incorporates the closing phrases of the State trials report which states that 'His Lordship then pronounced the sentence in the usual form, and the prisoner bowed, and retired.'[100] These stanzas pick out the rhetorical flourishes of Emmet's speech in a style which Maurice Harmon describes as 'both echoing and mocking the emotion of Emmet's speech from the dock and the patriotic flourishes of those who inflated his significance.'[101] The dual process of echoing and mocking characterises Kinsella's use of historical material in this poem which questions how we come to an understanding of political events and, in a parallel movement through his focus on family history, questions how we come to an understanding of the self.

The second scene in *St Catherine's Clock* is dated 1792, and the following section is titled '*Jas. Malton, del*' (P 11, C 271). The title refers to James Malton, from whose series of engravings of Dublin scenes the third and final image on which Kinsella draws in *St Catherine's Clock* is taken. This image depicts 'St Catherine's Church, Thomas Street, Dublin' and is a variant of a print from a volume called *A Picturesque and Descriptive View of the City of Dublin (1792–1799)* which was issued in monochrome in 1799 and later in colour aquatint by Dolmen Press in 1984.[102] The version that Kinsella uses differs slightly from the 1799 and 1984 prints in that it includes the figure of an old woman – 'Centre, barefoot, / bowed in aged rags to the earth, / a hag' – who will appear again at the end of St Catherine's Clock (P 11, C 271). Kinsella describes the scene in a relatively straightforward manner:

> a man and woman with buckets,
> a couple of mongrels
> worrying the genitals out of each other.

>   (P 11, C 271)

However, this view of Georgian calm and order contrasts sharply with the scenes of violence and disorder portrayed by the previous two images. As David Kellogg points out, 'the implication is that Malton's engravings specifically, and picturesque renderings of Ireland more generally, glossed over the brutality of colonial rule.'[103] By bringing together these three images of events and scenes relating to St Catherine's Clock, Kinsella questions the choices and perspectives involved in representing the past, whether through narrative or visual imagery.

The poet's eye takes in the scene around St Catherine's Clock, then moves towards the 'pale blue' which 'divides downhill into thin air':

> on a distant dream
> of Bow Lane
> and Basin Lane.

>   (P 12, C 272)

The poem shifts from the scene of a community's history to the scene of a family history, each taking place within the same area of Dublin. Brian John has emphasised the importance of dinnseanchas in Kinsella's poetry.[104] Here, in an echo of the earlier Nightwalker and other perambulatory figures in Kinsella's poetry, the poet links public and private histories as he moves 'Past the Watch House and Watling Street / beyond St James's Gate' towards the place from which his family comes (P 12, C 272). The next section takes us forward in time to 1938, to the ten year old poet's visit to his extended family of aunts and uncles. The section is written from the child's point of view which takes in the details of grandmother's shop, especially the gob-stoppers and barley-sugar sticks displayed in 'the square glass jars' (P 13).[105] Family is seen from a subjective rather than objective perspective which focuses on specific physical characteristics: Aunty Gertie has 'big slippers and a slow bum', while 'Little Uncle Ned' is small enough to fit in her pocket (P 14, C 273). A child's wonder at certain physical prowess is caught delicately by the lines:

> She could let a long belch
> up her neck, like a noise
> coming up out of a jug.
>
> (P 14, C 273)

St Catherine's Clock emphasises the importance of family as the way in which the individual gains a sense of self through time and within community. Whether it is the transient humour of the aunts or the success of the 'best cousins' (P 16, C 275), Kinsella's language captures the atmosphere of family with its tensions and releases, and conveys with an astute ear the sounds of adult phrases in a child's mouth.

Kinsella combines the exalted and the lowly in the scene which describes the young boy killing flies with a rolled-up newspaper in the back room. The impassive compassion of 'the Sacred Heart's face' elicits no response from the 'dead eyes' of the fly who sits on the glass covering the image (P 14–15, C 273). The insignificance of the imminent death of the fly is juxtaposed against the significance of the death of Christ. With this recollection Kinsella questions the significance we attach to events, elevating a certain kind to enormous cultural importance and relegating others to the mundane. Death is usually understood in the negative, as an absence of life. But the deaths of Lord Kilwarden and Robert Emmet have assumed powerful connotations in the context of Irish history as either martyrs or murderers according to conflicting historical perspectives. Emmet and Kilwarden are linked with the Christ figure which Kinsella invokes through the public and collective nature of their deaths. Georges Bataille explains the importance of death through sacrifice in terms of its importance to those who witness it:

> A violent death disrupts the creature's discontinuity; what remains, [. . .] is the continuity of all existence with which the victim is now one. Only a spectacular killing, carried out as the solemn and collective nature of religion dictates, has the power to reveal what normally escapes notice.[106]

In *St Catherine's Clock* Kinsella turns to us as witnesses of these deaths and asks us to make sense of a history which is still coming to terms with the legacy of bloodshed and sacrifice. The very different visual images which Kinsella draws on to evoke two deaths on opposite sides of a political divide, and one death common to both sides of that divide, demand that we question the ways in which these deaths are understood. These images are one of the means by which the differing histories of a community are written.

Kinsella emphasises the role of memory in the writing of history in the section which takes place in 'Grand Canal Place, / at the second hour' (P 20, C 277). The blood from Emmet's dislocated head assumes a symbolic status as it trickles through streets and communities, mingling with tears until it reaches the 'impossible magnificat: a river / coiling its potent flood' (P 23, C 280). Though the body is dead, the blood is animated with a sense of history:

> starting down with the hill slope,
> sensing the possibility of direction
>
> (P 23, C 280)

The 'brand new soul' of the dead man becomes a winged creature emerging from its chrysalis, 'struggling with wet wings' (P 23, C 280). This image of absolute and complete transformation from one state to another captures the transfiguration of Robert Emmet from executed man to living hero, and recalls the earlier vision of the poet as:

> A little boy, some kind of uncertain
> shade, started trying to get up
> with wings dragging.
>
> (P 18, C 276)

The poet contrasts the memory of the intellect which enables the subject 'to flourish a while in freedom / on the surface of our recollection', with the memory of the emotions which anchors the subject 'in our angry hearts' (P 23, C 280). Movement and stasis, surface and depth, are set against each other as Kinsella emphasises the contrast between the private death, after which the soul ascends; and the public death, after which the spirit of the dead remains anchored to the living through a process of martyrisation. As Emmet himself knew, the role of memory is crucial in the construction of history. In each of the versions of his speech, Emmet stresses his desire that his actions be understood properly, and it is from such a passage that Kinsella quotes in the penultimate stanza of this section (P 24, C 280):

> – it is a claim on your memory, rather than on your candour, that I am making. I do not ask you to believe implicitly what I say. I do not hope that you will let my vindication ride at anchor in your breasts; – I only ask you, to let it float upon the surface of your recollection, till it comes to some more friendly port to receive it, and give it shelter against the heavy storms with which it is buffeted.[107]

The consequences of Emmet's actions were suffered not only by himself. The 'long-lost' letter of the last stanza of this section recalls Emmet's letter to his fiancée Sarah Curran explaining the reasons for his actions and urging her to destroy their letters so that she might not be implicated in his deeds. It also recalls the letter Emmet wrote to his brother Thomas Addis Emmet and his wife Jane, asking them to receive and protect Curran as if she were family. Both these letters were suppressed by the authorities:

> Long-lost, a second-last letter,
> written almost in his own tears,
> was found years afterward
> in the stuffing of a sofa.
>
> (P 24, C 280)

Through this stanza Kinsella emphasises how the individual is inextricably linked with family and history, just as the poet's own identity is understood in terms of his resemblance to his Aunt Bridie: 'the pair of us so alike, / everybody agreed, / wherever we got our brains' (P 22, C 279). But family is not simply a matter of resemblances and associations. Like society, there are conventions and structures to which blood and family must adhere:

> Not fifty yards from here
> she took the certificate
> and slapped it down on the table.
> It took that to shut them up.[108]
>
> (P·21, C 278)

This scene provides the contexts for Kinsella's emphasis on inheritance and identity in the stanza in which the voice of a father figure links mother and son:

> A dead voice now
> in my ear: You can be certain
> from your own cold certainties
> that you are a son of hers.
>
> (P 21, C 278)

Identity is something both physical and social. The boy's internalisation of of the edicts and constraints of his elders: 'I never went with the cur next door / or those gets down the street'[109] forms an important part of his own identity: 'And I always remembered / who and what I am' (P 19, C 277). This phrase finds its echo later in the dead voice which leaves the poet with a sense of 'who and what you are' (P 22, C 279).

The distinction between the social identification of 'who' and the physical identification of 'what' is drawn out as the poet situates himself in the context of his extended family, but whose sense of origin lies firmly in the physical:

> One night we scrounged up together
> and felt the little eggs in each other.
>
> (P 19, C 277)

This exploration of immature bodies connects with the goose eggs which Aunty Gertie has in the shop, 'green and big, the fill of your palm' (P 14, C 273), in an echo of the 'egg of being' from Kinsella's 1973 poem 'Hen Woman' (C 99). These eggs, whether male or female, manifest the potential for life and its inevitable corollary, death. The egg, or the ball of dung in 'Hen Woman', can be read, as Maurice Harmon emphasises, as 'the potential, the substance in which life may begin, as well as the waste of death'.[110] As this section ends, time is made visible through the hands of St Catherine's Clock:

> On the right,
> up in the slatted turret,
> a tooth on the big measuring wheel
>
> re-engaged,
>
> (P 24, C 281 var.)

The passage of time from the first to the third hour incorporates the passage of history though a series of scenes from 1740 to the present. These scenes do not progress according to a linear or chronological system of time. Instead the poem moves backward and forward between centuries and scenes in a process which makes each moment in past time resonate in the present.

St Catherine's Clock is a nodal point at which multiple points of time converge. Like the Church of Saint-Hilaire in Marcel Proust's *Swann's Way*,[111] or the automobile in Michel Serres's *Conversations on Science, Culture and Time*,[112] Kinsella's St Catherine's Clock transforms time from a series of continuations into a grouping of immediacies. The clock marks the passing of time but the church bears witness to successive generations. As these writers emphasise, past time lives also in the present. Indeed, it is only by understanding the past that the present can be fully realised. History is no longer a narrative which occupies successive points in time. It has become figurative and, like the images from which Kinsella writes this poem, can be apprehended concurrently. Time is an amalgam of presents from different periods of history which contribute to the poet's immediate experience. In *St Catherine's Clock* Kinsella 'establishes a new form of temporality' in which 'the learning process involves a return journey from the past to the present and back again'.[113] Kinsella's transformation of time allows us to understand history as something which exists in the present as well as the past. By focusing on a single location: the area around St Catherine's Clock, Kinsella is able to explore his own sense of self in terms of the family history that takes place around Bow Lane and Basin Lane, and also in terms of the national history which takes place at Bridgefoot Street and Thomas Street.

By binding family and national histories Kinsella reminds us of the depth and diversity of the tradition from which we come. The 'protestant' measuring wheel which marks time in St Catherine's Clock emphasises the difficulty of either moving on in time, or leaving history behind, but it also reminds us of the integral nature of the Protestant community to Ireland's history and tradition. The poem ends with a vision of a figure emerging from the 'darkened market place:'

> out of Francis Street
> reading the ground, all dressed up
> in black, like a madwoman.

(P 25, C 281)

Though this shadow is 'like a madwoman, it is also 'man-shaped' and, through the conjunction of date and place, can be read as the figure of Jonathan Swift. In an echo which links Kinsella to his poetic forebears, Brian John recalls W.B. Yeats's sense of connection with Swift:

> Indeed, as if to anticipate Kinsella's poem, Yeats declared: 'Swift haunts me; he is always round the next corner.'[114]

The shade also echoes Kinsella's 'quiet brutal other // closer than a brother' in terms of the Jungian idea of the shadow as that aspect of the self which resists the ordering conventions of society (P 22, C 278).[115] It also recalls the shade which waits for the 'hag' toiling across Thomas Street at the beginning of the poem. The 'hag' of the section '1792' and the figure of '1740' can be read as forms of the *cailleach* which, in Kinsella's writing, represents the origin of the self in the figure of the grandmother,[116] and indeed, in Celtic mythology, represents the origin of the world: 'Mountains, lakes and islands owe their existence or their location to her, and cairns are said to be stones that have fallen from her apron.'[117] Kinsella has described *St Catherine's Clock* as 'a poem of blood and family'.[118] Blood, here, refers to the blood lines which bind a family and the bloodshed which binds a people through ideology. Family encompasses the immediate relations from which one gains a sense of identity, and the larger community which make up a country. Connecting these two terms is an interrogation of the idea of sacrifice as a transformative act. In these four Peppercanister volumes, *Songs of the Psyche*, *Her Vertical Smile*, *Out of Ireland* and *St Catherine's Clock*, Kinsella draws together the histories of Ireland, Britain and Europe from medieval times to the present in an exploration of personal and public identity. With an extraordinary virtuosity, Kinsella interweaves knowledge, violence, art and politics in a series of poems which trouble the position of accepted historical narratives and invite us to rethink our own perspectives within the context of blood and family.

4

POLITICAL MATTERS

One Fond Embrace

In the epigraph which prefaces the 1981 and 1988 editions of *One Fond Embrace*, Kinsella parodies the disclaimer familiar in cinema:

> The persons and circumstances in this poem are real, but their parts have been redistributed so as to make them unrecognisable. (P 5)[1]

Written in the tradition of Swift and Merriman, *One Fond Embrace* brings a critical and scathing eye to Ireland of the 1980s. The persons and circumstances of the poem may have had their parts redistributed, but the *saeva indignatio* which brings them together makes clear where the barbs of satire should fall. People and politics are excoriated equally as the poet takes to task the attitudes and institutions on which modern Ireland stands.

Kinsella conceives of the poem as a kind of 'Last Supper' at which the guest are invited to 'Take one another / and eat' (P 11, C 286). This theme is announced on the cover of the Peppercanister, developed by Brendan Foreman in collaboration with Kinsella, which redraws an etching by Albrecht Dürer, omitting the figures of Jesus and John. In a letter to John F. Deane of Dedalus Press, Kinsella explains the image he has of the cover:

> The idea I had was of taking out Jesus entire, with John, from the picture, then filling in the lines of the table, the dark background, radiation, etc., so that it looked like an empty place at the table.[2]

Kinsella also thought of using an image of the crucified Christ from another of Dürer's etchings, with the head replaced by the number thirteen. *One Fond Embrace* is the thirteenth Peppercanister, and thirteen figures are depicted on the cover. Thirteen is also the number of the dead remembered in the device used to illustrate the cover of *Butcher's Dozen*, and in his notes Kinsella makes an explicit link between both poems.[3]

Cover of *One Fond Embrace* (1988)

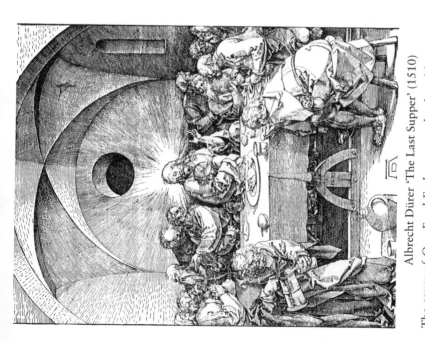

Albrecht Dürer 'The Last Supper' (1510)

The cover of *One Fond Embrace* was developed by Brendan Foreman in collaboration with Kinsella. The figures of Jesus and John have been removed from the centre of Dürer's woodcut, which is notable in that it features thirteen apostles.

Kinsella describes the volume as 'a poem of stocktaking & change' and as 'an occasion for friends and others'.[4] Given that the occasion depicted on the cover immediately precedes betrayal and sacrifice, it is hardly surprising that both friends and others are subjected equally to the excoriation of Kinsella's pen.

One Fond Embrace was first published in 1981 simultaneously by the Deerfield Press of Massachusetts and Peter Fallon's Gallery Press of Dublin, in a limited edition of 300 copies. The edition was illustrated by two woodcuts by Timothy Engelland and all copies were signed by the author. Written in 57 tercets divided into four sections, this is a shorter poem than the one which appeared seven years later under the imprint of Peppercanister Press containing 109 tercets. *One Fond Embrace* marks the beginning of Kinsella's connection with John Deane's Dedalus Press. The deluxe editions initiated by Peppercanister's association with Dolmen Press and produced from 1974 to 1987 do not form part of the arrangement with Dedalus. From 1988 to the present the Peppercanister poems appear simply in library and trade editions. There is a significant difference in the content of both editions. Kinsella's criticism of the business practices of multinational companies and their poor environmental records, underpinned by the blind eye that is turned by politicians eager for renewed employment in their constituencies, is expressed in stanzas which do not appear in subsequent versions of the poem. Through the cloacal image of being 'took sudden' the poet refers directly to the 1979 Whiddy disaster in which an oil tanker called the Betelgeuse exploded while discharging oil at the Whiddy Island terminal in Bantry Bay County Cork:

> Our bays and river valleys
> receptacles for our own
> and other's discharges;
>
> smooth film on our sea rocks;
> the sun turned red over Avoca
> Dungarvan Harbour charmingly set off –
>
> by a pall of chemical manures;
> tankers, took sudden,
> dumping on Bantry.[5]

One Fond Embrace provides an interesting example of how successive publication influences Kinsella's writing. The Gallery edition of the poem can be seen either as a draft, or a version of the Peppercanister edition which has substantial additions and revisions. When the poem was republished in Kinsella's *Collected Poems* by Oxford in 1996, the poem had once again been extensively revised, and reduced to 91 tercets.

The poem opens with the speaker rousing from a meditation with irritation and impatience: 'Enough / is enough' (P 7, C 283). The speaker's introspection is figured somatically as his 'knuckled' eyes 'answered with speckles and images' (P 7, C 283), and 'Time spurted in the narrows' of his wrists (P 7). Kinsella's eye moves from the close focus on 'this hearth and home / echoing with the ghosts // of prides and joys', to the wider frame of Dublin city, depicted with an affectionate unease:

> With a scruffy Nineteenth Century
> history of half-finished
> colonials and upstarts. Still with us.
>
> With a half charm,
> half gracious, spacious,
> and a miscellaneous vigour.
>
> (P 7, C 283 var.)

But within tercets, the affection gives way to sarcasm as Kinsella rails against the 'Invisible speculators, urinal architects, / and the Corporation hand in hand / in potent compliant dance' (P 8, C 284 var.). Kinsella levels criticism at the city planning in Dublin in the 1970s and 1980s which involved the construction of public housing without adequate facilities for the inhabitants, and caused the conflict between history and commerce over the proposed Civic Offices at Wood Quay. Also proposed was the demolition of Kinsella's Percy Place neighbourhood, against which the poet and Eleanor Kinsella protested.[6] The social planning which divided the inner-city communities and transplanted them to suburban tower blocks such as those in Ballymun (now scheduled for demolition) where sufficient local amenities were not provided, is linked, in Kinsella's lines, with the predilection for new developments to adopt Anglicised names rather than keep the older Irish place names:

> Southward from Fatima Mansions
> into the foothills
> to where the transplanted can trudge
>
> from Cherryfield Heights via Woodbine Crescent
> through Bridget's Terrace and Kennedy's Villas
> by Árd na Gréine and Cúl na Gaoithe
>
> to Shangri-La for a bottle of milk;
> Northward past our twinned experimental
> concrete piss-towers for the underprivileged;
>
> (P 9, C 284 var.)

In his revisions for the *Collected Poems* Kinsella excises most of these three stanzas to produce a tighter and more focused stanza formed from the first line quoted above and the last two lines. From Ballymun the poet turns to the banks of the Liffey. What follows is a criticism of Dublin Corporation's plan to build their Civic Offices on the site of an ancient Viking settlement, rich in archeological remains.[7] Kinsella was an active member of the 'Friends of Medieval Dublin' who attempted to get the site preserved. The attempt was unsuccessful, and by 1980 the building had begun. Kinsella conveys the frustration and anger of many, including the 20,000 who marched on Saturday 23 September 1978 from the Mansion House to Wood Quay in protest against the development, towards the 'city fathers' who are ready to pave over the 'Viking ghosts' of Dublin's origins,[8]

> laying flat an enduring monument to themselves,
> an office car park sunk deep in history.
>
> (P 9, C 285)

Kinsella closes with a curse reminiscent of early Irish maledictory poems: 'May their sewers blast under them!' (P 9, C 285).[9] But the poet includes himself in the apportioned blame. In lines which recognise the chance his generation had to forge a modern Irish society out of the dreams of the past and the realities of the present, Kinsella condemns an opportunity squandered: 'And we were the generation / of positive disgrace' (P 9, C 285).

The invective pauses for a moment as the poet echoes the medieval monastic glosses, meditations on the beauty of nature and the order of the world: 'Bright gulls, gracefully idling / in the blue and wholesome heights / above our aerials' (P 9, C 285). Into this idyllic vision is introduced the possibility of accepting human nature as is: 'I embrace / your grasping manners, your natural behaviour' (P 10, C 285). But this embrace lasts only 'an instant' as each guest of the impossible last supper is invited in: 'Here's a hug while the mood is on me. / Take your places around my table // one last time together' (P 10, C 286). Disparagement, depreciation and detraction are on the menu as the poet addresses each of his guests with an accusation which relates to past or present injustices. The guests are drawn from a wide variety of backgrounds in Irish society. Divided roughly into groups (or perhaps seated around the 'additional table or two' (P 11, C 286)) they are friends and family, figures from the worlds of art and criticism, journalism and politics, the quick and the dead.[10] The hurt of a betrayed friendship is conveyed in the characterisation of 'You, so hesitant, so soon presumptuous, / urgent and confiding, breathing close / about nothing' (P 11, C 286). The terrible waste of talent and opportunity intimated in the earlier poems *A Selected Life*, *Vertical Man*, and *Out of Ireland*, is stated bluntly here as Seán Ó Riada is remembered as:

You that with an ear
for the cold fathoms of the self
whistled up the Song of our own Earth,

turned a spirit off the rocks
into a fire in the gut
and, in the final phase,

losing our close attention,
became an entertainer
among the lesser gentry.

(P 12, C 288 var.)

The third stanza gains a slightly harsher edge in the lines revised for the
Collected Poems where 'losing our close attention' becomes 'happy with
our half attention' (C 288). A certain regret that the importance of
Ó Riada's legacy is not better remembered by those who continue the
tradition of Irish music is evident in Kinsella's characterisation of a key
member of the Chieftains:[11]

And you, handling the market direct,
uproarious, tangled in your pipes,
but serious behind the fun,

an artist to your elbow tips.
Forgotten your past master,
your training like an animal.

(P 13, C 289 var.)

Even journalism and critical misreading comes in for opprobrium as
Elgy Gillespie's reference to the possible influence of Alexander Pope on
Kinsella's *A Butcher's Dozen* is refuted. In her 1981 *Irish Times* inter-
view Gillespie explores what Kinsella means when he says (speaking of
'Wormwood' and 'Nightwalker') '"I took a dive, rather than a detour.
But in retrospect there is an impulse to unify everything." Everything,
including "Butcher's Dozen", an honest impulse, but a much lesser piece
of doggerel in literary terms as the Popean "Dunciad" it was modelled
upon?' asks Gillespie.[12] Kinsella's criticism takes a distinctly personal
turn. He addresses the writer as

You with the forthright frock
the fixed ideas
and the cast in your point of view,

that saw a lame Dunciad
in a haunted prowl through Christforsaken Derry
– no Pope here;

(P 13, cf. C 289)

This weak and inappropriate criticism against the kind of misrepresen-
tation that would appear to be not unusual in reportage is deleted from
the *Collected Poems*. Far more formidable adversaries are found in the
figures of C. J. Haughey and Conor Cruise O'Brien.

Kinsella's reference to Haughey as 'Our swift-mounted, tight-hammed /
hot tip: a ham-fisted / butterfingers in the saddle' (P 15, C 290 var.)
recalls his earlier characterisation of the politician in 'Nightwalker' in
which he was 'The Sonhusband / Coming in his power, [. . .] mounting to
glory / on his big white harse!' (C 80). In the light of recent revelations,
the description of 'Leeches clustered at his orifice' gains greater resonance
(P 15, cf. C 290). Conor Cruise O'Brien, in the guise of 'Pontifex
Minimus' (an ironic reversal of *Pontifex Maximus*),[13] is taken to task for
his attitude to Ireland's history:

> Tribal antagonisms merely;
> the intelligentsia not involved:
>
> (P 16, cf C 290)

The ten tercets concerned with O'Brien are reduced to three in the
Collected Poems and they sum up more clearly Kinsella's concerns:

> And you, our activist commentator,
> descending on London and the serious papers
> with a bundle of dirty linen
>
> ironed across your arm,
> your briefcase full of applied literature
> – baulked in Redmondite bafflement at human behaviour,[14]
>
> but complaining so melodiously
> we could forgive you
> almost anything.
>
> (P 15–16 var., C 290)

What is in dispute here is an analysis of the relationship between Britain
and the Republic of Ireland as it concerns Northern Ireland. Terence
Brown, in his *Ireland: A Social and Cultural History*, explains O'Brien's
central thesis as stated most clearly in his book *States of Ireland*:[15]
'Ireland's ideological ambivalence on the issue of partition was altogether
too dangerous a self-indulgence for the citizens of the Republic in a
period when a full-scale Irish war threatened.'[16] It is not just O'Brien's
political views that Kinsella objects to, but also the way in which these
views were accepted by the British reading public as an explanation of
violence in Northern Ireland as a self-contained tribal conflict. In an
interview with Philip Fried in 1986, Kinsella underlines the importance
of information and communication for a possible resolution of the

conflict in Northern Ireland: 'The use of modern devices, of advertising and publicizing, to make the detail of the situation unmistakable, so that it would be impossible for the problem to be understood at the current partial level.' Kinsella names O'Brien as someone with the necessary historical sense, but provides this caution: 'It could be Conor Cruise O'Brien, for instance – but he provides a digestible version of the problem, which does not require that his British audience should take any responsible part in the cure.'[17] A review from *The Times* quoted in a reprint of *States of Ireland* published by Granada in 1979 gives ground to Kinsella's concern: 'Here in public is a "southern" Irishman of unquestionable patriotism and high intelligence examining his own tribal myths, and finding them not only wanting but highly dangerous.'

With tones of brutal irony the poet suggests a 'modest proposal' (P 17, C 291) which can be understood as a rebuttal to O'Brien's fears for certain civil war with the removal of British presence in Northern Ireland: 'It can be predicted, with a probability amounting almost to certainty, that British disengagement would be followed by civil war in Ireland.'[18] Kinsella proposes a solution to the crisis in Northern Ireland which parodies the treaty of 1921, reworking Swift's suggestion for a mutually beneficial relationship between England and Ireland in *A Modest Proposal*:

> A channel a mile in width
>
> to be dug along the Border;
> link with the loose material
> Fair Head and the Mull of Kintyre;
>
> at the noon Angelus on St. Patrick's Day
> exchange governments.
>
> (P 17, cf. C 291)

His declaration that 'everything West of the Shannon [. . .] to be declared fair game' (P 17, C 291) recalls Cromwell's dictum that any 'of the dispossessed found east of the Shannon after 1 May 1654 might be killed by anyone who chose'.[19] Set against this vision of violence and division is the voice of the Christ figure absent from the last supper of *One Fond Embrace*, as Kinsella sends an ironic invocation to 'our holy distracted Mother' who watches over both sides of the divide: 'And he said, / Have love one to another / as I have loved the lot of you' (P 18, C 291). The poem draws to a close with the impatient exclamation 'Enough', which mirrors the similar exclamation at its beginning (P 19, C 292). Kinsella's reference to Diderot's 'Encyclopaedia' returns us to *A Technical Supplement* and the idea of an additional commentary on the main body of work. It is perhaps in this light that we can best read *One Fond Embrace*. Taken on its own merits, this poem does not rank with Kinsella's strongest. Though rooted in particulars, its characterisations operate on the level of generalisations, expressing criticisms of Irish society and politics through an intemperate and ill-considered persona, as the poet himself acknowledges: 'That there is more spleen / than good sense in all of this, I admit' (P 19, C 292).

As *A Technical Supplement* makes clear, Kinsella's poetic project is similar in its extensiveness and openness to Diderot's project to map an understanding of human knowledge. The quotation from section 15 of the earlier poem 'The pen writhed' (P [30], C 194; P 19, C 292) underlines the link between these volumes, as does the speaker's resolve, '– and back to the Encyclopaedia I go' (P 19, C 292), indicating Kinsella's return to the larger project at hand: the exploration of those 'personal places' from which an understanding of self and society comes. Kinsella closes with the image of his pen 'dipped again / in its organic pot' (P 19, C 292). The image of ink as both the medium and the material of poetry links with what Kinsella describes as the 'organically related meanings' of his poetry that become evident as they combine in the larger whole that includes all the Peppercanister Poems.[20]

Personal Places

Both *Personal Places* and *Poems from Centre City* focus on Dublin as the locus for the poet's increasingly cold-eyed judgment on himself and his society. The cultural, familial, and economic politics explored in *One Fond Embrace* are developed with a clearer focus in Peppercanisters 14 and 15.[21] Kinsella describes *Personal Places* as 'a "station" of Dublin data', and suggests in his drafts 'Stations of Dissatisfaction' as a possible title for the volume.[22] Here Kinsella alludes to the Stations of the Cross which mark out the successive stages of Christ's journey to Calvary. The themes of endurance and perseverance paticular to the Stations are evident in *Personal Places*, but the transformation and redemption implicit in the Passion are not to be found here.

Writing in *New Poems 1973* of his journey to retrace the route of *The Táin*, Kinsella connects the intellectual journey through which understanding is achieved with a physical movement or pilgrimage which provides a comprehension of place. The physical journey of 'The Route of the Táin' is conceived as 'the whole tedious enabling ritual' which makes possible a kind of enlightenment: 'something reduced shivering suddenly / into meaning along new boundaries' (C 125). The kind of understanding which is intrinsically linked to a sense of place is recalled again in the lines with which Kinsella opens his *Collected Poems* version of *Personal Places*:

> There are established personal places
> that receive our lives' heat
> and adapt in their mass, like stone.
>
> These absorb in their changes
> the radiance of change in us,
> and give it back
>
> to the darkness of our understanding,
> directionless
> into the returning cold.
>
> (P 25 var., C 293)

In the Peppercanister edition this poem prefaces the third section of the volume, and speaks of the more general 'time's heat' rather than 'lives' heat' (P 25). By prefacing the entire sequence with this poem Kinsella makes clear the interrelationship between place and person through which identity is formed, an interrelationship which is explored in a detailed manner through the individual poems. Kinsella makes considerable changes to *Personal Places* in his revisions for the *Collected Poems*. The tripartite division of the Peppercanister edition becomes a single sequence of poems which both rearranges the order of the poems, and omits or combines several. The thirteen poems of the Peppercanister edition become nine in the Oxford collection.

The Peppercanister *Personal Places* opens with an invocation to a trinity of powers which combines force, spirit and sense. The entreaty concerns a point of passage which can be construed in linguistic and corporeal terms, echoing the 'nutrient' and 'vertical smile' of the *Her Vertical Smile* (P 24, C 260): 'deign, o crushed lips, [. . .] // to separate beneath this kiss' (P 11, C 295–6 var.). Kinsella's revisions change 'this kiss' to 'his kiss', distancing the speaker from the proposed kiss, and connecting it instead with the 'Father' addressed in the first line (C 296). The lips of this poem are depicted on the cover of the Peppercanister edition in a stylised line drawing. They are also the lips of the poet's mother who is remembered in 'Dura Mater':

> Stiff necked, she put up her pursed mouth
> at her grown young – fish or flesh or whatever
> idea she had of it in her pinched eyes.

(P 12, C 300 var.)

The 'pinched eyes' of the Peppercanister become the somewhat harsher 'ill temper' in the *Collected Poems* (C 300). The ambivalent relation between mother and son is captured in the title which, as Donatella Badin points out, contains a 'semantic ambiguity (dura mater is the outer membrane enveloping the brain but also the Latin equivalent of hard mother)'.[23] But this is a poem of resolution rather than resentment, and the speaker returns the 'withheld kiss' onto the 'stone forehead' of the deceased who is remembered in characteristic pose, at home:

> She came along the passage in her slippers
> with a fuzz of navy hair and her long nails
> held away, wet out of the washing water.

(P 12, C 300 var.)

The subsequent two poems 'After the Service' and 'From my Journal' become part of 'Dura Mater' in the *Collected Poems*. Both are concerned with the poet's brother, the composer John Kinsella: 'The air was filled with music' (P 13, C 301). 'After the Service' remembers scenes from the funeral of the poet's mother. While the tone is measured and controlled, there is a hint also of censure: '[. . .] quick inviting hand gestures / repeated without meaning / and a motivous urging in the uplifted voice' which carries over to the next poem (P 13, C 301 var.). 'From My Journal' recalls a meeting years later between the poet and his brother in 'a crowded place, low ceilinged and obscure' (P 14, C 301). In this anonymous location, over a 'dish of eggs' which alludes to the brothers' common origin, an issue concerning inheritance needs to be broached: 'I have come to speak with him, after so long, / because I have a question' (P 14, C 301).[24] The polite exchange between the two men belies the lack of trust which has loosened those bonds of blood and family celebrated in earlier poems, and the assurances proffered ring hollow:

> I put the question. Yes. Why, certainly.

> Yes, of course. I am sad that you should ask.
> There should be something almost certainly
> next week in the post, or the week after.
> I'll see to that. And we must keep in touch.

(P 14, C 301 var.)

The three poems of section one detail the ending of familial relations, whether through death or distrust. In his notes, Kinsella joins 'Dura Mater' and 'From my Journal' together in the context of Stations of the Cross mentioned above: 'These poems, in this order, make one "station".'[25] Section two is also concerned with endings, but these are closures of a more public kind. The first, 'Apostle of Hope', brings the poet back to a city much like the Derry of *Butcher's Dozen* where hatred and the threat of violence haunt the streets:

> the squad of baby-looking troops
> with deadly undernourished faces
> kneeling and posing with their guns
> and waltzing across the cracked cement,
> our polite faces packed with hate.
>
> (P 17, C 293 var.)

The 'half-blind watch tower' (P 17, C 293) half-echoes Kinsella's allusion to Joyce in 'Nightwalker': 'Watcher in the tower / Be with me now. Turn your milky spectacles / On the sea, unblinking' (C 80). The social criticism integral to the earlier poem is also present in 'Apostle of Hope' in which the aspirations of local enterprise (the 'business breakfast' and 'worried flashy expedients') are contradicted by the prevailing situation and the 'silence of the stunned' (P 17, C 293). The condition of sacrifice and betrayal alluded to in *One Fond Embrace* is figured here in specifically visual terms as the image of the crucified Christ merges with Leonardo da Vinci's drawing of the right proportions of man from *De Architectura de Vitruve*:

> Man the Measure cruciforked
> upon His wheel, jacked up erect
> and splayed like a target against the grey,
> smooth as an ad.
>
> (P 17, C 294 var.)

The bleak 'Godforsaken' remembers Christ's anguish in Gethsemane (Mark 14: 32); and the following, repeated, 'Forgive. Forgive' (P 17, C 294) recalls his final absolution, 'forgive them; for they know not what they do' (Luke 23: 34). Through forgiveness and understanding the poet seeks to make sense of the violence and prejudice of Northern Ireland. The limitations of the human, whether as religious Christ-figure or humanist Renaissance man, are set against a larger 'Impulse' or 'Process' which 'labours into life' (P 17, C 294). By capitalising these and other nouns like 'Impulse' and 'Good', ('Scrutiny' and 'Waste' in the *Collected Poems*), Kinsella gives to this larger process of understanding a power which is beyond that of the individual:

> The Impulse, ineradicable,
> labours into life:
>   scrutiny;
> manipulation toward some kind
> of understanding; toward the Good.
>
> (P 17, C 294 var.)

The hate which packs the faces of the visitors in the first stanza is diminished and disempowered when placed within the greater history of betrayal, violence and forgiveness evoked through the Passion imagery of the penultimate stanza and the Biblical language of the final one:

> The Process as it hath revealed
> its higher waste . . .
>   Let our hate reach that.
>
> (P 17, C 294 var.)

Conflict of another kind occupies the second poem, 'Night Conference, Wood Quay: 6 June 1979'. Kinsella sketches a scene of resistence and compromise as the activists protesting against the development of the Wood Quay archeological site report back on negotiations with Dublin Corporation: '". . . We have a truce. They have made every mistake' (P 18, C 302). The achievement of their protest is imaged by 'A high crane hung in the dark, its swift hook locked / – and its steel spider-brain – by our mental force' (P 18, C 302 var.). The theme of betrayal announced in the first part of *Personal Places* is continued here as the truce celebrated by the protesters (the inclusive 'People') is threatened by the the new money, those 'Parvenus / with pickaxes' (reminiscent of 'invisible speculators' of *One Fond Embrace* (P 8, C 284) and the Corporation officials, 'white-cuffed marauders', who wait 'outside the circle of light' with 'Visages of rapine' (P 18, C 302 var.).

The next two poems, 'Departure' and 'Rituals of Departure' concern the Kinsella family's move from Crab Orchard, Illinois, to Wynecote, Pennsylvania in 1970. These poems provide a symmetry to Kinsella's earlier poem from *Nightwalker and Other Poems*, 'Ritual of Departure', which marks the family's move from Ireland to the United States in 1965. The richer diction of the earlier poem – 'A man at the moment of departure, turning / To leave, treasures some stick of furniture / With slowly blazing eyes, or the very door / Broodingly with his hand as it falls shut' (C 86) – contrasts with the calmly descriptive tone of 'Departure':

> We came out with the last suitcase strapped
> and nothing left to say
> onto the driveway under the giant red oaks.
>
> (P 19, C 296 var.)

The three short tercets provide a distilled image of the moment of departure, but the moment of leavetaking, experienced so keenly by the speaker of the 1968 poem ('The roots tear softly' (C 86)), is witnessed here at one remove:

> the children seen to and strapped in,
> speechless and taking us by surprise
> with their tears.
>
> (P 19, C 296 var.)

'Rituals of Departure' provides a meditation on leavetaking in the company of 'Melancholy, retiring / with her fingers to her lips' (P 20, C 296 var.). The *Collected Poems* version, 'Melancholy, retiring with her finger to our lips' (C 296) is more suggestive of the restrained emotion implicit in departure, the 'misery' assuaged by 'love':

> and the detailed care you have had here,
> and the rituals of departure,
> their ashes dying along our path.
>
> (P 20, C 296 var.)

The poem which faces 'Rituals of Departure' is an untitled meditation (like the opening poem of the volume) which returns to the primordial persona seen in earlier Peppercanisters and to the figure of the bat or bird which represents the speaker's shadow or unconscious. This poem becomes part of 'Seven' in the *Collected Poems*. The exhortation, 'Hurry darling, / myriads in me demand it' (P 21, C 294) echoes the forthright voice in *The Messenger*: 'Quick! / I am all egg!' (P 15, C 224 var.) and is suggestive of new beginnings. Through the airborne voice that 'flapped out haphazard / across a glowing glade' Kinsella draws our focus back from the individual event of departure and sets it within a larger context which concerns the development of the self, emphasised by the poet's use of the first person (P 21, C 294). The flapping figure is close to the 'bat-black, heron-slow' shadow of 'Song of the Night' (P 19, C 216); and as it settles 'on a nodding / solitary stem' (P 21, C 294) it recalls the lover / predator couple of that volume in the poems '1975' and '1975 (*an alternative*)' (P 8–9, C 207). 'Seven', the last poem of the second section of the Peppercanister edition develops the conjunction between lover and predator as a scene of lovemaking is shadowed on either side by animal or otherworldly movement:

> Our thoughts touched in waking.
> Breath stopped, blood held in a half beat
> restless in our loving dispute
> in the fragrance of arm and throat.
>
> (P 22, C 295 var.)

The 'Night foxes' of 'Songs of the Psyche' (P 29, C 237) appear again in the company of their namesake flower, the foxglove: 'A snapping fox shifted from doubt to doubt' (P 22, C 294). The 'carrion steel eyes' (P 22, C 295 var.) with which Kinsella's bird of prey surveys the midnight scene signals an appetite for destruction which countermands the generative appetite depicted in the daybreak scene as 'The bedroom curtain inhaled / and filled with light' (P 22, C 295). The title of the poem, 'Seven', is repeated in the penultimate stanza which describes the shadow distinctive to Kinsella's poetry advancing towards the cars which will take the family 'away from the West' (P 19, C 296). Five of the seven titled poems which precede 'Seven' each describes an ending that requires the speaker to resolve and forgive. Recollecting the image of Christ evoked in *One Fond Embrace*, we can understand the title in terms of the seven 'words' of the crucifixion which concern forgiveness, consolation, love and desolation, words which return us to Kinsella's exhortation in the 'Apostle of Hope': 'Forgive. Forgive' (P 17, C 294).[26]

The third part of *Personal Places* explores notions of inheritance and change in the context of the artistic act. 'Brothers in the Craft' describes a scene of interchange between established and aspiring writers:

> In the creative generations there is often
> a conspiracy of the mature and the brilliant young,
> a taking in hand, in hopes of a handing on.
>
> (P 26, C 297 var.)

With great clarity Kinsella explores the interdependence between generations in the development not only of a tradition, but also of an individual's work. These exchanges 'settle in the medium in their turn',

> a part of the essential colour of the work
> drawn from the early accidental particulars.
>
> (P 26, C 297 var.)

Kinsella turns to memories of his own apprenticeship and the lines of inheritance which stretch beyond the figure of Austin Clarke to include W. B. Yeats and Thomas Mann. In an interview with Dennis O'Driscoll in 1989 Kinsella explained the movement of influence and appropriation in Irish writing of the 1950s:

> Yeats was a major poet from the beginning. [. . .] Yeats's shadow certainly fell very heavily on Austin Clarke and his generation. But by the time we were growing up, in the nineteen-fifties, Yeats was a poet of the past, no more present, or 'threatening', than Joyce or anyone else.[27]

Yet in 'Brothers in the Craft' Yeats does cut a threatening figure: 'Out in the dark, on a tree branch near the Bridge, / the animus of Yeats perched

(P 26, C 297). Kinsella's tree branch connects with Clarke's home at the Bridge in Templeogue, and with the older poet's image of the oak-tree to describe the effect of Yeats's stature on younger writers:

> So far as the younger generation of poets are concerned, here in Ireland, Yeats was rather like an enormous oak-tree which, of course, kept us in the shade, and did exclude a great number of the rays of, say, the friendly sun; and of course we always hoped that in the end we would reach the sun, but the shadow of that great oak-tree is still there.'[28]

As an animus, Yeats belongs to the darkness or shadow of the poet's unconscious psyche and acts as a guide or necessary link to 'creative possibilities and instruments of individuation'.[29] Another important precurser is Thomas Mann, represented here by one of his fictions, Tonio Kröger. Yeats and Mann are set apart through geographical distinctions, the latter allied with the place of Kinsella's youth: 'Another part of the City / Tonio Kröger, maladorous, prowled Inchicore' (P 26, C 297 var.). By naming Tonio Kröger, Kinsella introduces the theme of division in a specifically personal context. Mann's story describes a young writer who is divided between the need for a stable and secure environment, and the excitement of the literary bohemian life. Kröger finds himself alienated from experience; his 'critical, sceptical, knowing stance conflicts with his craving for ordinary, unproblematic living'.[30] The poet's use of the adjective 'malodorous' refuses any reading which sees Kinsella placing himself in an elevated literary tradition. Instead, he is depicted as the evil-smelling outsider who haunts the shadows with the intent of a 'Nightwalker'.

The leavetakings of the Peppercanister *Personal Places* are expanded in the Oxford editions, *From Centre City* and *Collected Poems*, to include a poem in memory of Valentin Iremonger, the Irish poet and diplomat who died in 1988. 'In Memory' recalls Iremonger as a poet who, like Kinsella until the 1960s, combined art and business:

> Authoritative, from the Department.
> Published recently, and discussed.
> Managing both careers.
>
> (C 298)

Through the counterpoint of youth and old age Kinsella traces the development of those who 'were gathered at your [Iremonger's] feet' (C 298). The portrait of Iremonger drawn in the first section of the poem moves, in the second, to an account of the 'character of our generation' with the expected combination of fulfilment and failure of 'early promise' (C 298). Iremonger's funeral provides the poet with a vantage point from which to view the changes that time has wrought. There is an opportunity to re-evaluate old friends: '– one, quiet-spoken and confiding, / not to be trusted again; / one nursing an old dispute / and able behind the scenes' (C 299); and the surprised recognition that he, the speaker, has also, imperceptibly, grown old. In a wonderful image that captures the uniform effects of time, the speaker notes that

> When I turned around to go back
> it was a while before I discovered
> our people among the others
> – everybody everywhere with white hair.

(C 299)

The final poem of both the Peppercanister and Oxford editions of *Personal Places*, 'At the Western Ocean's Edge', traces a line of influence in Irish literature through the image of the hero as liberator and warrior. This hero is Cúchulainn: not the brutal and rough-edged figure of Kinsella's *The Táin*, but the tragic persona vital to Yeats's mature writing:

> Yeats discovered him through Lady Gregory
> but grew to know him well in his own right
> – the final crisis, sweating mental strife,
> renewal in reverse, the revelation –
> and found him helpful as a second shadow
> in his own sour duel with the middle classes.

(P 27, C 302 var.)

Through a recollection of Yeats's poem 'Cuchulain's Fight with the Sea' and his play *On Baile's Strand* in which Cúchulainn does battle with the sea until the waves master him, Kinsella connects the mythical hero with the eighteenth-century poet, Aogán Ó Rathaille, who is remembered through his poem 'Is Fada Liom Oíche Fhírfhluich' or 'The Drenching Night Drags On' in which he also rages against the waves:

> A thonnsa thíos is airde géim go hard,
> meabhair mo chinnse cloíte ód bhéiceach tá;
> cabhair dá dtíodh arís ar Éirinn bhán,
> do ghlam nach binn do dhingfinn féin id bhráid.

> You wave down there, lifting your loudest roar,
> the wits in my head are worsted by your wails.
> If help ever came to lovely Ireland again
> I'd wedge your ugly howling down your throat![31]

Kinsella's earlier commemoration of Ó Rathaille in 'The Poet Egan O'Rahilly, Homesick in Old Age' describes the elder poet at a moment of dissolution, which also draws on 'Is Fada Liom Oíche Fhírfhluich': 'The salt abyss poured through him, more raw / With every laboured, stony crash of the waves: / His teeth bared at their voices, that incessant dying' (C 73). By placing Ó Rathaille at the western ocean's edge Kinsella emphasises the poet's position on the cusp of the irrevocable shift from Irish to English and the consequent dissolution of the old bardic traditions:

> Aogán Ó Rathaille defined his part
> at the Western ocean's edge. A vagrant, turning
> the gale wailing inland off the water
> into a voice responding in his head,
> and answering the waves on their own terms
> – energy of chaos and a shaping
>
> counter-energy in throes of balance;
>
> (P 27, C 303 var.)

Kinsella also draws an implicit comparison between Ó Rathaille and the poet Amairgin depicted in *One*. When the Sons of Míl try to land in Ireland (for the second time) the sea is roused into a storm by the druids of the Tuatha Dé Danann, but is calmed by Amairgin through the power of his poetry.[32] Ó Rathaille, in Kinsella's rendition, no longer has access to such power:

> A wasted figure. Any substance left
> borne on waves of threat inside the mind.
>
> (P 27, C 303 var.)

Kinsella effects a symmetry between Amairgin, which he names as the first poet of Ireland,[33] and Ó Rathaille as the last of the ancient *filí*, through a reversal of the double landing described in the Lebor Gabála Érenn. In the original story the Sons of Míl are obliged to leave Ireland for three days, travelling a distance of nine waves from the island. This is the distance of the 'ninth shadow' beyond which Ó Rathaille has 'set his face [. . .] into dead calm' and beyond which, as we know from *One*, lies the land of the dead (P 27, C 303).

Poems From Centre City

The situations of conflict and anxiety which gave rise to *One Fond Embrace* are brought closer to resolution in *Personal Places*. This process of stocktaking continues in *Poems from Centre City*, focusing more directly on Kinsella's Dublin of the 1970s and 1980s. Once again

Kinsella returns to the contentious issues raised in *One Fond Embrace*. Kinsella's attention to the particulars of a given situation give these poems a rootedness in specific experience which can, occasionally, become exclusive. Kinsella's comments on Austin Clarke's poetry ring, at times, equally true also of his own:

> In its narrowness of reference, in fact, much of his work raises the whole question of legitimate obscurity in poetry. Some poems are virtually private, or so particular in their comments that it would be helpful to have the relevant newspapers handy.[34]

The relevant newspapers would, indeed, be handy for a reading of poems like 'Administrator' and 'Social Work'. Certainly an understanding of local politics, and details of Kinsella's life, allow for easier access to the poems. Donatella Badin emphasises this point, arguing that 'the reader, however, risks remaining in the dark if he is not given some vital facts about the biographical background [to Kinsella's poetry]'.[35] It is useful, as she points out, to know that O'Keeffe's stable at 47 Percy Lane became Kinsella's workplace, and also the shop where he and Eleanor Kinsella sold the Peppercanister editions, along with various artifacts including the collection of aboriginal art mentioned in 'Household Spirits'. But are these alone the 'essential facts [. . .] on whose basis the poem's statement communicates'?[36] As with Beckett on Proust, Kinsella's analysis of Clarke contains an understanding of poetry which illuminates his own:

> The poems accumulate, particularly the later ones. They illuminate each other and establish relationships among themselves so that a microcosm of the human scene is formed, small in scope but complete. Raising the question of obscurity, these poems, by their authority and integrity, lay the question to rest.[37]

Kinsella's *Poems from Centre City* forms such a microcosm. Each of the poems radiates from the centre city location of Kinsella's home in Percy Place, Dublin. The ten poems of the Peppercanister edition are joined in the Oxford *Collected Poems* by an eleventh poem, 'Departure Platforms', which was first written as part of drafts for *Song of the Psyche*.[38] As with *Personal Places* Kinsella has changed the order of the poems in the Peppercanister and Oxford editions. The Peppercanister opens with a backward glance at a world fast fading in 'The Stable', while the Oxford edition opens with a moment of contemporary conflict based on the incidents at Wood Quay in 'A Portrait of the Artist'. Both editions, however, close with the memory of W. H. Auden, the place from which Kinsella's poetry began.

As with *Personal Places*, the language of *Poems from Centre City* is descriptive and evenly paced. Kinsella's observational eye takes note of the details of its surrounds and of the mundane rituals through which life is measured. In 'The Stable' Kinsella evokes the passage of time and the erosion of a way of life through an image of ivy covering the wall of O'Keeffe's stable:

> The creeper opposite, crept at last
> over the date and initials painted
> big and uneasy on the stone.
>
> where he kept the dray, half stacked with sacks.
>
> (P 9, C 307 var.)

The stable, once home to a workhorse, becomes the workplace of the poet. O'Keeffe's departure marks the end of a city, familiar to Kinsella's childhood, in which horses were an integral part of commerce. The transformation of the stable also marks the change of occupation in the Kinsella family from the traditional employment in Guinness's Brewery to employment in government, education and the arts effected by Kinsella and his brother. This shift is not restricted to Kinsella's circumstance, but is indicative of the remarkable changes in Irish society between these generations. A sense of handing on from one generation to the next is subtly conveyed in the bargaining scene:

> I said Three Pounds, and he made it Five.
> We shook hands, and I wrote it down.
> The cash to be left on the window sill.
>
> (P 10, C 308 var.)

Yet there is a sense of loss conveyed by the line describing how O'Keeffe's wife 'waited back in the stable, crying' (P 9, C 308); and also a sense of foreboding: 'He was gone a week when the roughs were in' (P 10, C 308 var.).

The unsettling tone with which 'The Stable' closes is continued in 'The Stranger' which depicts that familiar figure of Kinsella's poetry, the shadow or shade. Described initially in straightforward terms as 'a clerk from somewhere in the area', the stranger gradually circles closer to the speaker until he is 'arab up close' (P 11, C 313). The orientalist sense (in Edward Said's understanding) of the word 'arab' underlines the stranger's position as other to the poet. But the initial description of the stranger as a clerk recalls Kinsella's own early days in the Civil Service. The stranger is conceived as both other to, and the double of, the speaker of the poem. He is a sign of upheaval and turmoil:

> In another time I might have put it down
> to evil luck or early death – the Stranger
> close upon our heels – and taken care.
>
> (P 11, C 313)

The trouble signalled by the stranger is Bloody Sunday, and the scene which Kinsella describes is the poet's search for 'a structure for my mess of angers' (P 12, C 313). The structure found is the *aisling* form of Irish poetry in which a vision of Ireland appears to the poet: 'the poet sinks to the earth and hides his face // in harrowed sleep. A kindly beauty approaches, / unworldly, but familiar – one of us – / comforts his misery, and turns his thoughts // toward some theatrical hope' (P 12, C 313 var.). Kinsella is writing here of the circumstances surrounding his composition of the first Peppercanister poem, *Butcher's Dozen*: the 'house was full of neighbours / met in upset' and the 'photographs and cuttings pinned in fury / around the wall' (P 11, C 312–13). The importance of form for the adequate expression of content is emphasised by Kinsella, who describes the *aisling* as 'A simple form, // adjusted easily to the situation, / open to local application; weakened / by repetition; ridiculed and renewed // at last in parody' (P 12, C 313–14 var.). Echoing his comments in *Fifteen Dead*, which explain his approach to *Butcher's Dozen*, 'One changed one's standards, chose the doggerel route, and charged. . .',[39] Kinsella describes how 'My pen quickened / in a pulse of doggerel ease' (P 12, C 314). The stranger, whose presence was a portent of the trouble which gave rise to *Butcher's Dozen*, stands now in judgment of the poet's attempts to give voice to the anger to which Bloody Sunday gave rise. As the poet writes, he notices the stranger:

> underneath the Moon, across the road,
> overacting, bowing with respect;
> resuming his night patrol along the terrace.
>
> (P 12, C 314 var.)

But of course, the stranger heralds not only the trouble which was to ignite over twenty years of bloodshed in Northern Ireland, but also the trouble which came to Kinsella as a result of *Butcher's Dozen*, and his increasing isolation from British markets estranged from his political views.[40]

As 'The Stranger' closes with a vision of the poet interrupted at work, 'my fingers stopped above the paper' (P 12, C 314), 'Household Spirits' opens with the poet also pausing in his work, meditating on nature in the fashion of the medieval Irish scribes. The location is the old stable in Percy Lane, where the poet now writes. Below is the shop in which the aboriginal carvings from Australia sit for sale. Through an image of eating Kinsella brings the pastoral vision of the thrush, 'pecking up / at a little black bunch of berries', into conjunction with a darker understanding of appetite:

> With the red juice on his mouth
> he is consulting
> the cannibal committee downstairs,
>
> (P 13, C 308)

Kinsella's description of the carvings as 'mongrel images shaped in wood / with a fluency as though it were dung: / collect of innocent evils –' connect them with the image of the síle-na-gig in *Out of Ireland* and the threatening images of pre-Christian deities of *One* (P 13, C 309 var.). The idea of 'innocent evils' suggests a moral judgment which recognises its lack of context, yet gives an indication – underlined by the word 'cannibal' – of beliefs which are anathema to contemporary morality but which have their place in the history of social development. In his study on cannibalism and human sacrifice, Gary Hogg quotes reports of Aboriginal cannibalism:

> They ate human flesh largely from superstitious beliefs. If they killed a worthy man in battle, they ate his heart, believing that they would inherit his valour and power. They ate his brain because they knew it represented the seat of his knowledge. If they killed a fast runner, they ate part of his legs, hoping thereby to acquire his speed.[41]

In Kinsella's work, particularly 'The Oldest Place' in *One* and later in 'Morning Coffee in *Madonna and Other Poems*, the idea of human sacrifice has links with Irish mythology through the idol of the Cromm Cruach in whose honour human victims were immolated, and the Formorians who demanded a tithe of two thirds of all newborn children.[42]

Sacrifice, this time of history to commerce, is also one of the subjects of 'A Portrait of the Artist'. The poem rewrites the aesthetic debates of Joyce's *A Portrait of the Artist as a Young Man* in a Dublin context. Kinsella looks back to the conflict surrounding the proposed development of Wood Quay, and in particular to a dinner party held by Miranda Guinness to which Kinsella and the architect of the Civic Offices, Sam Stephenson, were invited. Kinsella's drafts show that he initially intended to include a poem on this subject in *One Fond Embrace*:

> Sam Steveson [sic] lecturing
> an Taisce on his "reasons"
> for demolishing the Georgian
> terraces for the ESB offices
>
> *
>
> Brought Miranda Guinness
> on the Wood Quay site &
> assured her there was nothing
> of archaeological or historical
> value there.
>
> *
>
> She invited us to dinner with him.
> She likes to do that: set up
> "interesting" tensions, and "no
> politics please."[43]

In 'A Portrait of the Artist' Kinsella and Stephenson, poet and architect, are portrayed in argument over ideas of the aesthetic: 'The one, in crisis, nagging beauty / to her place among the senses. / And the fool lending an impatient quick ear: / *But what is beauty?*' (P 14, C 305 var.). The italicisation of the last line lifts the question beyond the argument of the two artists and addresses it to the reader. In lines marked by ellipsis, and bearing remarkable similarity to the poet's characterisation of his own writing, Kinsella approaches an answer:

> A jewel of process. . .
> The fugitive, exact in its accident,
> turned about on the fingers . . .
>
> (P 14, C 305 var.)

The prostitution of art to commerce, which Kinsella saw in the architect's complicity with the developers, finds its expression in the closing image of nightwalkers along Percy Place. But the final sentence, particularly in the *Collected Poems* revision ('Her eyes / and oyster mouth wet to my thoughts'), somehow implicate the poet in that which he wishes to reject:

> A silent soul in black and red leatherette
> bestirred herself to meet them. A second waited
> back against the railings in a short skirt,
> the tip of the cigarette pointing, her eyes hidden,
> wet to my senses, and her oyster mouth.
>
> (P 15, C 306 var.)

'Administrator' and 'Social Work' continue Kinsella's criticism of power and decision making in a Dublin context. This time it is the Catholic Church rather than Dublin Corporation and the developers that comes under scrutiny. The situation involves Church-sponsored refuge which has given rise to complaints from neighbours. The Administrator is a 'new breed' of the Church, 'Accustomed / to property and its management. Seldom seen' (P 16, C 306). In tones which echo Austin Clarke's sharp satire on the Catholic Church, Kinsella portrays the priest with quiet dislike:

> He appeared once, in response to a complaint.
> Entered the hall, quietly discourteous,
> suited in grey, easy to mistake
> for a Protestant colleague.
>
>   Sat across the table
> without really listening, his response ready,
> the track of his comb soft in the ordered hair,
> eyes looking past the speaker toward the window.
>
> (P 16, C 306 var.)

The lack of respect for his interlocutors is evident in the priest's rehearsed response: 'Our charges have certain needs. If these entail / annoyance for others that is unfortunate' (P 16, C 306). However, no alternative perspective is offered to the reader. 'Social Work' continues the theme of indifferent and unresponsive public servants here in the context, perhaps, of plans to demolish Percy Place to make room for public housing.[44] Church and City are complicit in plans from which the residents are excluded:

> I turned away to talk with a new neighbour.
> A voice at my ear: 'I think we may give it up'.
>
> (P 17, C 306 var.)

In his *Collected Poems* and the earlier *From Centre City* Kinsella adds a poem called 'Departure Platforms' to the Peppercanister *Poems from Centre City*, between 'The Stranger' and 'The Last'. This poem was composed in the seven-year period before *Songs of the Psyche*, and it joins an observation of swans on the canal with a childhood recollection of passengers at the train station.[45] A sense of decay amid progress is conveyed through the conjunction between the city detritus and the swan and cygnets who 'were busy, pecking and paddling / grey-furred among the heaps of worn tyres' (C 314). The flotating waste, 'A sack floated, half sunk, against the bank' contrast with the 'fat, fashionable barges' emblematic of the new Dublin (C 314). The second part of the poem describes two crippled figures on a train platform. Both are women, and both suffer from injuries to the legs. The first is a girl with 'one leg kneeling / in a metal thing' (C 314). The second is a woman returning from hospital, perhaps from an operation on varicose veins, 'her legs wrapped in reddened bandages' (C 314). Both of these observations are made from a child's perspective, conveyed by the conspiratorial repetition of 'I whispered' (C 314).

Kinsella moves from the private perspectives of 'Departure Platforms' to a more public stocktaking in 'The Last', which profiles two formidable figures of Irish life, the painter Jack Yeats and the politician Eamon de Valera.[46] Both men transformed the image of Ireland: Yeats through his vigorous and expressionist portrayal of Irish scenes, and de Valera through his involvement in the conflicts and resolutions from which the Republic of Ireland emerged. In a discussion on the value of poetic indeterminacy, Kinsella puts forward this argument:

> It seems to me that you must use your wits or the poem loses some of its voltage. Jack Yeats is the last survivor of the artistic renaissance and De Valera is the last of the political giants of the time.[47]

These two figures represent the end of an era in which culture and politics underwent a radical transformation which had as much to do with the developments of the twentieth century as it did with the individual circumstance of Ireland. Yet they are depicted in strangely static and almost monumental terms. Yeats is 'Stone still on the path' while de Valera stands 'Upright, stately and blind' in an attitude of diminished isolation, 'solitary on the lavatory floor' (P 18, C 315 var.). Kinsella's reference to Baggot Street down which Jack Yeats's 'aged eyes' are directed, recalls his early poem, 'Baggot Street Deserta'. The symmetry of endings and beginnings evoked by the street name give to 'The Last' less a sense of nostalgia for a lost era, and more a sense of meditation in the mode of the 1958 poem in which introspection is tempered by action:

> My quarter-inch of cigarette
> Goes flaring down to Baggot Street.

> (C 15)

'The Back Lane' returns Kinsella to the peripatetic subjectivity of poems such as 'Nightwalker' and 'St Catherine's Clock'. From his workshop in Percy Lane, the speaker embarks on a journey which parallels the steps O'Keeffe and his horse used to take:

> along the Canal in the morning from Mount Street corner
> into the Lane, and going home at night
> with the horse locked into the dark, by Haddington Road,
>
> over the main road to The Beggar's Bush,
> down into South Lotts, back to the house.
> And never a word at home of the day's work.[48]

The speaker's companion on his route is the austere figure of Dante Alighieri whose 'elderly down-tasting profile' Kinsella has placed on the cover of *Poems from Centre City* (P 19, C 310). The book which the speaker fetches – 'Close it / with one finger and gather it up' (P 19, C 310 var.) – is the book from which the cover image of Dante is drawn.[49] Though the journey Kinsella describes in 'The Back Lane' does not quite encompass a Dantean Heaven and Hell, it is none the less a venture 'into the world of waste' (P 21, C 311). Kinsella characterises Dante's era as a fortunate time 'when many things were shared' and in which 'complex utterances were possible', and contrasts that time with the condition of the late twentieth century in which

> What we share is a general sense of unease and distress, betrayal and disappointment. There are very few bases on which we can share an understanding of great, enormous nouns like love, faith, and so on.[50]

In the *Collected Poems* version Kinsella divides the speaker's journey into three sections, paralleling, perhaps, the triple division of Dante's journey.[51] Kinsella has made certain changes in his revision of the

Peppercanister edition for the *Collected Poems*. Most significant, perhaps, is the shift from quatrains to tercets which strengthens the connection with Dante's *Divine Comedy*, and the rearrangement of lines and stanzas to better effect, for example in these lines from the Peppercanister:

> And abstracted, with the pen patted
> in its proper pocket and the book next my heart,
>
> I started down the centre of the Lane,
> haunted by shifting horse shadows
> for the first twenty or thirty yards,
> past locked doors and dark gates
>
> in various use and ruin:
> scent of spinster flesh, mongrel
> and vegetable scents, the thick scent
> of clay and root company.
>
> (P 20)

are revised to read thus in the *Collected Poems*:

> and I started down the middle of the Lane
>
> with the book at my heart
>   and the pen patted in its pocket
> Past stables and back gates
>
> in various use and ruin:
>   vegetable and mongrel smells, a scent of clay
> and roots and spinster flesh.
>
> (C 310–11)

The repetition of the word 'scent' in the Peppercanister is replaced with the more varied 'scent' and 'smells' in the *Collected Poems*. Similarly, the repetition of 'cement' in the sixth and seventh stanza of the Peppercanister is varied with the addition of 'concrete' in the *Collected Poems*. Also, the capitalised 'Time' which watches the cement drying – 'and hardened in Time's face' (P 20) – is removed in the 1996 version.

The speaker's perambulations lead him away from the sanctuary of his writing-place into the familiar yet forbidding surrounds of the darkened Canal. The scene is squalid: 'My toe stirred a half-brain of cauliflower / on damp paper, in a mother-ghost of urine, // against the corrugated iron / and the neglect next door.' (P 20, C 310 var.). The midnight prowler resembles the malodorous Tonio Kröger of *Personal Places*, but this figure is closer to Thomas Mann's Adrian Leverkühn of *Dr Faustus*, since he carries with him the latter day tools of his search for under-standing. Faust's cauldron and key become the 'pen patted / in its proper pocket and the book next my heart' (P 20, C 311 var.). Mephistopheles gives way to Christ who is evoked in the 'Iron Trinity' of the 'three lamps' (P 21), which becomes the more specific 'Three Corporation lamps' in the *Collected Poems* (C 310), as the speaker allows himself:

> a sign, with open arms:
> right hand held up, hanging empty,
> the left lifting my book,
> wrists nailed back in resignation,
>
> (P 21, C 311 var.)

This sign becomes a 'prayer' in the *Collected Poems*, but in both versions the speaker identifies himself with the figure of the crucifixion. He makes an entreaty which concerns politics and poetry:

> Lord grant us a local watchfulness,
> accept us into that minority
> impelled toward totality of response,
>
> (P 22, C 312 var.)

This prayer is said under the light of the Corporation whose planning and work has been subject to the poet's ire in *One Fond Embrace*, *Personal Places* and earlier in 'The Back Lane', when the speaker notes 'the slovenliness of the City and its lesser works. / Cement mash emptied direct onto the dirt' (P 20, C 310 var.). The 'local watchfulness' about neighbourhood issues which proved the subjects for 'Administrator' and 'Social Work', is also the attention to minutiae from which Kinsella builds his poetry. While Christlike, the deity to whom the speaker prays is also connected to the Eternal Feminine or maternal god which features in volumes such as *One* and *Her Vertical Smile*. While conceived as the masculine 'Iron Trinity', the god to whom the speaker prays is also represented in the negative as a feminine 'shadow' (in the Jungian sense) through the figure of the prostitute on Warrington Place:

> And more than your shadow waiting
> against the wire and nettles, a mental sign.
> The smell of exit.
> The next, and last, excitement.
>
> The breath catching the hem of your skirt.
> My own footsteps passing dead
> among my dying neighbours,
> my material mixing with theirs.
>
> (P 21, cf 311)

In the *Collected Poems* Kinsella omits this reference to the feminine shadow figure and the 'Iron Trinity', leaving a skeletal tercet: 'But the smell of exit: / the next, / and last, excitement' (C 311). Just as Christ has his shadow, so the speaker has a 'brother figure' who startles the speaker from his Christ-like pose: 'Embarrassed suddenly from the right hand, / on the first beat of the Church bell, // by my brother figure' (P 22, C 312 var.). In the *Collected Poems* Kinsella splits the embarrassment of the speaker from the encounter with his brother figure:

> and I will lower these arms
> and embrace what I find.
> Embarrassed.
>
> Encountering my brother figure.
> – Startled likewise, in that posture
> of seeming shyness, then glaring,
>
> (C 312)[52]

so that the embarrassment relates more clearly to his self-identification with Christ, rather than to the disturbance of the brother figure whose night-time activities are betrayed by 'features withdrawn and set in shame' (P 22, C 312).

The 'first beat of the Church bell' which tolls in 'The Back Lane' is taken up by the subsequent poem, 'The Bell', which opens to a similar sound as 'The bell on Haddington Road rang, / a fumbled clang behind the flats' (P 23, C 309). In the drafts of 'The Bell', the crucified pose of 'The Back Lane' finds its exemplar inside the Church on Haddington Road: 'His arms hammered wide, / His head hanging on one side / in token abandonment.'[53] Similarly, O'Keeffe of 'The Stable' is a ghostly presence in 'The Bell' through drafts which reach back four decades to the Haddington Road church 'where O'Keeffe took her hand in marriage / forty years ago, nor held her / but by her granting, in summer brave'.[54] Through the sound of the bell, 'audible in Inchicore', Kinsella connects his younger self growing up in Inchicore with his adult self prowling around Percy Place.[55] This return to origins is evoked in a larger framework through the image of the tabernacle light which signifies a sacred presence and indicates both a material and spiritual genesis:

> Fluttering the sanctuary lamp,
> cup of blood, seed of light,
> hanging down from their dark height.
>
> (P 23, C 309 var.)

Poetic origins form the subject of the final poem in the Peppercanister *Poems from Centre City* as Kinsella writes in memory of his earlier exemplar, W. H. Auden. In conversation with Dennis O'Driscoll, Kinsella outlines his debt to Auden:

Reading Auden, it occurred to me that there was a need in myself, and that I could write poetry. For a while I wrote only imitations of Auden.[56]

In an earlier interview Kinsella gives an example, noting that 'the earliest poems that I still think are good were written quite specifically in Auden's manner: "A Lady of Quality" is specifically modelled, as an exercise, on a poem of Auden's.'[57] Another such poem is Kinsella's elegy 'Dick King' from the 1962 collection *Downstream*. 'Dick King' replicates the double structure of Auden's 'In Memory of W. B. Yeats', in which the long line of the first two sections gives way to a third section of shorter iambic lines which jog the reader along: 'Earth receive an honoured guest; / William Yeats is laid to rest: / Let the Irish vessel lie / Emptied of its poetry.' Kinsella's poem shifts from the longer line to what Brian John describes as a 'ballad stanza and rhythm':[58] 'Dick King was an upright man. / Sixty years he trod / The dull stations underfoot. / Fifteen he lies with God' (C 37).

'Dedication' – or 'Memory of W. H. Auden' in the *Collected Poems* – brings us back to the Baggot Street location of Kinsella's early poetry:

> A tangle of concerns above the dark
> channel of Baggot Street.
> Jesus in History.
> Man and his Symbols. Civilisation
> Surprised in her Underwear . . .
>
> (P 24, C 315 var.)

Like the father in *The Messenger*, whose reading of Carlyle, Dante, Shelley, Shakespeare and Moore characterises his intellectual development, so Kinsella's early self is characterised through his reading of Howard Clark Kee's *Jesus in History*, C. G. Jung's *Man and His Symbols*, and Sigmund Freud's *Civilisation and its Discontents*.[59] Out of this 'tangle of concerns' comes a vision of Auden from the 1930s:

> [. . .] Silver jowls
> half shaded with understanding: rapt, radiant
> with vision and opinion, displaced love,
> piercing intelligence, exhausted song.
>
> (P 24, C 315 var.)

Kinsella's description of Auden as his 'Secondary Father, with Cigarette' (P 24, C 315 var.) recalls the closing gesture of 'Baggot Street Deserta' – 'My quarter-inch of cigarette / Goes flaring down to Baggot Street' (C 15) – which, reread from the perspective of 'Dedication', works both as an identification with the elder poet, and also as a gesture of rejection. The ambivalence of poetic influence is aptly conveyed in the phrase 'scarred regard', which is used to describe Auden's 'corpsegaze' as it falls across the speaker's shoulder (P 24, C 315–16). In conversation with Daniel O'Hara, Kinsella argues against Harold Bloom's idea of the anxiety of influence, suggesting instead a generative, even predatory, notion of influence:

> No: the function of influence is a fructifying one; it helps, if the poet has to capacity to enlarge the influenced poet. It is also, however, a very predatory thing on the part of the influencee: He will take what suits him.[60]

The predatory aspect of the poet is conveyed through the image of his hands as 'spent claws picking the paint / off the sill at an upper window' (P 24, C 315). Yet, though the poet would like to think that he takes what suits him, he is aware of the lingering presence of the influence long abandoned. Auden's influence is described as a 'taint' as the speaker turns away from the vision of the elder poet, back to his own poetic project, that now concerns itself less with the formal harmonies of an Audenesque line and more with 'a pattern of some kind, some harmonious shape', which 'emerges automatically as a way of handling the material':[61]

> My hands
> rediscovered each other, and I turned away
> back into my den, his scarred regard
> across my shoulder, my fingers finding their way
> back about their business, with the taint upon them.
>
> (P 24, C 316 var.)

Madonna and Other Poems

From the political and social concerns of *One Fond Embrace*, *Personal Places* and *Poems from Centre City*, Kinsella turns to the the private concerns of love and endurance in *Madonna and Other Poems*. Published in 1991, in tandem with *Open Court*, Kinsella illustrates the cover of the Peppercanister edition with an image, taken from a woodcut attributed to Albrecht Dürer, of a 'Woman with the Zodiac'.[62] The pale blue cover of the volume evokes the Madonna of the title. The cover image reminds us of the astrological cover image of *Her Vertical Smile*, and of the powerful 'Eternal Feminine' figure which underpins that volume. Here, however, the female figure is embodied rather than alluded to. She stands, supported by the trajectories of the planets, her arms reaching to enclose the heavenly spheres which are named by the signs of the zodiac. Her curling tresses are echoed by the flourish of the conifer branches and cones which guard each corner of the image, both evoking fecundity and endurance.

In notes for a programme on RTÉ dated 3 December 1991, Kinsella describes *Madonna and Other Poems* as 'a set of 6 poems on the subject of the woman companion'.[63] The woman companion includes the mother, the wife and the artistic guide or muse. Kinsella connects this figure back to early Irish literature in which the woman appears in a number of shapes: as wife and companion, as queen, and as the old woman or witch who is 'wise with all the experiences of human life, and a mediator when it comes to death'.[64] This figure is associated with the gift of artistic creativity, and also with the creativity of the earth as manifested in 'the movement of the seasons and the tides'.[65] This early Irish view of the triple aspect of the woman is linked in these poems with the Christian figure of the Madonna as both mediator and mother.

Madonna and Other Poems comprises four titled poems, 'Madonna', 'Morning Coffee', 'Visiting Hour', and 'At the Head Table'. On either side of 'Madonna' Kinsella places two untitled poems, '*Better is an hand-full with quietness*' and '*I have known the hissing assemblies*'. As with his other Peppercanisters from the late 1980s and the 1990s, Kinsella makes some significant revisions to the poems of this volume, particularly in 'Morning Coffee'. And indeed, in the *Collected Poems* Kinsella moves the short poem '*I have known the hissing assemblies*' from *Madonna and Other Poems* to a section of meditations at the end of the edition which comment on Kinsella's work as a whole (C 335).

The volume opens with a meditation on the nature of strife within love. In a language which resembles the archaic diction of prayer, Kinsella offers this advice:

> Better is an handfull with quietness
> than both hands full
> with travail and vexation of spirit.
>
> (P 9, C 317)

Quoting from Ecclesiastes IV: 6, Kinsella evokes emotion in tangible terms. The lover is also a supplicant whose cupped hands hold the conflicting emotions of the 'loving upset' (P 9, C 317). And it is through these hands that the knowledge and understanding born of love is conveyed; unless they take leave: 'my blind fingers forsaking your face' (P 9, C 317). With a wisdom born of trial, the speaker attests to the necessity of endurance and communication. To turn away from the beloved, to turn in on oneself, is to destroy the self:

Yet worst is the fool that foldeth his hands
and eateth his own flesh.

(P 9, C 317)[66]

'Madonna' continues the themes of love, supplication and endurance
in a poem of five sections (revised to four in the *Collected Poems*), which
trace the development of love from the first encounter to the easeful
rituals of a long-established union. Kinsella continues the themes of
chapter four of Ecclesiastes which places great importance on partnership:
'Two *are* better than one; because they have a good reward for their
labour. For if they fall, the one will lift up his fellow: but woe to him *that
is* alone when he falleth; for *he hath* not another to help him up.'[67]
'Madonna' opens with a scene in which man and woman meet under the
figure of the crucified Christ whose pierced form is both masculine
and feminine:

She knelt beside me at the money-box
in the light of the candles,
under the Body with the woman feet.

(P 10, C 317)

The woman is apprehended through the senses: her high heels sounding
along the aisle; her body sensed in its proximity; her bowed head glimpsed
by the soft glow of the votive candles; her flesh breathed in, 'Her meat
sweet' (P 10, C 317). In a scene reminiscent of James Joyce's 'The Dead',
Kinsella describes the woman at her evening ritual, 'busy, minding her
hair / at the window, a long brushful held out' (P 10, C 317). The cold
light of the night 'coming in dead white' is transformed into shadow by
the body of the woman. This shadow is both a recognition of the unity
of the man and the woman whose bond is as close as that between self
and shadow. The suggestion of shadow 'invading / our urinary privacy'
intimates the beginnings of a third element born of love, but also brings
with it intimations of a darkness in human nature which the couple must
face (P 10, C 317 var.).

The physical union through which two become one is delicately
described in the third section as a movement of both 'concern' and
'familiarity' in which 'our two awarenesses / narrowed into one point, /
our piercing presences exchanged / in pleasantry and fright' (P 10,
C 318). While the couple are described in terms of the intangible, as
'awarenesses' and 'presences', the poet situates their union within a
somnolence described in animal terms: 'our thoughts disordered /
and lapped in fur', and the beloved's body is apprehended as tangibly somatic,
'your shoulder sleeping / distinct in my hand' (P 11, C 318). The curious
arithmetic by which the speaker counts these moments of union

> the tally of our encounters
> reduced by one
>
> (P 11, C 318)

makes sense in terms of a movement towards complete union. The speaker is counting down to a zero point in which each lover will be indistinguishable from the other in a union of one flesh. The morning brings a ritual which celebrates this union of flesh. With deliberate Eucharistic parallels the speaker cuts open the (appropriately enough) blood grapefruit and makes a pot of tea:

> Cut and fold it open,
> the thick orange, honey-coarse.
> First blood: a saturated essence
> tasted between the teeth.

> I held the kettle out high
> and emptied it
> with a shrivelled hiss
> boiling into the scalded pot.
>
> (P 11, C 318)

Grapefruit and tea are offered up in a thanksgiving for the union of body and blood made possible through love. Ghosting this ritual is the presence of the feminine deity or perhaps the muse who appears in a 'stubborn memory' and whose 'deliberate, tender incursions' (P 11, C 318 var.) echo the '"sudden and peremptory incursions"' of the muse in A *Technical Supplement* (P [30], C 194). Kinsella closes the *Collected Poems* 'Madonna' with this image of domestic sacrifice in which the couple's breakfast mirrors the breaking of the bread at the Last Supper. The earlier Peppercanister edition includes a fifth section, now included in the last page of the *Collected Poems* (C 335 var.), which presents the couple, sitting 'face to face at the table / in the morning cold' (P 12, C 335 var.). Outside, the sounds of a 'raven couple' are rendered by the exclamation '*Nought!*' which contains a reference to the zero point of love, which is also, as we know from *Notes From the Land of the Dead*, the beginning of life (P 12, C 335 var.). The ravens are emblematic of union since, as Kinsella notes, they stay together forever. As messengers from the gods, they are also emblematic of a union between heaven and earth.[68]

In the Peppercanister volume, 'Madonna' and 'Morning Coffee' are separated by a meditation which mirrors the opening verse of the book. '*I have known the hissing assemblies*' provides a pause in which the speaker-poet turns away from the public concerns of the previous three Peppercanisters, the 'hissing assemblies' which so frustrated the speaker of *One Fond Embrace*, *Personal Places* and *Poems from Centre City*. In a gesture of refusal the speaker turns his back on the 'foul ascending city' which gave rise to such frustration, filtering the city smell through the grass of the 'fragrant slope' on which he stands:

> and held a handful of high grass
> sweet and grey to my face.

(P 13, C 335)

This gesture writes in miniature Kinsella's own move in the mid-eighties from his city-centre home in Percy Place to the rural townland of Killalane in Wicklow, the county of his forefathers.

'Morning Coffee' explores ideas of love, sacrifice and self-knowledge through a movement of introspection. The differences between the Peppercanister version of the poem and that in the *Collected Poems* lies primarily in the rearrangement of the opening sections of the poem. The first section of the Peppercanister poem, 'a loving little boy', becomes the third section of the *Collected* poem. The second section of the Pepper-canister poem, 'I left the road [. . .]', moves from the *Collected Poems* 'Morning Coffee' to the last page of that volume (C 335), and is replaced by an entirely new set of stanzas which form the first section of the *Collected* poem, 'We thought at first it was a body'. Both poems are divided into two, and in both the first part has three sections. I shall read the first two sections of the first part of the Peppercanister version, then move to a reading of the opening section of the *Collected Poems* version, joining both readings at the third section of the first part, 'At a well beside the way', from which point both versions are roughly similar.

The Peppercanister 'Morning Coffee' opens with an image of Cupid in a reciprocal relationship with the speaker:

> A loving little boy
>   appeared on angel's wings
> and showed his empty quiver.
>   I filled it out of mine.

(P 14, C 319)

This short section, comprising two quatrains, reverses the mythical notion of love as that which strikes from without, borne on the tip of Cupid's arrow. Instead, the arrows which find their mark in the speaker are the speaker's own. Love given is always returned:

> He vanished, but remembered:
>   every dart
> returning furious
>   to my heart

(P 14, C 319)

The second section, which appears at the end of the volume of *Collected Poems*, describes the speaker entering a wood, symbolic, perhaps, of the unconscious: 'dry trees standing close in their own grain, / bare branches with sharp fingers out everywhere' (P 14, C 335 var.). He comes 'face to face' with a resting bat, its 'mouse body / upside down on a patch of bark' (P 14, C 335 var.). The figure of the bat is reminiscent of the 'bat-black, heron-slow' figure of *Song of the Night and Other Poems* (P 19, C 216). It evokes the 'other aspect' or 'dark brother' which represents the repressed aspects of the self, an aspect which is 'Meant only to be half seen, quick in the half light' (P 14, C 335 var.).[69] Through flight the bat merges with the cherubic figure of Cupid, becoming a 'little leather angel, falling everywhere, / snapping at the invisible!' (P 14, C 335).

The *Collected Poems* version of 'Morning Coffee' begins with a quite different approach. Kinsella returns to the *Lebor Gabála Erenn* and the story of the first peoples of Ireland, and to the rituals of sacrifice and cannibalism that link pagan and Christian worlds. Part of the drafts of this poem form the epigraph of *One*: 'A storyteller with his face in the shadow / hones his blade near the fire / for the voyage of the first kindreds.'[70] This section of 'Morning Coffee' was given the draft titles, 'Genesis' or 'A Parable'.[71] The opening lines bring together notions of birth and death through powerful images of a body with a 'blank belly' washed up on shore, and of a 'big white earthenware vessel' staring up 'open mouthed' (C 318–19). The alliterative negation of 'blank belly', and the 'open mouthed' vessel convey an idea of perverted fecundity, of a space which should bring forth life but which holds only death. The poetic voice, speaking in the first person plural, comes from the people of Nemed, the third invaders of Ireland after Cessair and Partholón. These are the people in thrall to the Fomorians, who demand a tithe of newborn children:[72]

> We thought at first it was a body
> rolling up with a blank belly onto the beach
> the year our first-born babies died.

(C 318)

However, there is another source for this section of 'Morning Coffee' which comes from farther afield, and relates to the 'cannibal committee' in 'Household Spirits' of *Poems from Centre City*. The second and third stanzas rewrite scenes from Gary Hogg's *Cannibalism and Human Sacrifice* from which Kinsella took notes:

> The [. . .] men had previously noticed several long earthenware pots cooking on the fires. Feeling curious, they took this opportunity of being alone to examine their contents. Approaching one pot, to their horror they

discovered the fingers of a human hand protruding from a mass of boiling meat, and, stirring the contents with the end of their bows, they saw next a foot. In another pot, when turning over a large, round piece of meat, a human face was exposed. They were filled with horror, disgust and terror, and fled immediately into the woods, making all haste to their homes.[73]

The figure of the crucifix in 'Madonna' and the ritual of sacrifice re-enacted by the breakfast scene in the closing lines of the poem gain an unsettling resonance in the context of the cannibalism and human sacrifice outlined above. We reread the last lines of the first poem, the 'fool' that 'eateth his own flesh', with both a literal and metaphorical understanding. The counterpoint that Kinsella establishes between the sacrificial iconography of Christianity and the role of sacrifice in the mythology of Ireland's origins echoes back to the private rituals between the lovers of 'Madonna', and reaches forward to the vision of the 'loving little boy' in the next section of 'Morning Coffee' to create a sense of life and loss – 'blood and milk' – experienced within the most private sphere. The importance of recognising both the generative and the destructive aspects of life is emphasised by Kinsella who stresses that 'it is a canni-balistic world, and very cruel in many ways, but it has among its major comforts the fact that we can make some kind of sense of it'.[74] One way of making sense is through art; the forging of narrative as a bridge between life and death:

> Soon we were making up stories
> about the First People
> and telling them to our second born.
>
> (C 319)

The third section of 'Morning Coffee', the point at which both versions of the poem meet, replays the introspection of earlier poems such as 'Mirror in February' and the twenty-second section of *A Technical Supplement*. Rather than the shaving mirror of 'Mirror in February' in which the speaker stops and stares – 'Riveted by a dark exhausted eye, / A dry downturning mouth' (C 54), or the diptych of selves glimpsed in the mirrors of *A Technical Supplement* – 'Two faces now returned my stare / each whole yet neither quite 'itself' (P [39], C 200), the speaker of 'Morning Coffee' chooses a pool of water to re-enact Narcissus's self-reflexive search:

> At a well beside the way
> I alighted and put down
> my lips to the water.
>
> You, lifting your face
> like a thirsty thing to mine,
> I think I know you well:
>
> (P 15, C 319)

The section, provisionally titled 'Travellers' or 'Pilgrims' in the drafts, rewrites the story of Narcissus, but rather than the impossible image that so enchants Narcissus, 'Not knowing what he sees, he adores the sight; / That false face fools and fuels his delight',[75] Kinsella's speaker gazes with clear recognition on the image of his own self. There is a calm acceptance of the attributes which make up the public and the private self. To others he appears 'of character retiring, / settled in your habits, / careful of your appearance;' (P 15, C 319). To himself, 'with eyes open inward' he is 'restless in disposition; / best left alone' (P 15, C 319). The speaker poses himself a series of questions which connect self-development with artistic development, asking

> What matter if you seem
> assured in your purpose
> and animal commitment
>
> but vague in direction
> and effect on affairs?
>
> (P 15, C 320)

The response is not so much an answer to this question, as a contextualisation which sees life as a pilgrimage, a journey through darkness and uncertainty: 'We are all only pilgrims. / Travelling the night' (P 15, C 320).

'Morning Coffee' ends with a scene from which the poem takes its title. The speaker is recognisably the figure of the young poet as civil servant, sitting alone in his basement canteen at work. He surveys the 'feet hurrying around the corner' of Merrion Square, their steps drawing his gaze outward, 'up the tenement stone stairs – / and closing in a lane by the library' (P 16, C 320 var.).[76] In an opposite movement, his thoughts turn inward, remembering the touch of his own flesh:

> Thumb and finger felt
> at my throat: the soft leather.
>
> (P 16, C 321 var.)

With this memory comes a vision of 'pain and pleasure', the primary sensations through which life is lived. In contrast with the suicidal protagonist of *The Good Fight* who soaks 'wrist in cold water / to numb the pain' (P 14, C 159), the speaker of 'Morning Coffee' holds his wrist 'too long at the hot tap' in a gesture of affirmation and endurance. The speaker's reverie is broken in the closing tercet, written loosely in the Peppercanister edition with a broken line, and spaces between each sentence, as he returns to his colleagues 'starting to wonder upstairs' (P 17, C 321 var.), leaving his cup 'for the woman waiting' (P 17, C 321).

Kinsella's attention to visceral processes is continued in 'Visiting Hour'. The speaker, confined to the hospital bed and connected to the technological paraphernalia through which healing is effected, entertains visions of the mother and brother last glimpsed in 'Dura Mater' of *Personal Places*. The scene is described in detail:

> The pale inner left arm pierced, and withdrawn
> A sweat-heated pillow flattened under my neck,
>   I lay and fingered my mental parts.

> (P 18, C 321)

The speaker's reverie emerges from images of red: the stirring of the 'red curtain' which announces the arrival of the brother, and the 'crimson drape' against which stands the vision of the mother. These chromatic notes underline 'the blood beating injected in the face' (P 18, C 321), emphasising the state of heightened somatic and noetic awareness in the poem. The physical and the abstract interchange through the 'aura' of sickness: 'Awareness, with an echo of memory, // fainted in the bowels, and inward / under the heart' (P 18). This line is rewritten in the *Collected Poems* to focus on the role of memory and the state of consciousness in which repressed thoughts and images surface: 'An aura like a cloud around the heart. / Memories intermixing, opening inward, / and melting in the loins with a ghost of pleasure' (C 321). The closing tercets address the figure of the Mother, who can be read as the speaker's own mother, and also as the Madonna of the volume's title. There is some considerable difference in tone between the Peppercanister version of this poem and that in the *Collected Poems*. The Peppercanister poem under-lines the connection between mother and child:

> Her thin palm on her womb, in memory.
> The sac of flesh and fervour where we met
>   and nourished each other for a while.

> (P 19)

It follows with the entreaty: 'be mindful of me now, with my lids / closed on the medicine dark. / Until I wake' (P 19). In contrast, the *Collected Poems* version describes the mother with 'One thin hand out, denying' (C 322). Rather than giving succour, the mother is described as 'taking refreshment at my well of illness' (C 322), and is offered a different kind of prayer: 'take my love back, into the medicine dark' (C 322).

'At Head Table' returns to the kind of communion offered in *One Fond Embrace*. Written in the third person, the protagonist resembles closely the retiring, careful character of 'Morning Coffee':

he kept an even temper
thinking:
            I have devoted
my life, my entire career,
to the avoidance of affectation,
the way of entertainment
or the specialist response.

                              (P 20, C 322 var.)

With a certain irony, the speaker addresses a muse-mother figure who is
deemed 'the source of trouble' (P 20, C 322).[77] This trouble turns out to
be the difficulty and challenge of art. He toasts her, 'Madam. Your
health!' (P 20, C 323 var.), raising before him a 'beaker' which is both
toast and sacrificial offering. The beaker is another version of the 'ordeal-
cup' of 'Phoenix Park' (C 89), that container for the 'enabling processes'
out of which poetry is formed.[78] The beaker with its 'slim amphibian
handles' (P 20, C 322) mirrors the snake-like aspect of the woman whose
smile is 'lipless like an asp' (P 23, C 325 var.). This smile evokes the serpent
and uroboros figures familiar to Kinsella's poetry, symbols which represent
the inextricability of destruction and creation. Creativity and, in particular,
art form the subject of the speaker's toast which opens with a mediation
on the craft involved in producing the ordeal cup:

            This lovely cup before us,
            this piece before all others,
            gave me the greatest trouble
            in impulse and idea
            and management of material
            – in all the fine requirements
            that bring the craftsman's stoop.
            Yet proved the most rewarding.
            Its structure its own statement,
            and perfect for its purpose:

                              (P 21, C 323 var.)

The last two lines encapsulate Kinsella's focus on the relationship between
form and content in art. Recalling Beckett on Joyce – 'here form *is*
content, content *is* form'[79] – Kinsella draws our attention to the balance
of elements which make up a work of art and enable it to fit its purpose,
'the weight tilted forward, / the rim moulded outward / pouring precise
and full' (P 21, C 323 var.). But 'ornament and pattern' (P 21), or, as
Kinsella puts it more succinctly in the revised *Collected Poems*, 'vital
decoration' (C 323) is also integral to the structure which, like Kinsella's
own poetry, seeks to weave 'a web of order' elicited from the 'shapes of
sand and water' (P 21–2), and the 'marks of waves and footsteps' (C 323).
Through an analogy with Amairgin's arrival in Ireland which was

marked by successive retreats and advancements – 'Nine waves out, a ship / lying low in the water' and 'Nine steps inland / where the two worlds meet, or divide' (P 22–3, C 324) – Kinsella lays down his own approach to poetry, his own version of Keats's Grecian Urn:[80]

> In fact, a web of order
> covering the surface
> with movement and real meaning,
> a system of living images
> inscribed in the material
> or modelled and imposed;
> each mark accommodating
> the shapes of all the others
> with none at fault, or false;
> making increased response
> to each increased demand
> in the eye of the beholder;
> with a final full response
> – a total theme – presented
> to a full intense regard:
>
> (P 22)[81]

Kinsella's reference to Amairgin, the 'absent shade' to whom the speaker drinks (P 23, C 325), underlines the extent to which the *Lebor Gabála Érenn* provides just such a 'web of order' through which the poet can elicit 'order from significant data'.[82] Kinsella's attention to the detail of that data, however unpalatable it may be, is an integral part of his poetic process, 'the process whereby one's experience is ingested, processed, deposited, prepared for use, made ready – brought to a condition where it can be "set off" by a new significant experience striking it'.[83] This is the 'totality of response' that Kinsella is driven toward in 'The Back Lane' of *Poems from Centre City* (P 22, C 312). It is a response which seeks to remove the 'merely linguistic characteristics' of poetry 'so that one is brought closer and closer to the data and to the form and unity embodied in the data' of experience.[84] This response demands as much of the reader as it does of the poet. Kinsella speaks of the reader 'completing an act of communication' through the poem.[85] Through an act of 'positive sympathy' the reader 'puts on this poetic sensitivity, engaged at this given time, with all its contexts, and extends his self; he extends his range of significant observation by this means, so as, in his turn, to ingest and understand.'[86] Out of this process of total engagement comes the 'full intense regard' with which poetry is best read. The final stanzas of the poem return us to the themes of sacrifice and ritual explored in the preceding poems, this time in a self-deflationary manner as the limping poet-speaker administers the sacrament of the Eucharist through the 'blood brandy', which is a visceral parallel to the alchemical 'lifewater' of *The Messenger* (P 6, C 219), taking care to wipe 'the rim often' (P 24). The inclusiveness of the muse-mother's open arms echoes the gesture of the cover image in which the 'Eternal Feminine' figure embraces the cosmos. This embrace is multiplied by the poet-speaker who underlines his engagement with the totality of experience as he 'danced off downward / out among the others, / everyone in turn' (P 24, C 325).

Open Court

Following Kinsella's characteristic migration back and forth between the personal and the public, *Open Court* switches from the personal meditation on love in *Madonna*, to a public stocktaking of the place of poetry in modern Irish society. Situated in that most public yet intimate of places, McDaid's pub just off Grafton Street, Kinsella draws out the Dublin literary scene of the mid-twentieth century. Taking its spirit, if not quite its form, from Brian Merriman's *Midnight Court*, *Open Court* begins with the speaker's customary perambulations around Dublin city:

> From Stephen's Green I set my feet
> contented into Grafton Street.
>
> (P 9, C 327 var.)

With Joycean attention to geographic detail, Kinsella's rhyming couplets draw the reader towards the doors of McDaid's public house, home to poets, journalists and civil servants. Outside, a dissonant dervish conjures images of a demented tradition in its last throes:

> [. . .] dives and swoops
> with bow and fiddle – living things –
> and, double-stopping, sweeps the strings
> with passionate inaccuracy.[87]
>
> (P 10, C 327 var.)

Inside, the decor of this 'overcrowded sty' is described in familiar detail. The 'Disputing hoards', whose 'slow turmoil' describes wonderfully the seething mass that is society of a Sunday evening, are reflected in the 'spotted mirror, vast in size, / and framed in bottles' (P 10, C 327). The condensation requisite of a pub coats 'the lofty walls' as 'A haze / of smoky light obscures the bar' (P 10, C 327).

Into this purgatorium steps the speaker. On one side 'Three poets sprawl / silent, minor, by the wall' (P 10, C 327). Kinsella sketches three portraits of poets active in the Dublin scene around the 1950s and 1960s, poets whose characters are described by association with literary figures from the English, or Anglo-Irish, tradition such as Matthew Arnold, W. H. Auden and Oscar Wilde:

> Locked in his private agony,
> showing the yellow of his eye,
> a ruined Arnold turns his face
> snarling into empty space,
> flecks of black about his lips.
> Next, a ruined Auden slips
> lower on the leather seat,
> his tonsure sunken in defeat
> – roused to fits and starts of life
> by the distant shrilling of his wife.
> Last, downcast and liquid-lipped,
> umbrella handle moistly gripped
> and staring inward, doomed and mild,
> a ruined, speechless Oscar Wilde.

(P 10–11, C 327–8)

Whether composite or individual, these portraits recall figures from Irish literary life. By associating these portraits of minor Irish poets with major figures from the English literary tradition, Kinsella implies the absence of a comparable tradition in Ireland, and the lack of a community from which a dynamic writing can emerge.[88] Kinsella describes his poet-figures as 'minor' and 'ruined', but it is clear from the context of *Open Court* as a whole, and especially reading the poem in tandem with 'The Dream', that Kinsella attributes the responsibility for this ruin not so much to the poets themselves, as to the cultural climate that failed to give the necessary support. These were people who, in Dillon Johnston's words, 'if nurtured in a different milieu, might have flourished as poets'.[89]

Kinsella's Swiftian eye moves from the ruined poets to the 'ageing author' whose self-regard relies as much on the adulation of the dependent 'female student' as it does on the quality of his writing. While perhaps modelled on an individual, this satirical portrait is so perfectly observed that it makes reference to any number of established figures:

> a giant bringing into town
> an atmosphere of vague renown,
> a female student, open-eyed,
> held to his patriarchal side.
> Once more, with slow authority,
> he tells her how it came that he
> was passed all day from hand to hand
> [. . .]
> He halts a moment, losing track.
> His hand slips lower down her back.
>
> (P 11, C 328 var.)

A similar relationship is observed between the 'novelist from Northern parts' – who is described as if on some anthropological field-trip 'collecting data in the South' – and his diminutive acolyte: 'On every word that leaves his mouth, / tiny – admiring – by his knee / a lecturer in history / hangs excited' (P 11–12, C 328 var.).[90] The indifferent cruelty of the young and ambitious is captured as a new arrival to the Dublin scene 'cuts short his chat' with the civil servant 'with his case / held in a desolate embrace; / once more passed over. . .' (P 12, C 329 var.).[91] The newcomer, eye always on the main chance, 'aims a grin' past the 'tragic bureaucrat' 'at one that (he has heard it said) / writes leaders on the local news / and manages the book reviews' (P 12, C 329).

Another character, less recently arrived from 'the provinces' speaks up from 'the farther wall' (P 12, C 329). In a voice which recalls the intermittant vitriol of Patrick Kavanagh, he rails against a city in which 'Truth' and 'Joy' hold no sway, and praises the simple pleasures of rural life:

> 'Accursed pity
> I ever came to Dublin city,
> packed my bag and left behind
> the very source I came to find.
> I'd more between my thumb and finger
> any Summer night I'd linger
> up against a wooden gate
> in simple pleasure. [. . .]
>
> (P 13, C 330)

This 'wooden gate' echoes a similar gate on which the frustrated Patrick Maguire of Kavanagh's 'The Great Hunger' 'fantasied forth his groan'.[92] The simple pleasure praised by 'ruined Anonymous' is the very one used by Kavanagh to evoke the bleak sterility of peasant life: 'His face in a mist / And two stones in his fist / And an impotent worm on his thigh.'[93] Kinsella had first-hand experience of Kavanagh's critical pronouncements during an exchange of views between both poets which included Stephen Spender and W. D. Snodgrass on the topic of 'Poetry Since Yeats'.

Kinsella's assessment of the state of poetry in Ireland after Yeats included this description of Kavanagh:

> Kavanagh came from the country to that literary Dublin, full of hope. He stayed to haunt its outskirts, and pour much sour – and largely incompetent – satire over it, with an anger proportionate to his disappointment rather than to the importance of his subject.[94]

Kavanagh's response to Kinsella's analysis, and that of Spender and Snodgrass, was to declare that 'Having listened to the three speakers I know that there couldn't possibly be any poetry in the world inhabited by such idiotic critics: such deadness and boredom and rubbish I have not listened to for many years.'[95] Kinsella's description of Kavanagh sounds similar to that expressed by Anonymous who regrets the 'simple conviction that I lost / in bothering with Dublin's loud / self-magnifying, empty crowd. / Double foolishness to flatter, / – by attack – what doesn't matter' (P 13–14, C 330 var.). Anonymous's gibe against the 'monthly magazine subscriber!' recalls the ultimatum issued by the penultimate edition of the Kavanagh brothers' *Kavanagh Weekly* threatening to cease publication unless it received an immediate donation from subscribers towards costs (P 13, C 330). Needless to say, the finance was not forthcoming.

As the 'ruined Anonymous' reaches the end of his rant, the pub begins the closing-time rituals: 'Last drinks are swiftly measured, then / the barman halts and, howling "Please!", / reaches back and rasps his keys / across an iron grating' (P 14, C 331). McDaid's assumes a surreal aspect: the stairs down to the Gents becomes a 'weeping ladder' and the unassuming lounge-boy is transformed into a 'dwarf official' (P 14, C 330). The drinkers, startled from their pints as the barman calls time, are transmogrified into beasts:

> The house lights flicker on and off.
> We lift our faces from the trough.

> (P 14, C 331 var.)

With an observant eye Kinsella details the nightly routine as 'with cries of sadness and dismay, / we exit'. The oblivious lovers who 'in liberated sex / collapse across eath others' necks' join with friends not noticed in the crowd, as all 'struggle, joking, through the door / and mingle in the dirty lane' (P 14–15, C 331). The aspirations, hesitations and delusions that fuel the gregarious Sunday night crowd (time was called at 'half-past ten') are reduced, like the remains of Beckett's Murphy,[96] to detritus:

> A man, with brush, behind our backs
> sweeps our waste across our tracks,
> wipes his feet and bolts the door
> against us, and is seen no more.
>
> (P 15, C 331)

Beckett's bleak humour is glimpsed as Kinsella effects an ironic reversal of pastoral norms, overturning the traditional priority of day over night, and satirising, perhaps, revivalist fetishisation of the 'green green grass of home':

> The dark is kind where day will bring
> some dew-drenched, green, revolting thing . . .
>
> (P 15, C 331 var.)

The bleakly surreal vision hinted at in 'Open Court' is fully fledged in the next poem 'Dream'. Styled as a dream or hallucination, and combining 'imagery taken from Yeats and Eliot', this poem depicts a similar, but more contemporary, gathering of literary society.[97] Draft titles for the poem were 'Fragment: from an old diary', 'Period Pieces', or 'A Riddle'. The Peppercanister version of poem is subtitled '(A puzzle for Bob Buttel)', and the drafts date the poem around 1985.[98] The elements of this riddle or puzzle are two creatures, one a monopod, situated in 'a stony desert, baked and still' who come into contact with two successive groups of 'human figures' (P 16, C 332). Taken in conjunction with 'Open Court', 'Dream' can be read as an allegory of the Irish cultural scene in Ireland around mid-century. While choosing the metaphor of wilderness rather than desert to characterise Ireland in the 1940s, Sean O'Faolain describes it as a 'thorny time when our task has been less that of cultivating our garden than of clearing away the brambles', the task made difficult by the diverse and conflicting voices of Ireland's 'bourgeoisie, Little Irelanders, chauvenists, puritans, stuffed shirts, pietists, Tartuffes, Anglophobes, Celtophiles, *et alii hujus generis*'.[99] A general indifference to culture is declaimed by Thomas Bodkin's 1949 *Report on the Arts in Ireland* which condemns the absence of a coherent policy in support of the Arts:

> We have not merely failed to go forward in policies concerning the Arts, we have, in fact regressed, to arrive, many years ago, at a condition of apathy about them in which it had become justifiable to say of Ireland that no other country in Western Europe cared less, or gave less, for the cultivation of the Arts.[100]

Into this cultural apathy, this 'stony desert, baked and still' Kinsella places two enigmatic creatures. The first 'scuffles among the rocks / and stops, harrying its own vitals', while the other 'stands still on one foot, / pulling its head down between its shoulders, / torn by a great extinct beak' (P 16, C 332). They are joined in this 'pitiless waste' by 'a group of human figures', two of whom stand out from the crowd (P 16, C 332). Bold, and perhaps foolish, they approach the two creatures, 'misjudging their apparent preoccupation' (P 16, C 332):

> One is caught and swallowed in an instant.
> The other is seized as a support.
>
> (P 16, C 332 var.)

Both human figures are devoured by the creatures, while their human companions 'squat on their heels', wailing 'with low voices' (P 16, C 332). In 1965 Kinsella described 'literary Dublin of twenty years ago, giving off the same faint odour of isolation, [. . .] expressing such strength as it has in one or two lonely figures'.[101] Is this 'pitiless waste' a metaphor for the cultural wasteland of Ireland in the 1940s and 1950s? Are these two strange creatures the figures of a dual or divided poetic tradition about which Kinsella has written in his study of 1995?[102] Or do they represent the stultifying power of poetic influence, such as that of Yeats, under which younger poets laboured? Are the two unfortunate humans the figures of Austin Clarke and Patrick Kavanagh – named by Kinsella in his introduction to *The New Oxford Book of Irish Verse* as two poets 'that demand special attention'[103] – each in his different way struggling to establish a distinctive poetic voice against the apathy of their environment and in the shadow of Yeats: Kavanagh rewriting Yeats's pastoral romanticism in terms of the gritty Monaghan soil, Clarke trying to connect contemporary poetry with the Irish-language poetic tradition through his use of distinctively Gaelic prosody? Kinsella sets his reader more questions than answers here, but read in conjunction with the second scene, these questions at least gain a distinctive shape.

Between the scenes is a period of three or ten years of darkness. When the darkness lifts, a fertile and bright desert is revealed:

> The desert is full of voices, and blossoming.
> A breeze ruffles a carpet of wild flowers.
>
> (P 16, C 332)

The two carniverous creatures still endure, the first surrounded by the evidence of its earlier meal and clutching a fist of laxative herbs to ease, perhaps, the passage of that repast:

> He holds a bunch of coarse herbs
> up to his snout; cassia, the purging flax.
>
> (P 17, C 332 var.)

This image recalls lines from *Madonna and Other Poems*, (placed on the last page of *Collected Poems*) in which the poet 'turned away in refusal, // and held a handful of high grass / sweet and grey to my face' (P 13, C 335 var.). The second creature is adorned with the poisonous weedy nightshade:

> The monopod, decked in bittersweet
> from head to foot, hops about, garrulous.

> (P 17, C 332 var.)

Of the first group of humans on this scene, there is little evidence: 'Most of the new arrivals have vanished. A few / are lying still among the prostrate figures' (P 17, C 332 var.). In his revisions for the *Collected Poems* Kinsella renames the 'new arrivals' the 'early group' (C 332) to distinguish them from the second group. This group forms the centre of a renewed literary scene in Dublin 'three years – ten years' on. The scene is characterised by 'new expression and attitudes' that 'range from faded sneer to witless discovery' (P 16–17, C 332). Interpreting these new attitudes are the critics, depicted in Kinsella's poem as 'a ring of ghosts / surrounding the scene', one of whom, Denis Donoghue, 'seven feet tall, / prods at random with a shadowy stick' (P 17, C333).[104] The lethargy evident in the first part of the poem is still pervasive in the second part in which poetry and its critical reception are portrayed as lacking dynamism or purpose. Even though there 'is some excitement in one corner', 'most of the ghosts are merely shaking their heads' (P 17, C 333).

The image that Kinsella chooses for the cover of *Open Court* depicts an image of a man's head 'for the purpose of the study of phrenology'.[105] Taken from Albrecht Dürer's woodcuts, it illustrates the now discredited science of phrenology which argued 'that the mental powers of the individual consist of separate faculties, each of which has its organ and location in a definite region of the surface of the brain' (OED). The relationship between surface and centre is crucial to Kinsella's poetry. His attention to the detail of experience as a means of understanding its import is integral to the poet's approach. In *Open Court* Kinsella gives us a phrenological examination of the state of poetry in Ireland in which the surface evidence does not always correlate with what is at work in the centre. Taking the cover of *Open Court* in tandem with the image on the cover of *Madonna*, we might remember the connection R.W. Emerson makes between astrology and phrenology: 'Astronomy to the selfish becomes astrology; . . . and anatomy and physiology become phrenology and palmistry' (OED). From the biting lampoon of *One Fond Embrace*, in which few friends or colleagues escaped censure, to the humorous satire of *Open Court*, Kinsella's work of the late 1980s and early 1990s gives us an anatomy of Ireland traced through a phrenology of Dublin.

His attention to location and place, especially in *Personal Places* and *Poems from Centre City*, describes a surface through which an analysis of the underlying situation may be written.

CONCLUSION

Five years elapsed between *Open Court* and the publication of Kinsella's next volume of poetry, *The Pen Shop*, issued by Peppercanister in 1997. In the intervening years Kinsella published an essay on poetry and politics called *The Dual Tradition* which came out with Carcanet Press of Manchester as the eighteenth Peppercanister. *The Dual Tradition* brings together Kinsella's previous critical writings on the Irish poetic tradition, such as his 1966 address to the Modern Language Association, 'The Irish Writer', and his research for the Irish Studies programme that he directed for Temple University. Kinsella envisages this essay as the start of a series of critical readings coming from Peppercanister which will work in tandem with the Peppercanister poems. A possible next project is a reading of Ezra Pound's *Cantos*. During this time Kinsella was also preparing a collection of his poems, *Thomas Kinsella Collected Poems 1956–1994*, which was published by Oxford University Press in 1996. The collection provided Kinsella with the opportunity to make revisions, especially in the writing from the previous two decades, and it gives the reader a sense, for the first time, of the interplay between each volume or section of his poetry. Describing the *Collected Poems* as a 'work-in-progress' Floyd Skloot emphasises the way in which Kinsella continues to 'revise and reorganize' the work so that the older poems gain a new understanding when read through the prism of the later work:

> He has habitually absorbed his past work into his new work, referring back to specific images and scenes, returning to situations dealt with in earlier poems, using the concluding lines of previous books as the opening lines of new ones, and developing a set of references that serve as the circulatory system for his body of work.[1]

These sets of reference have slowly shifted through the decades. The emphasis on Jungian psychology and Celtic mythology as enabling structures for the poetry of the 1970s and 1980s gives way, slowly, to a greater attention to the structures of geography and history as the poet explores self and society within the circumference of Dublin. The final volumes of the 1990s, *The Familiar* and *Godhead*, signal a movement of reappraisal and renewal which coincides with Kinsella's shift towards a more private and meditative poetry.

The Pen Shop

Like *Open Court*, *St Catherine's Clock*, and *Butcher's Dozen*, *The Pen Shop* continues what Michel de Certeau has called 'the long poem of walking'.[2] In these poems Kinsella uses the poet-speaker's journey through a specifically delineated urban geography to explore the relationship between place and politics from the perspective of both the present and the past. The act of walking in an urban space allows for connections to be made between disparate times through an identity of space. Kinsella's 1997 volume, *The Pen Shop*, enunciates a topography of Dublin through which the poet draws together the strands of personal and public history into the nodal point of writing. Divided into two sections – 'To the Coffee Shop' and 'To the Pen Shop' – with an prefatory poem at the beginning of the volume, *The Pen Shop* traces a journey from the General Post Office on O'Connell Street, over the Liffey, into Bewleys of Westmoreland Street, and on down to Nassau Street to the warm confines of 'The Pen Shop'. This journey also traces a movement from the mythical history of Ireland which so informed Kinsella's *One*, through a meditation on pre-independence history alluded to in books such as *The Messenger* and *St Catherine's Clock*, to an assessment of the poet's family history and his own mortality. The poem opens in the General Post Office as the speaker posts a letter to the muse-mother figure whose 'fierce forecasts' provoke this response: '*Rage, affliction and outcry!*' (P [7]). The italicisation of this phrase undercuts the seriousness of the sentiments, and is followed by a wry self-portrait: 'Wide awake at the faintest scent of trouble; / contented, nosing around among the remains' (P [7]). The journey '*To the Coffee Shop*' begins 'under the cathedral ceiling' of the post-office at the centre of which stands a statue of Cúchulainn, the mythical figure already familiar from 'At the Western Ocean's Edge' of *Personal Places*:

> [. . .] Around the bronze hero
> sagging half covered off his upright,
> looking down over one shoulder at his feet.
> The harpy perched on his neck.
>
> (P [7])

This 'bronze hero' is the dead Cúchulainn, no longer turning his 'struggle outward, against the sea' (P 27, C 302). Instead, he is lashed to a pillarstone with a crow, symbol and manifestation of Mórrígan, goddess of war, standing on his shoulder. She foretells the hero's death, and announces it by landing on his dead, but upright, body. The crow, or 'harpy' as Kinsella puts it, is also a version of the cailleach figure who can be read as Hecate or the Terrible Mother. By focusing on the representation of Cúchulainn depicted by the statue in the GPO, Kinsella situates an aspect of the Irish mythology which is fundamental to his poetry in a specifically political context. Through subject and situation Kinsella questions the use of mythology for political purposes, evoking the rhetoric of Pádraig Pearse, key figure in the Easter Rising of 1916, for whom Cúchulainn was 'the great prototype of the Irish patriot-martyr'.[3]

This rhetoric of blood-sacrifice embodied in the statue of the dead hero is subtly undercut in *The Pen Shop* by the appearance of James Joyce's pacifist 'Mr Bloom'. The introduction of Bloom adds a retrospective resonance to Kinsella's description of himself in *The Messenger* as a 'blackvelvet-eyed jew-child' who watches his father agitating against the fascist Blueshirts in *The Messenger* (P 13, C 222). As the speaker leaves the GPO he passes the 'souls' whose movements approximate Dantean circumambulation as they take their 'places in line at the glass grills / or bowing at the shelves. / Following one another / out through the revolving doors' (P [7]). On O'Connell Street Kinsella's speaker intersects with Leopold Bloom who travels northward to the Prospect Cemetery in Glasnevin:

> By Smith O'Brien. Dead thirty years, to the day,
> when Mr Bloom unclasped his hands in soft
> acknowledgement. And clasped them. About here.
>
> (P [8])

Drawing on the 'Hades' episode of Joyce's *Ulysses* (alluding, also, to a Dantean Inferno), Kinsella connects the statue of Cúchulainn with the statues of O'Connell Street, each of which commemorate a particular moment in Irish history. Here, Kinsella rewrites Joyce's passage:

> Mr Bloom unclasped his hands in a gesture of soft politeness and clasped them. Smith O'Brien. Someone has laid a bunch of flowers there. Woman. Must be his deathday. For many happy returns. The carriage wheeling by Farrell's statue united noiselessly their unresisting knees.[4]

William Smith O'Brien,[5] Cambridge-educated MP for Limerick, was involved in the insurrections of 1848 for which he was commemorated by a statue sculpted by Sir Thomas Farrell.[6] Another statue by Farrell, that of Sir John Gray,[7] continues the connection with Bloom for it was he who owned and edited the newspaper that Bloom carries around in his pocket, *The Freeman's Journal*: 'By Sir John Gray, of *The Freeman's Journal*'. Significantly for Kinsella's poem, it is in the offices of *The Freeman's Journal* that Stephen rejects the rhetoric of nationalist Irish culture. On his way to Glasnevin, Bloom passes Gray's statue: 'Mr Power, collapsing in laughter, shaded his face from the window as the carriage passed Gray's statue.'[8] Though Gray was commemorated for advocating disestablishment of the Church of Ireland, land reform, and free denominational education, he is now 'unremembered on his pedestal' and denigrated by a quotation drawn from Joyce's story 'Grace' of *Dubliners* in which Mr Power pronounces that 'None of the Grays was any good' (P [8]).[9] The speaker's journey continues:

> Under Larkin with his iron arms on high,
> conducting everybody
> in all directions, up off our knees.
>
> (P [8])

In *The Messenger* Kinsella remembers the role that James Larkin[10] played in the development of his father's political consciousness: 'He reaches for a hammer, / his jaw jutting as best it can / with Marx, Engels, Larkin' (P 17, C 226). Larkin's struggle against capitalism rather than colonialism is seen, in these lines, to be inclusive and empowering. He stands outside the rhetoric of blood-sacrifice promulgated by Pearse and provides a visual contrast, 'arms on high', with the 'sagging' figure of the dead Cúchulainn. Kinsella's Joycean connection underlines a certain antipathy to what Declan Kiberd, in his 1992 introduction to *Ulysses*, has called 'the Cúchulainn cult' which was 'objectionable to Joyce because it helped to perpetuate the libel of the pugnacious Irish overseas, while gratifying the vanity of a minority of self-heroicizing nationalists at home'.[11]

By ghosting *The Pen Shop* with the Hades episode of *Ulysses*, and 'Grace' of *Dubliners*, Kinsella strengthens his inquiry into the role of memory and the place of the hero in the formation of history. The shades which Odysseus meets in Hades become the shades in the GPO, and the statues that Kinsella's poet-protagonist passes as he walks through the centre of Dublin. Just before crossing the River Liffey the speaker encounters the state of Daniel O'Connell, aloft on his twenty-eight foot pedestal.[12] He is the 'Hero as liberator' of 'At the Western Ocean's Edge' in *Personal Places* (P 27, C 302), and the 'hugecloaked Liberator's form' of *Ulysses*.[13] O'Connell, MP for Clare and successful agitator for Catholic Emancipation, stands 'high in the salt wind' that blows in from the Liffey (P [8]). The depth of his commitment, and his exceptional abilities as a politician are conveyed by his stance, 'shirt thrown open and ready for nearly anything', and his attitude, 'with hand on heart and dealer's eye' (P [8]).[14] Below O'Connell's statue gather personifications of the debates and issues of his time: 'Church and Education in debate / around the hem of his garment; Honest Toil at his heel' (P [8]).

With *The Pen Shop* Kinsella moves from the public history of the nineteenth century to a more private history centred on the twentieth century. As the speaker crosses O'Connell Bridge, the smell carried by the river tells of the poet's origins and of his family's long tradition of employment in Guinness's Brewery :

> From Islandbridge. Under Kingsbridge,
> with the black currents turning among each other
> in among the black piles at the lower Brewery gates:
>
> (P [9])

The description of 'hogsheads, swinging high up off the jetty' recalls Kinsella's grandfather, the barge-captain, from *The Messenger* (P [9]). The diminutive 'loaded barge' is counterpointed against the much larger ship, the 'Lady Patricia moored beyond Butt Bridge' (P [7]). It is to her that Kinsella offers this prayer: 'Family queen, / accept him, fumbling at your flank' (P [9]). The deaths through which national and family history are formed come to rest in the body of the speaker, which experiences a suspension of its own active processes, a suspension conceived of in metaphysical terms: 'Cold absence under the heart. / Arrest of the will' (P [9]). The speaker's epileptic arrest provides a moment in which he is literally outside of time, a peculiar sensation described through the speaker's focus on a vision which is at once the same, yet different: 'My left hand distinct against the parapet. / The parapet distinct, with my hand against it' (P [9]). This is the moment in which the poet-protagonist's body rehearses the 'Cursus inter- / ruptus' of *The Messenger* which marked John Paul Kinsella's death in 1976 (P 8, C 220), and recalls the connection Bloom makes between the Paddy Dignam's death and that of Charles Stewart Parnell whose foundation stone the funeral party has just passed: 'Breakdown. Heart'.[15] This moment gains a greater, though undefined, significance – 'something was indicated' – which is connected to notions of need and capacity as they are linked to measure (P [10]). The subsequent stanza, situated in Bewley's of Westmoreland Street, enriches Kinsella's meditation through its focus on the grinding and measuring of the coffee which will become Kinsella's necessary 'black draft' (P [11]). His repetition of similar phrases, 'Measured to the need' and 'precise in their needs', links the specific measurement of coffee with the larger measurement of life as apprehended through a moment in which life is suspended (P [10]). Bewley's assumes the air of an alchemical laboratory where the coffee, elixir of life, combines with the speaker's tablets to restore him to health. The 'family queen', who oversaw his grandfather's labours, is invoked in a toast as 'the black draft / entered the system direct, / foreign and clay sharp' (P [10–11]).

The second poem, 'To the Pen Shop', continues the newly restored speaker's journey through the centre of Dublin. Moving towards College Green he passes by the Bank of Ireland, once Ireland's House of Lords, stepping out 'under the arms of Grattan' whose statue stands between three streams of traffic. With an accuracy that most Dubliners will recognise, Kinsella describes the old antagonism between the jaywalking pedestrian and the double-decker bus, which aims a 'broadside of bus windows against my face; // the green backside swaying and settling / with an organic blast' (P [13]). The bus acts as an excipient for Kinsella's thoughts which follow the retreating vehicle 'Down Dame Street' towards Kinsella's own birthplace and childhood haunts, past Dublin Castle and on 'to the Fountain and the Forty Steps':[16]

> toward Kilmainham, heading Westward.
> Past Inchicore. Toward the thought of places
> beyond your terminus.

(P [13])

These are the places beyond origin, the places glimpsed from the 'pale Western shore' which glimmer like 'the light of cities under the far horizon' (P [13]). Here Kinsella reverses the story of Ireland's origins, integral to the volume *One*, in which Ith sees a shadow or shape of Ireland from the distant Land of the Dead.[17] Instead, the speaker looks outward to other possible new worlds, not least the gleaming cities of the United States where Kinsella himself spent almost four decades.

Passing by the statues of Edmund Burke,[18] agitator for Catholic emancipation, and Oliver Goldsmith,[19] playwright and novelist, which stand on either side of the front arch of Trinity College, Dublin, the speaker's eye moves toward the shops at 'the far end' of Grafton Street which turn 'toward the South' (P [13–14]). This direction takes the speaker's thoughts to the Wicklow of his father's family and on to the Wexford from where his beloved comes. Hugging the 'high railings' of Trinity College, into which he sees the 'thick back of an enemy disappearing', the speaker moves into Nassau Street (P [14]). The traffic takes his thoughts eastwards to Dublin bay and beyond, remembering the diasporic movements of Irish people to Liverpool and beyond, 'rising out of Europe':

> clear in calibre and professional,
> self chosen,
>   rising beyond Jerusalem.
>
> (P [14])

The journey of *The Pen Shop* juxtaposes the larger social history marked by the statues encountered on the way from O'Connell Street to Nassau Street – and problematised through the figure of Cúchulainn – with the personal and mythic history glimpsed through the vistas of the north, south, east and west. At the centre of these directions is the monastic 'narrow cell' of the Pen Shop –

> I turned aside
> into the Pen Shop
> for some of their best black refills.
>
> (P [15])

– source of the poet's supplies, those Faustian tools of transformation through which Kinsella makes sense of a journey which is both personal and public.

The Familiar

The last two volumes of the 1990s, *The Familiar* and *Godhead*, turn from the political, historical and social concerns which characterised the earlier volumes of the decade to a reappraisal of love and spirituality.[20] Operating within a threefold circuit which links lover, beloved and child with the Christian trinity of Father, Son and Holy Spirit, Kinsella returns to the wisdom of the flesh celebrated in *Out of Ireland* and *Madonna and Other Poems*. *The Familiar* opens with an epigraph in which Cupid brings lover and beloved together. Figured as 'Love' the god joins husband and wife in a covenant marked by the bow with which he is associated:

> Love bent the sinewy bow
> against His knee,
> saying: *Husband, here is a friend*
> *beseeming thee.*

(P [4])

The epigraph is followed by a seven-part sequence called 'The Familiar', which explores the development of that love from its early stages in the Baggot Street flat in which the speaker wrote his first poems. Ghosted by the illness which provides a backdrop for poems such as 'A Lady of Quality', the beloved's arrival is a gift which places into perspective the inner confusion signalled by the speaker's 'fumbling at the neglect / in my attic':

> My last thoughts alone.
> Her knock at the door:
> her face bold on the landing.
> 'I brought you a present.'

(P [7])

The lovers' union is witnessed by the 'demons over the door', reminiscent of the *síle-na-gig* of *Out of Ireland* who joins mind and matter in her 'offered self' (P 11, C 262 var.). Lover, muse and guide, the beloved is glimpsed in the image of the 'three graces' pinned above the toilet cistern in the fifth section, and appears as the *aisling* figure, 'whispering: *Come*' in the sixth (P [11, 13]). The poem ends with a re-enactment of the breakfast ritual sacrifice first performed in *Madonna and Other Poems*. The 'two crows' ascending towards the 'tundra' of the Sally Gap mirror the pair of ravens who signal constancy in love of 'Madonna' (P [14]). The blood grapefruit and scalding tea of 'Madonna' are offered up again (in the company of tomatoes, cheese and toast) in a eucharistic rite signalled by the ringing of 'the little brazen bell'. Like the image of the bearded Celtic priest which follows the poem, the speaker stands, 'arms extended', to welcome the beloved who encompasses the domestic and the divine:[21]

> Her shade showed in the door. Her voice responded:
> 'You are very good.
> You always made it nice.'

(P [15])

Here, Kinsella rewrites the Calypso episode of Joyce's *Ulysses* in which Bloom prepares breakfast for Molly. Joyce's 'Gelid light' becomes the 'the frost on the window' in the kitchen where the poet-protagonist sets out the toast for his beloved, 'Arranged the pieces // in slight disorder

round the basket' (P [14–15]), just as Bloom prepares the slices of bread
for Molly, 'Another slice of bread and butter: three, four: right.'[22] Joyce's
cat, with her 'sleek hide' and 'green flashing eyes' is, in Kinsella's poem,
'Folded on herself. Torn and watchful' (P [14]).[23]

The two following poems counterpoint marriage from one generation
to another. The first, 'St John's', revisits the Enniscorthy church remem-
bered in 'Anniversaries' of *Song of the Night and Other Poems* as 'a
cage / of flowering arches full of light' (P 6, C 204) in which the speaker
and his beloved were married:

> Ghost hands,
> from behind, across your heart.
> Your head low
> in the confusion of assent.
>
> (P [19])

The hesitancy of remembered youth is contrasted with the quiet confidence
of the next generation in 'Wedding Evening' as the speaker remembers his
daughter on her wedding morning, 'in her white veil. / Sara in certainty'
(P [20]). That evening the speaker witnesses three women who appear
'on the Canal wall by the bridge opposite our house'. As three sides of the
cailleach figure who, for Kinsella, embodies the ancient mother, the beloved
'and everything else', the 'Three woman from the North side' evoke the
three tutelary goddesses of Ireland, Ériu, Banba and Fódla. By placing
this family event within the context of mythological origins Kinsella links
the succession of individual generations with a larger cultural history.
The poem ends on a note of sadness and hope as the speaker remembers
the vision of his daughter 'Where she stood this morning / in the front
window / in her white veil' (P [20]). The virginity and potentiality indi-
cated by the veil is embodied in the 'virginal drop' which issues from the
goddess Iris after whom the last poem is titled. Drawing the epigraph and
the closing poem together, Kinsella combines three of the aspects of Iris –
insect, flower and rainbow – in a vision which conveys the delicate tran-
sience of love through the adjectives 'shivering', 'whispering', and 'frail'.
The Familiar, with its connotations of otherworldly fidelity, and doubling,
attests to the endurance of a love celebrated through intimate gestures.

Godhead

Domestic and divine converge again in *Godhead* which explores a trinity of powers between the two shores of the North American continent. Recalling the waves against which Ó Rathaille and Cúchulainn railed, Kinsella writes of 'High Tide: Amagansett'. Set on Long Island, the poem describes the ebb and flow of the Atlantic ocean as it reaches towards the speaker's 'bare foot', recalling in reverse Amairgin's arrival to Ireland. Through a richly cadenced language, Kinsella conveys the rhythms of the tide:

> The ocean swell mounted, approaching the land;
> folded in a long crest, whitening along its length;
> and dismantled in thunder up the miles of shore,

> (P [9])

The conjunction between the rhythms of nature and the rhythms of poetry conveyed by 'High Tide: Amagansett' is picked up by the second poem, 'San Clemente, California: a gloss'. Situated on the opposite and more southerly Pacific shore of Southern California, 'San Clemente' questions the power of poetry through its quotation of Giolla Brighde Mac Con Midhe's 'A Defence of Poetry':[24]

> *All metre and mystery*
> *touch on the Lord at last.*
> *The tide thunders ashore*
> *in praise of the High King*

> (P [10])

Written in the thirteenth century, this poem is 'addressed to a priest claiming to bring from Rome a condemnation of the Irish bards', and it argues for the importance of poetry within the centre of economic and political life, for 'If decent men are told / to give no pay for poems / it is to say, No satire, / but praise all round, my priest!' The conflict between the Celtic and the Roman church here exposes a deeper conflict between the place of poetry in pagan and Christian society, recalling the Christian disavowal of *imbas forosnai* (and consequent disempowerment of the poet) alluded to in *Songs of the Psyche*. It is fitting, therefore, that

Kinsella sets these prefatory poems between the pagan and indigenous place name of Amagansett, and the Christian and colonial San Clemente. The sequence 'Godhead' comprises four poems – 'Trinity', 'Father', 'Son', and 'Spirit' – in which Kinsella situates the power of the poet within the larger force of the triune god. The cover of *Godhead* combines the bearded face of the paternal god with an image of a snake which signals the carnality of the son.[25] Both aspects of the deity are joined by an image of outspread wings, symbolic of the third facet of god, the holy spirit. In 'Father' the thunder of the tide from which poetic metre gains its force and rhythm is replaced by a 'palpable tongue' which, like the carnal knowledge of *Out of Ireland*, conflates the somatic and the noetic. In a language which mimics biblical pronouncements (see Leviticus 13 on leprosy), the speaker casts himself as an outsider, and outcast, who has a divine message to convey:

> And I said: O my Father,
> Thou hast spoken to Thy servant!
> But I am slow of speech – they will not believe me.
>
> (P [15])

'Son' rewrites the annunciation which signals the transformation of word into flesh, drawing a parallel between the body of the crucified Christ and that of the virgin whose body is also transformed for the sake of the word:

> A Stranger fallen across her
> in fierce relief, without love.
> And the Adjustment in her body.
>
> (P [17])

The sequence ends with a return to the pagan concerns with which it opened, as Kinsella situates the tension between the pagan and the Christian worlds within a perspective drawn from the *Lebor Gabála Érenn* which has witnessed the passing of successive peoples. The salvific first-born of 'Son' becomes the 'Dust of our lastborn' in 'Spirit'. The wind which whips the waves of Amagansett, 'shaking the night air' of San Clemente, is the same wind of the desert 'that passes and does not return'. This same wind is both body and spirit. It is the wind which elicits compassion from God, 'For he remembered that they *were but* flesh; a wind that passeth away, and cometh not again' (Psalm 78: 39), and comforts St Augustine in an acknowledgement of his own weakness, 'since I was *flesh and blood, no better than a breath of wind that passes by and never returns*', (*Confessions* I: 13). Situated on a liminal line between land and water, body and spirit, life and death, *Godhead* proposes a vision of continuity and transformation which promises renewal, not redemption. The 'dust of our lastborn' is the ground on which we stand.

*

Kinsella's poetry involves the intentional disavowal of the specifically aesthetic elements of poetry in favour of a fidelity to the elements or 'data' of experience through which the poet constructs his sequences. One example is Kinsella's detailed descriptions of the workings of the abbatoir in *A Technical Supplement*. The sequence uses the details of butchery to construct an anatomy of poetry, of the self, and (in a less direct way) of society. This approach can be taken as emblematic of Kinsella's direction as a whole in the Peppercanister poems whereby he isolates the details under consideration, then constructs a framework of interrelationships through which the details cohere. This framework began with the numerological system of one to five through which the poet structured *Notes from the Land of the Dead* and the initial Peppercanister sequences. This system links with Kinsella's interest in Jungian theory and Taoism, both of which work towards a notion of completeness signified by the number five and achieved through a process of self-knowledge (which involves acknowledging the unpalatable aspects of the self) which Jung called individuation. Through the number five, which is figured as the centre of the Quincunx or Mandala that features in sequences such as *Vertical Man* and *Her Vertical Smile*, Kinsella connects with Celtic mythology and in particular the voyage of the first kindreds of Ireland told in the *Lebor Gabála Érenn*. Mythology, both classical and Celtic, provides important reference points for the poetry, and works as an 'additional weight' behind the narratives of origin and identity.[26] However, the numerological framework which wove together the psychological, spiritual, and mythic strands of the poetry had to be abandoned because, as Kinsella explains, 'ordinary experience began to take over'.[27] Kinsella recognises that his programme for the Peppercanister series contained the seeds for its own undoing since the goal achieved through the figure five 'would be the ultimate solution, where totality would be understood'.[28]

The idea of an ultimate solution, or a totality of understanding, is contrary to the procedures and directions which characterise these poems. The great strength of the Peppercanister poems is their ability to remain open-ended, to allow for the possibility of further inquiry. David Kellogg situates Kinsella's poetry between the modern poetic sequence and the postmodern poetic series.[29] The former is defined by Rosenthal and Gall as 'a grouping of mainly lyric poems and passages, rarely uniform in pattern, which tend to interact as an organic whole. It usually includes narrative and dramatic elements, and ratiocinative ones as well, but its structure is finally lyrical'.[30] Contrasted with the organic nature of the modern poetic sequence is the often aleatory nature of the postmodern sequence which, in Joseph Conte's view, operates by discontinuous conjunction and 'forgoes the linear, thematic development' characteristic of the modern poetic sequence.[31] While Kinsella's Peppercanister poetry is not characterised by chance arrangement, it does eschew linear progression in favour of a doubling or reflexive movement by which the early poetry finds itself being read from the perspective of the later work, and indeed others' work: *The Pen Shop*, for example, casting new light on the social and familial concerns of *The Messenger*, and sending us back to a rereading of Joyce's *Ulysses*. Rather than strictly postmodern, Kinsella's attention to serial form is perhaps closer to the musical definition of 'total serialism' as a search for a forms of music that is consonant with its method. Just as serial music is composed with a very small degree of redundancy, requiring listeners to attend closely if they are to perceive serial differences, so Kinsella's Peppercanister poetry demands similar attention.

The integrity and courage of *Butcher's Dozen*, in which justice, violence, truth and power are put to the test, connects with Kinsella's examination of the expectations and disappointments of politics in *The Good Fight*. The latter sequence raises questions which are also pertinent to *A Selected Life* and *Vertical Man*. Drawing a parallel between art and politics Kinsella asks to what extent do we project our aesthetic or political needs on figures such as Ó Riada or Kennedy, and at what cost to them? The intertextuality of *The Good Fight*, which informs both the form and the content of that poem, becomes an integral part of subsequent Peppercanisters, especially *Her Vertical Smile*, establishing one form of the polyphony in which, as the epigraph of *Out of Ireland* makes clear, either a delightful melody or 'confused and disordered noise' can be heard (P 6, C 261). The ideal community which Kinsella describes in that epigraph, 'those who have a fine perception and can penetrate carefully to the secrets of the art', is evoked through the poet Amairgin in *One*. Distinguishing between artifice and creation (through a Faustian parallel) Kinsella questions the position of the poet in society, rewriting the first poet's confident conflation of self, society and nature with an interrogative slant:

> Who
>   is a breath
> that makes the wind
> that makes the wave
> that makes   this   voice?
>   (P [13], C 170)

The uncertainty of the poetic voice expressed here is explored in *A Technical Supplement* in which Kinsella scrutinises the craft of poetry, questioning the revision of lines and the selection of words until all that can really be affirmed is the solidity and usefulness of concrete words such as 'water' or 'root' and the ineffectiveness of larger, abstract terms such as 'Love' and 'Truth'. Kinsella explains his choice of the former lexicon over the latter by analogy with Dante:

> There have been times, fortunate times, when many things were shared, so that complex utterances were possible without questioning one's means, as in Dante's time. This is not one of those times. What we share is a general sense of unease and distress, betrayal and disappointment. There are very few bases on which we can share an understanding of great, enormous nouns like love, faith, and so on. Acts of communication involving objects of that kind have to be managed very carefully.[32]

Yet Kinsella does manage such acts of communication. Love, and the articulation of that love, is essential to his work. From the early poems celebrating the beloved, Kinsella has remained constant to an idea of love as an enabling force. Whether predatory in 'Anniversaries', revelatory in 'Song of the Night', unifying in *Out of Ireland*, or understood in terms of sacrifice and self knowledge in *Madonna and Other Poems*, love stands for a power that re-establishes a balance of perspective through which understanding and articulation is possible.

Throughout the Peppercanister poems, personal issues are developed within a larger political context, whether it is through the debate between socialism and nationalism in *The Messenger* or through the different representations of history in *St Catherine's Clock*. Though rooted in a specific local politics, the poems of the 1990s brings art and politics together. Kinsella's focus on the events surrounding the Wood Quay development in *One Fond Embrace* and *Personal Places* signal two diametrically opposed views of artistic process. An architecture which destroys the historical foundations on which it stands is contrasted with a poetry which gains its strength and form from local history and mythology. Art and politics are intertwined in the Peppercanisters on a number of levels. The counterpoint between music and war in *Her Vertical Smile* addresses the extent to which the material of life can be ordered, and raises questions regarding the complicity between art and violence. *Songs of the Psyche* alludes to the conflict between pagan rituals and the encroaching Christianity through the rite of *imbas forosnai*, which links the poet with a tradition of poetic apprenticeship as well as connecting him to a channel of enlightenment that is no longer available to the modern poet. The position of the writer within tradition is examined in *Personal Places* and *Poems from Centre City* as Kinsella names his brothers in the craft and places himself in the company of W. B. Yeats, Austin Clarke, Thomas Mann, Valentin Iremonger and W. H. Auden. In *The Pen Shop*, James Joyce joins Kinsella in a perambulation through Dublin which links personal and public history to a localised topography in a diminished *dinnsheanchas* through which the self is centred. A less measured portrait of literary company is drawn in *Open Court* which paints a bleak and barren picture of aesthetic reception. Some of the Peppercanister volumes, like *One Fond Embrace* and *Open Court*, appear to squander the energies of criticism on ill-judged or out-of-date targets, but yet, when read in the context of the sequence as a whole, their tone and subject matter finds a level among the other volumes as examples of the waste or detritus which must be acknowledged and assimilated in order that 'the poet can come to terms with his own significant experience'.[33]

Speaking of the role of entropy, dissolution and randomness in his poetry, Kinsella emphasises the importance of waste matter in the poetic process: 'waste is a significant part of the process, and [. . .] the process would have no significance unless the observing entity was present, making some sense of it'.[34] The responsibility to make sense does not lie only with the poet. As outlined by the epigraph to *Out of Ireland*, Kinsella envisages a readership that is willing to engage actively in the process of exploration in which the poet is involved. The reader, 'by an act of positive sympathy "puts on" the poem, so to speak, puts on this poetic sensitivity, engaged at this given time, with all its contexts, and extends his self; he extends his range of significant observation by this means, so as, in his turn, to ingest and understand.'[35] This extension of the self is a kind of journey in Ezra Pound's understanding of the Greek *periplus*.[36] Rewritten by Pound as *periplum*, the voyage is both one of continuous discovery and one of conquest and annexation: both deferral and resolution. But perhaps most importantly, it is a journey in which navigation relies on the lie of the land (or sea) rather than on schematic description: 'periplum, not as land looks on a map / but as sea bord seen by men sailing'.[37] A similar navigation is surely necessary for Kinsella's Peppercanister poems. The poet's 'responsibility toward actuality' requires a similar attention from the reader who, through the *dinnseanchas* of Kinsella's poetic territory, understands by 'reading the ground' (P 25, C 281).[38]

NOTES

Introduction

1 *Poetry Book Society Bulletin* 17, Mar. (1958).
2 John Haffenden, *Viewpoints: Poets in Conversation with John Haffenden* (London: Faber & Faber, 1981), pp. 100–13 (p. 101).
3 Dennis O'Driscoll, 'Interview with Thomas Kinsella', *Poetry Ireland Review* 25: Spring (1989): 57–65 (p. 58).
4 Michael O'Higgins, 'Poets of the Fifties: Thomas Kinsella', *Oxford Opinion* May (1960): 21–2 (p. 21).
5 Dillon Johnston, *Irish Poetry after Joyce* (Indiana: U of Notre Dame P; Mountrath: Dolmen, 1985), p. 102.
6 O'Higgins, 'Poets of the Fifties', p. 21.
7 *Poetry Book Society Bulletin* 55: Dec. (1967).
8 Kinsella prefaces the collection with a quotation from Apocalypse 8: 10–11.
9 Edna Longley, 'Spinning through the Void', *Times Literary Supplement*, 19 Dec. 1980: 1446.
10 John Montague, 'And an Irishman', *The New York Times Book Review*, 18 Aug. 1968: 5.
11 Eavan Boland, 'Kinsella: A New Direction', *The Irish Times*, 6 Apr. 1968.
12 John Haffenden, *Viewpoints*, p. 108.
13 Daniel O'Hara, 'An Interview with Thomas Kinsella', *Contemporary Poetry* 4 (1981): 1–18 (p. 6).
14 Ibid.
15 Johnston, *Irish Poetry after Joyce*, p. 104.
16 O'Driscoll, 'Interview with Thomas Kinsella', p. 60.
17 Haffenden, *Viewpoints*, p. 105.
18 This connection no longer exists in the revised poems of *Collected Poems*. See Maurice Harmon, *The Poetry of Thomas Kinsella: 'With Darkness for a Nest'* (Dublin: Wolfhound, 1974), p. 81.
19 Floyd Skloot, 'The Evolving Poetry of Thomas Kinsella' *New England Review* 18: 4 (1997): 174–87 (pp. 174–5).
20 Edna Longley, 'The Heroic Agenda: The Poetry of Thomas Kinsella', *Dublin Magazine* 5: Summer (1966): 61–78.
21 O'Driscoll, 'Interview with Thomas Kinsella', p. 65.

22 John MacInerney, 'Searching for Structure: Kinsella's Pause En Route', *Hibernia*, 4 Aug. 1972.

23 Seamus Heaney, 'The Poems of the Dispossessed Repossessed', *The Government of the Tongue* (London: Faber & Faber, 1988), pp. 30–5 (p. 32).

24 Haffenden, *Viewpoints*, p. 112.

25 Philip Fried, '"Omphalos of Scraps": An Interview with Thomas Kinsella', *Manhattan Review* 4: Spring (1998): 3–25 (p. 12).

26 Johnston, *Irish Poetry after Joyce*, p. 98.

27 Brian John, 'Contemporary Irish Poetry and the Matter of Ireland – Thomas Kinsella, John Montague and Seamus Heaney', *Medieval and Modern Ireland*, ed. Richard Wall (Gerrards Cross: Colin Smythe, 1988), pp. 34–59 (p. 38).

28 Kinsella explains that the decision to do an edition of the *Táin* 'had to do with the Dolmen Press maturing to a certain point: we wanted to do a new kind of work. The first idea was the Deirdre story; it was a manageable length. Then I got interested in such things for their own sake.' Fried, 'Omphalos of Scraps"', p. 11.

29 Carolyn Rosenberg, 'Let Our Gaze Blaze: The Recent Poetry of Thomas Kinsella', unpublished PhD thesis (Kent State University, 1980), pp. 120–1.

30 For a history of Dolmen see Robin Skelton, 'Twentieth-century Irish Literature and the Private Press Tradition', *Irish Renaissance: A Gathering of Essays, Memoirs and Letters for the Massachusetts Review*, ed. R. Skelton and D. Clarke (Amherst: U of Massachusetts, 1965), pp. 158–67; and Michael G. Freyer, 'The Dolmen Press', *The Private Library* (Apr. 1960). In 1976 Dolmen issued an illustrated bibliography of the first 25 years of the Press: Liam Miller, *Dolmen XXV: An Illustrated Bibliography of the Dolmen Press, 1951–1976* (Dublin: Dolmen Press, 1976).

31 Peter Lennon, 'Dolmen Dublin', *The Guardian*, 23 Oct. 1962.

32 Thomas Kinsella, 'A Note on Irish Publishing', *The Southern Review* 31: 3 (1995): 633–8 (p. 635). Also included in slightly revised form in Kinsella's *The Dual Tradition*, Peppercanister 18 (Manchester: Carcanet, 1995), pp. 107–10.

33 Rosenberg, 'Let Our Gaze Blaze', p. 209.

34 Kinsella, Preface to Stephen Enniss, *Peppercanister 1972–1997: Twenty-five Years of Poetry: A Bibliography* (Atlanta: Emory U, 1997), pp. 1–2. However, Kinsella did not abandon serial publication altogether. Certain poems in *Song of the Night and Other Poems*, published by Peppercanister in 1978, were first published in journals such as *Tracks*, *The Chowder Review*, and *The Sewanee Review*. Indeed this practice continues. Kinsella's recent journal publications include poems in *Agenda*, *Poetry* and *Ploughshares*.

35 Kinsella, Preface to *Peppercanister 1972–1997*, p. 1.

36 Ibid.

37 Ibid., p. 2.

38 Thomas Kinsella Papers, Woodruff Library, Emory University, box 24, folder 20.

39 For information on how Kinsella divides the editions into series, see the publicity pamphlets issued by Peppercanister in June 1978, 1985 and 1987.

40 Correspondence with Peter Fallon, 24 June and 12 Aug. 1980. Kinsella Papers, box 24, folder 1.

41 See Kinsella Papers, box 29, folder 10.

42 Ibid. See Dillon Johnston 'The Anthology Wars', *Times Literary Supplement*, 13 Sept. 1991 in which Peppercanisters 14 and 15 are listed under 'Dublin: Dedalus; distributed in the UK by Manchester: Password'.
43 Subsequent to the publication of the *Collected Poems*, OUP have ceased to publish their poetry list. Forthcoming commercial editions of Kinsella's work will be published by Carcanet Press, Manchester.
44 Skloot, 'The Evolving Poetry of Thomas Kinsella', p. 176.
45 Ibid.
46 Brian John, *Reading the Ground: The Poetry of Thomas Kinsella* (Washington: Catholic UP, 1996), p. 259.

1 Elegiac Concerns

1 Hugh McFadden, 'The Poet and Politics', *The Irish Times*. From Kinsella Papers, OBV 5.
2 In his preface to *Fifteen Dead*, Kinsella chooses to name the city 'Derry' rather than 'Londonderry.' Though this choice of name may on one level indicate a certain political view, this is not always borne out in practice. See James Simmons, 'Kinsella's Craft', *Fortnight*, 11 May 1972, p. 19.
3 Thomas Kinsella, *Fifteen Dead* (Dublin: Dolmen, 1979), p. 58.
4 John, *Reading the Ground*, p. 146.
5 Kinsella, *Fifteen Dead*, p. 57.
6 Quoted from promotional material for the first five Peppercanister volumes, produced by Peppercanister Press. See also Hayden Murphy, 'Thomas Kinsella: Inscapes of an Emotional Emigré', *Agenda* 33, 3–4 (1996): 176–98 (p. 183).
7 For bibliographic details of the Peppercanister series see Enniss, *Peppercanister 1972–1997*.
8 Kinsella Papers, box 8, folder 12.
9 Quoted by Desmond Rushe in 'Tatler's Parade', *Irish Independent*, 28 Apr. 1972.
10 David McCullough, 'David McCullough's Eye on Books', *Book-of-the-month-club News* Jan. (1974), pp. 6–7.
11 Kinsella Papers, Box 8, folder 12.
12 James Simmons, 'Kinsella's Craft', *Fortnight*, 11 May 1972, p. 19.
13 Enniss, *Peppercanister 1972–1997*, p. 6.
14 Kinsella, Preface to *Fifteen Dead*, p. 9.
15 Enniss, *Peppercanister 1972–1997*, pp. 5–9.
16 I am also grateful to Anthony Lioi of Rutgers University for drawing my attention to the connection between *Butcher's Dozen* and 'Mask of Anarchy'.
17 Kevin Sullivan, 'Thomas Kinsella's Public Poem', *The Nation* 214: 23 (5 June 1972): 725–6 (p. 725).
18 Longley, 'Spinning through the Void'.
19 Kinsella, *Fifteen Dead*, p. 58.
20 Brian Lynch, 'Kinsella falls short on Derry', *Evening Press*, 27 Apr. 1972.
21 See Elgy Gillespie, 'Thomas Kinsella: the poet', *The Irish Times*, Saturday, 20 June 1981, and Kinsella's response in Kinsella Papers, Box 23, folder 13.
22 Jonathan Swift, 'Ireland', in *The Faber Book of Political Verse*, ed. Tom Paulin, London: Faber, 1986, p. 185.
23 Kinsella, *Fifteen Dead*, pp. 57–8.

24 *An Duanaire 1600–1900: Poems of the Dispossessed*, ed. Seán Ó Tuama and trans. Thomas Kinsella (Dublin: Dolmen with Bord na Gaeilge, 1981, rpt. 1994), p. xxvii. In *Austin Clarke: Selected Poems* Kinsella describes the *Aisling* as a poem in which 'the poet meets a "sky woman" and describes her beauty; he asks her who she is, listing various Classical and Irish heroines as possibilities; she gives him a message of hope (or otherwise) for Ireland in its great troubles; and he "awakes", to find she has left him.' *Austin Clarke: Selected Poems*, ed. with an introduction by Thomas Kinsella (Mountrath, Portlaoise: Dolmen, 1976), p. 192.

25 Daniel Corkery, *The Hidden Ireland* (Dublin: Gill, 1967), pp. 126–30.

26 See Ó Rathaille's 'An Aisling' translated by Thomas Kinsella as 'The Vision' in *An Duanaire*, pp. 152–3.

27 Skelton, 'Twentieth Century Irish Literature and the Private Press Tradition'.

28 Bryan Merriman, *The Midnight Court: Cúirt an Mheadhon Oidhce*, trans. David Marcus, Dublin: Dolmen Press, 1966, p. 10.

29 For a description of Kinsella's visit to the site see W. J. McCormack's 'Politics or Community: Crux of Thomas Kinsella's Aesthetic Development', *Tracks* 7 (1987), 61–77, (pp. 70–1).

30 Harmon, *The Poetry of Thomas Kinsella*, p. 106.

31 'Report of the Tribunal appointed to inquire into the events on Sunday, 30th January 1972, which led to loss of life in connection with the procession in Londonderry on that day.' (London: HMSO, 18 Apr. 1972), p. 32. Quoted by Harmon in *The Poetry of Thomas Kinsella*, p. 106.

32 The form of these lines is echoed by Michael Hartnett's 1978 *A Farewell to English* in which he uses the image of the stew to describe the form of post-independence Irish poetry: 'Our commis-chefs attend and learn the trade, / bemoan the scraps of Gaelic that they know: / add to a simple Anglo-Saxon stock / Cuchulainn's marrow-bones to marinate, / a dash of Ó Rathaille simmered slow, / a glass of University hic-haec-hoc: / sniff and stand back and proudly offer you / the celebrated Anglo-Irish stew. In *The New Oxford Book of Irish Verse*, ed. Thomas Kinsella (Oxford: Oxford UP, 1986), p. 391.

33 See the Kinsella Papers, box 8, folder 12.

34 Desmond Rushe, 'Tatler's Parade', *Irish Independent*, 28 Apr. 1972.

35 Gerald Dawe, 'In the Violent Zone: Thomas Kinsella's *Nightwalker and Other Poems*', *Tracks* 7 (1987): 26–31 (p. 27).

36 Simmons, 'Kinsella's Craft', p. 19.

37 Note from Professor M. Roberts, Department of Modern History, The Queen's University of Belfast, to Professor D. Greene, MRIA, 7 May 1972, regarding *Butcher's Dozen*. Kinsella Papers, box 8, folder 12.

38 News bulletin of NICRA, *Civil Rights* 1: 9 (13 May 1972).

39 See 'New Bloody Sunday Twist', *The Belfast Telegraph*, 16 Sept. 1999; George Jackson, 'Experts say evidence to Widgery " worthless"', *The Irish Times*, 17 Sept. 1999; John Mullin, 'Bloody Sunday Revelation', *The Guardian*, 17 Sept. 1999.

40 Kinsella, *Fifteen Dead*, p. 58.

41 O'Driscoll, 'Interview with Thomas Kinsella', p. 64.

42 Thomas Kinsella, *Butcher's Dozen* (Dublin: Peppercanister, 1972, reissued 1992), p. 7

43 Donatella Abbate Badin, *Thomas Kinsella* (New York: Twayne, 1996), p. 178.

44 Denis Donoghue, *We Irish: Essays on Irish Literature and Society* (New York: Knopf, 1986), p. 187.
45 Tom Paulin, *The Faber Book of Political Verse* (London: Faber, 1986), p. 17.
46 Ibid., pp. 18–19.
47 *An Duanaire 1600–1800*.
48 Heaney, 'Poems of the Dispossessed Repossessed', p. 32.
49 'Unhappy and at Home: Interview with Seamus Heaney' in *The Crane Bag Book of Irish Studies (1977–1981)*, ed. Mark Patrick Hederman and Richard Kearney (Dublin: Blackwater Press, 1982), pp. 66–72 (p. 67).
50 Quoted by John Haffenden in *Viewpoints*, p. 105.
51 Floyd Skloot reviewing *Peppercanister Poems 1972–1978* in *Éire–Ireland* 15, Summer (1980): 141–6 (p. 143).
52 Celeste M. Schenck, 'When Moderns Write Elegy: Crane, Kinsella, Nemerov', *Classical and Modern Literature: A Quarterly* 6: 2 (1986): 97–108 (p. 98).
53 Kinsella, *Fifteen Dead*, p. 60.
54 Robert Welch, ed., *The Oxford Companion to Irish Literature* (Oxford: Clarendon, 1996), p. 454.
55 Aloys Fleischmann, 'Appréciation: Seán Ó Riada's *Nomos II*', *Éire–Ireland* 7: 3 (1972): 108–15 (p. 109).
56 Thomas Kinsella, 'The Irish Writer', *Éire–Ireland* 2: 2 (1967): 8–15 (p. 10).
57 John Engle, 'That Always Raised Voice: Seán Ó Riada and Irish Poetry', in *Contemporary Irish Writing*, ed. James Brophy and Raymond Porter (Boston: Twayne, 1983), pp. 33–47 (p. 33).
58 Kinsella, *Fifteen Dead*, p. 62.
59 John Montague, *The Rough Field* (Mountrath, Portlaoise: Dolmen, 1972, reprinted 1984), pp. 63–70.
60 Seamus Heaney, *Field Work* (London: Faber & Faber, 1979), pp. 29–30. In this edition Ó Riada's name appears neither in the English, as Reidy, nor the Irish, as Ó Riada, but in a hybrid of both: O'Riada.
61 Aidan Mathews, 'Modern Irish Poetry: A Question of Covenants', *The Crane Bag Book of Irish Studies (1977–1981)*, ed. Mark Patrick Hederman and Richard Kearney (Dublin: Blackwater Press, 1982), pp. 380–9 (p. 384).
62 Quoted from publicity produced by Peppercanister for their first four pamphlets.
63 Kinsella Papers, box 8, folder 20.
64 Thomas Kinsella, *Eire Ireland: Bulletin of the Department of Foreign Affairs* 843, Dublin, 14 Jan. 1972.
65 Engle, 'That Always Raised Voice', p. 44.
66 Daragh Smith, *A Guide to Irish Mythology* (Dublin: Irish Academic P, 1988), pp. 46, 126.
67 Correspondence with Kinsella, 27 July 2000.
68 Brian John notes that the contralto is Bernadette Greevy singing *Das Lied von der Erde*, *Reading the Ground*, p. 152. However, Kinsella stipulates that the singer was not Greevy, but rather the voice of an older recording (Correspondence with Kinsella, July 2000).
69 Sleeve notes for *Mahler: Das Lied von der Erde*, with Otto Klemperer, Christa Ludwig and Fritz Wunderlich (EMI Records, 1967). The notes describe the mezzo's first song, 'the lonely one in autumn', as a 'contemplation of autmnal colours and melancholy'.

70 For a description of Ó Riada's illness see Kinsella's commentary in *Fifteen Dead*, pp. 71–2.
71 John, *Reading the Ground*, p. 152.
72 Montague, 'Patriotic Suite: For Sean O Riada', in *The Rough Field*, p. 64
73 See Brian John's reading of this stanza in the light of Kinsella's commentary in *Fifteen Dead* in which he tells of an evening with Ó Riada masquerading as 'a pair of simple and lonely seamen from the Baltic.' John translates '*yob tvoyu mat*' as 'fuck your mother.' *Reading the Ground*, pp. 152–3. Also Kinsella, *Fifteen Dead*, p. 66.
74 See Kinsella's commentary in *Fifteen Dead*, p. 74.
75 Brian John, 'Irelands of the Mind: The Poetry of Thomas Kinsella and Seamus Heaney', *Canadian Journal of Irish Studies* 15: 2 (1989): 68–92 (p. 77).
76 Kinsella Papers, box 12, folder 26.
77 Kinsella, *Fifteen Dead*, p. 72.
78 Ibid.
79 Harmon, *The Poetry of Thomas Kinsella*, p. 44.
80 Kinsella, *Fifteen Dead*, p. 72.
81 John, *Reading the Ground*, 1996, p. 153.
82 Kinsella, *Fifteen Dead*, p. 60.
83 Lawrence Durrell, *Justine* (London: Faber & Faber, 1957). See Kinsella's review of Durrell's *The Tree of Idleness and Other Poems*, 'Poetry like a Punch-Bag says Thomas Kinsella', *Irish Press*, 19 July 1956.
84 Skloot, 'The Evolving Poetry of Thomas Kinsella', p. 184.
85 Apocalypse 8: 10–11; quoted by Kinsella in *Collected Poems*, p. 62.
86 John, *Reading the Ground*, p. 155.
87 Kinsella, *Fifteen Dead*, p. 72.
88 Fried, 'Omphalos of Scraps', p. 18.
89 Ibid. See also Brian John who includes in the possible sources for Kinsella's use of the term 'Quincunx' the division of Ireland into five provinces with the Stone of the Divisions standing at the centre. *Reading the Ground*, p. 154. See also Daragh Smyth, *A Guide to Irish Mythology* (Dublin: Irish Academic P, 1988), p. 178.
90 Arthur E. McGuinness, '"Bright Quincunx Newly Risen": Thomas Kinsella's Inward "I" ', *Éire-Ireland* 15: Winter (1980): 106–25 (p. 122). The quotation comes from C.G. Jung, *Symbols of Transformation* (Princeton: Princeton UP, 1970), p. 266.
91 John, *Reading the Ground*, p. 154, McGuinness, 'Bright Quincunx', p. 123
92 Kinsella, *Fifteen Dead*, p. 65.
93 Hans Bethge, after Li-Tai-Po, trans. Lionel Salter, 'Drinking song of Earth's Sorrows' or 'Das Trinklied vom Jammer der Erde' in sleeve notes for Mahler: *Das Lied von der Erde*, with Otto Klemperer, Christa Ludwig and Fritz Wunderlich (EMI Records, 1967, reissue 1998): 'Im Mondschein auf den Gräbern / hockt eine wild-gespenstische Gestalt! / Ein Aff' ist's! Hört ihr, wie sein Heulen / hinausgellt in den süssen Duft des Lebens!', p. 11. See also Kinsella's transcription of the poem in the notes to *Vertical Man*.
94 Kinsella, *Fifteen Dead*, p. 66.
95 Ibid., pp. 67–8.
96 Ibid., p. 70.

97 Kinsella, *Fifteen Dead*, p. 74

98 Kinsella Papers, box 13, folder 10.

99 Theodore H. White, *The Making of the President 1960* (New York: Atheneum, 1965), and Henry Fairlie, *The Kennedy Promise: The Politics of Expectation* (New York: Doubleday, 1973).

100 John, *Reading the Ground*, p. 157.

101 Fairlie, *The Kennedy Promise*, p. 287.

102 Gisela M.A. Richter, *The Portraits of the Greeks*, vol. 2 (London: Phaidon, 1965), pp. 164–7, The cover image and that facing part III comes from a head in the National Museum, Athens (plate 21, figs 957–8). The image on the frontispiece is held in the Fitzwilliam Museum, Cambridge (plate 16, fig. 946). The image facing part II comes from the Musée Granet, Aix en Provence (plate 14, fig. 939). The final image, facing the last page of the poem, is from the National Museum, Syracuse (plate 9, fig. 921).

103 Fairlie, *The Kennedy Promise*, pp. 210–11.

104 John, *Reading the Ground*, p. 159. See 'Morte D'Arthur', line 240.

105 See White, *The Making of the President*, p. 145.

106 Ibid., pp. 21, 331.

107 G. Lowes Dickinson, *Plato and his Dialogues* (London: George Allen & Unwin, 1931), p. 65. Kinsella notes phrases from an edition of this book in his drafts towards *The Good Fight*. I quote it here because Dickinson translates Plato somewhat differently to Desmond Lee's more widely read version which does not juxtapose the art of navigation with that of steering quite so directly: 'they think that it's quite impossible to acquire the professional skill needed for such control . . . and that there's no such thing as an art of navigation'. *Plato: The Republic*, trans. Desmond Lee (London: Penguin 1955, rpt. 1987), pp. 222–3. See Plato, *The Republic* book 6: 488.

108 Fairlie, *The Kennedy Promise*, p. 82.

109 Ibid.

110 Ibid, p. 83.

111 In his notes towards *The Good Fight*, Kinsella's quotations from Plato's *The Republic* and *The Laws* are taken from Lowes Dickinson's *Plato and his Dialogues*, pp. 96–7, also *The Republic*, book 6: 492–3.

112 In 1970 Kinsella joined the English Department of Temple University, Philadelphia.

113 Kinsella Papers, box 13, folder 8.

114 'There is a very close relationship between the "I" as narrator and the "I" as protagonist in the sick second section, where the assassin is preparing his state of mind.' Haffenden, *Viewpoints*, p. 110.

115 'The Shoals Returning: In memory of Gerry Flaherty, drowned 1959' in *Nightwalker and Other Poems*, 1968.

116 John Clellon Holmes, 'The Silence of Oswald', *Playboy* Nov. (1965): 101–2, 222–4 (p. 102).

117 Kinsella Papers, box 13, folder 6.

118 Plato, *The Republic*, book 8: 565–6: 'the popular leader [. . .] is inevitably and fatally bound either to be destroyed by his enemies, or to change from man to wolf and make himself a tyrant.'

119 Lowes Dickinson, *Plato and his Dialogues*, p. 119. *The Republic*, book 3: 401.

120 Lowes Dickinson, *Plato and his Dialogues*, p. 162.

121 Fairlie, *The Kennedy Promise*, p. 217.

122 Ibid., pp. 222–4. See also Martha Wolfenstein and Gilbert Kliman, eds, *Children and the Death of a President* (Gloucester, Mass.: Peter Smith, 1969).

123 Fairlie, *The Kennedy Promise*, p. 232.

124 John Fitzgerald Kennedy, 'Inaugural Speech', *The Irish Independent*, 21 Jan. 1961.

125 In the *Collected Poems* Kinsella omits the ellipsis after 'again' and brings the lines together into a single stanza.

126 John Haffenden, *Viewpoints*, p. 104.

127 Ibid., pp. 101–2.

128 Seán Lucy, 'The O Riada and Kennedy Poems', *The Irish Independent*, 30 Feb. 1974.

129 Ibid.

2 *Psychic Geography*

1 O'Driscoll, 'Interview with Thomas Kinsella', p. 59.

2 O'Hara, 'Interview with Thomas Kinsella', p. 16: 'The past has a psychic geography which is vitally important for the present.'

3 Kinsella Papers, box 14, folder 22.

4 John, *Reading the Ground*, p. 165.

5 H. D'Arbois de Jubainville, *The Irish Mythological Cycle and Celtic Mythology*, trans. Richard Irvine Best (Dublin: Hodges Figgis, 1903), p. 15

6 'Notes from the land of the dead', Thomas Kinsella, *Poems 1956–1973* (Mountrath, Portlaoise: Dolmen, 1980), p. 132. The revised version of the poem in *Collected Poems* omits these lines.

7 O'Driscoll, 'Interview with Thomas Kinsella', p. 61

8 Alwyn and Brinley Rees, *Celtic Heritage: Ancient Tradition in Ireland and Wales* (London and New York: Thames & Hudson, 1961), p. 118.

9 Fried, 'Omphalos of Scraps', p. 60.

10 In a discussion on the nature of cairn or burial mound in Ireland, A.and B. Rees report that any gathering of five things, or places, can be called a cairn; and given that 'every *cairn* in Ireland represents the whole' therefore 'Even children playing "fivestones" are unwittingly playing with symbols of the whole of Ireland.' Rees and Rees, *Celtic Heritage*, p. 188. The Reeses draw their material from 'Coir Anmann', in *Irische Texte*, ed. W. Stokes and E. Windisch (Leipzig 1897); and S. O Suilleabhain's *A Handbook of Irish Folklore* (Dublin 1942).

11 John, *Reading the Ground*, p. 179.

12 Enniss, *Peppercanister 1972–1997*, p. 18.

13 The copy from which Kinsella worked in preparation for *One* is held by the Woodruff Library, Emory University, Atlanta.

14 Erich Neumann, *The Origins and History of Consciousness*, trans. R.F.C. Hull, (Princeton: Princeton UP, 1954), p. 263.

15 C. G. Jung, *Collected Works*, ed. William McGuire et al., trans. R.F.C. Hull et al. (Princeton: Princeton UP, 1953–71), vol. 5.

16 Neumann, *Origins and History of Consciousness*, p. 10.

17 Brian John quotes from the Lebor Gabála Érenn, paragraph 23, *Reading the Ground*, p. 166.

18 In 'Dream Symbols and the Process of Individuation' Jung emphasises the relatedness of the self with all animate and inanimate life, and locates this self in opposite but interdependent poles: 'The self is not only the centre, but also the circumference that encloses consciousness and the unconscious', *The Integration of the Personality*, p. 96.

19 This is not the first of Kinsella's borrowings from Goethe. In conversation with Dennis O'Driscoll, Kinsella notes that the image of 'her dear shadow' in 'Nightwalker' 'is a borrowing from Goethe.' O'Driscoll, 'Interview with Thomas Kinsella', p. 63.

20 Johann Wolfgang von Goethe, *Faust*, Part II, Act 1, lines 6404–6, trans. Stuart Atkins (Cambridge MA: Suhrkamp/Insel, 1984), p. 164.

21 Rosenberg, 'Let Our Gaze Blaze', pp. 51, 54–6.

22 Ibid., p. 56.

23 A draft title for this poem was 'The Whole Temple', a phrase which is drawn directly from Goethe's text: 'the whole temple seems to me to sing' (line 6448). Goethe, *Faust*, p. 165.

24 'Goethe first wrote *Dichter*, poet, which he later changed to *Magier*, magician, sorcerer, magus; the equation is traditional', Stuart Atkins, 'Explanatory Notes, *Faust*, p. 321.

25 Goethe's use of the word 'conjurors' makes an allusion to 'the long popular identification of Faust with Gutenberg's associate Fust'. Stuart Atkins, 'Explanatory Notes', *Faust*, p. 321.

26 de Jubainville, *The Irish Mythological Cycle*, pp. 132–5.

27 When Ith arrived in Ireland he met three kings of the Tuatha Dé Danann who, seeing that it was Ith's intention to take possession of Ireland, slew him in a place which was subsequently called *Mag Itha* or the Plain of Ith. Ith's companions left Ireland for home, but resolved to avenge his death. Thirty-six chiefs, each with his company, returned to Ireland and overthrew the Tuatha Dé Danann. It is on this second journey that Amairgin chants his poem. See de Jubainville, *The Irish Mythological Cycle*, pp. 132, 136.

28 Neumann, *Origin and History of Consciousness*, pp. 39–101.

29 Alexander Gillies, *Goethe's Faust* (Oxford: Basil Blackwell, 1957), p. 116.

30 de Jubainville, *The Irish Mythological Cycle*, pp. 145–6

31 Ibid., p. 136, note 1.

32 Rees and Rees, *Celtic Heritage*, p. 96

33 de Jubainville, *The Irish Mythological Cycle*, p. 137. De Jubainville continues: 'the *file* is the personification of science, and science is identical with its object. Science is Being itself, of whom the forces of nature and all sensible beings are but manifestations. Thus it is that the *file*, who is the visible embodiment of science in human form, is not only man, but also eagle or vulture, tree or plant, word, sword, or spear; thus it is that he is the wind that blows over the sea, the wave of the ocean, the murmuring of the billows, the lake in the plain. He is all of these because he is the universal being, or, as Amairgin puts it, "the god who creates in the head" of man "the fire" of thought', p. 138.

34 de Jubainville, *The Irish Mythological Cycle*, p. 14.

35 Ibid., p. 16.
36 See John, 'Contemporary Irish Poetry', p. 38.
37 de Jubainville, *The Irish Mythological Cycle*, p. 58.
38 Carolyn Rosenberg links 'Agath, Kak' with the phrase 'Good, bad'. 'Let Our Gaze Blaze', p. 325. These two words are omitted from the *Collected Poems* edition.
39 Euhemeristic readings of the Irish mythology Kinsella uses in *One* have gained support from a recent study by Daniel G. Bradley and colleagues at Trinity College, Dublin, which links the DNA profile of Connaught men with similar profiles in the Basque region of Spain. See *The New York Times*, 23 Mar. 2000, p. A13. As the History of the Britons by Nennius states: 'Last of all the Scots out of Spain arrived in Ireland.' (de Jubainville p. 14). Spain was another name for the Land of the Dead.
40 John McCormack, 1884–1945.
41 For details of Kinsella's early family life see Rosenberg, 'Let Our Gaze Blaze', pp. 74–97.
42 Carolyn Rosenberg in an interview with Kinsella, 13 June 1975. 'Let Our Gaze Blaze', p. 560, n. 54.
43 Kinsella Papers, box 14, folder 18.
44 O'Hara, 'Interview with Thomas Kinsella', p. 17.
45 See de Jubainville, *The Irish Mythological Cycle*, p. 217.
46 John, *Reading the Ground*, p. 177. See also his 'Contemporary Irish Poetry and the Matter of Ireland', p. 40.
47 Haffenden, *Viewpoints*, p. 111.
48 Ibid., p. 112.
49 Enniss, *Peppercanister 1972–1997*, p. 23.
50 John F. Deane, 'A Conversation with Thomas Kinsella', *Tracks* 7 (1987): 86–91 (p. 88).
51 William Petty (1623–87). See William Petty's 'A General Mapp of Ireland' in *Hiberniae delineatio* (London: 1685). I am indebted to Ian Fleming's paper, '"Urinal Architects": Shining a light on Thomas Kinsella's Cloacal Construction (via Swift and Joyce)', Royal Holloway Research Seminars, 7 Feb. 2000, for this reference.
52 John O'Donovan, introduction to William Petty, *The Political Anatomy of Ireland: with the Establishment for that Kingdom and Verbum Sapienti* (London: D. Brown & W. Rodgers, 1691, rpt. Shannon: Irish UP, 1970), p. vi.
53 William Petty, 'The Author's Preface' in *The Political Anatomy of Ireland*, unpaginated.
54 Exodus 34: 29, Mark 9: 3.
55 Genesis 11: 1; Acts 2: 5–13.
56 Mc Cormack, 'Politics or Community', pp. 71–2.
57 O'Hara, 'Interview with Thomas Kinsella', p. 8.
58 M. L. Rosenthal and Sally M. Gall, *The Modern Poetic Sequence: The Genius of Modern Poetry* (New York and Oxford: Oxford UP, 1983), p. 9.
59 d'Alembert co-edited the *Encyclopédie* with Diderot until his resignation in 1758 after the publication of the seventh volume which brought Rousseau's attack on d'Alembert's article 'Genève'.
60 Denis Diderot, *Oeuvres Complets de Diderot*, ed. J. Assézat (Paris: Garnier Frères, 1876), vol. 14, p. 415.

61 John Morley, *Diderot and the Encyclopaedists* (London: Chapman & Hall, 1878. rpt. London: Macmillan, 1923), vol. 1, p. 184

62 Morley, *Diderot and the Encyclopaedists* (1878 edn, pp. 188–9).

63 Floyd Skloot, review of *A Technical Supplement Éire–Ireland* 12, Autumn (1977): 143–7 (p. 145). In his review of *A Technical Supplement*, Skloot attributes the illustrations in this volume to the section in Diderot's *Éncyclopédie* on anatomy: 'Kinsella has illustrated his poem with selections from the volumes of plates issued with Diderot's *Éncyclopédie* in 1772, choosing six of the 33 plates devoted to anatomy. The six are noteworthy: a scalpel on the cover; a hand poised with pen on the title page; heads and eyes in various stages of neat, calm dissection; a body straining upwards.'

64 This image is drawn from *Recueil de Planches* vol. 22 'Art d'écrire' planche iii, and is accompanied with the commentary: 'Pour accompagner la main dont je viens de parler, on a ajoûté trois instrumens convenables à l'art d'écrire.' [*sic*] 'Ecritures', p. 2.

65 Ibid.

66 Ibid. vol. 23 'Chirurgie' planche xxiv. fig.5.

67 *Colliers Encyclopedia*, ed. William D. Halsey (London: Cromwell, Collier & Macmillan, 1967), vol. 9, p. 520.

68 Section xv of *A Technical Supplement* was written as part of the earlier volume *One*, coming between the last two stanzas of 'The Oldest Place.' Kinsella Papers, box 14, folder 14.

69 Denis Diderot, *Selected Writings*, ed. Lester G. Crocker (London: Collier-MacMillan, 1966), p. 183.

70 Haffenden, *Viewpoints*, p. 101

71 Diderot, *Selected Writings*, pp. 180–181.

72 G. E. Lessing, *Laocoön: An Essay on the Limits of Painting and Poetry*, trans. E.A. McCormick (Baltimore: Johns Hopkins UP, 1984), pp. ix–x

73 'Dessein, Proportions de la Statue de Laocoon', planche xxxvi, fig. 1. "Laocoon vû de face" [Dessein, p. 12], vol. 23.

74 John Haffenden, *Viewpoints*, p. 113.

75 Ibid.

76 Skloot, review of *A Technical Supplement*, p. 145.

77 John Morley, *Voltaire* (London: Chapman & Hall, 1872), p. 336

78 John Morley, *Diderot and the Éncyclopaedist* (London: Macmillan, 1923), vol. 1, p. 157

79 Ibid.

80 Skloot, review of *A Technical Supplement*, p. 145.

81 Morley, *Diderot and the Éncyclopaedists*, vol. 1, p. 189

82 *Recueil de Planches* vol. 21. 'Anatomie'.

83 Claude Gandelman, *Le Regard dans le texte: image et écriture du Quattrocento au xxᵉ siècle* (Paris: Méridiens-Klincksieck, 1986), pp. 56–7

84 *Recueil de Planches*, vol. 21. 'Anatomie', p. 13, "suite de la planche xi et xii", fig.2

85 *Recueil de Planches*, vol. 23. 'Chirurgie' planche xvii. fig.1, p. 2.

86 Haffenden, *Viewpoints*, p. 113

87 Thomas Kinsella writing in the *Poetry Book Society Bulletin* 55, Dec. (1967)

88 Kinsella, *Poems 1956–1973*, p. 66.

89 Deane, 'A Conversation with Thomas Kinsella', p. 88.

90 Maurice Harmon, '"Move, if you move, like water": The Poetry of Thomas Kinsella, 1972–88', *Contemporary Irish Poetry: A Collection of Critical Essays*, ed. Elmer Andrews (London: Macmillan, 1992), pp. 194–213 (p. 194).

91 Ibid.

92 C.G. Jung, *Memories, Dreams, Reflections*, revised edn. Recorded and ed. Aniela Jaffé, trans. Richard and Clara Winston (New York: Pantheon, 1973).

93 Kinsella Papers, box 16, folder 14.

94 Jung, *Memories, Dreams, Reflections*, p. 8.

95 Ibid., pp. 10–12.

96 Kinsella makes greater use of ellipsis in the Peppercanister version.

97 Kinsella Papers, box 16, folder 14.

98 de Jubainville, *The Irish Mythological Cycle*, p. 100.

99 Ibid., p. xi.

100 *Thirty Three Triads*, trans. Thomas Kinsella, illust. Pauline Bewick (Glenageary, Co. Dublin: Dolmen, 1955), p. 5.

101 Kinsella Papers, box 16, folder 14.

102 Ibid., box 16, folder 24.

103 The river Nore runs into the river Barrow.

104 Another variant title for the poem is 'Tao and Unfitness. Inistiogue X June 1974'. Kinsella Papers, box 16, folder 17.

105 Public Record Office of Northern Ireland, The Tighe Papers (D/2685).

106 Kinsella Papers, box 16, folder 17.

107 *The Sewanee Review* 86 (June 1978): 123–6 (p. 125).

108 John, *Reading the Ground*, p. 188, n. 52; Andrew Samuels, Bani Shorter and Fred Plaut, *A Critical Dictionary of Jungian Analysis* (London: Routledge & Kegan Paul, 1986), p. 23.

109 C. G. Jung, 'Commentary on "The Secret of the Golden Flower"', *Alchemical Studies*, trans. R. F. C. Hull, *The Collected Works of C. G. Jung*, vol. 13 (London: Routledge & Kegan Paul, 1967), p. 21. Jung collaborated with Richard Wilhelm, director of the China Institute in Frankfurt, to publish the old Taoist text *The Secret of the Golden Flower* (Das Geheimnis der goldenen Blüte, Munich: Dorn-Verlag, 1929).

110 The *Collected Poems* version has 'mid-river'.

111 Liebestod means 'love-death'. Wagner used the term to describe the love duet in Act II of *Tristan und Isolde*, but the term is more usually applied to Isolde's aria in Act III. This aria or 'Liebestod' is often performed with the Prelude to Act I as a concert item. See Michael Kennedy, ed., *Oxford Dictionary of Music* (Oxford: Oxford UP, 1994), p. 509.

112 Edward A. Lippman, *The Philosophy and Aesthetics of Music* (Lincoln and London: U of Nebraska Press, 1999), p. 217

113 Wagner, *Tristan und Isolde*, Act III, 'Soll ich schlürfen, / untertauchen, / süss in Düften /mich verhauchen? / In dem vogenden Schwall / in dem tönenden Schall / in des Welt-Athems / wehendem All –' trans. Andrew Porter: 'Shall I taste them, / Dive beneath them? / Drown in tide / of melting sweetness? / In the rapturous swell, / In the turbulent spell, / In the welcoming wave, / Holding all.' *English National Opera Guide 6* (London: John Calder, 1981), p. 92.

114 Richard Wagner, *Tristan und Isolde: Oper in drei Aufzügen* (Frankfurt; London; New York: C. F. Peters [no date given]), pp. 654–5.

115 The *Collected Poems* version omits the phrase 'God in Heaven!'

116 Kinsella Papers, box 17, folder 3, contains drawings by Kinsella of herons and bats, and of the image used for the cover, title page and last page of the Peppercanister edition.

117 Carl Dahlhaus, *The New Grove Dictionary of Music and Musicians*, ed. Stanley Sadie, vol. 20 (London: Macmillan 1990), p. 121.

118 'Thomas Kinsella', *Poetry Book Society Bulletin* 17, Mar. (1958).

119 C.G. Jung, *Alchemical Studies*, trans. R. F. C. Hull, *The Collected Works of C. G. Jung*, vol. 13 (London: Routledge & Kegan Paul, 1967), p. 235.

120 Ibid., p. 223.

121 *Encyclopedia Britannica*, 13th edn, vol. 1, p. 520.

122 Rosenberg, 'Let Our Gaze Blaze', p. 89

123 Correspondence with Kinsella, 27 July 2000.

124 Jolande Jacobi cites Shakespeare's Caliban as a figuration of the unconscious in *The Psychology of C. G. Jung* (London: Routledge & Kegan Paul, 1942, 5th edn, 1951), p. 127

125 Jung, *Alchemical Studies*, p. 246; 'Mercurius as the lapis is a symbolic expression for the psychological complex which I have defined as the self.'

126 Brian John notes that the 'child in the Jungian child motif often appears as something precious (jewel, chalice, golden egg or ball, pearl) and indicates the integrated self' in *Reading the Ground*, p. 200.

127 Jung, *Alchemical Studies*, pp. 53, 67–8, 259. Andrew Samuels, Bani Shorter and Fred Plaut, *A Dictionary of Jungian Analysis* (London: Routledge & Kegan Paul 1986), p. 14.

128 Kinsella Papers, box 17, folder 11.

129 Jacobi, *The Psychology of C.G. Jung*, p. 139.

130 See F.S.L. Lyons, *Ireland Since the Famine* (London: Weidenfeld & Nicolson, 1971), pp. 267–84; and R.F. Foster, *Modern Ireland 1600–1972* (London: Penguin, 1988), pp. 434–46. See also Marx's and Engels's writings on *Ireland and the Irish Question* (London: Lawrence & Wishart, 1971).

131 Lyons, *Ireland Since the Famine*, p. 280.

132 In *Sartor Resartus* Carlyle develops his 'Clothes Philosophy' which has elements in common with C. G. Jung's theory of archetypal experience.

133 For Kinsella on Thomas Moore see *The Dual Tradition*, pp. 47–9.

134 O'Driscoll, 'Interview with Thomas Kinsella', pp. 61–2. See also Ian Flanagan, 'An Interview with Thomas Kinsella', *Metre* 2 (Spring 1997): 108–15 (p. 108).

135 Fried, 'Omphalos of Scraps', p. 18.

3 Historical Particulars

1 Kinsella, ed., *The New Oxford Book of Irish Verse*, p. vii.

2 See also Elgy Gillespie's mention in 'Thomas Kinsella, the poet', *The Irish Times*, 20 June 1981: 'He's just knocked off four new poems for Cecil King's print collection, commissioned by Monica Beck, and will be Peppercanistering the texts soon.'

3 Kinsella Papers, box 62, folder 1.

4 Ibid., box 18, folder 15.
5 Ibid., box 18, folder 15.
6 This verse is the second stanza of 'Four "Glosses"' from Kinsella's *The New Oxford Book of Irish Verse*, p. 30.
7 Kinsella Papers, box 18, folders 15–16. From notes in folder 16 it seems as if Kinsella envisaged having these glosses as an introduction to *Songs of the Psyche*. For an example of such a gloss see 'Ah blackbird, giving thanks', in Thomas Kinsella, ed., *The New Oxford Book of Irish Verse*, p. 55.
8 Kinsella Papers, box 62, folder 2.
9 Ibid., box 62, folder 2.
10 For a list of the titles of the chosen poems see the Ibid., box 62, folder 2.
11 Ibid., box 18, folder 12.
12 Ibid., box 18, folder 11.
13 Ibid., box 18, folder 8.
14 Kinsella Papers, box 18, folder 13.
15 George Brown; see Rosenberg, 'Let Our Gaze Blaze', p. 74.
16 Kinsella Papers, box 18, folder 13.
17 Notes from the *Irish Independent Eucharist Congress Souvenir*, 1932, in Kinsella Papers, box 18, folder 7. See also Lyons, *Ireland since the Famine*, pp. 70–7; and Foster, *Modern Ireland*, p. 304.
18 Maurice Harmon, '"Move if you move, like water": The Poetry of Thomas Kinsella, 1972–88', *Contemporary Irish Poetry: A Collection of Critical Essays*, ed. Elmer Andrews (London: Macmillan, 1992), pp. 194–213 (p. 197).
19 O'Driscoll, 'Interview with Thomas Kinsella', p. 60.
20 Fried, 'Omphalos of Scraps', p. 12.
21 John, *Reading the Ground*, p. 203.
22 Nora K. Chadwick, 'Imbas Forosnai', *Scottish Gaelic Studies* 4: 2 (1935), pp. 97–135 (p. 104).
23 Ibid., pp. 97–135, pp. 110–11.
24 John, *Reading the Ground*, p. 205.
25 James MacKillop, *Dictionary of Celtic Mythology* (Oxford: Oxford UP, 1998). See also Chadwick, 'Imbas Forasnai', pp. 98–100.
26 Kinsella Papers, box 18, folder 18.
27 See *An Duanaire*, pp. 276–355.
28 In *Collected Poems* Kinsella revises the lines, moving 'up' from the end of line 5 to the beginning of line 6.
29 For reference to Kinsella's interest in science fiction see Fried, 'Omphalos of Scraps', p. 5.
30 Dante Alighieri, *The Divine Comedy*, trans. Charles S. Singleton (Princeton: Princeton UP, 1970), p. 3.
31 Correspondence with Kinsella, 27 July 200. See also Floyd Skloot's 'The Evolving Poetry of Thomas Kinsella', pp. 175–6: '[. . .] only to interrupt himself once more with a mocking "Please." OR Puh-leeze, as we might read it. The man knows he can be a handful; his intimidating glower is softened by a mischievous grin'.
32 P. W. Joyce, *A Smaller Social History of Ancient Ireland*, 2nd edn (London: Longman, Green/Dublin: M.H. Gill, 1908), p. 294.
33 Jacobi, *The Psychology of C.G. Jung*, p. 158.
34 O'Driscoll, 'Interview with Thomas Kinsella', p. 63.

35 Promotional pamphlet, 'New Special Editions, Thomas Kinsella 1985' (Dublin: Peppercanister Press).
36 Kinsella, *Fifteen Dead*, p. 65.
37 Goethe, from *Faust* in *Mahler: Symphony no. 8*, with Colin Davis (BMG Music, 1996).
38 Mahler, trans. Lionel Salter, last lines of 'Der Abschied' or 'The Farewell' in sleeve notes for *Mahler: Das Lied von der Erde*.
39 Goethe, from *Faust* in *Mahler: Symphony no. 8*.
40 Gustav Mahler to Willem Mengelberg, 18 Aug. 1906, quoted in Egon Gartenberg, *Mahler: The Man and his Music* (New York: Schirmer, 1978), p. 319.
41 For images of Mahler conducting see Gartenberg, *Mahler: The Man and his Music*, pp. 181–5; also Michael Kennedy, *Mahler* (London: Dent, 1990).
42 John, *Reading the Ground*, p. 215.
43 Mahler's compositions were not always received favourably, indeed for the early part of his career he was considered primarily as a conductor rather than a composer. In addition he had to contend with the institutionalised anti-Semitism of Austria.
44 John, *Reading the Ground*, p. 215
45 Alma Mahler in *Gustav Mahler: Memories and Letters*, ed. Donald Mitchell, trans. Basil Creighton (London: John Murray, 1968), p. 180. See also Egon Gartenberg, *Mahler*, pp. 113–14.
46 Bruno Walter, *Theme and Variations*, trans. James A. Galston (New York: Alfred Knopf, 1946), p. 187.
47 Egon Gartenberg, *Vienna: Its Musical Heritage* (University Park: Pennsylvania State UP, 1968).
48 Other possible titles for *Her Vertical Smile* were *The Elect* and *Our Music Master*. See Kinsella Papers, box 21, folder 11.
49 *The Letters of Thomas Mann, 1889–1955*, trans. Richard Winston and Clara Winston, (Harmondsworth: Penguin, 1975), p. 69.
50 See Donald Prater's *Thomas Mann: A Life* (Oxford: Oxford UP, 1995), p. 99.
51 Thomas Mann's daughter Erika figured on the list of 8 June 1935 of those to be stripped of their German citizenship. While visiting her brother Klaus in Holland she met the English novelist Christopher Isherwood, and asked him for a marriage of convenience to enable her to get a British passport. He declined out of consideration for his partner who was a German exile and also because he did not want it to seem that he wished to pass as a heterosexual. However he suggested his friend W.H. Auden, who was amenable to the idea. Erika travelled to England on 12 June 1935 and was married to Auden three days later. See Prater, *Thomas Mann*, p. 238.
52 O'Driscoll, 'Interview with Thomas Kinsella', p. 58.
53 John, *Reading the Ground*, p. 219.
54 Ronald Hayman, *Thomas Mann: A Biography* (New York: Scribner, 1995), p. 494.
55 For a photo of a similar scene titled 'Mahler and his wife, Alma, in Rome in 1910' see Kennedy, *Mahler*.
56 Relations between Gustav and Alma went through a difficult period just after they arrived from the United States to Germany to prepare for the

première of the Eighth Symphony. During the summer of 1910 Alma went to Tobelbad to improve her health, where she met the young architect Walter Gropius who fell in love with her. He wrote her a declaration of love and addressed it inadvertently, perhaps, to Gustav Mahler. The arrival of the letter allowed for all the resentments of the marriage to be aired. Gustav was horrified at how he had treated Alma. It was as if he had just realised the consequences of his behaviour. Indeed he was in such distress that he consulted Sigmund Freud on the matter who, predictably, diagnosed mother fixation in Gustav and father fixation in Alma. One of Alma's complaints was that on their engagement Gustav had forbidden her to compose music and so deprived her of her creative outlet. She describes this interdiction in terms of a kind of death: 'and now I dragged my hundred songs with me wherever I went – like a coffin into which I dared not even look'. One of the outcomes of the confrontation between Alma and Gustav was the latter's reappraisal of the former's work and their subsequent publication and performance. Gustav and Alma resolved to stay together and, in the winter of 1910, Alma reports that 'we often went for walks together arm in arm'. See Alma Mahler, *Gustav Mahler*, pp. 76, 187.

57 James L. Zychowicz, Sleeve notes for *Mahler: Symphony no. 8*, with Colin Davis (BMG Music, 1996), p. 7.

58 John, *Reading the Ground*, p. 215.

59 Carol Tattersall, 'Thomas Kinsella's Exploration in *Notes From the Land of the Dead* of His Sense of Alienation from Women', *Canadian Journal of Irish Studies* 15: 2 (1989): 79–91 (p. 88). For another analysis on the feminine in Thomas Kinsella's poetry see also Peggy F. Broder, 'Images of the Feminine in the Poetry of Thomas Kinsella', *Canadian Journal of Irish Studies* 5: 1 (1979): 87–99.

60 Kinsella Papers, box 21, folder 4.

61 Ibid., box 21, folder 1.

62 W.B. Yeats, *W.B. Yeats: Selected Poetry*, ed. Timothy Webb (London: Penguin, 1991), p. 179.

63 Thomas Kinsella in conversation with John F. Deane, 'A Conversation with Thomas Kinsella', *Tracks* 7, p. 87

64 In his notes to *Out of Ireland* Kinsella refers to his earlier volume *A Selected Life: In Memory of Seán Ó Riada*, and in the preface to *Her Vertical Smile* Kinsella remembers an evening in the company of 'Reidy'.

65 The notes of the Peppercanister edition are included in *Blood and Family* but not in *Thomas Kinsella: Collected Poems 1956–1994*. It is not clear why it was considered necessary that the line "Tabhair dom do lámh" be translated into English for the Oxford editions? Expediency and ease of reading cannot be the answer since there are in both editions ample notes provided by the author to illuminate any obscure references. Why was this trace of an almost silenced tongue removed once the poem travels beyond the place where Irish is, at least nominally, the first language?

66 Kinsella, "The Irish Writer", p. 9.

67 Ibid, p. 10.

68 Pierre Riché, *Daily Life in the World of Charlemagne*, trans. Jo Ann McNamara (Philadelphia: U of Pennsylvania Press, 1978), p. 204.

69 Ibid.

70 Eriugena, *Periphyseon (The Division of Nature)*, trans. I.P. Sheldon-Williams, rev. John J. O'Meara (Montréal: Bellarmin, 1987), p. 15.
71 Ibid, p. 19.
72 Thomas Kinsella, mss notes and drafts towards *Out of Ireland*, held by the Robert W. Woodruff Library, Emory University, Atlanta. Box 11.
73 Group m, 'Douze bribes pour décoller en 40, 000 signes', *Revue d'esthétique: Collages* (Paris: Union Générale, 1978): 11–41 (p. 34). This passage is translated by Gregory Ulmer, 'The Object of Post-Criticism' in *The Anti-Aesthetic*, ed. Hal Foster (Washington: Bay Press, 1983), pp. 83–110 (p. 88).
74 Eriugena, *Periphyseon*, Book II, p. 132
75 Mary Anderson, 'Kinsella and Eriugena: "Out of Ireland"', *Canadian Journal of Irish Studies* 17, 2 (1991): 39–53 (p. 47).
76 John, *Reading the Ground*, p. 228, n. 28.
77 Riché, *Daily Life in the World of Charlemagne*, p. 204.
78 O'Meara in his introduction to Eriugena's, *Periphyseon*, p. 20.
79 Ludwig Bieler in *Ireland: Harbinger of the Middle Ages* (London: Oxford UP, 1963), p. 132
80 Eriugena quoted by Bieler in *Ireland: Harbinger of the Middle Ages*, p. 133.
81 Mc Cormack, 'Politics or Community', p. 71.
82 Daniel O'Hara, 'Appropriate Performance: Thomas Kinsella and the Ordeal of Understanding', *Contemporary Irish Writing*, ed. James D. Brophy and Raymond J. Porter (Boston: Twayne, 1983), pp. 65–81 (p. 66).
83 Jean A. Potter refutes this account of Eriugena's death in her introduction to *On the Division of Nature* where she writes: "We can be quite certain, however, that William of Malmesbury's account of Eriugena's return to Britain to spend his last years is based on a confusion of names and that the bizarre tale that he was stabbed to death by the pens of his infuriated students is pure legend". Eriugena, *Periphseon, On the Division of Nature*, trans. Myra L. Uhlfelder, summaries. Jean A. Potter (Indianapolis: Bobbs-Merrill, 1976), p. x.
84 Haffenden, *Viewpoints*, p. 107.
85 See Jean-François Lyotard, *The Differend: Phrases in Dispute*, trans. Georges Van Den Abbeele (Manchester: Manchester UP, 1988), ¶ 40.
86 Seamus Deane, *A Short History of Irish Literature*, London, 1986, p. 236
87 For an informed discussion of the notion of the Irish poet see David Kellogg's 'Kinsella , Geography, History', *South Atlantic Quarterly: Ireland and Irish Cultural Studies* 95: 1 (1996): 145–70, and Daniel O'Hara's 'Appropriate Performance', pp. 65–81.
88 See Brian John's reading of this section as a gloss on *St Catherine's Clock* in *Reading the Ground*, p. 236.
89 This epigraph is omitted from *Thomas Kinsella: Collected Poems 1956–1994*, although it appears in *Blood and Family* (Oxford: Oxford UP, 1988), p. 68.
90 National Library of Ireland, R.1378.
91 William Hamilton Maxwell, *History of the Irish Rebellion in 1798: With Memoirs of the Union, and Emmet's Insurrection in 1803* (London: Baily Bros, 1845).
92 Geraldine Hume and Anthony Malcomson, *Education Facsimiles 181–200: Robert Emmet – The Insurrection of July 1803* (Public Records Office of Northern Ireland), p. 3.
93 Ibid.

94 This engraving is *The Execution of Robert Emmet*, Anon., 1877.
95 Hume and Malcomson, 'Introduction', *Education Facsimiles*, p. 22.
96 Ibid., p. 3.
97 National Library of Ireland, Joly Pamphlets, 637.
98 (T.3069/D.21B)
99 Public Record Office of Northern Ireland, *Education Facsimile no. 192: Robert Emmet*, 'The Speech of Robert Emmett, Esq.'[sic] described by Hume and Malcomson as a 'loyalist or government sponsored broadsheet' (T.3069/D.21B).
100 Public Record Office of Northern Ireland, *Education Facsimile no. 193: Robert Emmet*, 'Emmet's speech: the *State Trials* version.'
101 Maurice Harmon, 'Nutrient Waters', *Poetry Ireland Review* 21, Spring (1988): 20–4, (p. 21).
102 James Malton, *Georgian Dublin: Twenty-five Aquatint Views in Colour*, intro. and notes by Maurice Craig (Portlaoise: Dolmen, 1984).
103 David Kellogg, 'Kinsella, Geography, History', *South Atlantic Quarterly 95*, 1 (1996): pp. 145–70 (p. 159).
104 Brian John explains *dinnseanchas* as the way in which 'a place's significance is communicated and sustained through the Gaelic place name and the myth, folklore, and history associated with the place' in his *Reading the Ground*, p. 244. Daragh Smyth explains '*dindshenchas*' as 'the book of legends and stories written by Amergin, poet of Diarmuid mac Cearbhaill.' Sections are to be found in the *Book of Leinster* and the *Yellow Book of Lecan*. See Smyth, *A Guide to Irish Mythology*, p. 182.
105 These lines are omitted in *Thomas Kinsella: Collected Poems 1956–1994.*
106 Georges Bataille, *Erotism: Death and Sensuality*, trans. Mary Dalwood (San Francisco: City Light Books, 1986), p. 22.
107 Public Record Office of Northern Ireland, *Education Facsimile no. 193: Robert Emmet*, Emmet's speech: the *State Trials* version.
108 As Brian John points out, the possible impropriety alluded to in this scene picks up on an earlier reference to a 'secret husband' in the 1978 volume *The Messenger* (C 224). John, *Reading the Ground*, p. 242.
109 For an explanation of the term 'gets' as 'British–Irish pejorative for "children"' and other colloquial phrases in these stanzas see Brian John's note in *Reading the Ground*, p. 241, n. 39. See also Eric Partridge, *A Dictionary of Historical Slang* (Harmondsworth: Penguin, 1972).
110 Harmon, *The Poetry of Thomas Kinsella*, p. 83.
111 Marcel Proust, *Swann's Way*, trans. C.K Scott Moncrieff (London: Penguin, 1957), p. 74.
112 Michel Serres, *Conversations on Science, Culture and Time: Michel Serres interviewed by Bruno Latour*, trans. Roxanne Lapidus (Ann Arbor: U of Michigan Press, 1995), p. 45.
113 Julia Kristeva's analysis of time in Proust's writing also illuminates Kinsella's work. See *Proust and the Sense of Time*, trans. Stephen Bann (London: Faber & Faber, 1993), p. 3.
114 Brian John, '"Brothers in the Craft": Thomas Kinsella and the Yeats Inheritance', *Irish University Review* 24: 2 (1994): 247–63 (p. 258).
115 Frieda Fordham *Introduction to Jung's Psychology* (Harmondsworth: Penguin, 1953), p. 49.

116 O'Driscoll, 'Interview with Thomas Kinsella', p. 62.

117 Rees and Rees, *Celtic Heritage*, p. 135.

118 Prospectus for 'New Publications Thomas Kinsella 1987' issued by the Peppercanister Press.

4 Political Matters

1 Thomas Kinsella, *One Fond Embrace* (Dublin: Gallery Press, and Deerfield, Mass.: Deerfield Press, 1981), [6].

2 Kinsella Papers, box 22, folder 22.

3 Kinsella Papers, box 24, folder 20: '(ending with 13; cf. *Butcher's Dozen. . .*).'

4 Ibid., box 24, folder 20.

5 Kinsella, *One Fond Embrace*, 1981 edn [12].

6 See 'An Irishwoman's diary' in *The Irish Times*, 11 Nov. 1974: 'A local government hearing at which Percy Place people whose homes may be demolished were refused an opportunity to speak angered many people, among them Thomas Kinsella, the poet.'

7 See John Bradley, ed., *Viking Dublin Exposed: The Wood Quay Saga* (Dublin: O'Brien Press, 1984). See also Kellogg's 'Kinsella, Geography, History', pp. 145–70.

8 See John Mulcahy, 'The Politics of Wood Quay', *Hibernia*, 28 Sept. 1978.

9 For example, 'Mallacht na Baintrí in *An Duanaire*, pp. 344–5.

10 For information on the identity of Kinsella's addressees see Kinsella Papers, box 24, folder 22.

11 As Terence Brown explains in his *Ireland: A Social and Cultural History 1922–1985*, 'The music of the traditional group, the Chieftains, which started life under the direction of the enormously respected composer, the late Seán Ó Riada (who in the 1960s became more and more preoccupied by the musical potential of the Irish tradition) created a market for recordings of Irish traditional music both in Ireland and abroad'. (London: Fontana, 1985), p. 276.

12 Elgy Gillespie, 'Thomas Kinsella, the Poet', *The Irish Times*, 20 June 1981.

13 A 'pontifex' is a member of the principal college of priests in ancient Rome, the head of which was the *Pontifex Maximus*, or chief priest (OED). See Mary Raymond Shipman Andrews, *Pontifex Maximus* (New York: Scribner, 1925).

14 John Redmond (1856–1918), MP responsible for the introduction of the Home Rule bill in 1912. Misjudged the mood in Ireland during the First World War when he supported Britain's war effort, leading to a split in the Irish Volunteers and events which culminated in the Easter 1916 Rising.

15 Conor Cruise O'Brien, *States of Ireland* (London: Hutchinson, 1972).

16 Brown, *Ireland: A Social and Cultural History*, p. 283.

17 Fried, 'Omphalos of Scraps', p. 21. See also Kinsella's comment in drafts of *One Fond Embrace*: 'CCO'B makes Irish stn. [situation] digestible in English for English so they could deal with it and "terrorism" and avoid yet again considering causes. It caused enormous harm.' Kinsella Papers, box 23, folder 12.

18 Máire Mhac an tSaoi and Conor Cruise O'Brien, *A Concise History of Ireland* (London: Thames & Hudson, 1972, 3rd edn 1985), p. 176.

19 Kinsella, *The Dual Tradition*, p. 29. See also Foster, *Modern Ireland*, pp. 107–16.

20 Haffenden, *Viewpoints*, p. 104.

21 Kinsella's notes for *Personal Places* and *Poems from Centre City* suggest that these two volumes were developed in tandem. A table of contents for *Personal Places* drafted in the spring of 1989 lists poems such as 'The Last', 'Dedication' and 'Household Spirits' which are now part of *Poems from Centre City*. Kinsella Papers, box 25, folder 30.

22 Kinsella Papers, box 24, folder 24.

23 Badin, *Thomas Kinsella*, p. 163. Kinsella's papers for *Personal Places* include a typed quotation from *Gray's Anatomy*: 'To examine the brain with its membranes, the skull-cap must be removed. In order to effect this, saw throguh the external table. . . Then break the internal table with the chisel and hammer . . . loosen and forcibly detach the skull-cap, when the dura mater will be exposed. . .'. Kinsella Papers, box 25, folder 31.

24 Kinsella Papers, box 25, folder 32. Excised lines from the poem read: 'She has told me / she wanted [to make certain] / above all [that] everything to / [would] come to me.'

25 Ibid., box 25, folder 23.

26 W.R.F. Browning, *Oxford Dictionary of the Bible* (Oxford: Oxford UP, 1996), p. 341. Also, Luke 23: 34, Matthew 27: 46, John 19: 26–7.

27 O'Driscoll, 'Interview with Thomas Kinsella', p. 58.

28 Austin Clarke speaking on a BBC broadcast in 1949. W. R. Rodgers, ed., *Irish Literary Portraits* (London: British Broadcasting Corporation, 1972), p. 19.

29 Andrew Samuels, Bani Shorter and Fred Plaut, *A Critical Dictionary of Jungian Analysis* (London: Routledge & Kegan Paul, 1986), p. 23.

30 Martin Swales, *A Student's Guide to Thomas Mann* (London: Heinemann, 1980), p. 30.

31 Translation Kinsella. *An Duanaire*, pp. 140–1.

32 Rees and Rees, *Celtic Heritage*, pp. 96–7.

33 O'Hara, 'Interview with Thomas Kinsella', p. 2.

34 Kinsella's introduction to Austin Clarke's *Selected Poems*, ed. Thomas Kinsella (Mountrath, Portlaoise: Dolmen, 1976), p. x.

35 Badin, *Thomas Kinsella*, p. 166.

36 Kinsella's introduction to Austin Clarke's *Selected Poems*, p. x.

37 Ibid.

38 Thomas Kinsella Papers, box 18, folder 11.

39 Kinsella, *Fifteen Dead*, p. 58.

40 The reception of *Butcher's Dozen* is discussed in chapter one of this study. In conversation with the poet in Philadelphia, Jan. 1999, Kinsella described how his career took a decisive turn as a result of *Butcher's Dozen*.

41 Gary Hogg, *Cannibalism and Human Sacrifice* (London: Robert Hale, 1958), p. 172.

42 See de Jubainville, *The Irish Mythological Cycle*. De Jubainville connects Celtic mythology with the Athenian legend of the Minotaur who exacted an annual tribute of seven youths and seven maidens, p. 58.

43 Kinsella Papers, box 23, folder 13.

44 See 'An Irishwoman's diary' in *The Irish Times*, 11 Nov., 1974.

45 Drafts of the poem are among the papers for *Songs of the Psyche*. Kinsella Papers, box 18, folder 11. See also box 29, folder 7.

46 Jack Butler Yeats (1871–1957), brother of W. B. Yeats. One of the most significant Irish painters in the twentieth century, see Bruce Arnold, *Jack Yeats* (New Haven, Conn.; London: Yale UP, 1998). Eamon de Valera (1882–1975), see Foster, *Modern Ireland*, p. 485, n. xx; and Tim Pat Coogan, *De Valera: Long Fellow, Long Shadow* (London: Hutchinson, 1993).

47 Badin, *Thomas Kinsella*, p. 166.

48 Kinsella Papers, box 26, folder 9.

49 See the photocopy of Dante's profile 'from the bronze bust at Naples' in Kinsella Papers, box 27, folder 17.

50 O'Hara, 'Interview with Thomas Kinsella', p. 7.

51 In a 1962 interview Kinsella names Dante as one of his influences: 'But the poems which I really admire [. . .] are the conscious, constructed real fabrications of the human intellect and spirit like Dante and Keats, and the later Yeats.' Peter Orr, ed., *The Poet Speaks: Interviews with Contemporary Poets conducted by Hilary Morrish, Peter Orr, John Press and Ian Scott-Kilvert* (London: Routledge & Kegan Paul, 1966), pp. 105–9 (p. 108).

52 The Peppercanister versions of these lines are more descriptive, but have a looser focus: 'and I will lower these arms / and embrace what I find. / Embarrassed suddenly from the right hand, / on the first beat of the Church bell, // by my brother figure. Startled likewise, / in that posture of seeming shyness, / then glaring, lips set and dark, / hands down and averted' (P 22).

53 Kinsella Papers, box 26, folder 8.

54 Ibid., box 27, folder 8.

55 As Hayden Murphy recounts, 'Kinsella, his wife Eleanor and their three children in Percy Place were within walking distance of Haddington Road's Catholic church where they regularly attended Sunday mass. There they saw the remains of Patrick Kavanagh (1905–67) lie in state before being removed for burial in Innishkeen in his native Monaghan in the north of Ireland.' 'Thomas Kinsella: Inscapes', p. 177.

56 O'Driscoll, 'Interview with Thomas Kinsella', p. 58.

57 Haffenden, *Viewpoints*, p. 101.

58 John, *Reading the Ground*, p. 52. In correspondence (July 2000) Kinsella notes that 'Dick King' was not a conscious rewriting of Auden's poem.

59 Kinsella Papers, box 27, folder 10.

60 O'Hara, 'Interview with Thomas Kinsella', p. 5.

61 Ibid., p. 9.

62 Noted on the colophon of the Peppercanister edition. See *The Complete Woodcuts of Albrecht Dürer*, ed. W. Kurth (New York: Dover, 1963), plate 172: 'Nude Woman with the Zodiac. Single sheet with the Prognosticon of the Astronomer Stabius for the year 1503–04', p. 25.

63 Kinsella Papers, box 29, folder 10.

64 Ibid., box 29, folder 10.

65 Ibid., box 29, folder 10.

66 Once again Kinsella quotes from Ecclesiastes, rewriting IV:5: 'The fool foldeth his hands together, and eateth his own flesh.'

67 Ecclesiastes IV: 9–10.

68 Kinsella Papers, box 28, folder 9.

69 Jacobi, *The Psychology of C.G. Jung*, p. 126.
70 Kinsella Papers, box 18, folder 8.
71 Ibid., 'Genesis' box 30, folder 1; 'A Parable' box 19, folder 12.
72 de Jubainville, *The Irish Mythological Cycle*, pp. 57–8. Kinsella's notes situate the scene of 'Morning Coffee' thirty years after the plague which did away with the previous arrivals in Ireland, the people of Partholón. The notes also make mention also of Cessair (daughter of Bith who is the son of Noah) who was the first to arrive in Ireland, fleeing from the biblical flood because she was refused entry to the Ark. Cessair, and her womenfolk, are abandoned by the last man of the company, Fintan mac Bóchra: 'She died at last, of a broken heart. / The sea took her body in slow instalments as it rotted and dried. / The seawind swept / the swell away.' Kinsella Papers, box 18, folder 8.
73 This is a report from W. Barbrooke Grubb of the South American Missionary Society regarding the cannibals of the Amazon Basin. Garry Hogg, *Cannibalism and Human Sacrifice* (London: Robert Hale, 1958), p. 73. See the Kinsella Papers, box 19, folder 4. Kinsella makes notes from pages 25, 73–74, 79–80, 178–79.
74 Fried, 'Omphalos of Scraps', p. 18.
75 Ovid, *Metamorphoses*, trans. A. D. Melville, intro. E. J. Kenney (Oxford: Oxford UP, 1986, rpt. 1992), Book III: 431–32, p. 64.
76 The *Collected Poems* version differs slightly: 'up the tenement stone stairs – / then narrowed in a lane along by the Library' (C 320).
77 This is also, perhaps, the 'vanity and vexation of spirit' spoken of in Ecclesiastes IV: 16.
78 O'Hara, 'Interview with Thomas Kinsella', p. 10.
79 Samuel Beckett, 'Dante . . . Bruno .Vico . . Joyce', *Disjecta*, ed. Ruby Cohn (London: John Calder, 1983), p. 27.
80 I am grateful to J.C.C. Mays for this reference.
81 The *Collected Poems* version lacks lines 2–5 of the stanza and is divided into three quatrains.
82 Fried, 'Omphalos of Scraps', p. 15. See also 'Ancient Myth and Poetry: A Panel Discussion, David Greene, Thomas Kinsella, Jay MacPherson, Kevin Nowlan, Ann Saddlemyer' in Joseph Ronsley, ed., *Myth and Reality in Irish Literature* (Waterloo, Ontario: Wilfred Laurier UP, 1977), pp. 8–15 (p. 8).
83 O'Hara, 'Interview with Thomas Kinsella', p. 8.
84 O'Driscoll, 'Interview with Thomas Kinsella', p. 65.
85 O'Hara, 'Interview with Thomas Kinsella', p. 12.
86 Ibid., p. 12.
87 Kinsella's phrase recalls the opening of Oscar Wilde's *The Importance of Being Ernest*. Algernon: 'I don't play accurately – anyone can play accurately – but I play with wonderful expression.' *Wilde: Three Plays*, intro. H. Montgomery Hyde (London: Methuen, 1981).
88 Kinsella Papers, box 29, folder 11.
89 Johnston, *Irish Poetry after Joyce*, p. 41.
90 The *Collected Poems* version has 'agrees excited' (C 328).
91 The *Collected Poems* version places a colon after 'embrace' and omits the ellipsis after 'over.'
92 Patrick Kavanagh, *Patrick Kavanagh: Collected Poems* (1964) (London: Martin Brian & O'Keeffe, 1972), p. 44.

93 Ibid., p. 37.

94 Stephen Spender, Patrick Kavanagh, Thomas Kinsella, W. D. Snodgrass, 'Poetry Since Yeats: An Exchange of Views', *Tri-Quarterly* 4 (1965): 100–11 (p. 106).

95 Ibid., p. 109.

96 Samuel Beckett, *Murphy* (New York: Grove Press, 1957), p. 275: 'By closing time the body, mind and soul of Murphy were freely distributed over the floor of the saloon; and before another dayspring greyened the earth had been swept away with the sand, the beer, the butts, the glass, the matches, the spits, the vomit.'

97 Peter Denman, Book review of *Madonna and Other Poems* and *Open Court*, *Irish University Review* 22, 1 (1992): 190–2 (p. 192).

98 A note on a draft of 'Dream' provisionally titled 'Fragment: from an old diary' reads: 'sent to Donald Radkin for "bouquet" for Bob Buttel. 26.2.85. To be presented as a riddle: he to guess the main characters & the dates.' Kinsella Papers, box 29, folder 7.

99 Sean O'Faolain, 'Signing Off', *The Bell* 12: 1 (1946): 1.

100 Thomas Bodkin, *Report on the Arts in Ireland* (Dublin: Stationery Office, 1949), p. 9; quoted in Brown, *Ireland: A Social and Cultural History*, pp. 232–3.

101 Spender, Kavanagh, Kinsella and Snodgrass, 'Poetry Since Yeats', pp. 105–6.

102 Kinsella, *The Dual Tradition*.

103 Kinsella, *The New Oxford Book of Irish Verse*, p. xxviii.

104 Correspondence with Kinsella, July 2000. See also Denis Donoghue's, 'Irish Writing' *Month,* ns, 17: March (1957): 180–5

105 *The Complete Woodcuts of Albrecht Dürer*, plate 93.

Conclusion

1 Skloot, 'The Evolving Poetry of Thomas Kinsella', p. 174.

2 Michel de Certeau, *The Practice of Everyday Life*, trans. Steven F. Rendall (Berkeley: U of California Press, 1984), p. 101; quoted in Kellogg's 'Kinsella, Geography, History', p. 156.

3 Father Francis Shaw, 'The Canon of Irish History – A Challenge' (1972), reprinted in *The Field Day Anthology of Irish Writing*, ed. Seamus Deane (Derry: Field Day Publications, 1991), vol. 3, pp. 590–5 (p. 593).

4 James Joyce, *Ulysses* (1922) intro. Declan Kiberd (London: Penguin, 1992), p. 116.

5 William Smith O'Brien (1803–64).

6 Sir Thomas Farrell (1827–1900).

7 Sir John Gray (1816–75).

8 Joyce, *Ulysses*, p. 117.

9 James Joyce, *Dubliners*, ed. Terence Brown (London: Penguin, 1992), p. 170.

10 James Larkin (1876–1947).

11 Joyce, *Ulysses*, pp. xii–xiii.

12 Daniel O'Connell (1775–1847).

13 Joyce, *Ulysses*, p. 117.

14 R. F. Foster describes O'Connell as 'the greatest leader of Catholic Ireland.' *Modern Ireland*, p. 291, n. iii.

15 Joyce, *Ulysses*, p. 119.

16 For details of Kinsella's childhood and family history see Rosenberg, 'Let Our Gaze Blaze', pp. 72–97. For photographs of the Forty Steps and environs see Thomas H. Jackson, *The Whole Matter: The Poetic Evolution of Thomas Kinsella* (Dublin: Lilliput, 1995), pp. 143–4 (p. 46).

17 de Jubainville, *The Irish Mythological Cycle*, pp. 129–30.

18 Edmund Burke (1729–97).

19 Oliver Goldsmith (1728–74).

20 Extracts from both books were published in the *PN Review* 23, 6 (1997): 9.

21 The two images in *The Familiar* are taken from Courtney Davis, *Celtic Ornament: Art of the Scribe* (London: Blandford, 1996), pp. 13, 81. According to Davis, the cover image is one of 'various ornaments from the book of Kells' and the image of the priest is a 'Portrait of Christ, centrepiece of a three panel triptych 'Spirit of the Gael', pp. 92–3.

22 Joyce, *Ulysses*, p. 65.

23 Ibid.

24 See *The New Oxford Book of Irish Verse*, pp. 98–102.

25 Kinsella draws his image from Klaus Holitzka, *Mandalas of the Celts* (New York: Sterling, 1996).

26 O'Hara, 'Interview with Thomas Kinsella', p. 2.

27 Flanagan, 'Interview with Thomas Kinsella', p. 108.

28 Ibid.

29 Kellogg, 'Kinsella , Geography, History', p. 169, n. 40.

30 Rosenthal and Gall, *The Modern Poetic Sequence*, p. 9.

31 Joseph M. Conte, *Unending Design: The Forms of Postmodern Poetry* (Ithaca: Cornell UP, 1991), pp. 3, 20.

32 O'Hara, 'Interview with Thomas Kinsella', pp. 6–7.

33 Ibid., p. 12.

34 Fried, 'Omphalos of Scraps', p. 17.

35 O'Hara, 'Interview with Thomas Kinsella', p. 12.

36 My thanks to J. C. C. Mays for suggesting this connection.

37 Ezra Pound, Canto 59, *The Cantos of Ezra Pound*, (1954) (London: Faber & Faber, 1975), p. 324.

38 Haffenden, *Viewpoints*, p. 102.

SELECTED
BIBLIOGRAPHY

Works by Thomas Kinsella

Books of Poems

The Starlit Eye. Dublin: Dolmen, 1952.
Three Legendary Sonnets. Dublin: Dolmen, 1952.
Per Imaginem. Dublin: Dolmen, 1953.
The Death of a Queen. Glenageary: Dolmen, 1956.
Poems. Dublin: Dolmen, 1956.
Another September. Dublin: Dolmen, 1958.
Moralities, Dublin. Dolmen, 1960.
Three Irish Poets: John Montague, Thomas Kinsella, Richard Murphy. Dublin: Dolmen, 1961.
Poems and Translations. New York: Atheneum, 1961.
Downstream. Dublin: Dolmen, and London: Oxford UP, 1962.
Wormwood. Dublin: Dolmen, 1966.
Nightwalker. Dublin: Dolmen, 1967.
Nightwalker and Other Poems. Dublin: Dolmen, and London: Oxford UP, 1968.
Nightwalker and Other Poems. New York: Knopf, 1968.
Poems: Thomas Kinsella, Douglas Livingstone, Anne Sexton. London: Oxford UP, 1968.
Nightwalker and Other Poems. New York: Knopf, 1968.
Tear. Cambridge, Mass: Pym-Randall Press, 1969.
Butcher's Dozen. Peppercanister 1, Dublin: Peppercanister Press, 1972.
A Selected Life. Peppercanister 2, Dublin: Peppercanister Press, 1972.
Finistère. Dublin: Dolmen, 1972.
Notes from the Land of the Dead. Dublin: Cuala Press, 1972.
Notes from the Land of the Dead and Other Poems. New York: Knopf, 1973.
Selected Poems: 1956–1968. Dublin: Dolmen, and London: Oxford UP, 1973.
New Poems 1973. Dublin: Dolmen, 1973.
Vertical Man. Peppercanister 3, Dublin: Peppercanister Press, 1973.
The Good Fight. Peppercanister 4, Dublin: Peppercanister Press, 1973.
One. Peppercanister 5, Dublin: Peppercanister Press, 1974.
A Short Sequence: Thomas Kinsella. Storrs: U of Connecticut Library, 1975.

A Technical Supplement. Peppercanister 6, Dublin: Peppercanister Press, 1976.
Song of the Night and Other Poems. Peppercanister 7, Dublin: Peppercanister Press, 1978.
The Messenger. Peppercanister 8, Dublin: Peppercanister Press, 1978.
Fifteen Dead. Dublin: Dolmen, 1979.
One and Other Poems. Dublin: Dolmen, 1979.
Poems 1956–1973. Winston-Salem, North Carolina: Wake Forest UP, 1979.
Poems 1956–1973. Montrath, Portlaoise: Dolmen, 1979.
Peppercanister Poems 1972–1978. Winston-Salem, North Carolina: Wake Forest UP, 1980.
One Fond Embrace. Dublin: Gallery Press, and Deerfield, Mass.: Deerfield Press, 1981.
Songs of the Psyche. Peppercanister 9, Dublin: Peppercanister Press, 1985.
Her Vertical Smile. Peppercanister 10, Dublin: Peppercanister Press, 1985.
Out of Ireland. Peppercanister 11, Dublin: Peppercanister Press, 1987.
St Catherine's Clock. Peppercanister 12, Dublin: Peppercanister Press, 1987.
One Fond Embrace. Peppercanister 13, Dublin: Peppercanister Press, 1988.
Blood and Family. Oxford: Oxford UP, 1988.
Personal Places. Peppercanister 14, Dublin: Peppercanister Press, 1990.
Poems from Centre City. Peppercanister 15, Dublin: Peppercanister Press, 1990.
Madonna and Other Poems. Peppercanister 16, Dublin: Peppercanister Press, 1991.
Open Court. Peppercanister 17, Dublin: Peppercanister Press, 1991.
Butcher's Dozen. Reissue of Peppercanister 1, Dublin: Peppercanister Press, 1992.
From Centre City. Oxford: Oxford UP, 1994.
Thomas Kinsella: Collected Poems 1956–1994. Oxford: Oxford UP, 1996.
The Pen Shop. Peppercanister 19, Dublin: Peppercanister Press, 1996.
The Familiar. Peppercanister 20, Dublin: Peppercanister Press, 1999.
Godhead. Peppercanister 21, Dublin: Peppercanister Press, 1999.

Translations, Anthologies and Editions

Longes Mac Unsnig: Being the Exile and Death of the Sons of Usnech. Dublin: Dolmen, 1954.
Thirty-three Triads, Translated from the XII Century Irish. Dublin: Dolmen, 1955.
Thirty Three Triads. Trans. Thomas Kinsella, illust. Pauline Bewick, Glenageary, Co. Dublin: Dolmen, 1955
The Breastplate of St Patrick. Dublin: Dolmen, 1954; revised as *Faeth Fiadha: The Breastplate of St Patrick.* Dublin: Dolmen, 1957.
The Dolmen Miscellany of Irish Writing. Ed. with John Montague, Dublin: Dolmen, 1962.
Austin Clarke: Selected Poems. Mountrath, Portlaoise: Dolmen, 1976.
The New Oxford Book of Irish Verse. Oxford: Oxford UP, 1986.
The Táin. Dublin: Dolmen, 1969 limited edn, reprinted in trade edn 1986.
Myth, History and Literary Tradition. Extracts from *The Táin*, Dundalk: Dundalk Arts Publications, 1989, pp. 5–7.
The Táin. Trade edn, Oxford: Oxford UP, 1970.

An Duanaire 1600–1900: Poems of the Dispossessed. Ed. Seán Tuama and trans. Thomas Kinsella, Dublin: Dolmen with Bord na Gaeilge, 1981, reprinted 1994.

Essays, Notes and Exchanges

'Note on *Another September'*. *Poetry Book Society Bulletin* 17: March (1958).
'Note on *Downstream'*. *Poetry Book Society Bulletin* 34: Sept. 1962.
Stephen Spender, Patrick Kavanagh, Thomas Kinsella, W.D. Snodgrass, 'Poetry Since Yeats: An Exchange of Views'. *Tri-Quarterly* 4 (1965): 100–11.
'The Irish Writer'. *Éire-Ireland* 2: 2 (1967): 8–15.
'Note on *Nightwalker and Other Poems'*. *Poetry Book Society Bulletin* 55: Dec. (1967).
'The Divided Mind'. *Irish Poets in English*. Ed. Seán Lucy. Cork: Mercier, 1973, pp. 208–18.
'Ancient Myth and Poetry: A Panel Discussion, David Greene, Thomas Kinsella, Jay MacPherson, Kevin Nowlan, Ann Saddlemyer'. *Myth and Reality in Irish Literature*. Ed. Joseph Ronsley. Waterloo, Ontario: Wilfred Laurier UP, 1977, pp. 8–15.
'W.B. Yeats, the British Empire, James Joyce and Mother Grogan'. *Irish University Review* 22: Spring–Summer (1992): 69–79. Also published in *PN Review* 19: 3 (1993): 10–14.
'Origins of Anglo-Irish'. *PN Review* 20: 1 (1993): 20–8.
The Dual Tradition: An Essay on Poetry and Politics in Ireland. Peppercanister 18. Manchester: Carcanet, 1995.
Thomas Kinsella, 'A Note on Irish Publishing'. *The Southern Review* 31: 3 (1995): 633–8.

Secondary Sources

Anderson, Mary. 'Kinsella and Eriugena: "Out of Ireland"'. *Canadian Journal of Irish Studies* 17: 2 (1991): 39–53.
Andrews, Mary Raymond Shipman. *Pontifex Maximus.* New York: Scribner, 1925.
Anon. 'New Bloody Sunday Twist' *The Belfast Telegraph*, 16 Sept. 1999.
Arnold, Bruce. *Jack Yeats.* New Haven, Conn. and London: Yale UP, 1998.
Badin, Donatella Abbate. *Thomas Kinsella.* New York: Twayne, 1996.
Beckett, Samuel. 'Dante . . . Bruno . Vico . . Joyce'. *Disjecta.* Ed. Ruby Cohn, London: John Calder, 1983.
——. *Murphy.* New York: Grove Press, 1957.
Bedient, Calvin. *Eight Contemporary Poets.* London: Oxford UP, 1974.
Bieler, Ludwig. *Ireland: Harbinger of the Middle Ages.* London: Oxford UP, 1963.
Boland, Eavan. 'Kinsella: A New Direction' *The Irish Times*, 6 Apr. 1968.
Bradley, John, ed. *Viking Dublin Exposed: The Wood Quay Saga.* Dublin: O'Brien, 1984.
Broder, Peggy F. 'Images of the Feminine in the Poetry of Thomas Kinsella'. *Canadian Journal of Irish Studies* 5: 1 (1979): 87–99.

Brown, Terence. *Ireland: A Social and Cultural History 1922–1985*. London: Fontana, 1985.

Browning, W. R. F. *Oxford Dictionary of the Bible*. Oxford: Oxford UP, 1996.

Certeau, Michel de. *The Practice of Everyday Life*. Trans. Steven F. Rendall. Berkeley: U of California P, 1984.

Chadwick, Nora K. 'Imbas Forosnai'. *Scottish Gaelic Studies* 4: 2 (1935): 97–135.

Conte, Joseph M. *Unending Design: The Forms of Postmodern Poetry*. Ithaca: Cornell UP, 1991.

Coogan, Tim Pat. *De Valera: Long Fellow, Long Shadow*. London: Hutchinson, 1993.

Coughlan, Patricia and Alex Davis, eds. *Modernism and Ireland: The Poetry of the 1930s*. Cork: Cork UP, 1995.

Dante Alighieri. *The Divine Comedy*. Trans. Charles S. Singleton. Princeton: Princeton UP, 1970.

Davis, Courtney. *Celtic Ornament: Art of the Scribe*. London: Blandford, 1996.

Dawe, Gerald. 'Poetry as Example: Kinsella's Peppercanister Poems'. *Poetry in Contemporary Irish Literature*. Ed. Michael Kenneally. Gerrards Cross: Colin Smythe, 1995, pp. 204–15.

——. 'In the Violent Zone: Thomas Kinsella's *Nightwalker and Other Poems*'. *Tracks* 7 (1987): 26–31.

Deane, John F. 'A Conversation with Thomas Kinsella'. *Tracks* 7 (1987) 86–91.

Deane, Seamus. *A Short History of Irish Literature*. London: Hutchinson, 1986.

——. *Celtic Revivals: Essays in Modern Irish Literature, 1880–1980*. London: Faber, 1985.

Denman, Peter. Review of *Madonna and Other Poems* and *Open Court*. *Irish University Review* 22: 1 (1992): 190–2.

Dickinson, G. Lowe. *Plato and his Dialogues*. London: George Allen & Unwin, 1931.

Diderot, Denis. *Oeuvres Complets de Diderot*. Ed. J. Assézat. Paris: Garnier Frères, 1876.

——. *Recueil de planches, sur les sciences, les arts libéraux, et les arts méchaniques, avec leur explication*, Paris 1762–72.

——. *Selected Writings*. Ed. Lester G. Crocker. London: Collier-MacMillan, 1966.

Donoghue, Denis. *We Irish: Essays on Irish Literature and Society*. New York: Knopf, 1986.

Dürer, Albrecht. *The Complete Woodcuts of Albrecht Dürer*. Ed. W. Kurth. New York: Dover, 1963.

Durrell, Lawrence. *Justine*, London: Faber & Faber, 1957.

Engle, John. 'That Always Raised Voice: Seán Ó Riada and Irish Poetry'. *Contemporary Irish Writing*. Ed. James Brophy and Raymond Porter. Boston: Twayne, 1983, pp. 33–47.

Enniss, Stephen. *Peppercanister 1972–1997: Twenty-five Years of Poetry, A Bibliography*. Atlanta: Emory University, 1997.

Eriugena. *Periphyseon (The Division of Nature)*. Trans. I.P. Sheldon-Williams, rev. John J. O'Meara. Montréal: Bellarmin, 1987.

Fairlie, Henry. *The Kennedy Promise: The Politics of Expectation*. New York: Doubleday, 1973.

Flanagan, Ian. 'An Interview with Thomas Kinsella'. *Metre* 2: Spring (1997): 108–15.

Fleischmann, Aloys. 'Appréciation: Seán Ó Riada's *Nomos II*'. *Éire-Ireland* 7: 3 (1972): 108–15.

Fordham, Frieda. *Introduction to Jung's Psychology*. Harmondsworth: Penguin, 1953.

Foster, R.F. *Modern Ireland 1600–1972*. London: Penguin, 1988.

Fried, Philip. '"Omphalos of Scraps": An Interview with Thomas Kinsella'. *Manhattan Review* 4: Spring (1988) 3–25.

Gandelman, Claude. *Le Regard dans le texte: image et écriture du Quattrocento au xxe siècle*. Paris: Méridiens-Klincksieck, 1986.

Garratt, Robert F. *Modern Irish Poetry: Tradition and Continuity from Yeats to Heaney*. Berkeley: U of California Press, 1986.

Gartenberg, Egon. *Mahler: The Man and his Music*. New York: Schirmer, 1978.

——. *Vienna: Its Musical Heritage*. University Park: Pennsylvania State UP, 1968.

Gillespie, Elgy. 'Thomas Kinsella: the poet'. *The Irish Times*, Saturday, 20 June 1981.

Gillies, Alexander. *Goethe's Faust*. Oxford: Basil Blackwell, 1957.

Goethe, Johann Wolfgang von. *Faust*. Trans. Stuart Atkins, Cambridge MA: Suhrkamp/Insel, 1984.

Group m. 'Douze bribes pour décoller en 40,000 signes'. *Revue d'esthétique: Collages* 3/4 (1978). Paris: Union Générale: 11–41.

Haffenden, John. *Viewpoints: Poets in Conversation with John Haffenden*. London, Boston: Faber & Faber, 1981.

Halsey, William D. ed. *Colliers Encyclopedia*. London: Cromwell, Collier & Macmillan, 1967.

Harmon, Maurice. 'Ancient Lights in the Poetry of Austin Clarke and Thomas Kinsella'. *Éire-Ireland* 29: 1 (1994): 123–40.

——. '"Move, if you move, like water": The Poetry of Thomas Kinsella, 1972–88'. *Contemporary Irish Poetry: A Collection of Critical Essays*. Ed. Elmer Andrews, London: Macmillan, 1992, pp. 194–213.

——. 'Nutrient Waters'. *Poetry Ireland Review* 21: Spring (1988): 20–4.

——. *The Poetry of Thomas Kinsella: With Darkness for a Nest*. Dublin: Wolfhound, 1974.

Hayman, Ronald. *Thomas Mann: A Biography*. New York: Scribner, 1995.

Heaney, Seamus. 'Poems of the Dispossessed Repossessed'. *The Government of the Tongue: The 1986 T. S. Eliot Memorial Lectures and Other Critical Writings*. London: Faber & Faber, 1988, pp. 30–5.

——. *Field Work*. London: Faber & Faber, 1979.

Hogg, Gary. *Cannibalism and Human Sacrifice*. London: Robert Hale, 1958.

Holdeman, David. *Much Labouring: The Texts and Authors of Yeats's First Modernist Books*. Ann Arbor: U of Michigan Press, 1997.

Holmes, John Clellon. 'The Silence of Oswald'. *Playboy*: Nov. (1965): 101–2, 222, 224.

Hufstader, Jonathan. 'Thomas Kinsella and Irish Music'. *Canadian Journal of Irish Studies* 21: 2 (1995): 19–31.

Hume, Geraldine, and Anthony Malcomson. *Education Facsimiles 181–200: Robert Emmet – The Insurrection of July 1803*. Public Records Office of Northern Ireland.

Jackson, George. 'Experts say evidence to Widgery "worthless"'. *The Irish Times*, 17 Sept. 1999.

Jackson, Thomas H., *The Whole Matter: The Poetic Evolution of Thomas Kinsella*. New York: Syracuse and Dublin: Lilliput, 1995.

Jacobi, Jolande. *The Psychology of C.G. Jung*. London: Routledge & Kegan Paul, 1942, 5th ed. 1951.

John, Brian. *Reading the Ground: The Poetry of Thomas Kinsella*. Washington: Catholic UP, 1996.

———. '"Brothers in the Craft": Thomas Kinsella and the Yeats Inheritance'. *Irish University Review* 24: 2 (1994): 247–63.

———. 'Irelands of the Mind: The Poetry of Thomas Kinsella and Seamus Heaney'. *Canadian Journal of Irish Studies* 15: 2 (1989): 68–92.

———. 'Contemporary Irish Poetry and the Matter of Ireland – Thomas Kinsella, John Montague and Seamus Heaney'. *Medieval and Modern Ireland*. Ed. Richard Wall. Gerrards Cross: Colin Smythe, 1988, pp. 34–59.

Johnston, Dillon. 'The Anthology Wars'. *Times Literary Supplement*, 13 Sept. 1991, p. 26.

———. *Irish Poetry after Joyce*. Indiana: U of Notre Dame P/Mountrath: Dolmen, 1985.

James Joyce. *Ulysses* (orig. 1922). Intro. Declan Kiberd. London: Penguin, 1992.

Joyce, P.W. *A Smaller Social History of Ancient Ireland*. 2nd ed. London: Longman, Green/Dublin: M.H. Gill, 1908.

Jubainville, H. D'Arbois de. *The Irish Mythological Cycle and Celtic Mythology*. Trans. Richard Irvine Best, Dublin: Hodges Figgis, 1903.

Jung, C. G. *Memories, Dreams, Reflections*. Revised edn. Recorded and ed. Aniela Jaffé. Trans. Richard and Clara Winston. New York: Pantheon Books, 1973.

———. *Symbols of Transformation*. Princeton: Princeton UP, 1970.

———. *Collected Works*. Ed. William McGuire et al. Trans. R. F. C. Hull et al., Princeton: Princeton UP, 1953–71, vol. 5.

Kavanagh, Patrick. *Patrick Kavanagh: Collected Poems* (orig. 1964). London: Martin Brian & O'Keefe, 1972.

Kearney, Richard. 'Myth and Modernity in Irish Poetry'. *Contemporary Irish Poetry: A Collection of Critical Essays*. Ed. Elmer Andrews, London: Macmillan, 1992, pp. 41–62.

Kellogg, David. 'Kinsella, Geography, History'. *South Atlantic Quarterly: Ireland and Irish Cultural Studies* 95: 1 (1996): 145–70.

Kennedy, John Fitzgerald. 'Inaugural Speech'. *Irish Independent*, 21 Jan. 1961.

Kennedy, Michael, ed. *Oxford Dictionary of Music*. Oxford: Oxford UP, 1994.

———. *Mahler*. London: Dent, 1990.

Kristeva, Julia. *Proust and the Sense of Time*. Trans. Stephen Bann. London: Faber & Faber, 1993.

Lee, J. J. *Ireland 1912–1985: Politics and Society*. Cambridge: Cambridge UP, 1989.

Lennon, Peter. 'Dolmen Dublin'. *The Guardian*, 23 Oct. 1962.

Lernout, Geert. 'The Dantean Paradigm: Thomas Kinsella and Seamus Heaney'. *The Clash of Ireland: Literary Contrasts and Connections*. Ed. C.C. Barfoot and Theo D'haen, Amsterdam/Atlanta, GA: Rodopi, 1989, pp. 248–77.

Lessing, G. E. *Laocoön: An Essay on the Limits of Painting and Poetry*. Trans. E.A. McCormick. Baltimore: Johns Hopkins UP, 1984.

Lippman, Edward A. *The Philosophy and Aesthetics of Music*. Lincoln and London: U of Nebraska Press, 1999.

Longley, Edna. 'Spinning through the Void'. *Times Literary Supplement*, 19 Dec. 1980, p. 1446.

——. 'The Heroic Agenda: The Poetry of Thomas Kinsella'. *The Dublin Magazine* 5: 2 (1966): 61–78.

Lucy, Seán. 'The O Riada and Kennedy Poems'. *Irish Independent*, 23 and 30 Feb. 1974.

Lynch, Brian. 'Kinsella falls short on Derry'. *Evening Press*, 27 Apr. 1972.

Lyons, F.S.L. *Culture and Anarchy in Ireland 1890–1939*. Oxford: Clarendon, 1979.

——. *Ireland Since the Famine*. London: Weidenfeld & Nicolson, 1971.

Lyotard, Jean-François. *The Differend: Phrases in Dispute*. Trans. Georges Van Den Abbeele. Manchester: Manchester UP, 1988.

MacKillop, James. *Dictionary of Celtic Mythology*. Oxford: Oxford UP, 1998.

MacInerney, John. 'Searching for Structure: Kinsella's Pause En Route'. *Hibernia*, 4 Aug. 1972.

Mahler, Alma. *Gustav Mahler: Memories and Letters*. Ed. Donald Mitchell. Trans. Basil Creighton. London: John Murray, 1968.

Malton, James. *Georgian Dublin: Twenty-five Aquatint Views in Colour*. Intro. and notes by Maurice Craig. Portlaoise: Dolmen, 1984.

Mann, Thomas. *The Letters of Thomas Mann, 1889–1955*. Trans. Richard Winston and Clara Winston. Harmondsworth: Penguin, 1975.

Marx, Karl and Friedrich Engels. *Ireland and the Irish Question*. London: Lawrence & Wishart, 1971.

Maxwell, William Hamilton. *History of the Irish Rebellion in 1798: With Memoirs of the Union, and Emmet's Insurrection in 1803*. London: Baily Bros, 1845.

Mc Cormack, W. J. 'Politics or Community: Crux of Thomas Kinsella's Aesthetic Development'. *Tracks* 7 (1987): 61–77.

McCullough, David. 'David McCullough's Eye on Books'. Book-of-the-month-club *News*, Jan. 1974, pp. 6–7.

McGuinness, Arthur E. 'Fragments of Identity: Thomas Kinsella's Modernist Imperative'. *Colby Library Quarterly* 4 (1987): 186–205.

——. '"Bright Quincunx Newly Risen": Thomas Kinsella's Inward "I"'. *Éire-Ireland* 15 (1980): 106–25.

Miller, Liam. *Dolmen XXV: An Illustrated Bibliography of the Dolmen, 1951–1976*. Dublin: Dolmen, 1976.

Montague, John. 'Patriotic Suite: For Sean Ó Riada'. *The Rough Field*. Mountrath, Portlaoise: Dolmen, 1972, rpt. 1984.

——. 'And an Irishman'. *The New York Times Book Review*, 18 Aug. 1968, p. 5.

Moran, Dermot. 'Nature, Man and God in the Philosophy of John Scottus Eriugena'. *The Irish Mind*. Ed. Richard Kearney, Dublin: Wolfhound, 1985, pp. 91–106.

Morley, John. *Diderot and the Éncyclopaedist*. London: Macmillan, 1923

——. *Voltaire*, London: Chapman & Hall, 1872.

Mulcahy, John. 'The Politics of Wood Quay'. *Hibernia*, 28 Sept. 1978.

Mullin, John. 'Bloody Sunday Revelation'. *The Guardian*, 17 Sept. 1999.

Murphy, Hayden. 'Thomas Kinsella: Inscapes of an Emotional Emigré'. *Agenda* 33: 3–4 (1996): 176–98.

Neumann, Erich. *The Origins and History of Consciousness*. Trans. R. F. C. Hull, Princeton: Princeton UP, 1954.

O'Brien, Conor Cruise. *States of Ireland*. London: Hutchinson, 1972.

O'Brien, Conor Cruise and Máire Mhac an tSaoi. *A Concise History of Ireland*. London: Thames & Hudson, 1972, 3rd edn 1985.

O'Driscoll, Dennis. 'Interview with Thomas Kinsella'. *Poetry Ireland Review* 25 (1989): 57–65.

O'Faoláin, Seán. 'Signing Off'. *The Bell* 12: 1 (1946): 1.

Ó Glaisne, Risteard. 'Thomas Kinsella'. *An tUltach* 65: 11 (1988): 24–6.

O'Hara, Daniel. 'Appropriate Performance: Thomas Kinsella and the Ordeal of Understanding'. *Contemporary Irish Writing*. Ed. James D. Brophy and Raymond J. Porter, Boston: Twayne, 1983, pp. 65–81.

——. 'An Interview with Thomas Kinsella'. *Contemporary Poetry*. 4: 1 (1981): 1–18.

O'Higgins, Michael. 'Poets of the Fifties: Thomas Kinsella'. *Oxford Opinion*, May (1960): 21–2.

Orr, Peter, ed. *The Poet Speaks: Interviews with Contemporary Poets conducted by Hilary Morrish, Peter Orr, John Press and Ian Scott-Kilvert*. London: Routledge & Kegan Paul, 1966.

Ovid. *Metamorphoses*. Trans. A. D. Melville. Intro. E J. Kenney. Oxford: Oxford UP, 1986, rpt. 1992.

Paulin, Tom. *The Faber Book of Political Verse*. London: Faber & Faber, 1986.

Petty, William. *The History of the Survey of Ireland, Commonly called the Down Survey*. Ed. T. A. Larcom. Dublin: Irish Archaeological Society, 1851.

——, *The Political Anatomy of Ireland: with the Establishment for that Kingdom and Verbum Sapienti*. London: D. Brown & W. Rodgers, 1691, rpt. with intro. by John O'Donovan, Shannon: Irish UP, 1970.

Pound, Ezra. *The Cantos of Ezra Pound* (orig. 1954). London: Faber & Faber, 1975.

Rees, Alwyn and Brinley. *Celtic Heritage: Ancient Tradition in Ireland and Wales*. London and New York: Thames & Hudson, 1961.

Rosenthal, M. L., and Sally M. Gall. *The Modern Poetic Sequence: The Genius of Modern Poetry*. Oxford: Oxford UP, 1986.

Partridge, Eric. *A Dictionary of Historical Slang*. Harmondsworth: Penguin, 1972.

Plato, *The Republic*. Trans. Desmond Lee, London: Penguin 1955, rpt. 1987.

Prater, Donald. *Thomas Mann: A Life*. Oxford: Oxford UP, 1995.

Pratt, William. 'Thomas Kinsella, *The Pen Shop*'. *World Literature Today* 21: 1 (1988): 147–8.

Proust, Marcel. *Swann's Way*. Trans. C. K. Scott Moncrieff. London: Penguin, 1957.

Riché, Pierre. *Daily Life in the World of Charlemagne*. Trans. Jo Ann McNamara. U of Pennsylvania Press, 1978.

Richter, Gisela M. A. *The Portraits of the Greeks*, vol. 2. London: Phaidon, 1965.

Rodgers, W.R., ed. *Irish Literary Portraits*. London: British Broadcasting Corporation, 1972.

Ronsley, Joseph, ed. *Myth and Reality in Irish Literature*. Waterloo, Ontario: Wilfred Laurier UP, 1977.

Rosenberg, Carolyn. 'Let Our Gaze Blaze: The Recent Poetry of Thomas Kinsella'. Unpublished PhD. dissertation: Kent State University, 1980.

Rosenthal, M. L. and Sally M. Gall. *The Modern Poetic Sequence: The Genius of Modern Poetry*. New York; Oxford: Oxford UP, 1983.

Rushe, Desmond. 'Tatler's Parade'. *Irish Independent*, 28 Apr. 1972.

Sadie, Stanley, ed. *The New Grove Dictionary of Music and Musicians*, vol. 20. London: Macmillan, 1990.

Samuels, Andrew, Bani Shorter and Fred Plaut. *A Critical Dictionary of Jungian Analysis*. London: Routledge & Kegan Paul, 1986.

Schenck, Celeste M., 'When Moderns Write Elegy: Crane, Kinsella, Nemerov', *Classical and Modern Literature: A Quarterly* 6: 2 (1986): 97–108 (p. 98).

Serres, Michel. *Conversations on Science, Culture and Time: Michel Serres interviewed by Bruno Latour*. Trans. Roxanne Lapidus, Ann Arbor: U of Michigan Press, 1995.

Simmons, James. 'Kinsella's Craft'. *Fortnight*, 11 May 1972.

Skelton, Robin. 'Twentieth-Century Irish Literature and the Private Press Tradition: Dun Emer, Cuala, and Dolmen Presses: 1902–1963'. *Irish Renaissance: A Gathering of Essays, Memoirs, and Letters from The Massachusetts Review*. Ed. Robin Skelton and David R. Clarke, Amherst: U of Massachusetts, 1965, and Dublin: Dolmen, 1965.

Skloot, Floyd. 'The Evolving Poetry of Thomas Kinsella'. *New England Review* 18: 4 (1997): 174–87.

——. Review of *A Technical Supplement*. *Éire-Ireland* 12: Autumn (1977): 143–7.

Smith, Daragh. *A Guide to Irish Mythology*. Dublin: Irish Academic P, 1988.

Sullivan, Kevin. 'Thomas Kinsella's Public Poem'. *The Nation* 214: 23 (1972): 725–6.

Swales, Martin. *A Student's Guide to Thomas Mann*. London: Heinemann, 1980.

Swift, Jonathan. 'Ireland'. *The Faber Book of Political Verse*. Ed. Tom Paulin. London: Faber, 1986, p. 185.

Tattersall, Carol, 'Thomas Kinsella's Exploration in *Notes From the Land of the Dead* of His Sense of Alienation from Women'. *Canadian Journal of Irish Studies* 16: 2 (1989): 79–91.

Ulmer, Gregory. 'The Object of Post-Criticism'. *The Anti-Aesthetic*. Ed. Hal Foster. Washington: Bay Press, 1983, pp. 83–110.

Virgil. *The Aeneid*. Trans. W.F. Jackson Knight. London: Penguin, 1986.

Richard Wagner, *Tristan und Isolde: Oper in drei Aufzügen*. Frankfurt, London and New York: C. F. Peters [no date given].

Walter, Bruno. *Theme and Variations*. Trans. James A. Galston. New York: Alfred Knopf, 1946.

Welch, Robert. Ed. *The Oxford Companion to Irish Literature*. Oxford: Clarendon, 1996.

White, Theodore H. *The Making of the President 1960*. New York: Atheneum, 1965.

Wilde, Oscar. *Wilde: Three Plays*. Intro. H. Montgomery Hyde. London: Methuen, 1981.

Wolfenstein, Martha, and Gilbert Kliman, eds. *Children and the Death of a President*. Gloucester, Mass.: Peter Smith, 1969.

Woodbridge, Hensley C., 'Thomas Kinsella: A bibliography'. *Éire-Ireland* 2: 2 (1967): 122–33.

Yeats, W. B. *W. B. Yeats: Selected Poetry*. Ed. Timothy Webb. London: Penguin, 1991.

INDEX

aisling, 17, 81, 186, 222, 233n
alchemy, 108, 112, 206
Amairgin, first poet of Ireland, 64, 66, 95, 183, 204–5, 224, 227, 238n
anatomical inquiry, 77–8, 83, 85, 130, 249n
Another September (1958), 1–2
Arnold, Matthew, 207
astronomy, 37, 134, 138
Auden, W. H., 1, 207
  influence on Kinsella, 1, 193–5
  'Nones', 2
  'To Christopher Isherwood', 32, 139–40

Bacon, Francis, 77
Badin, Donatella Abbate, 10, 23, 176, 184
Beckett, Samuel, 29, 146, 184, 204
  Murphy, 210
Bethge, Hans, 39
Bewick, Paul, 119
Biblical references in Kinsella's poetry, 37, 59, 122, 128, 139, 143–4, 196–7
birds in Kinsella's poetry, 28–9, 30, 98, 198, 217, 222
Blood and Family (1988), 155
Bloody Sunday, 22–3, 186
Bloom, Harold, 195
Bodkin, Thomas, 210

Boland, Evan, 2–3
Brown, Terence, 172
Browne, Liam, 6
Butcher's Dozen (1972), 6, 7, 14, 177, 186, 227
  critical reactions to, 21–4
  eighteenth-century poetic influences, 17–18
  newspaper reactions to, 15–16
  relation to previous poetry, 24
  rhythm of, 17
  voices in, 18–21
Butler, Samuel, 16

cailleach figure, 75, 165, 223
cairn, 165, 237n
Cambrensis, Giraldus, 59
Cannibalism and Human Sacrifice, 70, 187, 200–1
cartography, 77
Catholic Church in Ireland, 112, 188
Catholic ritual, 14, 135–6, 143, 177, 198, 205, 222
Celtic mythology *see under* mythology
Chien Andalou, Un, 85
Children and the Death of a President, 52
Christ, images of in Kinsella's poetry, 70, 78, 96, 161, 166, 177, 180, 192

Christian imagery in Kinsella's
    poetry, 74
Clarke, Austin, 2, 180–1, 184, 211
Clarke Kee, Howard, 194
Collected Poems (1996), 4, 9, 120,
    127
    'Departure Platforms', 120
    'Dura Mater', 176
    'Midsummer', 96
    'Personal Places', 175
    'Prologue', 76
    revisions incorporated into,
        108
Conte, Joseph, 226
Corkery, Daniel, 17
creation myths, 59, 61–2, 66–9,
    108, 143, 165
crows, 28–9, 30, 217, 222
Cruikshank, George, 156–7
Cúchulainn, 29, 119, 182, 216–18,
    221, 224
Cushing, Cardinal, 52

Dantean allusions in Kinsella's
    poetry, 29, 127, 190–1,
    217–18, 227–8, 250n
data, Kinsella's concept of, 4
Daviel, Jacques, 85
Dawe, Gerald, 21
Deane, John F., 8, 10, 77, 93, 166
Deane, Seamus, 10, 24
de Certeau, Michael, 216
Dehmel, Richard, 139
de Jubainville, H. D'Arbois, 58, 66,
    67, 97
democracy, 41, 45, 46
de Valera, Éamon, 189–90
Diderot, Denis
    Encyclopédie, 7, 82–3, 90–1,
        240n
    Le Rêve d'Alembert, 86
    letter to Voltaire, 89, 93
Dillon, Eilís, 21
dinnseanchas, 160, 228, 229, 247n
Dolmen Press, 5–6, 231n
Donoghue, Denis, 23, 212

Downstream (1962), 32
    'Chrysalides', 2
    'Dick King', 32, 194
    'Downstream', 34
Dr Faustus, 191–2
Dryden, John, 23
Dublin, topography of, 12, 216
Dublin literary scene, 206–14
*Duanaire 1600–1900: Poems of
    the Dispossessed, An* (1994),
    4, 16, 23, 118
Dürer, Albrecht, 166, 195, 213
Durrell, Lawrence, 36

Easter Rising 1916, 124, 217
Eliot, T. S., 2, 125, 210
Ellmann, Richard, 33
Emerson, R. W., 213
Emmet, Robert, 11, 154, 155,
    157, 158, 161
    letters to Sarah Curran, 162–3
    speech of, 159
Encyclopédie, 7, 82–3, 90–1,
    240n
Engelland, Timothy, 168
Engle, John, 26
English/Irish language division
    in Ireland, 26, 121, 147,
    182–3, 208
Enniss, Stephen, 6
Eriugena, Johannes Scotus, 11,
    148–50, 152, 153
Eucharist, 198, 205, 222

Fairlie, Henry, 42
Fallon, Peter, 8
Familiar, The (1999), 221–3,
    253n
family and childhood, 165,
    252n
family history, 123–4, 160, 219
family relationships in Kinsella's
    poetry, 69–70, 71–4,
    105–117, 124, 161–3
Farrell, Sir Thomas, 218
Faust, 61–2, 63, 132, 140, 143

female figures in Kinsella's poetry,
63, 69, 74–5, 99, 108, 135,
143–5, 164
see also Great Mother, mother,
women,
feminine deities, 133, 143–4, 192,
198, 206
Fifteen Dead (1979), 9, 186, 232n,
235n
filí, 66, 183, 238n
First World War, 70, 133, 135–7, 139
Flaherty, Jerry, 40
flayed body in art and literature, 90
Foreman, Brendan, 166
Freud, Sigmund, 194
Fried, Philip, 57, 172
Friel, Brian, 23
    Freedom of the City, 23, 77
    Translations, 77
From Centre City (1994)
    'Departure Platforms', 120
From My Desk, May 1981, 118–19
Frost, Robert, 42, 43
    'The Gift Outright', 52–3

Gall, Sally M., 226
Gandelman, Claude, 90
Garratt, Robert F., 10
gender, 149–50, 197
Gillespie, Elgy, 16, 171, 242
Godhead (1999), 224–5
Goethe, Johann Wolfgang von,
61–2, 63, 132, 140, 143
Good Fight, The (1973), 41–55,
227, 236n
    and the Kennedy presidency, 52,
54
    Kinsella's research for, 41–2
    Lee Harvey Oswald, 42–3,
48–50
    Platonic ideas in, 45–6, 47–8
    revisions to, 45
    and Robert Frost, 43, 52–3
    structure of, 43
    and 'The New Frontier', 47–8, 49
    typography in, 50–1

grandmother figures, 108
Great Mother Jungian archetype,
69, 124, 126, 143
Greene, Professor D., 22

Haffenden, John, 54
Harmon, Maurice, 3, 9–10, 123
    on Butcher's Dozen, 18
    and Out of Ireland, 159, 164
    and Song of the Night and Other
        Poems, 94
    and Vertical Man, 34
Hartnett, Michael, 233n
Haughey, Charles, J., 171
Hayes, Jarlath, 107, 154
Heaney, Seamus, 4, 23–4, 26
Hermes, 97
Her Vertical Smile (1985), 71, 104,
126, 132–46, 227–8
    and Alma Mahler, 136, 142–3
    and female figures, 135, 143–5
    and Gustav Mahler, 132–3,
134–6, 137–8
    illustrations in, 134
    and Michelangelo, 133, 135,
138, 143
    and Ó Riada, 133
    and the responsibilities of love,
141–2
    revisions to, 140
    and Thomas Mann, 133, 139–40
    and First World War, 137,
138–9, 145
Hidden Ireland, The, 17
Hogg, Gary, 187, 200
Hölderlin, Johann Christian
    Friedrich, 25
Holmes, John Clellon, 42, 43, 45,
49, 50
Holocaust, the, 112
human sacrifice, 70, 187, 200–1
Hume, Geraldine, 157, 159

identity, search for, 69–70, 72, 163
imbas forosnai, 125–7, 224, 228
Inistiogue, 100–1

Ireland, 117
  legacy of imperialism in, 20
  primeval peoples of, 58, 63
  story of origins, 201, 220,
    250–1n
Iremonger, Valentin, 181
Irish/English language division in
  Ireland, 26, 121, 147, 182–3,
  208
Irish history, 154, 157, 172–4
Irish labour movement, 107,
  109–110, 111–13, 218
*Irish Mythological Cycle and Celtic
  Mythology, The*, 58–9, 67
Irish University Review (1983), 10
Isherwood, Christopher, 139

Jackson, Thomas L., 10
Jesus *see* Christ
John, Brian, 10, 32, 135, 143, 160,
  165
  and *Fifteen Dead*, 235n
  and *The Good Fight*, 42, 43–4
  and *One*, 57, 74
  and *A Selected Life*, 31
  and *Songs of Psyche*, 125
  and *Vertical Man*, 35, 36, 38
Johnston, Dillon, 2, 5, 10, 207
Journal of Irish Literature, The, 43
journals and Kinsella's poetry, 94,
  101, 207
Joyce, James, 16, 58, 177, 187, 204
  The Dead, 197
  The Holy Office, 16
  Ulysses, 217–19, 222–3, 227
Joyce, P. W., 130, 134
Jung, C. G., 38, 57, 95–6, 194,
  238n, 242n
Jungian concepts, 58, 61, 62, 63,
  74–5, 131
  communal memory, 95
  Great Mother, 69, 124, 126, 143
  imago, 98, 101
  shadow, 123, 127, 134, 193
  snake, 59
  Taoism, 102, 108

Kavanagh, Patrick, 208, 211
Keating, Geoffrey, 59
Keats, John, 135, 205
Kellogg, David, 160, 226
Kennedy, John F., 41, 45–7, 52, 54
Kennedy Promise, The, 42, 52
Kiberd, Declan, 218
Kilwarden, Lord, 154, 156, 158,
  161
King, Cecil, 118
King and Kinsella, 118
Kinsella, Thomas
  'A Country Walk', 34
  'A Hand of Solo', 108
  and America, 3, 48, 102, 178–9
  'Ancestor', 108
  on art and politics, 55
  artistic response of, 153
  critical works on, 10–11
  criticism of poetry, 9–10
  early poetry of, 1–2
  and the Irish language, 26
  language of poetry, 2, 34
  'Mirror in February', 201
  mother of in poetry, 175–6
  move to Wicklow, 199
  poetic influences of, 1, 180,
    193–5
  and poetic process, 82, 85–6, 93
  'Poetry Since Yeats', 209
  publication history, 1–12
  public events and poetry, 13
  'Tear', 108
  translations of Irish poetry, 4–5
  US editions of his poetry, 6
Kliman, Gilbert, 52
knives, 83, 85
knowledge, 125–7, 151, 224

language and Kinsella's poetry, 2,
  34
language division in Ireland, 26,
  121, 147, 182–3, 208
Larkin, James, 114, 218
Lebor Gabála Érenn, 61, 64, 200,
  205, 226

Lennon, Peter, 5
Li, Tai Po, 39
Lied von der Erde, Das, 30, 35, 37–9, 133, 143
Life Studies, 3
Longley, Edna, 2, 4, 16
love in Kinsella's poetry, 97, 98–9, 105, 119, 141–2, 196–8, 217, 222, 228
Lowell, Robert, 2, 3
Lowes Dickinson, G., 50–1
Lucy, Seán, 54
Lug, 97
Lynch, Brian, 16
Lyotard, Jean-François, 153

Mac Con Midhe, Giolla Brighde, 224
MacInerney, John, 4
Madonna and Other Poems (1991), 195–206, 222, 228
 'At Head Table', 203–6
 illustration in, 195–6
 'Madonna', 197–8
 'Morning Coffee', 120, 199–202, 250–1n
 revisions to, 196, 198, 199, 203, 204
 treatment of love in, 196–8
 'Visiting Hour', 203
 women and, 196
Mahler, Alma, 136, 142–3, 244–5n
Mahler, Gustav, 11, 30, 35, 132–3, 134–6, 137–8, 244–5n
 Eighth Symphony, 30, 35, 37–9, 132–46, 235n
 see also Lied von der Erde, Das
Making of the President 1960, The, 42, 46, 52
Malcomson, Anthony, 157, 159
Malton, James, 159
Mann, Thomas, 42, 133, 139, 180–1, 191
Marcus, David, 17
Mathews, Aidan, 26
Maxwell, W. H., 157

McCormack, John, 69
Mc Cormack, W. J., 79, 152
McCullough, David, 15
McFadden, Hugh, 13
McGuinness, Arthur, 38
Mercury, 97, 114
Merriman, Brian, 16–18, 166, 206
Messenger, The (1978), 97, 105–117, 179, 217, 218, 228
 Christian imagery in, 106–7
 and death of Kinsella's father, 105, 115–16
 and Dublin lockout of 1913, 114
 illustrations of, 107
 and John Kinsella's political actions, 109–10, 111–12
 and John Kinsella's private persona, 110–11, 115, 194
 poet's own place in, 113
 relation to other poetry, 108, 113, 116–17
 revisions to, 108, 110
 and *Songs of Psyche*, 126, 129
Michelangelo, 133, 135, 138, 143
Midnight Court, The, 16–18, 206
Miller, Liam, 5, 6, 7, 15, 21
Mise Éire, Ó Riada's film score for, 36–7
Model Schools, 121–3
modern elegy, 25
modern poetic sequence, 82
montage technique, Kinsella's, 42, 140
Montague, John, 2
 memoriam for Ó Riada, 26, 31
Morley, John, Viscount, 83
mother figures, 63, 69, 203–4, 223
Murphy, Seamus, 27
Murphy, William Martin, 114
music and Kinsella's poetry, 4, 27, 30, 62, 104, 132–3, 134, 138, 145, 152, 227
 see also Gustav Mahler

mythology
  Celtic, 91, 97, 125, 128, 165
  Christian, 128
  the crow in, 28–9
  Greek, 62, 74, 87, 97, 201–2
  Irish, 4–5, 58–9, 61, 62, 64,
    66–9, 187, 217, 226,
    238n, 239n
  Kinsella's use of, 56
  pre-Celtic, 58, 66–9
  Roman, 74, 97, 114

Narcissus, 201–2
nationalism, 114, 117, 228
Neumann, Erich, 59, 63
New Oxford Book of Irish Verse,
  The (1986), 118, 119, 211,
  213
New Poems (1973), 3
Nightwalker and Other Poems
  (1968), 2–3, 178
  'Nightwalker', 112, 155–6, 160,
    171–1, 177, 181, 238n
  'Phoenix Park', 3, 148, 149,
    204
  'The Shoals Returning', 40
Northern Ireland Civil Rights
  Association, 22
Notes from the Land of the Dead
  (1972), 3, 4, 6, 105, 122,
  141
  numerology in, 74–6
  and *One*, 56–7, 63
  'Survivor', 5, 68
numerology in Kinsella's poetry,
  57, 74–6, 82, 116, 121, 226,
  235n, 237n
  Irish, 38, 63

O'Brien, Conor Cruise, 172–3
O'Casey, Seán
  The Plough and the Stars, 114
O'Connell, Daniel, 218–19
O'Driscoll, Dennis, 132, 180–1,
  193–4
O'Faoláin, Seán, 210–11

O'Hara, Daniel, 153, 195
Old Irish literature, 57, 119
Lebor Gabála Érenn, 61, 64, 200,
  205, 226
Táin, The, 5, 231n
One (1974), 34, 56–75, 76, 95,
  121, 141, 220, 227
  connection with earlier writing,
    56–7
  family relationships in, 71–4
  female figures in, 63, 69, 74–5
  'Finistère', 58, 62, 63, 64, 70,
    74
  and Goethe's *Faust*, 61–2, 63
  'His Father's Hands', 59, 69,
    71
  illustrations in, 58
  and Irish mythology, 58–9, 61,
    62, 64, 66–9, 187
  and Jungian psychology, 58–9,
    61, 62, 63
  'Minstrel', 59, 69, 70
  'Mister Cummins', 69–70
  numerology in, 57–8
  '38 Phoenix Street', 59, 69,
    70, 71, 78
  'Prologue', 58, 70
  revisions to, 58, 63, 71
  'The Entire Fabric', 58, 62,
    63, 125
  'The Oldest Place', 58, 62,
    66–8, 70
  'The Storyteller's Face, 58
  use of the familiar in, 69–71
  Yeats's drawings in, 58–9, 63
One Fond Embrace (1981), 16,
  166–74, 180, 228
  Conor Cruise O'Brien, 172–3
  illustrations in, 167–8
  revisions to, 168
  Seán Ó Riada in, 170–1
  and social planning, 169
  and *A Technical Supplement*,
    173–4
  and Wood Quay protest, 170,
    187

Open Court (1991), 206–14, 228
  'Dream', 208, 210–13, 252n
  illustrations in, 213
  and Irish poets from the 1950s,
      207–8
  and Patrick Kavanagh, 208–9
  revisions to, 212
Ó Rathaille, Aogán, 4, 17, 182–3,
    224
Ó Riada, Seán, 11
  in Kinsella's poetry, 27, 30,
      33, 34, 40, 133, 146–7,
      170–1
  life of, 25–6
origin myth in Kinsella's poetry, 59,
      61–2, 66–9, 108, 143, 165
  see also under Ireland
Oswald, Lee Harvey, 42–3, 48–51
Ó Tuama, Seán, 4
Out of Ireland (1987), 40, 69, 129,
    146–54, 187, 227–9
  and John Scotus Eriugena,
      148–50, 152, 153
  and Kinsella's poetic project,
      149–51
  'Native Wisdom', 119, 150–1
  and 'Phoenix Park', 148, 149
  revisions to, 147
  and *A Technical Supplement*,
      150, 153
  and two languages of Ireland,
      147–8
Oxford University Press, 9

pamphlet form for poems, 14
Parnell, Charles Stewart, 219
Paulin, Tom, 23
Pearse, Pádraig, 217
Pen Shop (1996), 216–21, 228
  and Cúchulainn, 216–18, 221
  and Kinsella's family, 219–20
  and *Ulysses*, 217–19
Pentecost, 14, 135–6, 143
Peppercanister poems
  reader and, 77
  summation of, 11–12, 225–9

Peppercanister Press, 1, 6–7
  Kinsella's control over, 7
  and Kinsella's longer sequences
      of poems, 9
  publicity material for
      Peppercanister, 8
Personal Places (1990), 174–83,
    228, 249n
  'Apostle of Hope', 177
  'At the Western Ocean's Edge',
      182–3, 216–17, 218
  'Brothers in the Craft', 180–1
  'Dura Mater', 175–7, 203
  'Godforsaken', 177–8
  revisions to, 175–6
  'Rituals of Departure', 178–9
  and *The Táin*, 174–5
Petty, William, 77, 117, 239n
phrenology, 213
place names, 38, 169
Plato and His Dialogues, 50–1,
    236n
Plato's works in Kinsella's poetry,
      35, 38
  in *The Good Fight*, 41, 42, 43,
      45–6, 47–8, 53–4
  in *A Technical Supplement*, 78
Poems (1956)
  'A Lady of Quality', 1, 194, 222
Poems from Centre City (1990),
    183–95, 228
  'Administrator' and 'Social
      Work', 188–9, 192
  'A Portrait of the Artist', 187–8,
      188
  'Departure Platforms', 189–90
  and details of Kinsella's life, 184
  'Iron Trinity', 192–3
  revisions to, 190, 193
  'The back Lane', 190–2, 193
  'The Bell', 193
  'The Stable', 185
  'The Stranger', 16, 185–6
  and W. H. Auden, 193–5
Poetry Book Society Bulletin
    (1958), 105

Poetry of Thomas Kinsella (1974),
     9–10
Political Anatomy of Ireland, The,
     77
Pope, Alexander
     'Dunciad', 16, 171
Pound, Ezra, 2, 4, 11, 42, 229
     Cantos, 3, 124
power of poetry, 224
primordial energies in Kinsella, 70,
     102, 113, 179
Prometheus, 62
Proust, Marcel, 164, 184
publishers of Kinsella's poetry, 5–9,
     94, 101, 207

quincunx, 58, 121, 226, 235n

ravens, 222
*Reading the Ground: The Poetry of
     Thomas Kinsella* (1996), 10
Reidy, John, 146–7
revisions, 215, 245n
     see also under each set of poems
Richter, Gisela, 43
Roberts, Professor M., 22
Rosenberg, Carolyn, 10, 62
Rosenthal, M. L., 226
Rushe, Desmond, 15, 21

Said, Edward, 185
Saville inquiry, 19, 22
Schenck, Celeste M., 25
Scotus Eriugena, Johannes, 11,
     148–50, 152, 153
sean-nós, 40, 49, 55
Selected Life, A (1972), 25–32,
     227
     'Coolea: 6 October 1971', 28–30
     Ó Riada in, 27, 30, 33, 34
     'St Gobnait's Graveyard,
          Ballyvourney: that
          evening', 30–2
     symbolism of crow in, 28–9
     treatment of death in, 31–2
Serres, Michel, 164

Shakespeare, William
     The Tempest, 62, 64, 110, 126
Shelly, Percy Bysshe
     'Mask of Anarchy', 16
síle-na-gig, 129, 151, 187, 222
Simmons, James, 15, 21
Skloot, Floyd, 4, 9, 215
     and *A Technical Supplement,* 87,
          240
     and *Vertical Man,* 37
Smith O'Brien, William, 218
snakes in Kinsella's poetry, 59, 74,
     103, 121, 204
Snodgrass, W. D., 209
social concerns in Kinsella's poetry,
     166, 168–70, 189
Song of the Night and Other Poems
     (1978), 94–117, 123
     'Anniversaries', 94, 96–8, 99,
          102, 223
     'C.G. Jung's "First Years"', 94,
          95
     childhood and, 95–6
     revisions to, 94, 101
     and *Songs of Psyche,* 123–4
     'Tao and Unfitness at Inistiogue
          on the River Nore', 94,
          99–104, 131
Songs of Psyche (1985), 224
     'Bow Lane', 124
     'Departure', 120
     illustrations in, 130–1
     'Invocation', 124, 125, 130
     'Man's Love', 119
     'Model School, Inchicore', 121–2
     'Notes', 128–30
     papers relating to, 119–20,
          120–1
     'Phoenix Street', 123–4
     revisions to, 127, 129
     significance of cover image,
          130–1
     'Songs of the Psyche', 124–5,
          180
     and *A Technical Supplement,*
          121, 129–30

Spender, Stephen, 209
St Catherine's Clock (1987),
    154–65
    division of poems in, 154–5
    and family, 161–3, 165
    historical engravings, 156–7,
        159–60
    'Nightwalker', 155–6, 160
    revisions to, 155
    'Seamus of the Smart Suit', 147
    and time, 156, 164
    and versions of Emmet's speech,
        159
Stevens, Wallace, 2
Sullivan, Kevin, 16
Swift, Jonathan, 16, 17, 79, 154,
    165, 166, 173
Symbols of Transformation (Jung),
    38

Táin, The, 5, 174–5, 231n
Taoism, 94, 131
Tattersall, Carol, 143
Technical Supplement, A (1976),
    75–93, 201, 227
    anatomical inquiry and, 78–8,
        83, 85
    'Blessed William Skullbullet',
        77–8
    central metaphor in, 86
    and Diderot and Voltaire letters,
        89, 93
    illustrations in, 7, 82–5
    and Laocoön statue, 87
    mythology in, 90–1
    'No one did anything at first', 76
    numerology in, 75–6, 82
    and the poetic act, 80–2
    and poet's self-analysis, 82, 90
    revisions to, 76
    slaughterhouse scene in, 79
    'The Station of the Depths', 79
Tennyson, Alfred, Lord
    'Morte d'Arthur', 45
Thirty Three Triads (1957), 97
Thomas Kinsella (1996), 10

Three Legendary Sonnets (1952),
    6
Tighe family, 100–1, 117
translation work of Kinsella, 4–5,
    26, 118–19, 231
Tristan und Isolde, 98, 104, 116,
    241n

Vertical Man (1974), 25, 32–41,
    115, 227
    examination of artistic process
        in, 36–8
    and Kinsella's friendship with
        Ó Riada, 40–1
    Mahler and, 35, 38–9
    and score for film Mise Éire,
        35–6
    structure of, 34–5
    'The Ghost of Seán Ó Riada
        Attends a Private Musical
        Evening in Philadelphia',
        33
violence in Kinsella's poetry, 13,
    42, 70, 145, 158
Virgil, 87

Wagner, Richard, 98, 105
Walter, Bruno, 136
Whiddy disaster, 168
White, Theodore H., 42
Whole Matter: The Poetic
    Evolution of Thomas
    Kinsella, 10
Widgery Tribunal and Report, 6,
    14, 18–19, 21, 22
Wilbur, Richard, 2
Wilde, Oscar, 207
Williams, William Carlos, 3, 11
Wolfenstein, Martha, 52
women in Kinsella, 195–296
    see also female figures
Wood Quay protest, 170, 178,
    184, 187
World War One, 137, 138–9, 145
Wormwood (1966), 2, 37, 93
    'Wormwood', 126, 141, 171

Yeats, Anne, 7, 58
Yeats, Jack, 189–90
Yeats, W. B., 3, 153, 165, 210,
    211
  'All Soul's Night', 32–3

'Cuchulain's Fight with the Sea',
    182
'Easter 1916', 152
'Remorse for Intemperate
    Speech', 146